BRITAIN AND THE DICTATORS

BRITAIN
AND
THE DICTATORS

A Survey of Post-War British Policy

BY

R. W. SETON-WATSON

We shall be found in our place when actual danger
menaces the system of Europe: but this country cannot and will not act upon abstract and speculative
principles of precaution.
    CASTLEREAGH (in a Minute to
    the Four Powers, May 1820)

With a gentleman I am always a gentleman and a half,
and when I have to do with a pirate, I try to be a pirate
and a half.   BISMARCK (1877)

NEW YORK

Howard Fertig

1968

First published in 1938

HOWARD FERTIG, INC. EDITION 1968
Published by permission of the Cambridge University Press

Library of Congress Catalog Card Number: 68-9600

PRINTED IN THE UNITED STATES OF AMERICA
BY NOBLE OFFSET PRINTERS, INC.

To
HUGH AND CHRISTOPHER
and to
THEIR GENERATION

Was du ererbt von deinen Vätern hast,
Erwirb' es, um es zu besitzen!

"MILTON! THOU SHOULDST BE LIVING AT THIS HOUR!"

Certainly then that people must needs be mad or strangely infatuated, that build the chief hope of their common happiness or safety on a single person; who, if he happen to be good, can do no more than another man; if to be bad, hath in his hands to do more evil without check than millions of other men.

JOHN MILTON, *Areopagitica*

> But what more oft in nations grown corrupt
> And by their vices brought to servitude,
> Than to love bondage more than liberty.

JOHN MILTON, *Samson Agonistes*

Jamais les hommes n'accepteront le pouvoir arbitraire d'un seul s'il ne sont des pleutres.

EMILE FAGUET

The longer I live, the more I am convinced that to understand revolutions and revolutionists, one must have lived in the midst of them.

HENRY REEVE

> Nie gelingt es der Menge, für sich zu wollen, wir wissen's:
> Doch wer verstehet, für uns alle zu wollen, er zeig's!

GOETHE

The more I see of the Tsar, the Kaiser and the Mikado, the better I am content with democracy.

THEODORE ROOSEVELT (1905)

> Träumt Ihr den Friedenstag?
> Träume wer träumen mag!
> Krieg ist das Losungswort!
> Sieg! und so klingt es fort!

Die Welt ist ein grosses Narrenhaus, nur sind die grössten Narren nicht eingesperrt.

FERDINAND GREGOROVIUS

PREFACE

THE present volume, planned as in some sense a sequel to my recent study of British Foreign Policy from 1789 to 1914 (*Britain in Europe*, Cambridge University Press), cannot fail to be highly controversial in character, owing to the many still unsolved problems of which it treats and the parlous state to which the cult of rival "ideologies" has reduced contemporary Europe. We have reached a moment when the fate of the whole British Commonwealth is in the balance, and with it, I profoundly believe, the fate of free institutions throughout the world. Herein lies my excuse, if excuse there be, for my extreme outspokenness.

In our Victorian dislike for the practice of calling a spade a bloody shovel, it is not necessary to go to the opposite extreme of calling it an agricultural implement. Even so mild-mannered a man as the late Lord Balfour was not always content to speak of mere "terminological inexactitudes": and if he were still with us today, he would certainly be one of the first to endorse our present Prime Minister's view that unprecedented measures are needed for altogether unprecedented times. For myself, I have always been attracted by the phrase of Joseph de Maistre: "Je continuerai toujours à dire ce qui me paraît bon et juste sans me gêner le moins du monde: c'est par là que je vaux si je vaux quelque chose."

This book is in no sense a full survey of British policy since the War, still less of European history in that period. It is rather an attempt to extract from the crowded chronicles of the last two decades the essence of the issues involved, to seek an explanation for the present state of our relations with the principal European countries, and in particular with Germany, and to analyse so far as is possible for the uninitiated, the alternatives that lie before us. If it be contended that only those who direct affairs can really do this, and that my self-imposed task is therefore the height of presumption, I can only reply that the whole theory of foreign policy in Britain rests, by the admission of successive Governments from Canning to Baldwin, upon an informed public opinion, conscious of the issues and ready to follow leaders whom it trusts, when it realises that they too understand those issues. How far recent British Governments have fulfilled the duty of responsible enlightenment—a duty more incumbent upon them in this age of propaganda than ever before—is a question better not answered at this early stage.

Maria Theresa's great Foreign Minister, Prince Kaunitz, once said, "It is prodigious how much the English do not know of Europe!" Under the stimulus of dictatorial menace, British opinion is more alive to problems of foreign policy than it has ever been in the past. May this book, in its own more modest way, contribute to the process of enlightenment!

Apart from written sources, this volume is the fruit of long and detailed discussions for years past with many friends and acquaintances of every shade of political opinion and of almost every nationality in Europe. But as there are many among them whose names it would, for hatefully obvious reasons, be unsafe to quote, and as a mangled list would give a false impression, I decided to limit myself to a general and impersonal expression of thanks for much good advice and many valuable suggestions.

R. W. SETON-WATSON

17 *February* 1938

P.S. In view of the momentous events which have occurred while this book was in the press, I have added an "Austrian Epilogue" (pages 435–46). But all that has happened seems to me to reinforce my arguments, and I have scarcely altered one word of the text.

25 *March* 1938

CHRONOLOGY OF EVENTS (1919–1938)

1919

18 Jan.	First Plenary Session of Peace Conference.
6 Feb.	Meeting of German National Assembly at Weimar.
11 ,,	Election of Fritz Ebert as President of German Republic.
21 Mar.	Bolshevik Government in Hungary.
28 Ap.	Covenant of League adopted by Conference.
23 June.	German National Assembly authorises unconditional signature.
28 ,,	Treaty of Versailles.
31 July.	New German Constitution adopted by Weimar Assembly.
1 Aug.	Fall of Béla Kun in Hungary.
10 Sept.	Treaty of St Germain (Allies and Austria).
22 Oct.	British Coalition Cabinet replaced by Conservatives under Bonar Law.
27 Nov.	Treaty of Neuilly (Allies and Bulgaria).

1920

10 Jan.	League of Nations created by exchange of ratifications.
4 Feb.	Declaration of Conference of Ambassadors against Habsburg Restoration in Hungary.
10 ,,	Slesvig Plebiscite (14 March, 2nd vote gives German majority).
18 Ap.	Supreme Council meets at San Remo.
5 May.	Mesopotamian Mandate assigned to Britain.
5–16 July.	Spa Conference.
11 July.	Second East and West Prussian Plebiscite.
10 Aug.	Treaty of Sèvres (Allies and Turkey).
14 Aug.–29 Sept.	Polish counter-offensive under General Weygand against Russia.
23 Sept.	Millerand elected French President.
12 Oct.	Treaty of Riga (Poland and Soviet Russia).
15 Nov.–18 Dec.	First Assembly of League of Nations.

1921

7 Mar.–4 Ap.	First Habsburg Putsch in Hungary.
13 Mar.	Kapp Putsch in Berlin.
16 ,,	Trade Agreement between Britain and Soviet Russia.
20 ,,	Upper Silesian Plebiscite.
1–5 May.	Allied Ultimatum on Reparations.
23 Aug.	Emir Faisal installed as King of Irak.
26 ,,	Murder of Dr Erzberger.
4 Oct.	League Protocols for financial reconstruction of Austria.
20 ,,	Second Habsburg Putsch in Hungary.

1922

6–13 Jan. Allied Conference at Cannes.
12 Jan.   Briand replaced by Poincaré as French Premier.
12 Mar.   Republics of Armenia, Georgia and Azerbaijan federated under Soviet Russia.
17 „   Italian Government orders occupation of Fiume.
1 Ap.   Death of Emperor Charles at Madeira.
16 „   Treaty of Rapallo (Germany and Soviet Russia).
24 June. Murder of Walther Rathenau, German Foreign Minister.
26 Aug.–9 Sept. Turkish offensive against Greece and occupation of Smyrna.
27 Sept. Abdication of King Constantine of Greece.
10 Oct.   Treaty between Britain and Irak.
11 „   Armistice Convention at Mudania (Allies and Turkey).
26 „   Fascist March on Rome.
12 Nov.   Treaty of Rapallo (Italy and Jugoslavia).
18 „   Abdul Medjid elected by Turkish National Assembly.
26 Dec.   Reparations Committee declares German default, against vote of British member.

1923

11 Jan.   Occupation of Ruhr by French and Belgian troops.
31 Mar.   Execution of Mgr Butkiewicz by Soviets.
20 May.   Mr Bonar Law succeeded as Prime Minister by Mr Baldwin.
8 June.   Bulgarian Coup d'État. Murder of Stambolisky.
24 July. Treaty of Lausanne (Allies, Turkey and Greece).
27 Aug.   Murder of General Tellini on Greek-Albanian frontier.
31 „   Mussolini's ultimatum to Greece; bombardment of Corfu.
12–14 Sept. Spanish Coup d'État under General Primo de Rivera.
29 Oct.   Turkish Republic proclaimed under Mustafa Kemal Pasha.
31 „   Sham Rhineland Republic proclaimed (collapses, Feb. 1924).
1 Nov.   Turkish Assembly abolishes Sultanate and Empire.
8 „   Munich Putsch of Hitler and Ludendorff.
1 Dec.   Stresemann, German Foreign Minister.
6 „   British Elections—Unionists lose 88 seats.
18 „   Expulsion of George II of Greece.

1924

14 Jan.   Dawes Commission first meets in Paris.
21 „   Labour Government under Ramsay Macdonald succeeds Baldwin. Death of Lenin.
22 „   Poincaré succeeded by Herriot as French Premier.
1 Feb.   Britain recognises Soviet Government.
3 Mar.   Abolition of Turkish Caliphate.
25 „   Proclamation of Greek Republic.

14 Ap. Dawes Plan accepted by Reich Government.
4–16 Aug. Conference of London ratifies Dawes Plan and Ruhr evacuation.
23 Sept. German Cabinet decides in principle to enter League.
8 Oct. British Election.
26 „ Zinoviev letter published. Second Baldwin Cabinet.
24 Dec. Ahmed Bey Zogu proclaims Albanian Republic.

1925

28 Feb. Death of President Ebert.
10 Mar. Rejection of Geneva Protocol by Britain.
16 Ap. Cathedral outrage at Sofia.
18 „ Austria invites League to appoint experts to examine her financial
state.
26 „ Marshal von Hindenburg elected German President.
1 Dec. Pact of Locarno signed in London.

1926

11 Jan. Ibn Saud proclaimed at Mecca as King of Hejjaz.
24 Ap. German-Russian Treaty.
12 May. Polish Military Coup under Marshal Pilsudski (1 June, Moscicki,
President).
28 „ Revolution in Portugal.
22 Aug. Greek Coup d'État: Kondylis overthrows Pangalos.
14 Sept. Ratification of Locarno.

1927

15 Mar. Italo-Hungarian Agreement.
7 June. Murder of Soviet Minister to Poland.
23 Oct. Expulsion of Trotsky and Zinoviev from executive of Communist Party.
11 Nov. Franco-Jugoslav Treaty.
22 „ Treaty of Tirana (Italy and Albania).

1928

20 June. Shooting of Croat deputies in Jugoslav Parliament. (8 Aug., death
of Stephen Radić.)
13 „ Italo-Jugoslav Convention of Nettuno ratified in Belgrade.
27 „ Pact of Paris (Briand-Kellogg Pact).
1 Sept. Ahmed Bey Zogu proclaimed King of the Albanians.
5 „ Franco-German negotiations for evacuation of Rhineland.
16 „ Agreement reached between six Powers.

1929

6 Jan. Proclamation of Dictatorship by King Alexander of Jugoslavia.
24 „ German-Soviet Treaty of Conciliation.

9 Feb. Litvinov Protocol for putting into force Pact of Paris (Russia and neighbours).
4 Mar. Mr Hoover inaugurated as U.S. President.
7 June. Signature of Young Report.
10 „ Establishment of Vatican City as independent State.
23 July. Lord Lloyd resigns as High Commissioner in Egypt.
31 Aug. Approval of Young Plan by Hague Conference.
14 Sept.–13 Dec. Withdrawal of British troops from Rhineland.
3 Oct. Death of Dr Stresemann.
24 „ Break on Wall Street.
30 Nov. Evacuation of second Rhineland zone by French and Belgian troops.

1930

21 Jan. Naval Conference opens in London.
13 Mar. Young Plan ratified by President von Hindenburg.
16 „ Death of General Primo de Rivera.
27 „ Dr Brüning, German Chancellor.
22 Ap. Naval Treaty signed by Britain, U.S. and Japan.
17 May. Young Plan comes into force.
8 June. Proclamation of Carol II as King of Roumania.
30 „ Final evacuation of Rhineland.
21 July. M. Litvinov succeeds M. Chicherin as Foreign Commissar.
14 Sept. German General Elections (Nazis win 107, Communists 77 seats).
5–12 Oct. First Balkan Conference held at Athens.
25 Nov.–7 Dec. Trial of technical experts at Moscow.

1931

21 Mar. Austro-German Customs Union (Curtius-Schober) (3 Sept. abandoned).
14 Ap. Spanish Republic proclaimed under Señor Zamora.
4 May. President Hoover's speech on World Depression.
11 „ Austrian Kredit-Anstalt in difficulties.
19 „ Launch of pocket-battleship *Deutschland*.
20 June. President Hoover proposes moratorium.
20 July. French Memorandum on Disarmament. Seven-Power London Conference.
24 Aug. National Government formed under Ramsay Macdonald.
3 Sept. King Alexander promulgates new Jugoslav Constitution.
19 „ Invasion of Manchuria by Japanese.
21 „ Britain abandons Gold Standard.
3 Dec. Statute of Westminster Bill passed.

1932

2 Feb. Disarmament Conference opens at Geneva.
7 Mar. Death of Aristide Briand.

13 Mar.–10 Ap. Hindenburg re-elected German President.
6–10 May. Assassination of President Doumer. M. Lebrun succeeds.
9 July. Reparation Agreement signed at Lausanne.
30 ,, German Elections (Nazis win 230 seats).
20 Aug. Ottawa Trade Agreements between Britain and Dominions.
3 Oct. Irak admitted to League of Nations.
17 ,, M. Avenol succeeds Sir Eric Drummond as Secretary General of League.
8 Nov. Election of Mr Franklin Roosevelt as U.S. President.
17 ,, General von Schleicher succeeds Herr von Papen as Chancellor.

1933

30 Jan. Herr Hitler becomes German Chancellor.
27 Feb. Burning of German Reichstag: suppression of Communist Party.
24 ,, League Assembly Resolution on Manchuria.
16 Mar. Dr Schacht succeeds Dr Luther as Chairman of Reichsbank.
27 ,, Japan gives notice of withdrawal from League.
12–18 Ap. Trial of Metropolitan Vickers employees at Moscow.
12 June. Opening of World Economic Conference in London.
1 July. President Roosevelt rejects joint declaration on Gold Standard.
14 Oct. Germany withdraws from League of Nations and Disarmament Conference.
16 Nov. U.S. recognises U.S.S.R.
29 Dec. Assassination of Roumanian Premier, Ion Duca.

1934

21 Jan. Devaluation of American Dollar.
26 ,, German-Polish Agreement.
7 Feb. Paris Riots. Doumergue-Barthou concentration Cabinet.
12–14 Feb. Suppression of Austrian Socialist Party.
17 Feb. Death of King Albert, succeeded by Leopold III.
1 Mar. Mr Pu Yi enthroned by Japanese as Emperor of Manchuria.
14 June. Meeting of Hitler and Mussolini at Venice.
30 ,, "The Thirtieth June"—Executions in Germany.
25 July. Austrian Putsch: murder of Chancellor Dollfuss. Succeeded by Herr von Schuschnigg.
2 Aug. Death of President von Hindenburg. Herr Hitler becomes Chancellor and Führer.
13 Sept. Poland repudiates Minority obligations, pending general system.
18 ,, U.S.S.R. admitted to League of Nations.
9 Oct. Assassination of King Alexander and M. Barthou at Marseilles.
15 ,, Death of ex-President Poincaré.
5 Dec. Fighting at Wal Wal between Italian and Abyssinian troops.
14 ,, Italy rejects Abyssinian request for arbitration.

1935

7 Jan.   Franco-Italian Agreement.
9 Mar.   Announcement of creation of German Air Force.
16 „   Re-introduction of Conscription in Germany.
25 „   Visit of Sir J. Simon and Mr Eden to Berlin (Mr Eden goes on to
          Moscow, Warsaw, Prague).
25–31 Mar. Belgian Devaluation under M. van Zeeland.
11–14 Ap. Three-Power Conference at Stresa.
17 Ap.   Special Session of League Council condemns unilateral denuncia-
          tion.
2 May.   Franco-Soviet Pact signed.
12 „   Death of Marshal Pilsudski. General Rydz-Smigli succeeds.
16 „   Czechoslovak-Soviet Pact.
7 June.   Reconstruction of National Government by Mr Baldwin.
          Sir S. Hoare succeeds Sir J. Simon.
18 „   Anglo-German Naval Agreement.
2 Oct.   Italy invades Abyssinia.
20 „   Death of Arthur Henderson.
14 Nov.   General election returns National Government by 431 to 184.
18 „   Economic Sanctions applied against Italy.
25 „   Restoration of Greek Monarchy under George II.
8–9 Dec. Hoare-Laval Agreement in Paris.
9–20 „   Five-Power Naval Conference in London.
18 Dec.   Dr Beneš succeeds Dr Masaryk as Czechoslovak President.
19 „   Sir S. Hoare resigns and is succeeded by Mr Eden.

1936

20 Jan.   Death of King George V. Edward VIII succeeds.
22 „   Resignation of M. Laval.
16 Feb.   Victory of Frente Popular at Spanish Elections.
7 Mar.   Re-occupation of Rhineland.
23 „   Rome Protocols (Italy, Austria, Hungary).
28 Ap.   Death of King Fuad of Egypt, succeeded by his son Faruk.
3 May.   Victory of Front Populaire in French General Election.
9 „   Italy annexes Abyssinia.
10 „   Election of Señor Azaña as Spanish President.
4 June.   M. Blum, French Premier.
9 „   Count Galeazzo Ciano, Italian Foreign Minister.
4 July.   Withdrawal of Sanctions.
11 „   Austro-German Convention.
13 „   Murder of Calvo Sotelo.
17 „   Outbreak of Spanish Civil War.
18 „   Montreux Convention (Turkey, Russia, Bulgaria, Roumania,
          Greece, Jugoslavia, France, Britain, Japan). Italy abstains.

4 Aug. General Metaxas becomes Dictator of Greece.
11   „   Herr von Ribbentrop, German Ambassador in London.
19   „   Trial of Zinoviev and other leaders in Moscow.
24   „   German military service increased to 2 years.
29   „   Dismissal of M. Titulescu, Roumanian Foreign Minister.
8–14 Sept. Nuremberg Party Congress proclaims Nazi Four Year Plan and
        world crusade against Bolshevism.
1 Oct. General Franco proclaims himself Dictator.
10   „   Dissolution of Austrian Heimwehr.
3 Nov. Re-election of President Roosevelt.
4   „   Largo Caballero reconstructs Spanish Cabinet to include Anarcho-
        Syndicalists.
9 Dec. Abdication of Edward VIII. George VI.

1937
2 Jan. "Gentleman's Agreement" (Britain and Italy).
17 Feb. British Rearmament Scheme.
16 May Spanish Cabinet reconstructed under Dr Negrin.
29 May, 18 June. *Deutschland* and *Leipzig* Incidents.
12–14 Sept. Conference of Mediterranean Powers at Nyon.
14 Sept. Death of ex-President Masaryk.
25–29 Sept. Visit of Signor Mussolini to Germany.

1938
4 Feb. Reconstruction of German High Command.
13   „   Hitler-Schuschnigg Meeting at Berchtesgaden.
21   „   Resignation of Mr Eden. Succeeded by Lord Halifax.
6–15 Mar. Trial and execution of Jagoda, Bukharin and others.
12 Mar. Hitler's Invasion and Conquest of Austria.

CONTENTS

I

INTRODUCTION

"O, I have ta'en too little care of this."
King Lear

I
T is no exaggeration to affirm that not in the lifetime of
any man living has the European situation been as obscure
and nebulous as it is today: never has there been so direct
a challenge not only to institutions which we had come to
regard as fundamental, but even to that idea of Progress which
many were only too apt to identify with Liberalism, or even
with Christianity itself.

It is also true that—despite the superficialities and vulgarities
of the popular press—a wider body of public opinion in this
country takes an active and intelligent interest in foreign
affairs, and in the conduct of our foreign policy, than at any
previous epoch in our history. This body of opinion quite
genuinely believed in "The War to end War", took quite
seriously President Wilson's ideal of "making the world safe
for democracy", and followed with sympathy and interest the
great experiment in international government at Geneva. There
was therefore corresponding disillusionment when it became
apparent that Europe was once more turning away from democracy and disarmament, and that the League of Nations was
unable to prevent the outbreak of war or to penalise a declared
aggressor. Faced with these harsh realities, public opinion
during 1936–37 passed through an acute spiritual crisis, clearly
reflected in the correspondence columns of such journals as
The Times, the *Manchester Guardian* and the *Spectator*. Since
then it has been following Mr Eden's good advice and "thinking
deeply", and its hesitations have been reflected in a staggering
gait and in a readiness to clutch at any straw that may save it
from being swept along in the gathering current of destiny.
And all the time the foreign critic, who never shared either

British ideals or British illusions, has been looking on with mingled incredulity and contempt, and asking himself whether these latest moods of Britain, and her seeming indecision and reluctance to face new facts, are a proof of that decadence in which he had believed until the Great War gave him the lie, or perhaps rather the façade of a subtle and double-minded policy such as is implied in the ancient nickname of "Perfide Albion".

The critic who reasons thus has an ancient tradition at his back, fortified by more than one historical precedent from the eighteenth century. But even among our Continental friends—and there are happily still many left—it is being pointed out that today Britain is the only country in Europe whose foreign policy remains obscure and undefined: and this is all the more exasperating to them because, since Britain is believed to hold the finger on the balance, certainty as to her attitude in given circumstances would have a decisive effect in shaping the policy of most other Powers. "We are all kept in uncertainty", it is often said, "because Britain refuses to make plain her ultimate aims and intentions: and so long as this continues, Europe must remain in a fever of apprehension. If once it were possible to calculate whether she would act, or remain inactive, in the event of a Continental war, the two possible groups of Powers would make their calculations accordingly, certain bargains and readjustments would result, and there would be no war. But her present attitude fills each side with hopes and fears and encourages, nay forces, it to speculate upon securing the support of Britain for itself and against its rival." If we think it out, we must of course admit that implicit in any such calculations is the unspoken doubt as to how far the incessant professions of British statesmen—on the major questions of peace, disarmament, collective security—are entirely sincere, or how far at the moment of supreme crisis they would not take refuge in a semi-isolation which could not be permanently upheld, but which might put a premium upon an aggressor's gamble by increasing his hope of rapidly creating accomplished facts.

In a certain sense it cannot be denied that we have reverted to the position of 1914, when the certainty (if expressed at a sufficiently early date) that we should remain neutral would have forced France and Russia to abandon Serbia, and conversely the certainty that we should intervene would have deterred Germany from invading Belgium, and perhaps Austria-Hungary from declaring war on Serbia. Undoubtedly there are many foreigners today who, recognising the only too patent fact that British intervention would weight the scales in one direction or the other, suspect that, while her sentimentalists talk the language of Geneva, her statesmen are waiting to throw that weight on to the strongest side, quite irrespective of international right or declared principle, and are trusting to the future to find the same sort of hypocritical justifications for such a course as, according to their reading of history, she has so often adduced in the past. I trust that in the course of my argument it will be possible to explode these suspicions, at any rate as regards British policy in the present century. In the meantime it may suffice to insist upon a fact which no serious student of modern history can fail to grasp—that hitherto, while Britain has often enough held aloof from secondary conflicts in Europe, she has never yet held entirely aloof from a struggle of the first magnitude, and that in such an event she has invariably thrown her weight on to the weakest, not on to the strongest, side. The inference is clear—that she has hitherto regarded the hegemony of any one Power over the Continent as incompatible with her own interests: and there is absolutely nothing to suggest that she is likely to abandon this attitude in the near future. It is an inference which our would-be "Isolationists" would do well to study, for it is part of the essential interdependence of European and overseas problems.

What at first sight gives a certain plausibility to the suspicions alluded to above, is the undoubted fact that almost from the armistice, and certainly from the conclusion of the first peace in June 1919, British policy has repeatedly shown reserve and hesitation. Faced by Germany's clear bid for hegemony, she reacted as she had reacted in the past to similar bids of France or Spain. But no sooner was the danger dispelled than she became once more conscious of her hybrid position, as of the Continent and yet not of it. She virtually proclaimed her *désintéressement* in all problems east of the German frontier; she receded, under cover of the United States Senate's action, from the triple guarantee originally contemplated; she withheld her backing from the League in the crucial Corfu affair: her wavering and vacillations, first during the discussions on the Geneva Protocol, and later during the Disarmament Conference, were the main factor in the failure of both. Above all, the fluctuations of her policy towards Italian aggression in Abyssinia —as exemplified by the Hoare speech in Geneva, the Hoare-Laval agreement and the final collapse of Sanctions—have alarmed even her firmest supporters and brought her prestige lower than it had been since Lord John Russell left the Danes in the lurch in 1864.

The post-war years illustrate perhaps better than any other period the "intermittent" character of British policy in Europe, the extent to which, after a gigantic emergency nobly met, we are capable of relaxing our efforts, putting off our moral no less than our material armour, and playing at make believe with shadows, while our backs are turned to grim realities. Certainly this mood has been followed by a rude awakening, and we may perhaps thank Britain's lucky star if we have been left the time to stretch and rub our eyes, before the next blow falls. Indeed the one good feature in the present situation is that whereas in July 1914 the nation was fast asleep and almost entirely blind to the omens of war, today it is at last wide awake, feverishly groping towards the light, and canvassing alternative lines of action. Upon our friends abroad this process has doubtless a depressing effect: but the day may come when they will be glad that we have gone through such searchings of heart, for that may mean all the difference between a clear programme and chaos. If it be true that our democratic form of government makes it impossible to carry through any constructive policy save with the backing of an informed public opinion, then the prolonged effervescence of that public opinion during the summer of 1936 may prove to have been a stage of dangerous, yet necessary, preparation for supreme decisions. And while it is difficult for any close student of affairs, whatever his party alignment, not to deplore the Government's failure to provide leadership, constructive ideas, and even essential information on the main European issues, it still remains possible for Government apologists to reply that never before has so much depended upon our right choice of allies—or better said, colleagues and comrades—in Europe; never before have the alternatives been so distasteful; never has it been so difficult to accept alignment with this or that Power, without at the same time sacrificing those fundamental principles upon which our own past liberties were built up. A hundred years ago we could ally ourselves with Austria to check Russo-Prussian aggressive aims, or we could combine with Austria in bringing back France to the comity of nations, or we could construct a quadruple western system as balance to the Holy Alliance, or, a little later, we could join Russia and France to isolate Austria in the Near East, or again join the three Eastern Courts in a plan for isolating France, only to revert to a series of more or less cordial ententes with France herself. In all these permutations we consciously bestowed a somewhat condescending favour upon all who stood for the Victorian panacea of "Progress": we frowned upon the absolutism of Nicholas I or "Bomba". But there was never any serious prospect that our weight in the scales might plunge all Europe under a despotism which tolerates neither variance nor shadow of turning. And that is rapidly becoming our dilemma today—to renounce that dream of a new World Order to which we pledged our troth in 1919, and in its place to submit to a choice between a Brown "Totalitarianism" and a Red "Totalitarianism" (the third, or Black, variety—as will, it is hoped, become clear from this analysis—is not a real alternative at all). If this be true—the official apologist may plausibly argue—we must think not once but twice and thrice, before taking any irrevocable decision: and both official and unofficial opinion must follow Mr Eden's advice and "think deeply" on the crucial issues that face the world of today.

It is as a contribution to this process of clearing our minds of the claptrap, fallacies and illusions that are so rampant in our midst that this little book has been planned. I am only too conscious of my presumption in attempting the analysis of so fluid a situation. And yet I feel impelled to the task in the belief that there are certain broad and enduring principles of policy which we have been in danger of forgetting, and in the hope that reader and writer may together help to clear their ideas, and by flinging out the dross of controversy reach an agreed platform where party plays a secondary part, and where great national interests may be reconciled with a higher international aim.

II

THE ESSENTIALS OF PRE-WAR POLICY

To attempt even a general summary of British foreign policy in previous centuries would be to stultify the whole purpose of this book, which is concerned with the problems produced by the Great War and the Peace Settlement and their bearing upon contemporary policy.[1] None the less, it is necessary at the outset of my task to consider whether our policy has in the past been determined by certain fundamental underlying principles, or, as some critics would have us believe, has rested upon pure opportunism and egotism, shifting and veering as the winds of the political world rise and fall. As my thesis must open with a direct and overwhelming denial of the latter of these theories, it is obviously incumbent upon me to marshal quite briefly the argument in favour of the former, before passing to their practical application in the post-war world.

In the first place, it may safely be affirmed that the apparent hesitations and half-measures of Britain's foreign policy are the natural expression of her hybrid, intermediate, geographical position as part of Europe, and yet detached from it. "One foot in sea and one on shore", and yet it would be an error to complete the quotation and assume her to be "to one thing constant never". There has, it is true, been a certain alternation between the wish for isolation and an extreme policy of interference, and foreign observers have sometimes sought to explain this by farsighted and calculated policy. Hence on the one hand the title of "Perfide Albion", and set against it the long since established fact that William Pitt, the great organiser of resistance to French hegemony, was for the first half of his career Britain's peace minister *par excellence*, and aimed above all at

[1] The reader may be referred to my earlier volume, *Britain in Europe* 1789–1914 (1937, Cambridge University Press), a volume of 650 pages.

a close understanding with France, and again that Edward Grey, whom an uninformed German opinion used to denounce as the organiser of encirclement and war, really had as his main aim the preservation of European peace and had, when the war broke out, almost completed negotiations for an understanding with Germany, intended to supplement and complete the earlier agreements with France and with Russia. The main explanation for apparent fluctuations is probably to be found in a phrase of Jules Cambon—that "the geographical position of a nation is the chief factor determining its foreign policy, and indeed the chief reason why it must have a foreign policy at all".

Already in the days of purely dynastic policy, when England's foreign Angevin kings had an unlimited appetite for French soil and even when the Plantagenets pursued their designs upon the French Crown by the help of English national prejudice, she was always faced by the problem of finding a golden mean between aloofness and intervention. With the Age of Discoveries and the slow growth of world communications this problem assumed new forms, and expressed itself in the expedient of the Balance of Power—a conception which had first arisen in divided Italy during the fifteenth century, but assumed a wider European character after the French invasions, from 1492 onwards, had provoked a rival combination of the Powers. First consciously used by Wolsey for the promotion of English interests, his principle of equilibrium was adopted by Elizabeth and Cecil and gave directive to the long struggle of the English nation against monopolistic and proselytising Spain. The Union of the English and Scottish Crowns and the final triumph of Protestantism in both halves of the island brought added security at home: yet the seventeenth century was, save for the glorious interlude of the Commonwealth, a period of eclipse and sometimes of ignominy in foreign policy, and the true upholders of the Balance of Power were Henry IV and Richelieu. Indeed, the Treaty of Westphalia (1648), the first general diplomatic settlement of European affairs, rested above all upon a certain equilibrium between Protestant and Catholic, alike in Germany and in Europe as a whole.

The downfall of the Stuarts, though of course due to domestic issues, was intimately bound up with the new position created on the Continent by Louis XIV's bid for hegemony. There is no stranger or more providential fact in our history than the emergence of William III, as the son and husband of Stuart princesses, the link of genius which united Britain and Holland in a common defence and drove them into alliance with the Austrian Habsburgs and some of the lesser German princes. Unless the whole struggle that fills the reigns of William III and Anne is to be dismissed as futile and avoidable—and it is difficult to believe that any serious historian could ever impart such twisted meaning to now notorious facts—we may also describe it as a signal illustration of the impossibility of Britain holding aloof from Continental affairs. The story is also full of warnings as to the extreme dangers of isolation and its immediate reactions upon the safety of our overseas dependencies.

The War of the Spanish Succession, then, was fought to prevent a French hegemony in Europe, but the modern isolationist is too apt to overlook the fact that on the part of Britain colonial ambitions played an equally strong part. In actual fact it resulted in Holland, who had borne its brunt on her own soil, falling behind in the race, and in France emerging temporarily enfeebled, while Britain, aggrandised by vast accessions of strategic strength in America—notably Nova Scotia, Newfoundland and Hudson Bay—was ready, after a period of recuperation, for a fresh and more decisive bout in the middle of the century.

The eighteenth century is indeed the classic example of the interconnection of Continental and overseas interests in our policy. The settlement of 1713, ending a war waged mainly in Europe, laid the foundations of British world power and maritime expansion. The peace policy pursued by Stanhope and Walpole while France plunged into the quicksands of the Austrian Succession, made it all the easier for Britain to pursue her ambitions in the New World. Her skilful intervention in the Continental struggle that centred round Maria Theresa and Frederick the Great, served as a diversion from the colonial field, and strengthened her naval power. The Seven Years' War in Europe enabled Britain to establish her predominance in India and America, and to strengthen her naval power in the Mediterranean. The elder Pitt was hardly exaggerating when he argued that "Hanover ought to be as dear to us as Hampshire, and that he would conquer America in Germany": and in this connection it may be profitable to quote a kindred passage in a letter of the Duke of Richmond to the younger Pitt. "Holland", he writes in 1795, "seems lost to us both in Europe and in the East Indies: and should the Emperor and Russia unite with France, Sweden must follow, and Denmark dare not be our friend. Under such circumstances what are we to look for but utter ruin! If France is disengaged on the Continent and assisted by Spain, Holland and Russia (to say nothing of America), we must be attacked with greatly superior force in the East and West Indies, and perhaps in Canada: but what is still worse, we shall undoubtedly have the war brought into Ireland....In short, the natural and political advantages of France are such that I very much fear the consequences. To divert her attention by stirring up some powerful enemy on the Continent had been long and universally considered as our only resource." This may not have been particularly estimable or scrupulous, but it showed a clear sense of realities as they were understood in that grasping century.

If the Seven Years' War illustrates the colonial advantages accruing from a skilful policy of European alliances, so the period of the American War shows the dangers of isolation. George III added to his many other follies the rash assumption that the Bourbons would never ally themselves with colonial rebels: the help of France and Spain completed and assured what the colonials had won by their own valour, and at the Peace of 1783 Britain not merely recognised the independence of the United States, but had to cede to Spain Minorca and Florida, and to France quite a number of strategic and trading points in America, Asia and Africa.

The dangers of isolation with which Britain was threatened during the long revolutionary and Napoleonic Wars are too obvious to require recapitulation: and it is also clear that we had no choice in making war, at first owing to the aggressive political philosophy of the Revolution, and later to the inordinate ambitions of Napoleon. But it cannot be too strongly emphasised that the Napoleonic Wars prove up to the hilt the twin lessons of the Spanish Succession and the Seven Years' Wars—namely, the extent to which success overseas was due to a sober, but never passive, policy in Europe, and the impossibility of aloofness from the major problems of the Continent. For Britain the settlement, following upon twenty years of effort, created a situation in which she was able to replace the lost colonial empire in America by another empire still more widely flung, to leave British sea-power almost unassailable, to secure a whole series of vital strategic points—Gibraltar, Minorca, Corfu in Europe, St Helena, the Cape, Mauritius on the route to India—and to prepare the way for that vast trade which then still "followed the flag". At the same time Castlereagh, by his moderation towards defeated France, had made a reality of that "just equilibrium" which was his ideal for Europe, and rendered possible the co-operation between France and Britain which ripened later into a series of *ententes cordiales*. Throughout the century sea-power enabled Britain to keep her distance from Europe, and to pursue a mainly peaceful policy of economic expansion overseas, but it never rendered her indifferent to Continental problems, and it was above all the contrast between her own negligible army and the vast, yet highly trained, conscript armies of the Continent, that was responsible for a temporary experiment in "splendid isolation", as a reaction alike from Disraeli's anti-Russian "forward" policy of the 'seventies and from Gladstone's signal lack of success, in such different spheres as South Africa, Egypt and Afghanistan. But it is to be remembered that splendid isolation never was the ideal of him who coined the phrase, but far rather a temporary and uncomfortable expedient, intended to save him from entanglements with the Powers whom he felt bound to distrust while Continental politics remained in so fluid a state.

Salisbury was indeed keenly aware of the danger that "if England was left out in isolation", the Great Powers might combine to "treat the English Empire as divisible booty" and again that "when once war has broken out in Europe, we cannot be secure from the danger of being involved in it": and this was at the back of his mind when he concluded the short-lived Mediterranean Agreements and weighed the possibility of adhering to the Triple Alliance. When the Boer War brought a Continental coalition within sight, Salisbury was already too old to assume a fresh initiative: but Lansdowne, his successor at the Foreign Office, hastened to conclude an alliance with Japan which put an end to all danger of our isolation in the Far East, and ere long followed it up with the Anglo-French Convention. By the twentieth century there was once more an obvious connection between the problem of isolation and the problem of the Balance of Power: and in proportion as the trend of German policy towards continental hegemony became more marked, so was Britain forced, somewhat hesitatingly, towards the rival camp, though never to the last abandoning all hope of forming the finger on the balance between the two main political and military groups in Europe.

The deciding factor is, however, to be found in Germany's naval ambitions—the simple, basic, fact that the Power already possessed of the strongest army in the world was making a definite bid for equality with the greatest naval Power also. In the words of A. J. Balfour, "Without a superior fleet Britain would no longer count as a Power. Without any fleet at all Germany would remain the greatest Power in Europe." In 1911 Grey found the Committee of Imperial Defence and all the Dominion Premiers in unanimous agreement with his confidential view that "it is the naval question which underlies the whole of our European foreign policy"; that there could be no question of British aggression against Germany, so long as the British army was kept "within its present small dimensions", whereas Germany, if she had a bigger fleet, "could not only defeat us at sea, but could be in London in a very short time with her army": and that if we stood aside from existing friendships and agreements, "we should be left without a friend", and in order to keep a command of the sea should have to reckon "with a combination against us of not two, but five, Powers". Here Grey was merely restating in modern terms the experience of Pitt, the greatest of our Prime Ministers, and of Castlereagh, the greatest of our Foreign Secretaries, that isolation is an altogether impracticable policy for a country with such world-wide interests as ours.

From this brief sketch it transpires that for at least two centuries there have been three constant factors at the root of British policy: the impossibility of isolation, opposition to the Continental hegemony of any single Power, and a resolve to maintain British naval supremacy as the only guarantee of the Empire and the basis of "Pax Britannica". We must next consider certain problems of practical detail which derive from these general principles.

In the first place it is obvious that the Narrow Seas that separate us from the mainland and command the Thames Estuary, the North Sea, and access to London, have always been a matter of vital concern to this island: and this problem in its turn is bound up with the fate of the Low Countries, from the mouths of the Rhine and Scheldt to the Channel ports, Dunkirk, Calais, Boulogne. Already fitfully under Edward III, in the great days of the Flemish wool trade, during the conflict with the Hansa, still more while Alba and Parma held the Netherlands for Spain, England was prompted to play for her own hand. For a time commercial and naval jealousy obscured the common interests of Britain and Holland and even led to war; but dire necessity brought them together again and under the leadership of men of such supreme genius as William III and Marlborough they together held France in check. The whole complicated structure of the Barriers, embodied in successive treaties, was above all the outcome of British interest in the Low Countries. Austrian rule in Belgium proved a workable device from the Treaty of 1713 through most of the eighteenth century. But Pitt was at once apprehensive when Joseph II began to meddle with the Barrier provisions, and it was French aggression in Belgium that first roused Pitt's powers of resistance and did as much as anything to convert him from a peace to a war minister. Britain lacked the military force to prevent the revolutionary armies from overrunning both Belgium and Holland: but from the purely tactical point of view the effect was to provide the nation with a visible witness to its danger, to touch a peculiarly sensitive nerve in its anatomy, in very much the same way as the German invasion in 1914. Concern for the fate of the Dutch and Flemish coast is a thread that runs right through the history of the revolutionary and Napoleonic wars, and is a strong factor in silencing opposition in quarters not indisposed to sympathise with the Revolution. Grenville voiced the views of the Cabinet and of the King when he treated the fate of the Netherlands at the end of the war as "so important for the interests of this country, that they ought to form the primary objects of attention in any discussion respecting a continental peace": and though at the Treaty of Amiens Britain weakly went back upon this and acquiesced in French control of the Low Countries, events soon forced her to revert to her former attitude, and the question did indeed assume a capital importance at the final settlement of 1814.

The attempt to guard against any repetition of foreign conquest by uniting Belgium and Holland under the House of Orange was in one sense an attempt to find a modern substitute for the now obsolete Barrier system. After fifteen years this experiment collapsed as the result of mutual antipathies and divergent traditions. This time it was Palmerston who played an even more decisive part than Castlereagh in 1815 in finding a new and workable basis: and he is justly regarded as one of the makers of the independent Belgian kingdom. From first to last he exercised a definite influence in restraining French territorial ambition, in preventing intervention on the part of the three Eastern Courts, and in ensuring general recognition of Belgian neutrality: and he turned the scale in favour of Prince Leopold of Coburg, in the well-founded belief that he would "make a good *Belgian* King, neither French nor

English". The Treaty of London (1839) formed a sound compromise between the two impossible policies of enforcing the broken union with Holland and partitioning Belgium between her neighbours: and it worked admirably for seventy-five years, especially in 1870, when the Gladstone Government's insistence on neutrality prevented the Franco-German War from becoming general. This was all the more satisfactory because in 1867 British statesmen had seemed disposed to take refuge in sophistical distinctions between "several" and "collective" guarantees, such as might well have encouraged aggression against Belgium. It is true that Belgian opinion showed periodical nervousness as to the British official attitude on the subject of neutrality—notably during the War Scare of 1887, when a newspaper credited with special access to Salisbury questioned the country's readiness to risk war in such a cause, and twenty years later, when the Congo agitation caused friction and polemics between Brussels and London. But all serious observers continued to regard Belgium as one of the strategic keys of the whole European system, and the crisis of 1914 at once revealed it as a sure touchstone of the British attitude towards our Continental engagements. The suddenness with which the strong movement for British neutrality in the impending war collapsed on the news of the German invasion of Belgium is one of the most remarkable instances in our history of *unconscious* political instinct: for neither the statesmen who regarded it as a *casus belli*, nor the young men who flocked to join the new armies, stopped to reflect that failure to implement our bond or undue delay in responding to the call would have meant the almost certain downfall of France as well as Belgium, and would probably ere long have left us alone to face a hostile coalition. The ensuing months and years were to demonstrate that the French Channel ports are more than ever bound up with the Flemish coast, that their possession intimately concerns us, and that modern communications being what they are, the defence of France no less than of Belgium has become part of the problem of the defence of these islands.

Intimately connected with the problems of sea-power and

foreign commerce is that of Britain's position in the Mediterranean. Already under Elizabeth the Levant Company assumed considerable importance, and it is characteristic that for nearly two centuries it bore the expenses of British diplomatic representation at the Porte. Under Cromwell the British fleet conducted operations in that sea, and Charles II received Tangier as part of the dowry of his Portuguese Queen. With the eighteenth century the problem of strategic bases was advanced two steps further by the acquisition of Gibraltar, which is still held, and of Minorca, which was lost in the War of American Independence. Needless to say, the ancient alliance with Portugal—dating originally from 1373 and renewed in 1642 after she had shaken off her Spanish conquerors—also had an eminently strategic quality, and in the eighteenth century it enabled us to threaten Spain from both west and east during the various naval wars in which we were engaged. In the struggle against France the Mediterranean formed a vital element in the wider factor of sea-power: the seizure of Malta, and of Corfu, Nelson's victory off Aboukir and the successful defence of Acre, put an end to Napoleon's dream of dominion in the Near East, and of course after Trafalgar our naval power could no longer seriously be challenged. A last effort on the part of Napoleon was frustrated by Captain Hoste's great Adriatic victory off Lissa in 1811. It should be unnecessary to add that sea-power alone made possible the Peninsular campaigns which Napoleon himself regarded as the ulcer that proved fatal to his career.

It is not too much to affirm that for a hundred years after Waterloo Britain pursued a policy of live and let live in the Mediterranean, and contributed more than any other Power to the comparative peace which reigned in that most dangerous of seas. Such wars as occurred were short and localised, and no Power ever aspired to dominate the whole sea or to threaten the main sea routes, though the vital importance of sea-power was amply illustrated by such examples as Navarino, the French conquest of Algiers, the course of the Crimean War, the blockades of Crete, Italy's seizure of Tripoli and Greek naval superiority in the Balkan Wars. Needless to say, Britain's attitude has been determined not merely by the profitable Levantine trade—rendered still more attractive by low tariffs and capitulations—but still more by her interest in a short route to India and the Far East. After the opening of the Suez Canal the question of its control, or of free passage through it, led us to concern ourselves increasingly with Egyptian affairs, and this for a time injured our relations with France. The surrender of the Ionian Islands to the free Kingdom of Greece in 1864 was politically an act of justice, but from the purely strategic point of view a serious blunder: and this partially determined Disraeli's search for a *place d'armes* in the Near East, from which to hold Russia more effectually in check. Cyprus—assigned to us on false pretences, for we could never have provided the promised equivalent of defending Turkey's Asiatic frontiers against the armies of the Tsar—proved to be perfectly useless for the purposes for which it was acquired: and it is only in the post-war transformation wrought by aviation that it is acquiring a new and unsuspected value.

Intimately connected with the problem of Mediterranean strategy has been Britain's active interest in the Eastern Question —as it were galvanised into activity by Bonaparte's memorable Egyptian expedition in 1798, and from time to time stimulated by suspicions of Russia. This problem may be defined as that of filling the vacuum created by the shrinkage and decay of the once conquering Ottoman Empire—whether by the reviving Christian states of the Balkan Peninsula or by the Great Powers with their endless conflicting ambitions and interests. Historians are sometimes reproached with exaggerating Britain's interest in these complications at the opposite end of Europe: but nothing can alter the fact that no less than eleven times were we involved in major international crises owing to Near Eastern complications. The bare catalogue is highly instructive—the Greek revolution, culminating in triple intervention in 1827: the two conflicts between the Sultan and Mehemet Ali of Egypt (1832–3 and 1839–41), in the latter of which Palmerston nearly involved us in war with France: the Crimean War:

the double Bosnian and Bulgarian crisis, leading to the Russo-Turkish War and the Congress of Berlin: the Bulgarian crisis of 1887: the Cretan rising of 1897: the Macedonian troubles of 1903–8: the Bosnian annexation crisis of 1908–9: the First and Second Balkan Wars, and finally the Great War itself. Even those who, like myself, are most critical of the Eastern diplomacy of our statesmen, above all of Palmerston and of Disraeli, will not dream of suggesting that the frequency with which they all became involved in the problems of the Near East was merely the result of folly or ignorance, and recognise that it was due to an interlocking of interests in many directions. That they radically misjudged the intentions of Russia and exaggerated her powers of threatening our Indian Empire, does not mean that they were not fully justified in giving the closest attention to anything that might affect either the sea or the land routes to the East. Where they were most at fault was in the incredible optimism with which, especially in the mid-Victorian period, they assumed that the Turkish state was still susceptible of speedy reform and, like Palmerston, denounced the idea of "its being a dead body or a sapless trunk" as "pure and unadulterated nonsense". This strange illusion lingered till the very eve of the Great War among a small group of gifted soldiers and travellers, who lightly brushed aside the policy of outrage and extermination pursued by Turkey towards the Armenians (still unsurpassed amid all the surfeit of horrors of the last twenty years!), and forgave anything to a bonny[1] fighter. Lord Salisbury, who in the crisis of the 'seventies had stood midway between the extremes of Disraeli and Gladstone, was far too great a realist to be deceived, and his famous avowal that in the Crimean War we had put our money on the wrong horse, marked the turn of British opinion to a juster appreciation of the facts. This was rendered easier by the proofs which every year of the 'eighties and 'nineties brought with it, that the emancipated nations of the Balkan Peninsula, once freed from the Turkish blight, were capable of turning dunghills into rose gardens, and that, so far from becoming the slaves and vassals

[1] The survivors of Kut in 1915 did not accept the adjective.

of an autocratic Russia, each of them was fully resolved to live its own life and develop its own national culture. Till the very eve of the great disaster of 1914, the worst feature of the Near East situation was not the conflict of rival races or the atrophy of government in what remained of the Turkish dominion in Europe, but the selfish intrigues by which the Great Powers envenomed the situation and set the free peoples at each others' throats.

There remain other more abstract considerations which yet have a highly practical bearing upon the development of British policy. Time and again Britain, entering upon an alliance or a common enterprise, perhaps belatedly or inadequately prepared, has turned the scale by her stubborn endurance, only to resume at once an attitude of masterly inactivity, holding aloof from the friends whose confidence she had gradually acquired and seeking to redress, in favour of a beaten foe, the balance which she herself had done more than any other to destroy. In particular, it was her action at the settlement of Utrecht, from 1711 to 1713, and at the settlement of Paris in 1763, that gave weight to the legend of "Perfidious Albion", inspired by far-reaching and unscrupulous calculations and owing her own safety and success to the practice of embroiling her neighbours. In both these cases a certain plausibility is imparted to the argument by two undoubted facts. In the first place it cannot be contested that she made peace before her allies had achieved anything approaching their full hopes, and secured her own future by extremely advantageous extra-European arrangements: and in the second place, the peculiar circumstances of British party politics, envenomed by rancorous personal intrigue and dynastic ambition, surrounded the whole transaction, to the senses of the outside world, with a strong flavour of perfidy and doubt.

This is not the place to argue the question in detail, but it need not take long to place it in truer perspective. The War of the Spanish Succession had been waged to prevent the union of the Crowns of France and Spain on a single head—a contingency which the treaty itself described as incompatible with

"the safety and liberties of Europe". But just as that danger
had been brought within reach by a series of deaths in the
Spanish royal family in 1699 and 1700, so now the death of
the Emperor Joseph I in 1711 without male heirs opened up
the possibility of his brother reuniting the Crowns of Spain,
the Indies, the Empire, and the Sicilies in his own person—
a result equally contrary to that European Balance of Power
for which he had fought as the ally of Britain. It was felt to
be contrary to good sense to oppose a Franco-Spanish union
which was only contingent, and then to accept the revival of
Charles V's imperial power under his descendant Charles VI.
The Treaties, therefore, rested upon a solemn and public recognition of "equilibrium between the Powers" as a foremost aim,
and of the Balance of Power as "the best and most solid foundation of mutual friendship". Nor can it be argued that the
interests of our two chief allies were left out of account in the
final settlement: for Charles was compensated for his loss of
Spain by acquiring the Spanish possessions in Italy, while the
transfer of the Spanish Netherlands to Austria—intended of
course as a substitute for the system of Barrier fortresses in its
original form—accrued greatly to the advantage of the Austrian
Habsburgs and interposed a Great Power between Holland and
France. Again, while it is clear that Britain was bent upon
strengthening her naval position in the Mediterranean by the
retention of Gibraltar and Minorca, she also secured two other
key positions for two of her allies—Sardinia for Austria and
Sicily for the Duke of Savoy. The most serious criticism points
in other directions. The concealment of major Anglo-French
negotiations from the Dutch and from the Emperor was equally
discreditable as regards form and motives, and it is not too
much to speak of the treachery of Bolingbroke. But the Asiento
bargain, by which Britain secured a lucrative slave trade monopoly at the expense of France, was taken by everyone at home
as perfectly legitimate and a matter of course: the nerves which
since the days of Wilberforce react to humanitarian instincts
were then still numbed or non-existent. Lastly, it is apposite
at the present moment to insist upon our cruel and quite

unnecessary abandonment of Catalonia, while adding that contemporary opinion does not appear to have felt the discredit
as modern writers do.

The indictment against Britain in connection with the Peace
of 1763 is in essence the same as in 1713—that for her own ends
she concluded a separate peace without consulting her principal
allies, and that the motives behind this were once more blended
with party rancour and intrigue. Above all, George III was
anxious to rid himself of his great, but perhaps overpowering,
minister, the elder Pitt, and chose as a substitute the miserable
Bute, who embroiled our relations with the Continent by his
ignorance and perfidy. Once more, it is possible to affirm
that the main objects of the war had been attained, and that
Prussia was no longer in danger when we made our own terms
with France, since the death of the Empress Elizabeth had
utterly transformed the whole situation by placing an ardent
devotee of Frederick on the Russian throne. It is true that
Frederick, as soon as Russia drew back, had no difficulty in
making terms with Austria direct, on the basis of retaining his
essential conquests in Silesia. It is also true that in Britain there
was keen resentment and indignation at the desertion of
Frederick, who (as many old inn-signs still attest) was a very
popular figure; that Bute was widely suspected of having been
bribed, and that Pitt's great speech against the peace preliminaries
voiced the true feelings of the nation. Lastly, it is true that
Frederick, whose whole policy rested upon breaches of faith
and sudden acts of aggression, was the last who had much right
to complain of a little sharp practice on the part of an ally.
But nothing can alter the fact that Britain, by this crude return
to the diplomacy of 1711, acquired a reputation for inconstancy
as an ally which was to become a fixed idea in many continental
minds. No one did more to propagate this than Frederick,
who was always harping on "the indecent, I might almost say,
infamous" way in which England had treated him, and on
one occasion succeeded in frustrating an Anglo-Russian alliance.
"The late frequent changes in England", wrote Sir Andrew
Mitchell, our envoy to Frederick, "have created a degree of

diffidence in foreign Powers, which renders all negotiations with them difficult and disagreeable."

Among the autocratic Powers especially there grew up, even in much later times and in cases where perfidy was not imputed, a feeling that continuity of policy could not be expected from a country where parliamentary changes were chronic and brought opposing parties into power. A classic instance of this attitude is provided by Bismarck, who in theory genuinely favoured an Anglo-German alliance, but was deterred by what he summed up as "the absolute impossibility of confidential intercourse, in consequence of the indiscretions of English statesmen in their communications to Parliament, and the absence of a security in alliances for which the Crown is not answerable in England, but only the fleeting Cabinets of the day".[1] This was, however, an overstatement on the part of a statesman who had his own Parliament well in hand, since the ultimate control of military and foreign policy lay with the Emperor. Bismarck did not perhaps grasp the extent to which the seeming fluctuations of British policy were in reality determined by considerations of the balance of power, with the result that at every fresh settlement in Europe Britain tended on the whole to throw her weight in favour of compromise, and against the unlimited triumph even of her own allies.[2] Much the most statesmanlike example of this was the settlement of 1815, in which Castlereagh, ably supported by Liverpool and Wellington, prevented some of the extremer solutions favoured by the Tsar and the King of Prussia. But the same tendency is visible in most other transactions of the nineteenth century, with

[1] Commenting upon the situation in 1804, Dr Holland Rose asks: "How could Russia and Austria bind themselves to an Administration which might at any time be succeeded by one which was under the domination of the Prince of Wales, Fox and Sheridan?"

[2] Bismarck would, however, have been interested in the following phrase which I culled from an unpublished letter of Salisbury to Layard, then Ambassador to Turkey, dated 18 April 1878: "The point to which your attention should be most distinctly drawn is that *this country, which is popularly governed and cannot therefore be counted on to act on any uniform or consistent system of policy*"... etc.

the characteristic exception of the Peace of Paris in 1856, when Palmerston was hot for a continuance of the war until Russia could be docked of most of her non-Russian provinces, and only yielded to pressure from the now pacific Napoleon III and his Staff.

If, as we saw, there have been occasions when party rancour dictated a change of policy, the explanation of British reserve has far more frequently been found in a refusal to be drawn into what is now called a "conflict of ideologies", and an instinctive feeling, a hundred times justified in practice, that the words "intervention" and "non-intervention", so far from being crystal-clear, as might seem at first sight, are really among the most equivocal in the whole political vocabulary. Their interpretation lies between two extremes. On the one hand there is the assumption that every state, being sovereign, is entitled to govern or misgovern itself without any interference from without: the weak spot in this theory being that a certain degree of misgovernment makes a state so easy a prey to ambitious or interested neighbours, as to render interference well nigh inevitable. On the other hand there is the view that any assault upon the established order in one country is a menace to all other governments, and that intervention on each other's behalf is not only a right but a positive moral duty. This theory in its turn obviously breaks down over the impossibility of inducing autocratic governments to support even lawfully constituted democratic governments, or *vice versa*, neither side being content to perpetuate political systems distasteful to them. The trouble is that so often orthodoxy is claimed to be *My Doxy*, while heterodoxy is *Your Doxy*, and who shall judge between us?

The classic example of interventionist theory is that of Burke, who spoke of a "Revolution of doctrine and theoretic dogma". Arguing that it was an error to rely too much "on the formality of treaties and compacts", he went on to contend that "men are not tied to one another by papers and seals. They are led to associate by resemblances, by conformities, by sympathies. It is with nations as with individuals. Nothing is so strong a tie of amity between nation and nation as correspondence in laws, customs, manners and habits of life". It followed logically that the nations of Europe had both the duty and the right to combine, as "the Grand Vicinage of Europe", in order to destroy the pest which had found its way into their midst. But for all the genuine alarm, and at times even panic, kindled in this country by the revolutionary doctrines proclaimed in Paris and soon finding expression in a policy of European conquest, Pitt never ventured far upon the thin ice of political theory and made more than one overture of peace to the new rulers of France. He must have realised only too clearly that one main reason why his allies of the Coalition proved such broken reeds was that behind all their high-sounding phrases they were more than ever bent upon territorial aggrandisement (their conclusion of the Second Polish Partition in the very week of Louis XVI's execution is the classic example), and looked upon England mainly as a source of subsidies for the furtherance of their designs. Moreover, without seeking to detract from Pitt's noble qualities of resolution, courage and endurance— the structure upon which his successors at last climbed to victory—it must be said that he was never closely conversant with the details of the European situation (the very opposite of the French myth which saw Pitt's personality at the bottom of every act of policy or war!) and that the most famous of all his orations, proclaiming "Security" as Britain's supreme aim, silenced by its eloquence, but did not meet, the charge of "ambiguity" levelled against him.

Equally remote from Burke and from Pitt was the cautious attitude of Castlereagh towards the at first veiled, but increasingly open, "interventionism" of the Holy Alliance. The idea of a "Confederation of Europe", ostensibly based on "the precepts of the Christian religion—justice, charity and peace", but really intended to establish the allied Powers as "delegated by Providence" to conduct the affairs of Europe, was too much for Castlereagh, who, for all his conservatism, freely recognised the extent to which British liberties rested upon the Revolution of 1688—doubtless the most conservative of all revolutions, in that it asserted ancient constitutional rights against a perjured King. Treating this "Holy Alliance" as "a piece of sublime mysticism and nonsense", Castlereagh found it necessary to humour Tsar Alexander as its author and motive force, and indeed he was only too ready to co-operate in the new system of "Diplomacy by Conference" as Professor Webster has aptly called it. The value of personal contact between the statesmen of different countries was one of the main lessons of the Grand Alliance, and Castlereagh while he lived did more than any man to make it a reality. But he grew increasingly reserved as it became apparent that to the three autocrats the Holy Alliance was an instrument for upholding authority, checking progressive ideas and acquiring a pretext for interference in countries where such ideas seemed to be gaining ground. The slightly cumbrous phrases in which he clothed his objections to the Tsar's later suggestion of a mutual guarantee of "the existing order of things in thrones as well as in territories", still have their practical bearing on the affairs of the world: and indeed the dilemma which faced Castlereagh once more faces his successor in a somewhat modified form. "The idea of an 'Alliance Solidaire'", he argued, "by which every state shall be bound to support the state of succession, government and possession within all other states from violence and attack, upon condition of receiving for itself a similar guarantee, must be understood as morally implying the possessor's establishment of such a system of general government as may secure and enforce upon all Kings and nations an internal system of peace and justice. Till the mode of constructing such a system shall be devised, the consequence is inadmissible, as nothing could be more immoral or more prejudicial to the character of government generally than the idea that their force was collectively to be prostituted to the support of established power, without any consideration of the extent to which it was abused". Here lay already the unbridged gulf between the two ideologies that were soon to divide Europe, and that confront us once more today, stripped of their legitimist husk and therefore not always immediately recognisable.

The difference between the somewhat icy Castlereagh and the ever impetuous Canning has often been pointed out: the details are to be found in the classical biographies of Professors Webster and Temperley. But it is of capital importance for a right understanding of the main trends of British policy throughout the century, to realise that even before Castlereagh's death in 1822 Europe was rapidly falling into two main camps, and that, despite a certain difference in outlook towards the first tentative experiment in international government (a difference which forces us to deny to Canning the claim which we allow to Castlereagh, of being one of the spiritual ancestors of the League of Nations), there was in fundamentals an agreement between Castlereagh and Canning which the brilliant Metternich, misled by his personal likes and dislikes, never fathomed. Already in 1820 Castlereagh had warned his allies that Britain could not approve of "any attempt to reduce to an abstract rule of conduct possible cases of interference in the internal affairs of independent states", and while no less eager than they to avert revolutions, objected to their ambition of becoming "the armed guardians of all thrones". He boldly faced the fact that "the House of Hanover could not well maintain the principles on which the House of Stuart forfeited the throne". The idea propounded at the Congress of Troppau, that the Powers were entitled, "by peaceful means, or if need be by arms, to bring back the guilty state into the bosom of the great alliance", was one to which Castlereagh was not for a moment ready to subscribe.

In view of the events of our own time, it is permissible to linger over the situation of a century ago, which amid very obvious differences presents so many curious analogies. For it was the Spanish Revolution of 1820 and the series of incidents which it provoked in Italy, that finally brought to a head the conflict of opinion between the three Eastern and the two Western Powers. France of the Restoration, it is true, could not as yet, despite her thin constitutional veneer, be reckoned in the same category as Britain: and indeed French intervention on behalf of the Spanish Bourbons was condemned in terms of extraordinary openness and severity not merely in the debates of the House of Commons, but in the Speech from the Throne. But a collision was averted, and British annoyance died down as it became apparent that at least one aim of the French had been to forestall the threatened intervention of Russia and Austria in the cause of extreme legitimism, and also that France, on her own vexed admission, drew little or no profit from the expedition. Never was the Duke of Wellington a better prophet than when he declared that "there is no country in Europe in the affairs of which foreigners can interfere with so little advantage as Spain": and it is a maxim more than ever deserving of close attention today. Canning himself held that Wellington's attitude turned the scale: "I dislike the Spanish mutiny, revolution and everything that has been the consequence", the Duke told Canning, but "I dislike still more the conduct of the French Government". But with all the prestige of the Peninsular victor he upheld "the principle, not to interfere in the internal affairs of any foreign country, except in a case of necessity, being convinced that we could not interfere with advantage to such country, or with honour to ourselves". This is not very far from Canning's own maxim, that we should "not interfere except in great emergencies, and then with commanding force".

Canning, then, laid down three specific conditions of neutrality—that our ancient Portuguese ally should not be attacked, that there should be no French interference in Spanish America, and that France *should in no case "push military occupation of Spain into political possession"*. Subject to these three reservations, he would not go to war, though he considered that the support given to Ferdinand VII against his people "struck at the root of the British Constitution". Even earlier he had taken the line that "as Great Britain did not put forward her own political institutions as the model on which those of other states were to be framed, or as the only system from which national freedom and happiness could flow, so neither could she allow France to make her own example a rule for other nations...". It is open to argument whether Canning always carried this maxim into practice: it is certain that some of his successors, and Palmerston in particular, acted quite otherwise, and gave active help to one of the rival factions in Spain and in Portugal, with the deliberate object of entrenching constitutional, as against autocratic, government.

Spain has, indeed, for all its geographical and spiritual apartness, only too often raised European issues in an acute form. The extreme case for "our most decided interference" was then put by Sir James Mackintosh, when he declared that "never until the fatal Congress of Vienna was England regarded in any other light than as the champion of the independence of nations and the liberties of mankind", and again by Hobhouse, who claimed that "the honour of England was involved in the preservation of the free institutions of the Continent". Brougham denounced "the conspiracy of the great band of tyrants against the liberties of free states"; but Peel, in words to which Mr Eden might conveniently appeal, deprecated the idea of "a war of principles", while hoping that "England would never be the advocate of despotism": and Canning backed him with a sarcastic reference to "those who think that with a view of conciliating the Continental Powers and of winning them away more readily from their purpose, we should have addressed them as tyrants and despots, trampling on the rights and liberties of mankind". A year later Canning was still more cautious: he doubted the Spanish people's support for the constitution, and asked whether it was "policy to hold no communion except with states which possess free constitutions". "He knew it was maintained by some that England ought to set herself up as a barrier for all Europe, against principles of a despotic tendency: but he could not be persuaded that it was the policy of England to do lightly any act which might plunge herself and all Europe into a bloody and unceasing war". And "of all wars," he added, "wars of opinion have been decidedly the most fatal".

Events amply justified Canning in the Spanish crisis: but it is useless to pretend that he adopted a consistent or logical attitude in South America, Portugal or Greece. Indeed it is to him that we trace the growing difficulty of defining "intervention" and "non-intervention" which reached its height under Palmerston. With the memory of his decisive part in sending troops for the defence of Portugal against Napoleon, Canning did not hesitate for a moment in 1826 to send the military help for which the Government of the child Queen Maria appealed. In one of his most famous speeches he now reminded the House of Commons that a few years earlier he had pleaded for "neutrality, not only between contending nations, but between contending principles", as the sole means of maintaining that balance of power which he believed to be "essential to the welfare of mankind". But in the Spanish threat to Portugal he now saw the imminence of a war "not so much of armies as of opinions", though he made it clear that French policy no longer caused him alarm, and argued that the Balance of Power on which he set such store was "a standard perpetually varying as civilisation advances and as new nations spring up".

It was on this same occasion that Canning uttered his famous phrase, "I called the New World into existence to redress the balance of the Old". His steady policy of "Hands Off" to other European Powers, even more than the attitude of President Monroe, rendered possible the independence of the South American colonies: and in the same way the recognition which he accorded to the Greek insurgents was one of the principal factors which eventually brought a free Greece into existence. In both cases Canning's policy was compounded of theory and practice: considerable commercial interests were at stake, and in allowing this fact to turn the scale in favour of belligerent rights, he could argue that sooner or later a Government's inability to quell an insurrection gives the organiser of the latter a right to *de facto* recognition. Whether a real distinction can be drawn between a national uprising against foreign rule and a civil war between co-nationals, is a knotty problem of international law, which could not be solved within the bounds set to this volume.

Canning's policy remained a torso, but in effect he had completely drawn back from what he sarcastically called the "Areo-pagitic" method of diplomacy, and for the time had substituted a Triple Alliance with France and Russia, cutting across the alignments of the Holy Alliance and leading logically to inter-vention in the Greek question. Canning's great crime, in the interested eyes of Metternich, was that he laid fresh stress upon "the interests of England", while admitting her intimate con-nection with the system of Europe; that he frankly recognised the incompatibility of aims between the Western and the Eastern Powers, and refused to be dragged at the heels of the latter. That he too, like Metternich and Nicholas, tended to interpret "intervention" and "non-intervention" according to whether progressives or reactionaries in any particular country stood most in need of outside help, can hardly be denied, and thus renders it almost inevitable that his statesmanship should today be judged by predilections of the Right or Left.

This tendency was greatly accentuated in the middle of the century under Palmerston and Russell, who, indeed, sought to turn the point of intervention against its original advocates. In 1836 Palmerston tried to convice his rather easy-going chief Melbourne, that "the division of Europe into two camps" was already an accomplished fact, as a result of the July Revolution of 1830. The three Eastern Powers—Russia, Austria, Prussia—so he argued, "fancy their interests lie in a direction opposite to that where we and France conceive ours to be placed. The separation is not one of words, but of things: not the effect of caprice or of will, but produced by the force of occurrences. The Three and the Two think differently, and therefore they act differently, whether it be as to Belgium, or Poland, or Spain." But already in 1832 Palmerston, while arguing before the House England's great interest in the maintenance of European peace, gave it as the Government's view that this could "most easily, most safely and most securely be attained by the maintenance of a firm and strict alliance between France and this country". Later in the same year he elaborated further the principles on which he sought to rest his policy, and openly declared "constitutional states to be the natural allies of this country" and their independence something that could "never be a matter of indifference to the British Parliament, or, I should hope, to the British Public". "Let persons recommend", he went on, "as much as they will, the propriety of England withdrawing itself from all political connection with the rest of the world, my opinion is that as long as our commerce is of importance to us, as long as Continental armies are in existence, as long as it is possible that a Power in one quarter may be dangerous to a Power in another, so long must England look with interest on the transactions of the Continent."

Amid the gathering force of revolutionary current in the 'forties, while other Governments sought the remedy in dams rather than in canalisation, Palmerston steadily preached to other Governments the doctrine of timely and "spontaneous concession" as in every way far less dangerous than concessions "wrung from them by the pressure of imperious circumstances" and only too apt to disturb the relations of Crown and people. Events proved him only too right, though he unfortunately had not possessed the tact or persuasiveness needed to convert recalcitrant rulers. In the year that preceded the great explosion of 1848, during a debate on Portugal, he openly avowed that "the recall of the [Portuguese] Parliament" was "the main-spring" of his policy, and proceeded to state this as a generally applicable principle. "Our duty, our vocation, is not to enslave, but to set free, and I may say, without any vainglorious boast or without great offence to anyone, that we stand at the head of moral, social and political civilisation. Our task is to lead the way and to direct the march of other nations. I do not think we ought to goad on the unwilling or force forward the reluctant: but when we see a people battling against difficulties and obstacles in the pursuit of their rights, we may be permitted to encourage them with our sympathy and cheer them with our approbation, and even, if occasion requires, to lend them a helping hand." It is not surprising that such phrases were widely misunderstood and resented in authoritarian circles, while kindling corresponding elation among all advocates of liberal and constitutional reform. It is necessary to add the reminder that the unpalatable form in which Palmerston offered advice, for instance to Austria or the Pope, had the very opposite effect from that intended, and created an entirely false impression as to his true aims. Prince Schwarzenberg and Francis Joseph in particular looked upon him as favouring revolution at the time when he was refusing to recognise the Hungarian exiles and writing instructions in the sense that the maintenance of the Austrian Empire was a vital European interest.

Whatever else may be said of Palmerston, it must be admitted that he meant what he said, and when he gave a warning or a threat, followed it up by equivalent action—and not merely against the lesser Powers, though his treatment of Greece can only be described as that of a big bully. But Russell as Foreign Secretary in the 'sixties combined with a passion for interference a still more didactic and irritating tone, and an unfortunate tendency to take up positions which he was not always prepared to defend. His admirers generally adduce the decisive moral and diplomatic support which he gave to the cause of Italy as his most lasting title to fame: but it is necessary to qualify this by a reminder that to the very last he lacked any clearly thought-out policy on this burning problem of his time, as is shown by his statement in Parliament as late as February 1861 (eighteen months after Solferino, nine months after Garibaldi's Sicilian triumph, and on the eve of the King of Naples surrendering his last fortress), expressing a preference for "*two Kingdoms of Italy* rather than one!" There was, moreover, a striking contrast between his support of nationality in Italy and his reactionary and hostile attitude towards the Serbian and Roumanian movements. Under him the policy of interference reached its supreme fiasco in the questions of Poland and of the Danish Duchies, in each of which Russell receded from his original position with great loss of prestige to Britain and grave injury to the small nations which had rashly relied upon his support. The soreness engendered by this and by his simultaneous bungling of our relations with America, led to a rebound in favour of strict non-intervention: and this coincided with decisive changes in the balance of forces in Europe, as a result of Prussia's successive victories over Austria and France and the reconstitution of the old alliance of the three Eastern Powers. Britain's almost impregnable naval position at that period atoned for her consciousness of impotence on land, in face of the new conscript armies of the Continent: and for a time Conservatives and Liberals, who had alternately inclined towards insular ideas, were agreed in their desire to keep out of European entanglements. None the less, in the 'seventies the eclipse of France and the insignificance of Italy left Britain uncomfortably isolated in face of the three great Empires: and this time it was the Conservatives under Disraeli who favoured a resumption of active intervention, spurred on in the first instance by suspicion of Russia and by the strong remnants of the old Turcophil illusion. One great difference between 1854–6 and 1876–8 is that the nation, so firmly united in its earlier frenzy that two such recent heroes as Cobden and Bright found themselves slighted and flung aside when they opposed war, was now deeply divided on the issue of supporting Turkey against her Christian subjects, at the risk of a conflict with Russia. In the great Eastern Crisis precipitated by the Bosnian rising and the Bulgarian massacres, neither Disraeli nor Gladstone was able to impose his will, and the ultimate settlement more nearly reflected the mind of Salisbury, who in all Near Eastern questions stood almost exactly between them, and who was very rightly Turcophobe without being Russophil.

If the rebound from Palmerston's and Russell's "muddle and meddle"[1] to isolation had spent itself by the time of Disraeli's victory in 1874, the second rebound was all the stronger owing to the deep dissensions of the Eastern Crisis and the dissatisfaction of the extremists with the final settlement, and resulted in a fresh attempt to avoid Continental commitments. The 'eighties and 'nineties—during which France steadily revives, but in a hypersensitive and challenging mood, and in which the scramble for colonies, especially in Africa, reaches its height —are also the classical period of Britain's would-be isolation, and simultaneously of a growing perception of its dangers.

[1] The phrase of their enemy the elder Lord Derby.

In this connection it remains to indicate one increasingly important factor in the sphere of foreign policy, namely the influence of public opinion, as voiced in the press no less than in Parliament itself. Since the days of Canning, who first based diplomatic action on an appeal to public opinion, to those of Balfour, who finally asserted Parliament's authority as to any cession of territory, and of the post-war period, when the precedent of submitting treaties to Parliament before ratification became well nigh, if not absolutely, irrevocable, there has been a steady decline in the Crown's control of foreign policy, though the short reign of Edward VII shows what immense, if imponderable, influence it still possesses: and this decline is undoubtedly due in part to the increased dependence of the Cabinet, both collectively and individually, upon a vocal, if not necessarily well-informed, public opinion. The skill with which ministers controlled or manipulated that opinion has of course varied according to characters and circumstances, long before what we now call propaganda was invented: much depended also upon the readiness or reluctance of individual governments to keep the public properly informed, to give it a lead at the right time and thus to prevent outbursts of passion or of panic. The origins of the Crimean War reveal what havoc can be wrought by an ill-informed and ill-led public opinion.[1] The Eastern Crisis of the 'seventies shows how even a strong and aggressive Government's policy can be deflected or paralysed by open dissensions in the country. The extent to which public opinion is sensitive to moral issues, and thereby exercises restraint upon its Government, finds abundant illustrations throughout the nineteenth century—from Wilberforce's agitation against the Slave Trade to Cobden and Bright's periodic intervention in the sphere of foreign policy, to the wrath kindled by "Bulgarian Horrors" in the 'seventies and by the Armenian massacres in the 'nineties. Hand in hand with such outbursts of idealism went the growing demand in intel-

[1] Mr Kingsley Martin's book, *The Triumph of Lord Palmerston*, deserves the closest study of all interested in the background of *imponderabilia* which so often sways policy to and fro.

lectual circles for the extension and vindication of a system of international law and for the application of methods of arbitration. Such problems assumed a new and more insistent form about the turn of the century, when America and Japan began to be factors in European as well as Pacific problems, and when the conception of "World Affairs" rapidly took on a new meaning. These are realities which cynical statesmen must take into account: and there is no more signal example in our history than the movement of opinion which swept the country when the news of Germany's attack upon Belgium arrived.

This country has never insisted upon identity of political outlook as a basis of alliance and friendship, as our relations with the Second Empire, with Turkey, with Tsarist Russia, and now with the U.S.S.R., amply testify. There have indeed been many obvious cases in which geography or economics or military necessity render an alliance, or at the least parallel diplomatic action, between a free and a despotic country both possible and effective. We shall have to consider later how far such co-operation has been rendered more difficult in our own day by the rise of totalitarian ideas, and by a militant intolerance of all other political views for which the great autocracies of pre-war days offer no precedent.

This brief summary of tendencies has deliberately relied for its most frequent illustrations upon earlier periods rather than that immediately preceding the Great War: for this method tends to bring home the lesson of continuity and unchangeable interests. It would be a fatal error to overload such a sketch with any enquiry into the question of War Origins. Today, despite profound divergences of view on many vital points, almost all historians are at least agreed upon the utility of distinguishing between the two categories of causes—the immediate and the ultimate—and admit that responsibility for the latter must rest with all the Great Powers and with some lesser Powers also. The exact proportions of that responsibility it will perhaps never be possible to estimate: but I do most earnestly believe that we have already reached a stage at which the supporters of conflicting views can discuss them together with conviction, and it may be even with passion, but without mutual insult and in a sincere endeavour to add a few stones to the dam which is to protect humanity against a fresh bursting of the floods. Speaking for myself, I would even go so far as to accept the view, put forward by Dr Friedrich Hertz in his penetrating study of the deeper causes of the Great War,[1] that no nation had deliberately planned the catastrophe which actually befell Europe in August 1914. This is of course a very different thing from saying that no nation had war plans, or was prepared to risk war to attain its immediate aim: in each case the facts overwhelmingly bear out the contrary. And again, while acquitting William II and his entourage of any concrete plan for war in the summer of 1914, I fail to see how any close student of the diplomatic documents now available (and not least of all, of the reports of successive German Ambassadors in London to the Berlin Government) can fail to reach the conclusion that those who controlled German policy in the opening years of the century were pursuing aims which involved hegemony by land and sea, and consequently a surrender on the part of all three Powers of the Triple Entente such as neither safety nor prestige could permit. It is simply futile to suggest that your attitude is not aggressive because it is at any moment open to your opponent to abandon the struggle and place himself in an inferior position. Sir Eyre Crowe put his finger on the main clue when he wrote of Germany in 1912: "She wants to have an absolutely free hand in dealing with any problem of foreign policy, without fear of meeting with the opposition of third parties. She wants to make herself so strong that she can dictate terms to every Power."

The crucial points in Britain's attitude towards Germany in those years may be summed up very succinctly in the three following directions. Firstly Britain sought to promote general peace by a series of *ententes* and understandings such as would remove existing points of friction—in other words, first with France as the nearest, and as the neighbour with whom there

[1] *Nationalgeist und Politik*, vol. 1 (Zurich, 1937).

were the largest number of unregulated questions, then with Russia, *and then with Germany* (and that this was no mere platonic wish is shown by Grey's dealings with Germany during the Ambassadorial Conference in the Balkan Wars, and still more by the agreements respecting the Portuguese colonies and the Bagdad Railway, which were ready for signature by the spring of 1914). Secondly, so far from trying to isolate Germany, she tried to act as a bridge between the two groups of Powers, and thereby to diminish friction and make a reality of the Concert of Europe: but at the same time she could not be blind to the fact that Germany, so far from reciprocating this desire, was above all bent upon detaching Britain from existing alignments. Then, as now, there could, and can, be no final settlement between Britain and Germany until the latter realises that our aim is not to transfer our allegiance from one Power or group to another, but to add her friendship to those friend-ships which we already possess,[1] and thus promote a general appeasement, but never to hoist any Power to hegemony on our shoulders. Thirdly, a sure instinct taught her the absolute necessity of naval superiority for a Power whose interests were world-wide and who, if her fleet were once defeated, would be instantly at the mercy of every plunderer. She recognised this to be no less true of the German army (1918 proved this), but in no way whatever of the German navy: she never pre-sumed to dictate to Berlin the size of that navy, but from every rejection of a naval holiday and from every fresh effort of Admiral Tirpitz to steal a march upon us, she grimly drew her own conclusions.

With regard to immediate responsibility in 1914 it must suffice to point out the strange fluctuations of the German barometer for measuring war-guilt. At first the chief villain was Grey, but long before the publication of the "British Diplomatic Documents" (edited by Gooch and Temperley) had overwhelmingly disproved his guilt, other exculpatory evidence had led to a toning down of the attack upon him.

[1] "To bring the two groups nearer", so Lichnowsky summed up Grey's programme, and no one has ever summed it up more tersely.

For a time Poincaré and Izvolsky shared the blame between them, and while the latter cannot be altogether acquitted, it has long since become clear that he had far too little influence upon his own Government to qualify as the maker of a Russian war policy, and of a conspiracy between them there has never been any real evidence. The attack was then concentrated upon the Russian mobilisation order as the actual cause of war, until it transpired that the three mobilisations—Russian, Austro-Hungarian and German—all took place quite independently of each other. As a last attempt to discover a scapegoat, there was a determined onslaught upon Serbia, whose Government was alleged to have been privy to the plot against the Archduke's life: and for a time the apparent indifference shown by the Pašić Cabinet to these charges, and its failure to publish the necessary documents, lent a certain plausibility to the campaign among those unacquainted with the complex party situation in post-war Jugoslavia and its bearings upon the problem. But latterly this campaign also has languished, in proportion as the relations of Berlin and Belgrade grew positively cordial. Today, by a process of exclusion, suspicion is turning back to the Austro-Hungarian Government, whose motives in risking and eventually precipitating war had nothing to do with a possible complicity of Serbia, for which they admittedly had no evidence whatsoever till a much later date. For them the all-important question was whether or not Vienna would have the full military backing of Berlin in the event of war.

There are many grounds for sharing Grey's view, expressed in cold blood long afterwards, that if the Ambassadorial Committee which was so successful in handling the problems of the Balkan War in the winter of 1912–13 had still been in existence, or could have been reconstituted, it would have been possible to avert the break-down of negotiations in July 1914. On the other hand, the best case that can be made out for Germany is that put forward soon after the War by Professor Erich Brandenburg—that if she had not given her full backing to Austria-Hungary in 1914 (after having decisively held her back in 1913) she would have lost her only reliable ally and perhaps found herself in complete isolation. But this cannot obscure the ominous meaning of the Hoyos mission to Berlin, of Viktor Naumann's mission to Vienna, and of Jagow's interference with the date of delivery of the ultimatum to Serbia: and there remains as a still more decisive factor the "Schlieffen Plan" for hacking through Belgium before Russia could be ready. It is this which gives to the Belgian question its immense double significance, at once from the moral and from the strategic point of view.

In matters of foreign policy the first requirement—so successive Governments have told us, though not always acting according to their own principle—is an informed and sane public opinion, knowing the essentials of our past history, proud of our free institutions and ready for sacrifice in their defence, and not least of all, strenuously avoiding that blend of aggressiveness and jumpiness which characterised it in mid-Victorian days. A sober realism must be our ideal, recognising that interference is undesirable, but isolation either impossible or fraught with appalling danger, and that the main problem of statesmanship is to reconcile specifically British interests with that wider internationalism which alone offers hope of peace and progress in our distracted Europe. I have the firm hope that those who desire to face hard facts and to profit by them will not be angry with me for the plain speaking of the following pages.

III

SOME ASPECTS OF BRITISH WAR POLICY

I T lies quite outside my present purpose to give the full history of British policy during and since the Great War. But there are certain aspects of it which it may be well to stress as part of that readjustment of focus which is so necessary under the altered circumstances of the present day.

It has long since become the merest truism that what turned British opinion and the man in the street from neutrality to action was not any real perception of our own danger or even of what may be regarded as political commitments, but a wave of sentiment against the German invasion of Belgium, against the cynical phrases by which the German Chancellor sought to justify it and against the terrorist measures by which it was hoped to quell Belgian resistance. It only gradually became clear that our attitude was compounded of three things: (1) our determination to uphold Belgian independence, not merely as part of our obligations under the Treaty of 1839, but as a restatement in modern times of Britain's vital concern in the Narrow Seas and Low Countries, which had repeatedly shaped our policy ever since the days of Elizabeth; (2) the perception that the conquest of Belgium might well be followed by the complete overthrow of France as a factor in European politics, and that the German offer to abstain from naval action in the Channel could in no way be a substitute for this; and (3) the conviction that Germany, the chief military Power in Europe, could have no motive in seeking naval equality with the chief naval Power also, unless she aimed at absolute hegemony in Europe, and that with her victory over France our naval security, and indeed our general security, would be at an end. In one word, prompt intervention was necessary to prevent Germany—either directly or through her Allies—becoming master of the Continent: and it was only after the war had been waged for some time that it became apparent that the much-

vaunted Balance of Power—which Britain then unquestionably
wished to uphold—was also a thing of the past, and that France
and Russia, even if supplemented by Britain and Italy, were not
in a military sense a match for the German Powers, and this
not merely because of the superior geographical and strategic
advantage conferred by interior lines of communication, but
absolutely, on the basis of man-power, equipment, mobility,
and organisation. The confident pre-war calculations of military
pundits like Colonel Repington were drastically disproved by
events.

THE SECRET TREATIES

For quite a long period in the War there was no attempt
to define British war-aims. All else was subordinated to the
desperate need of warding off a succession of victorious enemy
offensives on different fronts: and there was a very pardonable
reluctance on the part of our statesmen to divide up the skin
of the bear before he had been killed—a phrase which I
remember Sir Edward Grey once using in private conversation
in the first winter of the war. They did, it is true, pledge themselves in honour to restore the integrity and independence of
Belgium and of Serbia: and Mr Asquith's eloquent version of
this pledge was more than once officially renewed. "We shall
never sheathe the sword until...the rights of the smaller
nationalities of Europe are placed upon an unassailable foundation, and until the military domination of Prussia is wholly
and finally destroyed." They also assumed mutual undertakings against separate peace. On the other hand certain secret
treaties were concluded: (1) the Treaty of London (26 April
1915) which conceded to Italy the mastery of the Adriatic,
the possession of Istria and half Dalmatia and the control of
Albania; (2) the Convention which recognised Russia's claim to
Constantinople and the Straits (18 March 1915); and (3) the
Treaty of August 1916, which recognised Roumania's right to
annex not only all the Roumanian districts of Austria and
Hungary, but also large tracts of purely Magyar territory as
far as the river Tisza. All three treaties were wholly incom-

patible with that settlement on a basis of nationality and self-determination to which the Allies paid constant lip-service. It was not really till January 1917 that the attitude of President Wilson compelled the rival belligerents to define their war aims more closely: and it was then that the Allies announced their desire for "the reorganisation of Europe",[1] on the triple basis of "respect for nationalities and of the right to full security and liberty of economic development possessed by all peoples small and great, and at the same time upon territorial conventions and international settlements such as to guarantee land and sea frontiers against unjustified attack": and this was to involve the restitution of lost territory, "the liberation of the Italians, as also of the Slavs, Roumanians and Czechoslovaks from foreign domination", and the ending of Turkish rule in Europe. This answer, though in some respects vague and equivocal, was a landmark in the war, for the contrast between it and the German attitude, leading logically to a policy of "frightfulness", turned the scale in favour of American intervention. This, following so soon upon the Russian Revolution, ushered in a period of competitive programmes between the two groups. The catchword "Peace without Annexations" was canvassed to and fro, and great and well-merited embarrassment was caused when the new Bolshevik Government, at the end of 1917, began to publish the texts of the secret treaties as proof of the incorrigible Imperialism of all the bourgeois Governments, and in the hope of driving a wedge between them and their American allies, who had undertaken no such obligations. As a result the Allies, individually and collectively, drifted into a sort of competition of pledges, seeking to keep up their own morale, to outbid or take the edge off Russia's revolutionary professions and to retain the favour of America and of Wilson, the prophet of democracy.

In the opening months of 1918 confusion grew worse confounded. Revolutionary Russia, till so recently the foremost

---

[1] It is perhaps allowable to mention that two months earlier I had published in *The New Europe* (9 November 1916) an article bearing this very title, "The Reorganisation of Europe".

champion of self-determination, had fallen into the hands of the Bolsheviks, who abolished the Constituent Assembly and substituted a dictatorship of the proletariat—degenerating into open terror and civil war—for the political liberties to which the Provisional Government had aspired: and it was upon this no longer free state that Germany imposed on 3 March 1918 the Treaty of Brest-Litovsk, by which Finland, the Baltic Provinces, Poland and Ukraine passed from Russia's control. Germany's ambitions were sufficiently revealed by her military occupation of Kiev, Odessa, Riga and Kovno, by her attempts to maintain both Poland and Ukraine as vassal states, and by the drastic Peace of Bucarest (May 1918), which she imposed upon the now completely isolated Roumanians, and which, while reducing them to economic and financial vassalage, left them free to seek compensation in Bessarabia and thus to ensure Russian hostility to United Roumania.

SELF-DETERMINATION

It is absolutely essential, for any right understanding of the sequel, to bear in mind the rigorous and far-reaching terms imposed by Germany under these treaties, and the complete contrast between her public professions—especially in answer to Pope Benedict's peace move—and the secret aims which her statesmen and soldiers were all the time pursuing. It is a simple fact that while Chancellor Michaelis had in September 1917 welcomed "the simultaneous and reciprocal limitation of armaments" and "compulsory arbitration in international disputes", there had been discussions at the German Crown Council tending to insist upon the economic control of Belgium, the annexation of Luxembourg and some of the French mining districts, and similarly the economic control of Poland in the East, a great extension of territory in Silesia and on the Vistula, and virtual control of the Baltic Provinces. The full terms which Germany, at various stages of the war, thought of imposing on the Allies, still remain a jealously guarded secret: but there are grounds for supposing that the restitution of Belgian and French territory was in any case to have been made contingent upon France, Britain and Belgium surrendering to Germany the greater part of their African possessions and in particular the linking up of "South-West" with "East" by means of the Congo, effectively barring the way to the "Cape to Cairo" idea. Brest-Litovsk first taught the world what might be expected from a German peace, and its elaborate economic clauses, far too complex and technical to recapitulate here, left no possible doubt as to Germany's intention of laying her hands, for generations to come, upon the agricultural and mineral resources—above all the wheat and oil—of the Ukraine and of Roumania.

LLOYD GEORGE'S AND WILSON'S CONDITIONS OF PEACE

While these vast changes were being rapidly consummated, Mr Lloyd George, with his instinct for political strategy, realised that some further attempt to define our all too nebulous war-aims could hardly be postponed much longer, after all the eloquent discussions at Stockholm during the preceding summer and autumn on "self-determination" and kindred theories. Moreover, a double incentive was provided by the secret evidence of Austria's exhaustion and eagerness for peace talks,[1] and by the need for forestalling President Wilson's imminent definition of terms. On 5 January 1918 he delivered to the Trade Union Conference a speech previously approved by the Cabinet and by the Dominions. Declaring that "the days of the Treaty of Vienna are long past", he put forward as the three main Conditions of Peace the re-establishment of the sanctity of treaties, a territorial settlement based on self-determination, and "an international organisation to limit the burden of armaments". While of course demanding "the complete restoration" of Belgium, Serbia, Montenegro and Roumania and of occupied French and Italian territory, he disclaimed any desire

[1] General Smuts met Count Mensdorff in Switzerland on 18 and 19 December 1917.

to destroy Germany or to alter her constitution. He further declared that "the break-up of Austria-Hungary is no part of our war-aims", but qualified this by demanding "genuine self-government" for her nationalities, and independence for Poland, adding two extremely vague phrases about "the legitimate claims of the Italians" and justice for "men of Roumanian blood and speech". It is essential at this point to remember that when Revolutionary Russia repudiated the secret bargain with the Allies and gave them an excuse for regarding the Asia Minor pledges towards Italy as no longer valid, they unfairly ignored the latter's claim to compensation and thus left her with a fatal grievance.

As regards Turkey, Mr Lloyd George drew a significant distinction between "the homelands of the Turkish race" and the four non-Turkish provinces of her Empire, Arabia, Mesopotamia, Syria and Palestine. He hinted darkly that "new circumstances" such as the Russian collapse and separate negotiations had modified the attitude of the Allies towards the treaty pledges made to Russia earlier in the war. Of the German colonies he repeated earlier declarations, that "they are held at the disposal of a Conference whose decisions must have primary regard to the wishes of the native inhabitants".

The ambiguity of many of these phrases merely reflected the doubts and hesitations of the British Cabinet, and the extent to which, in the fourth year of the war, it was waiting upon military events and uncertain of the ultimate issue. A perusal of General Smuts's secret report to the War Cabinet[1] reveals the further fact that the Cabinet itself, at this time, did not know "the revised views of our Allies", and had not reached "even provisional conclusions" on the questions discussed with Mensdorff. In any case, there was still a complete deadlock, for the new German Chancellor, Count Hertling,[2] acting under pressure from German Headquarters, altogether repudiated Mr Lloyd George's conditions, refused to discuss Alsace, Poland

[1] Published *in extenso* by Mr Lloyd George in Chapter LXX of his *War Memoirs* (see especially v, p. 2473).
[2] Reichstag speech of 24 January 1918.

(or even Belgium, save as part of a general discussion) and explicitly rejected the integrity of Allied territory as a basis of negotiation. This led the Supreme War Council of the Allies on 4 February to denounce Germany's "now openly disclosed plans of conquest and spoliation", and to preach renewed military effort until "a change of temper" could be produced " in the enemy Governments and peoples".

AUSTRIA-HUNGARY AS THE KEY

Meanwhile the real initiative in constructive peace terms passed to President Wilson, whose "Fourteen Points" were given to the world only three days after the speech of Lloyd George. It will be necessary to examine them more fully in a later chapter in their bearing upon the actual terms of peace imposed by the Allies: for the moment their essential features may be summed up very briefly as follows: "Open covenants of peace" instead of secret diplomacy, freedom of the seas, the removal of economic barriers, reduction of armaments, adjustment of colonial claims with due regard for the interests of native populations, evacuation of all Russian territory, restoration of Belgium and France and also of Alsace-Lorraine, frontiers for Italy on a basis of nationality, "autonomous development" for the peoples of Austria-Hungary, evacuation of occupied Balkan territories and independence of all Balkan states, autonomy for "the non-Turkish portions" of the Ottoman Empire, Polish independence and "a general association of nations under specific covenants". The Fourteen Points caught the imagination of the peoples and throughout 1918 became increasingly the rallying point for all who sought an agreed democratic peace. It cannot, however, be emphasised too strongly that the President himself subsequently modified their contents in certain very vital particulars, in his three speeches of 11 February, 4 July and 27 September 1918: and that the many writers who today argue that Germany's acceptance of the Armistice was contingent upon the enforcement of the Fourteen Points, as such, are guilty of very grave misrepresentation. This is a matter of fundamental importance in any discussion of the Peace and of allied undertakings or allied good faith.

After these three pronouncements from London, Washington and Berlin, the deadlock seemed absolute between the two belligerent groups, and on the side of the Central Powers Ludendorff and the soldiers completely dominated the civilian advisers of the Emperor. In actual fact, the Allies stood irrevocably committed to the territorial *status quo* in the West and to the restoration of Alsace-Lorraine to France: in the East the collapse and disintegration of Russia was rapidly ousting them from all control over events. For that very reason, however, statesmen hitherto unfamiliar with Continental problems directed increased attention to that intervening section of Europe which included the many races of the Dual Monarchy and of the Balkan Peninsula. Their interest was stimulated by the secret overtures of the Emperor Charles to London through the Smuts-Mensdorff conversations and to Washington through still more informal discussions between Wilson's freelance confidant George Herron and the Austrian international jurist Heinrich Lammasch. By now many things were working up to a climax. Germany was preparing a desperate offensive in the West: Italy, sobered by the grave reverse at Caporetto, and alarmed at British and American disclaimers of all designs against Austro-Hungarian integrity, realised the vital necessity for reaching a timely and direct agreement with the other nationalities under Habsburg rule, for a reconstruction of the Dual Monarchy on national lines, if the war was not to end without any gains for Italy at the expense of her major enemy. Moreover, the creation of an Enemy Propaganda Department under Lord Northcliffe revealed the Cabinet's tardy comprehension of the need for a constructive British policy. Before the German attack could be launched on 21 March, it had become abundantly clear to Herron, and perhaps even to General Smuts, that Austria-Hungary was far too enmeshed in the German toils to be able to conclude a separate peace: and meanwhile a series of preliminary conferences in London between representative but unofficial Italians and Jugoslavs had prepared the ground for a joint statement of policy. Northcliffe had accepted his new post without realising the fundamental fact that propaganda must rest on policy, not on mere negation: but his alert mind quickly reacted, and as a preliminary to action against the Habsburg Monarchy he invited the War Cabinet to endorse one of two alternative policies: (A) "to work for a separate peace"—a policy already tried without success, or (B) "to try to break the power of Austria-Hungary, as the weakest link in the chain of enemy states, by supporting all anti-German and pro-Ally peoples and tendencies". On 26 February Mr Balfour, as Foreign Secretary, and in the name of the Cabinet, approved the adoption of Policy B, though declining to give any explicit promise of complete independence to individual nationalities. It was on the double basis of the Balfour-Northcliffe correspondence (endorsed by the French and Italian propagandist departments) and of the Italo-Jugoslav agreement of 7 March, that a Congress of the Subject Races of Austria-Hungary was organised on the Capitol in Rome,[1] and a joint programme of action was drawn up and solemnly ratified. The propagandist activities which followed on the Italian front had a disintegrating effect upon the non-German and non-Magyar regiments in the opposite trenches, in some cases rendered necessary their withdrawal or re-grouping, and contributed very materially to the failure of the last Austrian offensive on the Piave in June 1918. The last hope of an Austrian separate peace had vanished with the public controversy between Clemenceau and Czernin, which left the luckless Emperor Charles no alternative save to cry "Peccavi" and to surrender himself to the control of William II and the German High Command.

[1] Among its leading delegates were Beneš, first Foreign Minister and now President of Czechoslovakia, Stefaník, the first Czechoslovak War Minister, Trumbić, first Foreign Minister of Jugoslavia, Skirmunt, future Polish Foreign Minister and first Polish Ambassador in London, and Mironescu, a future Roumanian Premier. Among the Italian representatives were Salvemini and Borgese, now both in exile, Amendola, afterwards done to death by Fascist gangsters, and Bissolati, the Socialist Minister.

The Roman Congress awakened echoes inside the Dual Monarchy, where under the flimsy cover of allegiance to the Crown the various movements in favour of national unity— Polish, Ukrainian, Czechoslovak, Roumanian and Jugoslav— rapidly gained ground. But even more important were its diplomatic effects. In the first place the U.S. Government, much impressed by the proceedings in Rome, announced its "lively sympathy with the national aspirations of the Czecho-slovaks and Jugoslavs for liberty" (29 May): and this was promptly endorsed by the three Entente Powers on 3 June. Attempts were at once made to water this down by assuming that it could not mean more than the "autonomy" referred to in the tenth of the Fourteen Points: but this evoked a much more explicit statement from Washington, on 28 June, to the effect that "all branches of the Slav race should be completely freed from German and Austrian rule".

Step by step during the summer the Allies and America moved towards a far more drastic policy. On 30 June France formally recognised the Czechoslovak National Council as "the first step towards a future Government", and on 9 August the British Government recognised it "as the present trustee of the future Czechoslovak Government" and its army as a regular belligerent, and on 3 September recognised it "as a *de facto* belligerent Government". Meanwhile the Polish forces fighting on the Allied side obtained similar recognition, and the Jugoslav Legions would also have acquired this status but for the un-fortunate disagreement between the Serbian Government and the exiled Jugoslav Committee, and the opposition of the Italian Foreign Minister. Even as it was, Mr Balfour at the Mansion House, in August, openly spoke in favour of Jugoslav Unity. In a word, by the autumn of 1918, the Allies already stood committed to a programme which was wholly incompatible with the survival of Austria-Hungary as a Great Power: and the only really moot point was whether Roumania, by her forced conclusion of a separate peace, had forfeited her claim to be considered.

The explosive effect of these successive pronouncements upon the peoples inside the Dual Monarchy was still further heightened when, after the collapse of the Bulgarian and Turkish fronts, Austria-Hungary found it necessary to make peace overtures to President Wilson, and the decisive battle was now waged with diplomatic Notes rather than with shells and machine-guns. Too late the Emperor Charles pronounced in favour of the federalisation of his dominions, only to find his project stultified by Hungary's insistence that it should be restricted to the Austrian half only, and her threat that any attempt to extend it would lead Hungary to cut off food supplies from starving Vienna. Blocked at home by Hungary's intransigeance, he was almost simultaneously reminded by President Wilson that Point Ten, advocating "mere autonomy" for the Habsburg races, was now precluded by his explicit pledges of independence to the Czechoslovaks and Jugoslavs. Not since the trumpets of Joshua made the walls of Jericho to fall had so magical an effect been wrought. Wilson's Notes were undoubtedly the foremost instrument of Austria-Hungary's downfall.

It will thus be apparent that during the spring and summer of 1918 the Allies were engaged in adjusting their focus towards Central and South-Eastern Europe, of which in the earlier stages of the war they had been profoundly ignorant, though some of them were shrewd enough to realise its strategic possibilities. When at last the Turkish and Bulgarian fronts crumbled, the political effects were far-reaching, and today we have the testimony of many representative Germans, beginning with Ludendorff, as to the farsightedness of Mr Lloyd George and Mr Winston Churchill in advocating attacks upon the "back door", and the obtuse lack of imagination of some of our greatest generals in hammering upon the main defences.

In the closing months of the war even those few who had time to look ahead and plan a new order were outstripped and left breathless by events. The Revolution which had transformed Russia and given birth to the Border States was now succeeded by a whole series of revolutions in the defeated states, varying infinitely in motive and in form, but in each case confronting the Allies with accomplished facts, some of which they had failed to anticipate, and which left them puzzled and embarrassed. For my present purpose the essential facts are that Britain reached the Armistice without any clearly evolved peace policy, save upon obviously fundamental matters as Belgium or Alsace, and that no agreed common programme had ever been reached even among the principal Allies: that the ferment of popular opinion throughout the world, which was scarcely less responsible for the final issue than the actual military decisions, took but small account of the secret compacts with the Allied Governments to which she stood committed, and indeed that in some cases the rush of events was rendering them inoperative: and not least of all, that the great Associate Power, America, was expressly dissociating herself from such discredited old-world compacts and was, through the mouth of her President, assuming an initiative in the settlement that was almost apocalyptic.

IV

THE PEACE SETTLEMENT
AND BRITISH POLICY

STRATEGIC CHANGES IN EUROPE

THE period of upheaval which lasted from the military collapse of the Central Powers to the close of the Paris Peace Conference has no exact parallel in modern history, not even in the period following the downfall of Napoleon. For it was not merely the liquidation of the greatest and most devasting of all wars: it was also a revolution, or rather a series of revolutions—at once national, political and social—throughout large tracts of Europe. In a word, 1918–19 was at one and the same time 1815 and 1848, and it was in its second aspect that the greatest changes were wrought. The old Balance of Power was for the moment blown to smithereens, and with it vanished not only the Concert of Europe in its pre-war form, but both the main political systems, the Triple Alliance and the Triple Entente. Four ancient Empires fell, and with them four of the great dynasties of the world—Hohenzollern, Habsburg and Romanov in Europe, the House of Osman in Europe and in Asia. Two of the oldest national states of Europe—Poland and Bohemia—recovered their lost independence. The four small Baltic races which had hitherto been uncomfortably balanced between the Slav, German and Scandinavian worlds—Finns, Estonians, Letts and Lithuanians—achieved full independence, the first and fourth after a lapse of centuries, the second and third for the first time in history. Farther south the three western branches of the Southern Slavs, till then divided between six different systems, were for the first time united in a single state: the Roumanians achieved the boundaries of Roman Dacia, and with this the union of their entire race. This, and the union of Slovakia and Carpathian Ruthenia with the revived Bohemian state, involved a fresh partition of the historical Hungary, but on exactly inverted lines from that of 1540–1690. For in the first case it was the Magyar kernel of the country which was conquered by the Turks, while Slovakia and Transylvania, the bulk of whose peoples were Slav and Latin, remained centres of Magyar (or more properly Hungarian) resistance: while in the latter case the central districts became an overwhelmingly (though not exclusively) Magyar state, and the non-Magyars of the periphery united with their kinsmen in independent states.

Meanwhile Albania's precarious independence was confirmed under a native Moslem aristocrat, first as President, later as King. Greece expanded to her full capacity in Europe and united all her islands save Cyprus and the Dodecanese, but was driven from her points of vantage in Asia Minor: while Turkey, though her loss of every European province save Thrace was confirmed, proved better able than any of her allies to resist the exaggerations of the peace treaties, and leaving the Arab world to go its own way, and renouncing the seductions of both Sultanate and Caliphate, re-established her power on a far sounder, and strictly national, Anatolian basis.

Thanks to its revolutionary origin and to the fact that such vast tracts of territory in both hemispheres were affected, the Peace Settlement necessarily acquired a certain hybrid character to which public opinion has hardly done justice. For on the one hand its results have been far more drastic and sweeping than any others ever imposed by a European congress; yet on the other hand, it is the first international settlement which its authors deliberately tried to erect upon definite ethical principles.[1] For let there be no mistake: its critics may be right in arguing that the statesmen who made the peace did not live up to their own principles, or twisted them to subserve their own selfish designs: but that it rests upon a foundation of far-reaching political theory, which is not affected even by grave imperfections of detail, cannot seriously be disputed.

[1] Mr Gathorne Hardy, in his *Short History of International Affairs*, p. 12, in no way exaggerates when he says, "there has surely seldom or never been constructed a peace of a more idealistic character".

And indeed herein lies the real tragedy, that the exaggerated, and in some cases humiliating, demands imposed upon the defeated nations should have created in them a certain prejudice against that international co-operation upon which alone the hopes of peace rest, but which new prophets have led them to suspect as mere camouflage for an objectionable *status quo*. It has slowly become clear that the device which President Wilson envisaged as one of the main guarantees of permanence—the inclusion of the Covenant as an integral part of the Peace Treaties—has, on the contrary, done a good deal to compromise the League, and that a complete separation is an essential feature of League reform.

THE CAMPAIGN AGAINST THE VERSAILLES "DIKTAT"

Almost from the outset an elaborate and systematic propaganda was set on foot, which aimed at discrediting the settlement as a whole: and the British public—as ever, good-humoured, easy-going, superficial, incapable of a sustained vindictive effort and resenting such an attitude on the part of its Allies, and above all predisposed to espouse the cause of the underdog even in cases where Britain herself has been the upper dog—was only too prone to accept the most sweeping generalisations put forward as to the iniquities of the Treaty. Hence, before going any further, it will be well for us to clear our ideas on a question which has given rise to many misconceptions in both the main camps of Europe: did Germany surrender freely on certain specific conditions which the Allied and Associated Powers afterwards failed to implement, thereby relieving her of any moral obligation to observe the settlement any longer than *force majeure* compelled her?

The answer cannot be given in a single phrase: for never were so many complex issues involved as in the Peace Settlement of 1919. It is only necessary to cast the mind back to the other six great European settlements—1648, 1713, 1763, 1815, 1856, 1878—in order to realise that all were child's play compared with that of 1919. Indeed, in this connection it is helpful to remember that the Great War which preceded it was in reality five or six major wars rolled into one, and can only be fully understood as such. Franco-German and Anglo-German rivalry, Austro-Russian rivalry in the Near East, the Southern Slav question, the triangular Adriatic question, the Ukrainian question, became hopelessly interlocked with each other and eventually with colonial, American and Pacific interests and ambitions. Before we begin to criticise the many admitted blunders committed by the Conference, we are bound in fairness to take note that never in history had so difficult, so exacting and so urgent a task confronted the leading statesmen of Europe, and to wonder whether it was not altogether beyond human powers.

The practice, so widespread in Germany, of alluding to the settlement as "the *Diktat* of Versailles", is misleading in two directions: for the territorial settlement in particular is the outcome not merely of Versailles, but of St Germain, Trianon, Neuilly, Sèvres and Lausanne also,[1] while the phrase "Diktat" or "imposed peace" is not the special monopoly of Versailles, but is applicable to most of the treaties ending a victorious war that has been fought to a finish. It would apply to the treaty by which Frederick the Great took Silesia from Austria, or to that which Bismarck imposed upon France in 1871. The argument against the authority of an "imposed peace" is historically not tenable for a moment. From this angle the real criticism against Versailles is not that it was imposed, but that the German Government—and this not the Government which had made the war, but one which held office by reason of the overthrow of the old regime, and which accepted the democratic principles then favoured at Paris—was excluded from the preliminary discussions and negotiations, and treated with insult and ig-

---

[1] Brest-Litovsk also should perhaps be added: for though it is true that the Armistice of 11 November expressly laid down the "annulment" of both Bucarest and Brest-Litovsk, and of the "supplementary treaties", many of the changes scored by Brest-Litovsk upon the map of Europe did actually survive, whereas Bucarest was completely overthrown. After the Greek *débâcle* in Asia Minor Lausanne took the place of Sèvres.

nominy such as every German was bound to resent. It is usual to lay the chief blame for this upon Clemenceau, but London and Washington cannot escape their share, and even those who can recapture the atmosphere of hysteria in which we then lived must marvel at conduct so shortsighted and so tactless on the part of the victors. It was the first cause of that keen sense of grievance which has so long obsessed the German nation and which gave added impetus to the deep and at first unsuspected groundswell of the Nazi storm. Our disregard of national psychology blinded us to the fact that the Germans are more than usually sensitive, and swing easily from the over-confidence of arrogant militarism to what is little short of an inferiority complex. But if it be admitted that a just Nemesis befell the Allies for their lack of consideration towards a beaten foe, it is on the other hand impossible to admit that only an "agreed" peace is binding, for that would render most peace treaties worthless. It is a peculiarly illogical argument in the mouth of a dictator whose whole system is built up on a belief in Power Politics and Brute Force.

ARMISTICE CONDITIONS

Let us turn back to the really essential question, namely whether the Armistice was signed on the basis of certain specific conditions, and whether the final Treaty was, as is so often glibly asserted, a complete violation of those conditions. The clue to this question lies in the text of the various Notes exchanged between President Wilson and the German or Austro-Hungarian Governments during the period from 15 September to 11 November 1918: and it should be perfectly possible, without attempting a detailed analysis of them, to give within short compass their essential features. The first peace overture came from Austria-Hungary on 15 September, but it was Germany who on 4 October accepted the Fourteen Points as the basis of discussion. President Wilson, in his replies, reminded both Governments that since the Fourteen Points were first announced in January 1918, events had taken their course, and that they must now be accepted as modified in "subsequent addresses", and particularly that of 27 September. On 7 October Austria-Hungary, and on 12 October Germany, unreservedly accepted this qualification, the latter "in the name of the German Government and people". The American response to the two Governments differed very materially; for Austria-Hungary was told that American commitments to the Czechoslovaks and Jugoslavs ruled out Point Ten altogether, while to Germany three further conditions were addressed. They were as follows: (1) that the actual conditions of evacuation and armistice must remain in the hands of the military advisers of the Allied and Associate Powers; (2) that "inhuman practices" such as submarine warfare must cease; and (3) "the destruction of every arbitrary power that can...disturb the peace of the world", and in particular in Germany itself. Germany replied on 14 October by accepting the first, protesting against the wording and inferences of the second, and suggesting that the third had already been met by the fundamental changes introduced into the German Constitution. On the 23rd the President again stressed "the five Particulars" of 27 September, and on the 27th Germany claimed that it now possessed "a People's Government" and had therefore complied with Wilson's demands. On the same day Austria-Hungary accepted unconditionally terms which really involved her own dissolution: but this (as we shall see later) actually precipitated the collapse, and while the armistice terms were still actually being negotiated on the Italian front, the dynasty was overthrown and the Habsburg Monarchy broke up into its component parts. In its case the question of what obligations, if any, the Allied and Associate Powers had assumed was infinitely complicated by the fact that they no longer had to deal with a single enemy Great Power, but with no less than seven legatees—some, like Italy, Serbia and Roumania, within their own ranks, others, like Poland and Czechoslovakia, newly restored to nationhood, and two unhappy remnants, Austria and Hungary, obviously incapable of shouldering all responsibility or meeting all claims.

The position of Germany was, of course, quite different. All her allies were prostrate and forced to surrender, she herself was already in the throes of revolution, the Crown and General Staff alike had lost control of events or of policy and as the retreat went on, the new Government was kept waiting until President Wilson could consult his associates in victory and draw up a unitary programme with them. The final stage came on 5 November, when the Allies endorsed the President's terms to Germany, subject to two very vital reservations, which he accepted as his own. On the one hand they ruled out the second of the Fourteen Points, on "the Freedom of the Seas", and on the other hand they insisted upon the "restoration" of the invaded territories, defining this as "compensation for all damage done to civilian populations of the Allies and their property by the aggression of Germany by land, sea and air". Thus the Armistice of 11 November was concluded on the basis of twelve only of the Fourteen Points, as modified and interpreted in the pronouncements of 11 February (the so-called Four Principles), 4 July (the Four Ends), and 27 September (the Five Particulars), and also subject to evacuation and "restoration" of a far-reaching character.

THE FOURTEEN POINTS AND THEIR SUPPLEMENTS

It is obvious that in so complex and fluid a situation the insistence upon so many abstract principles inevitably opened the way for much misunderstanding and rival interpretation: and before we go further we must recapitulate, as briefly as may be, the essence of the Twelve Points, and consider in what respects the later pronouncements may be said to have modified them.

I. "Open covenants of peace openly arrived at", and the end of "Private international understandings".

[II].

III. "The removal, so far as possible, of all economic barriers and the establishment of equality of trade conditions."

IV. Reduction of armaments "to the lowest point consistent with domestic safety".

V. "A free, open and absolutely impartial adjustment of all colonial claims", the interests of the populations being equally considered with "the equitable claims" of the Governments.

VI. Evacuation of Russia, and her "welcome into the society of free nations, under institutions of her own choosing" (her treatment by other nations being "the acid test" of their goodwill and sympathy).

VII. Complete restoration of Belgium. ("Without this healing act the whole structure and validity of International Law is for ever impaired.")

VIII. Restoration of French territory, and with it of Alsace-Lorraine.

IX. Readjustment of Italy's frontiers, "along clearly recognisable lines of nationality".

[X].

XI. Restoration of the Balkan states, and international guarantees of their independence and integrity.

XII. "A secure sovereignty" for the Turkish portions of the Ottoman Empire, but "security of life" and "opportunity of autonomous development" for all non-Turkish nationalities: and freedom of the Dardanelles.

XIII. Polish independence on a racial basis, with access to the sea and international guarantees.

XIV. "A general association of nations, under specific covenants."

The Four Principles:

1. "Each part of the final settlement to rest on the essential justice of that particular case and on such adjustments as are most likely to bring permanent peace."

2. No more bartering of "peoples and provinces" as "mere chattels and pawns in a game".

3. "Every territorial settlement" to be made in the interests of the populations concerned.

4. "Utmost satisfaction" to "all well-defined national aspirations".

The Four Ends:

I. "The destruction of any arbitrary power anywhere, that can ...disturb the peace of the world."

II. Settlement of every question on the basis of "a free acceptance by the people immediately concerned".

III. "The consent of all nations to be governed in their conduct towards each other by the same principles of honour and respect for the common law of civilised society that governs the individual citizens of all modern states."

IV. "The establishment of an organisation of peace", to check "every invasion of right".

The Five Particulars:

I. Impartial justice to all, without discrimination.

II. No special interest of any single nation or group, to be "the basis of any part of the settlement which is not consistent with the common interest of all".

III. "No leagues or alliances within the general and common family of the League."

IV. "No special selfish economic combinations within the League."

V. Publication of all international treaties.

It will at once become obvious that the three supplementary statements, to which the President attached so much importance, cover the whole field of moral obligation between sovereign states, and would, if genuinely applied in practice, create a new heaven and a new earth; but also that on many points they are so abstract and general in character as to open the way to infinite divergence of interpretation. To take but two examples, no indication whatsoever is given as to how satisfaction can be given to "well-defined national aspirations" where they are in direct conflict with other no less well-defined aspirations on territory of inter-racial character: and again, the first of the "Four Ends", demanding the destruction of every arbitrary power, may have been accepted at the time by those in control of the Weimar Republic, but must be regarded with distinctly mixed feelings by those who since 1933 have directed German propaganda against the "Dictated Peace". Of the "Five Particulars", indeed, they must undoubtedly reject the 3rd and 5th as altogether obnoxious doctrine: having repudiated the League, they cannot support the 4th: and the 1st and 2nd then remain as mere pious aspirations amid a flowing tide of force.

Turning to the Fourteen Points themselves, as illustrating the German contention of wholesale violation, we may narrow the field still further. Two and Ten, as we saw, were excluded in advance. Fourteen was fulfilled by the creation of the League of Nations, and the fulfilment of One has followed logically from it, since no post-war treaties and conventions concluded by the member states have any validity unless registered at Geneva. The interpretation afterwards put upon it by President Wilson—that it excluded secret treaties, but not confidential negotiation—merely corresponds to obvious common sense and is now generally accepted: but the present German regime would presumably have preferred that this Point should *not* have been laid down or observed.

Every reasonable student of Wilsonian principles must admit that Six, on Russia, was framed on impracticably vague lines, and that the Russian regime was an overwhelming obstacle to its fulfilment, but also that Germany, with her present views of Russia, is the last country likely to object to non-fulfilment in this case, or alternatively, that German evacuation of former Russian territory is the last programme which any post-war German Government (whether Nazi or pre-Nazi) could have favoured. The admission of Russia to the League, which might be regarded as a necessarily tardy fulfilment of this Point, is a foremost count in Germany's indictment of the League.

Seven and Eight, relating to France and Belgium, have been fully executed, and this fact does indeed give some plausibility to the German contention that only where fulfilment suited the Allied cause was it made a reality. Eleven is vaguely worded and gives little or no clue to the actual situation in the Balkans, but it certainly cannot be said to have been violated, and in any case it only affects Germany very indirectly. In the same way

Twelve, on Turkey, may be said to conform broadly with the situation as it eventually evolved, but it too only affects Germany very indirectly. Thirteen, on Poland, has also been observed in all essentials, though it of course proved almost impossible to establish an exact racial frontier between Pole and German: and indeed the adoption of the plebiscite method in Allenstein and Silesia,[1] and its admittedly correct application, have often been cited as a model of what should have been attempted in other disputed areas also.

By a certain irony there is only one of the Fourteen Points which can be said to have been clearly violated, in the teeth of established facts, namely Nine, which enjoins that Italy's new frontier shall follow "clearly recognisable lines of nationality". In actual fact the settlement disregarded such lines and assigned to Italy over three-quarters of a million Germans and Jugoslavs in South Tirol and Venezia Giulia. This did not, of course, concern Germany as a state, but it did, and does, concern her as a nation, to whom the fate of so famous a German province as Tirol can never be a matter of indifference.

There remain three other Points—Three (on economic barriers), Four (on reduction of armaments), and Five (on colonial claims)—which involve issues of the widest and most controversial kind, and which must therefore be reserved for the next stage of the discussion. Point Three has, it is true, been robbed of much of its virtue by the insertion of the vague qualifying phrase "as far as possible": but we should be guilty of contemptible quibbling if we tried to shelter behind it from an obvious *moral* obligation. In view, however, of the vast amount of loose talk in England and America about wholesale violation by the Allies of the Wilsonian principles on which the peace was founded, it is not a mere academic exercise, but a practical duty, closely affecting our relations with Germany, to elucidate the fact that *only one* out of the Fourteen Points has been openly violated, while three others are open to criticism (and the reader will soon see that no attempt will be made to minimise the

[1] The Teschen dispute between Poland and Czechoslovakia was eventually settled without a plebiscite, but left a wound that has suppurated.

very great importance of these three). This already puts a very different complexion on the whole problem. It is not a case of wholesale violation: and there can in any case be no question of wholesale repudiation, for that would create a *vacuum juris*, and leave naked force as the sole foundation of international relations. Those who advocate repudiation are, consciously or unconsciously, advocating a reversion to war on the most catastrophic scale.

GERMANY'S GRIEVANCES

It remains to consider Germany's legitimate grievances: and for this purpose it is convenient to divide the Peace Settlement into certain main categories. These are (A) questions relating to the League and a new world order; (B) questions of private property and national resources; (C) general economic and financial questions; (D) questions of territorial readjustment; (E) colonial questions. Curiously enough, many of those who indulge in wholesale condemnation of the Settlement reserve their main anger for its territorial provisions. I submit that, on the contrary, it is just the territorial section of the Treaty of Versailles which has best stood the test of time (territorially the main blemishes are to be found in the Treaties of Trianon and Neuilly,[1] and do not affect Germany), whereas the section classed above as B partook of sheer spoliation for which there is no precedent in civilised history, and class C included absurdities so patent that it broke down by its own weight and twice underwent drastic revision before ever repudiation came to be adopted as the official German policy.

It is not necessary to labour this point in a volume devoted to political rather than economic problems. Mr Keynes, in refreshingly comprehensible and picturesque language, has once for all proved up to the hilt the monstrosity of the economic and financial settlements which it was sought to impose upon Germany. For once the logical French mind was incapable of realising that it was clamouring not merely for the impossible,

[1] With Hungary (4 June 1920) and Bulgaria (27 November 1919).

but for the fantastically impossible: and the book of that once prophetic and ever ingenious publicist, M. André Chéradame, remains as a fatal record. Even at the time the dire effects of a long delay in fixing the total liabilities of the enemy were sufficiently obvious to all who had retained their mental balance: and indeed the solitary excuse for this lies in the fact that such astronomical figures were involved as to render it difficult to draw a clear distinction between the "determinate" and "indeterminate" parts of Germany's debt. It took the Allies till January 1921 to agree upon a total figure, and that figure has been described as "double the highest figure any competent person here or in the United States has ever attempted to justify".[1] Let it then suffice for our present purpose to say that British opinion has long since been unanimous in accepting the two first points of the Keynes thesis—that the claims against Germany were impossible of payment, and that the attempt to enforce them might be ruinous to all Europe. French insistence upon them and the tergiversations of British policy in those early years after the war—first launching the campaign of "Making Germany pay for the War", then afraid to tone down or publicly acknowledge the exaggerated character of the demand, eternally wrangling with the French behind the scenes and shifting the action from one abortive conference to another—culminated quite logically in the fatal occupation of the Ruhr and the collapse of the Mark. It may further quite reasonably be argued that the British expert advisers, by pressing for the inclusion of pensions in the claim against Germany, made matters worse, since this increased the proportion of the British claim at the expense of the real sufferers, the French, and made them proportionately intransigeant.

That the German Government itself pursued a more than disingenuous financial policy—which resulted in disencumbering itself of its internal debt at the expense of the savings of its middle class—does not for one moment exculpate the Allies: for the mood in which Germany acted was in large measure due to a psychology of despair and recklessness in-

[1] See especially J. M. Keynes, *Economic Consequences of the Peace.*

creased tenfold by our folly. The knowledge of defeat and harsh conditions was bitter, but was accepted as inevitable: it followed from the German creed in respect of war and force. But that Germany should be indefinitely at the mercy of taskmasters who could not agree among themselves and some of whom openly advocated a policy of turning the whole German nation into "Nibelungs" for a couple of generations—this induced in German public opinion an atmosphere of pathological frenzy which was to unload itself in due season. That this aspect of the question has not won more general recognition may perhaps have a very elementary explanation. In the words of an expert, "it is difficult, when dealing with figures of the magnitude of £5 milliards, to convey any real impression of their significance"[1] or of their endless ramifications.

With Mr Keynes's further contention, that the inclusion of pensions and allowances in the Allied and Associate claim upon Germany was an actual breach of faith, I again do not propose to deal. I am free to confess that his arguments on this highly technical question seem to me entirely convincing. It is also permissible to express the view that the provisions of the Treaty of Versailles relating to "private property, rights and interests" (Articles 297–8, with Annex, and Articles 252, 260)—for instance, the confiscation of patent rights, to take perhaps the crudest instance of all—are in many ways its most drastic section, and go much further than any previous international treaty in their disregard for individual rights. They are an essential factor in those general confiscatory and overriding tendencies of the State towards the Individual, of which the Bolshevik experiment was merely the most ruthless and comprehensive. Those who endorsed the Treaty's inroads into the most elementary rights of private property have no right to protest against the logic by which all the dictatorial states are step by step extending these inroads. Mr Charles Buxton does not go too far when he claims that certain of the provisions of the Treaty were deliberately designed to destroy the economic position of Germany in Europe and have had

[1] *History of the Peace Conference* (ed. Temperley), II, p. 54.

disastrous effects upon the whole fabric of world trade and industry.

On the matter of Reparation, however, it is most material to add that among the conditions of the Armistice, as signed on 11 November 1918—in addition to all the drastic clauses regarding evacuation of territory and surrender of war material—are to be found clauses annulling the Treaties of Bucharest and Brest-Litovsk (par. 15) and ordering *"reparation for damage done"* (par. 19), subject to the express reservation that "subsequent claims...remain unaffected". This makes it quite impossible for Germany to argue that the draconic reparation terms of the Treaty were a violation of Allied undertakings, though it does not of course acquit the Allies of extreme unwisdom in demanding the impossible, or of an unworthy and tactless attitude towards a beaten foe.

THREE UNFULFILLED POINTS

We are left with Points Three, Four and Five. It has already been pointed out that Point Three, on the removal of economic barriers, was far too loosely worded in the first instance to be capable of forming the basis of an indictment of the Treaty as a whole. The most formidable criticism which could be directed against it is that the Allies themselves, in their blindness, destroyed the invaluable economic machinery which they had laboriously built up together and which, as Mr Garvin gallantly but vainly preached in his *Economic Foundations of Peace*, might have become the foundations of the new World Order.

In a word, the failure to implement Point Three is part of the general economic madness which assailed Europe from one end to the other after the War, and which, it must in common fairness be added, was stimulated by revolution, internal chaos and uncertainty, and the temporary breakdown of communications.

Point Four demanded "adequate guarantees given and taken, that national armaments will be reduced to the lowest point consistent with domestic safety". In pursuance of this, Article

VIII of the Covenant laid down that "the maintenance of peace requires the reduction of national armaments to the lowest point consistent with national safety and the enforcement by common action of international obligations" and required the Council to "formulate plans for such reduction". Moreover, Part V of the Treaty (containing the military, naval and air clauses) opens with the phrase: "in order to render possible the initiation of a general limitation of the armaments of all nations, Germany undertakes strictly to observe...etc." Today no reasonable person will attempt to deny that these two provisions constitute a moral obligation of the strongest kind, and that Germany has a legitimate grievance of the very first order against her former enemies, for not following up her disarmament by a reduction of their own forces. In arguing thus, we must not allow the Covenant and Part V of the Treaty, which in no way concerned Geneva and the League, to be mixed up together: this is only to make confusion worse confounded.

Where we still join issue with Germany is in refusing to recognise her right to unilateral repudiation, on her own interpretation of the facts. The question of armaments has from the first day been the crux of the European situation, irrevocably tied up with the question of security, and round it all other international discussions have always revolved. That it was still unsolved when Hitler repudiated the Treaty, was above all due to divergent interpretations of the obligations assumed under the Covenant: but that it was further than ever from being shelved is shown by the whole history of the Disarmament Conference, which could not be said to have failed until Hitler administered the *coup de grâce*. In other words, the problem of reduction or limitation of armaments continued to exercise public opinion in every country and would have continued to do so but for the action of Germany, or—perhaps it would be more accurate to say—still continues to do so amid the present welter of discouragement. Hence the Germans, while they have very real grounds for complaint in the tergiversations and delays of the Powers, are not entitled to claim that they are thereby dispensed from their international obligations. There is the further very vital claim that Britain, at any rate, *did* reduce her armaments to a level which almost every one at home and abroad now recognises to have been highly dangerous, and which, to take a most practical example, gave Signor Mussolini his chance of armed aggression in Africa.

There remains Point Five, which prescribes "a free, open-minded and absolutely impartial adjustment of all colonial claims": and who dare maintain today that the colonial clauses of the Treaty were a fulfilment of this principle? The relevant clauses (119–127) simply laid down that "Germany renounces...all her rights and titles over her oversea possessions", in favour of the principal Allied and Associated Powers, who thereupon proceeded to divide them among themselves. In this process the British Empire acquired the lion's share, and the incontestable fact that on this point London could not, even if it had wished, have held back Australia, South Africa and New Zealand from asserting their various claims, is a plea which, so far from appeasing Germany's soreness, has in her ears an ominous ring of hypocrisy.

It must of course at once be added that the victors, while laying their hands upon all Germany's colonies, did introduce into the Covenant (Articles 22 and 23) new principles of colonial administration such as the world had not hitherto known. The mandatory system, which in these eighteen years has on the whole functioned effectively, rests on a genuine attempt to make a reality of the second portion of Point Five, which insisted that in assigning colonial territory "the interests of the populations concerned must have equal weight". Article XXII starts from "the principle that the wellbeing and development of such peoples form a sacred trust of civilisation": and the distinction which it draws between the degrees of ripeness attained by the backward peoples in Turkey, in Central Africa and in the South Seas, is an altogether sound one. There can, however, be very little doubt that President Wilson, if he were here to interpret his famous Points, would be less than ever disposed to regret Germany's loss of her colonies, on the ground that a people which had lost, or renounced, its own freedom at home, was not qualified to administer colonies in the interest of native races. Yet it may well be doubted whether this is a tenable proposition today: and it is certain that to uphold it rigidly, or to maintain the insulting claim so often put forward at the end of the War, that the Germans are essentially unfit to govern native populations, is simply another way of rendering all agreement between Britain and Germany impossible. The whole issue is one of such importance that it must be reserved for fuller treatment in a later chapter.[1]

We have now reached a conclusion which may come as a surprise to many readers—namely that, next to Point Nine (on Italy's frontiers), the least fulfilled of all the Wilsonian principles is Point Five, relating to the colonies: in other words, on a matter in which Britain bears a very direct and special responsibility.

THE "WAR-GUILT" CLAUSE

Finally, brief reference must be made to Article 231,[2] which opens Part VIII of the Treaty, relating to Reparation, and which is loosely but inaccurately described as "the War-Guilt clause". In view of the widespread misapprehensions which have centred round this clause and which have been fanned by deliberate propaganda, it is well to quote it in full. "The Allied and Associated Governments affirm, and Germany accepts, *the responsibility of Germany and her allies for all the loss and damage* to which the Allied and Associated Governments and their nationals have been subjected as a consequence of the war imposed upon them by the aggression of Germany and her allies."

It has often been pointed out—and yet it is today realised less than ever—that this Article "was not, and was not intended to be, an affirmation of German 'war-guilt' in the moral sense—as the German Delegation were informed at Versailles

[1] See *infra*, pp. 416–24.
[2] Probably the clearest and most succinct statement on this vexed question is to be found in *L'article 231 du Traité de Versailles: sa genèse et sa simplification* (Paris 1932), by Camille Bloch and Pierre Renouvin (reprinted from *Revue d'Histoire de la Guerre Mondiale*).

when they made enquiry on this very point. It was a legal statement of claim against Germany and her allies for such reparation as they could make for damage done in a war which their aggression had brought on. Indeed, the next Article, 232, recognised that 'the resources of Germany are not adequate... to make complete reparation for all such loss and damage'."[1]

In Germany, however, an inaccurate translation of Article 231 is current. The passage, which I have placed in italics, runs: "dass Deutschland und seine Verbündeten *als Urheber für alle Verluste und Schäden verantwortlich sind*": whereas it should really run "für alle Verluste und Schäden als Veranlasser derselben verantwortlich sind", which has a very much narrower meaning. To illustrate the manner in which it has since been interpreted, it will suffice to quote (1) the speech of the German Chancellor Gustav Bauer who, during the discussions at the Weimar Parliament in June 1919, quoted this phrase as "als Urheber des Krieges" (as originators of the war); and (2) the claim of Herr von Wegerer, editor of the propagandist monthly *Die Kriegsschuldfrage*, that Article 231 is "the scientific foundation upon which the Treaty of Versailles was built".

It is impossible to read the real text of the Treaty without realising that Article 231 followed the much more limited aim of establishing a legal basis for reparation claims: and in actual fact two of the main commissions of the Conference, on Responsibility and on Reparations, rejected the suggestion of including in the text of the Treaty a moral judgment on the defeated nations. On the other hand, the Allies in their Note of 20 May 1919 put forward the perfectly concrete claim that Germany, in accepting the Lansing Note of 5 November 1918,[2] had recognised her responsibility for the damage caused, and that this, having remained unchallenged for over six months, could no longer be reversed in June 1919. It is of course true that the Allied Note of 16 June 1919 to the German delegation took

[1] H. W. Steed, *Vital Peace*, p. 149.

[2] This insisted on the invaded areas being not only evacuated but *restored*: i.e. there must be "compensation for all damages to the civilian population and their property by the fact of Germany's aggression".

a very strong line on the subject of "War Origins", and that all the Allied statesmen laid the blame for the outbreak of war in varying degrees upon Germany and Austria-Hungary—in other words, that in 1919 they were not yet calm enough to draw a distinction between "immediate" and "ulterior" or indirect causes. But the whole emphasis of the Note in question was in quite another direction—namely the search for adequate grounds on which to indite the Kaiser and "persons guilty of criminal acts": and here the relevant articles are 227–230, which eventually proved futile, and which today no one attempts to defend. The essential point to grasp is that Article 231 did not pass a moral judgment upon Germany (and was never intended to do so), but aimed solely at establishing a legal basis for claims of damage against her.[1] Germany (and of course Austria-Hungary, but by the time of the Armistice of 11 November she had already ceased to exist) had taken the initiative of war— according to Germany's own public admission, in violation of existing obligations—and must therefore be required by the terms of peace to repair the damage caused by that initiative. The whole "Kriegsschuldlüge" (War-Guilt Lie) agitation in post-war Germany rests on a phrase which does not occur in the Treaty of Versailles.

TERRITORIAL RESULTS

Let us in conclusion sum up quite briefly the main territorial results affecting Germany.

A. *On the West*

(1) Alsace-Lorraine was restored to France, without the plebiscite demanded by Germany. It is possible to regret the denial of this plebiscite while maintaining that the result would have been the same in any case, and while also recognising the French insistence on restitution as a *point d'honneur*. While,

[1] It is, however, important to add that the very next Article, 232, begins by a frank recognition "that the resources of Germany are not adequate... to make complete reparation for all such loss and damage".

however, the Third Reich, through the mouth of its Leader, has endorsed the renunciation as final, the question at issue becomes one of procedure, and of tact, rather than one of principle.

(2) Eupen-Malmédy were assigned to Belgium, of which they had formed part till 1815: and here the Allies, instead of a plebiscite, resorted to the highly unsatisfactory and not very honest expedient of "voting registers", in which the inhabitants during a period of six months would be entitled to "record their desire to see the whole or part remain under German sovereignty" (Article 34). It is not surprising that German opinion should have treated this as a means of avoiding any genuine consultation of the population concerned who, it was held with much plausibility, would have voted overwhelmingly in favour of Germany.

(3) Luxemburg's pre-war customs union with Germany was dissolved, and this was strongly endorsed by a plebiscite in the Grand Duchy, which at that time was actually ready for some similar kind of relationship with France.

(4) Articles 42–44 laid down the permanent demilitarisation of the Left Bank of the Rhine and a specified district on the Right Bank, while Articles 45–50 assigned to France for a period of fifteen years the Saar Basin and its mines, as compensation for the destruction wrought in the French mining districts during the German retreat. These clauses may be broadly described as a compromise—and a not unreasonable one— between the extremist demand for the Rhine frontier or a Rhenish buffer state (which neither Britain nor America was prepared to accept) and a situation in which French industry would have been fatally handicapped in face of German industry. The establishment of the League "in the capacity of trustee" (Article 49) and the decision in favour of a plebiscite at the end of the prescribed period were fully in accord with general Wilsonian principles, and now that the sequel also belongs to history we can claim that in this particular the settlement was fully justified.

(5) In the Western settlement may, for convenience' sake, be included the provisions relating to Slesvig, where a plebiscite

was ordered in the northern and predominantly Danish districts (Articles 109–111). The German Government, while pointing out that Slesvig was not mentioned in President Wilson's Points, accepted the principle of a plebiscite, and the exception which it took to "the formation of the voting districts" was a more or less technical affair. In the event, the result of the plebiscite was generally accepted as both fair and workable.

B. *On the East*

If the problem of re-drawing Germany's eastern frontiers proved to be even more difficult and thorny, and could not be completed for several years, it can at least be fearlessly maintained that despite all hesitations and errors, the settlement followed in the main Wilsonian principles, and was above all directed towards a solution on national lines, with special provisions for those districts where the two races were too intermixed to permit a "clean cut" on racial lines.

(1) Frontiers of Poland. (*a*) In East Prussia (Articles 94–99) plebiscites were ordered for the districts inhabited by Slavs—whom it had been the policy of the Prussian state to differentiate as "Mazurians" from their Polish kinsmen, but who were beyond all question of the same stock. Two plebiscites were held in July 1920 in the districts of Allenstein and Marienwerder, and resulted in an overwhelming vote in favour of the *status quo* and against Poland.

The main controversy centred round the so-called "Polish Corridor", the territory now known as Pomorze, which was an integral part of Poland till 1308 and again from 1464 to 1772,[1] and had in the half-century preceding the Great War

---

[1] Pomorze was under the Teutonic Order from 1308 to 1466, and under the Kingdom of Poland from 1466 to 1772. Its population at the three last censuses was as follows:

1910 (German Census) 552,733 Poles, 437,412 Germans.
1921 (Polish Census) 757,801 Poles, 177,842 Germans.
1931 (Polish Census) 976,499 Poles, 109,645 Germans.

For a reasoned account of this problem see V. Poliakov in "The Valley of the Vistula" (*Slavonic Review*, No. 34).

been subjected, like the province of Posen, to intensive Germanisation.[1] There was a clear choice between two evils—to deprive East Prussia of direct contact with the rest of Germany, or to deprive all Poland of direct contact with the sea: and at Paris it was held that the interests of twenty-five million Poles outweighed the interests of two million East Prussians. This decision was in full accord with Point Thirteen, and with the pronouncement of the British, French and Italian Premiers of 3 June 1918, claiming "free access to the sea" for Poland, and is therefore to be regarded as a fulfilment rather than a violation of Allied obligations. In one word, what propagandists call the "Polish Corridor" is the valley of the Vistula, today, as ever, Poland's only possible access to the sea, while East Prussia is on the sea, and thus has direct access to the rest of Germany. The system of sealed trains running across the "Corridor" is admittedly irksome, but it also admittedly attains its object of direct transit without any interference from the Polish authorities, and of course the growth of air communication is almost day by day driving this aspect of the question into the background.

(*b*) Danzig (Articles 100–108). The decision regarding Pomorze necessarily involved the separation of Danzig also from the Reich, but as it was incontestably a German city, a special status was provided for it, which was again in obvious conformity with Wilsonian principles and was genuinely intended as a compromise between the German and Polish points of view. It had the further advantage of being a reversion, subject to modern conditions, to the city's century-old status as an Imperial free city. Under Article 102 it was proclaimed as a Free City under the protection of the League, which was also to appoint the High Commissioner and to guarantee a

---

[1] The "Kashubs" of West Prussia, like the "Mazurians" of East Prussia, are as much Poles as the "Dalmatians" and "Bosnians" are Serbo-Croats, or the "Moldavians" Roumanians. The insistence on these and other local names was part of those tactics of "Divide et Impera" which formed so important a feature of pre-war assimilationist policy, alike in Germany, Austria-Hungary, Russia and Turkey.

constitution drawn up in agreement between him and "duly appointed representatives" of Danzig itself. If the compromise thus reached is now in danger of breaking down, this is certainly not the fault either of the League or of the Allied Powers, but of the two nations more specially concerned.

(*c*) The western boundary between Germany and Poland had already been drawn, under Articles 27–30, to include the Polish districts of the Prussian province of Poznania (Posen), which had been the centre of Prussianising policy ever since the middle of last century. The Allied Note of 16 June gave, as one of its main reasons for this, that "the seizure of the western provinces of Poland was one of the essential steps by which the military power of Prussia was built up". But their second ground was a far more valid one—that "districts inhabited by an indisputably Polish population" must be included in the restored Poland: and this too was a clear fulfilment of the Thirteenth Point and could not therefore have come as a surprise to German opinion.

(*d*) Most difficult of all was the question of Upper Silesia, where the two races were inextricably interwoven and where Germany was fully entitled to argue that too drastic changes might cause grave economic dislocation. Though this question excited equally intense feeling among the Germans and Poles, and though there was at times a regrettable tendency on the part of the Allies to take sides with one or other, it remains true that in the end the principles of arbitration and self-determination asserted themselves. No imaginable solution could have fully satisfied both parties or unravelled the tangled economic knot: but the plebiscite principle, conducted in a series of zones, was successfully applied, though the partition of Silesia which inevitably followed from it was strongly opposed by the Polish extremists and their French supporters, and at the same time roused a perfect storm of anger in Germany, leading to the overthrow of the Wirth Cabinet. It is possible to understand how, in the tense atmosphere of those days, the decision came to be received as a fresh proof of Allied partiality, and yet at the same time to regard it as, in effect, a vindication of Wilsonian principles. Nor indeed was there any question towards the solution of which the League has rendered greater services. In Silesia, as in the Saar, "it is very difficult to see how the conflicting interests involved could have been reconciled without some serious violation of justice, if the machinery of the League had not been available for a solution".[1] A mixed Commission and arbitral tribunal were set up and a kind of economic *condominium* proved not unworkable: and gradually ordered conditions returned to this highly industrialised but also highly nationalised district.

C. *Lithuania*

Germany, under Article 99, had to surrender to Lithuania the town of Memel and a strip of territory running from the Baltic along the former Russo-German frontier. This was based on the claim that the majority of the population was "Lithuanian in origin and in speech" (though the town of Memel itself was admittedly German) and that the latter port was the new state's "only sea outlet". In this case no opportunity was given for a plebiscite; and it may be doubted whether, if it had been held, it would have gone in favour of Lithuania. This was in many ways the most questionable of all the territorial decisions affecting Germany, though the argument as to a seaport is a valid one.

FIVE CRITICISMS OF THE TREATY

If our survey of the territorial settlement as it affects Germany is distinctly exculpatory for the Allies, it is but fair to set against this the five following facts:

(1) That our refusal to admit enemy representatives to the discussions at Paris was unworthy and humiliating on the moral side, and tactically a grave blunder.

(2) That the linking up of the League Covenant with the Treaties, though prompted by the best intentions and intended to impart added solemnity and validity, was in reality a blunder,

[1] *History of the Peace Conference*, II, p. 183.

in that it led large sections of German opinion to regard the League as a mere instrument of ruthless victors, bent upon perpetuating an unjust peace, and not the foundation stone upon which an entirely new order in Europe was to be constructed.

(3) That the charge of exclusive "War-Guilt" sometimes levelled against Germany is as absurd and untenable as the charge once levelled by German opinion against Sir Edward Grey as the real author of the War, and now universally abandoned as ridiculous. (This does not affect the arguments—in my opinion conclusive—in favour of the thesis that it was Germany's attitude in July 1914 which decided Austria's ultimatum, the event from which all subsequent events logically followed, and that therefore in summing up the *immediate* causes of the War we must place the name of Austria-Hungary first and of Germany second on the list, while frankly admitting that every Power, Great and Small, must share the responsibility for the *ulterior* causes, with roots stretching far back into history.)

(4) That the convenient thesis of Germany's unfitness to administer colonies is as untrue as it is insulting, and should be recanted.

(5) Above all, that the economic clauses of the Treaty were a defiance of plain commonsense and that by an undue and prolonged insistence upon altogether excessive and impossible economic terms, which destroyed the whole mechanism of German finance, they in the end did infinite mischief to the whole world.

The time is surely ripe for public admission of these five points, as tardy amendment to sensitive German opinion. It would not be a sign of weakness, but of strength and sanity of judgment.

The failure to distinguish between the two systems in Germany—the old Imperial regime which had made the war and had then clung to the last moment to impossible terms of peace, and the new democratic and constitutional regime of Weimar—was nothing short of a denial of the professions of Allied statesmen and of the main arguments of allied public opinion. If the Weimar republic was in the end discredited, the blame for this falls first and foremost upon the short-sightedness, intransigeance and disunion of the former Allies.

Some readers may at this stage exclaim that so lukewarm a defence of the Peace Settlement, coupled with such damning admissions, is more futile and at the same time more insincere than to allow the whole Treaty to go by the board. My reply is that my halftones, drab though they may be, correspond to realities, and that in major political issues it is the rarest of things to find all the shades on one side and all the high lights on the other. In effect, I have been trying to demonstrate that all the fine phrases about a "Carthaginian Peace" are little more than hot air. After all, Carthage was destroyed and ploughed with salt. Germany suffered dire defeat, the victors imposed many severe terms upon her and even tried to exact impossibilities.[1] But German unity was untouched—firstly no doubt because it proved itself superior even to the internal hates and discords of the Revolution, but also because the main body of Allied opinion recognised to Germany the same natural rights as to the reconstructed national states of Europe. There is no credit in this (and those who played with a mythical Rhenish separatism covered themselves with ignominy): but the fact remains that as between Germany and the rest of Europe a genuine attempt was made to make nationality as far as possible the main determining factor, and that (subject to certain not unimportant details) the attempt was successful.[2]

[1] Arthur Balfour, in his Memorandum of 4 October 1916, deprecated all idea of trying "to control or modify" Germany's internal policy. "The motto of the Allies should be, 'Germany for the Germans, but only Germany'." And it was on this principle that the Allies acted at Paris.

[2] In view of one particular argument often adduced, it is important to add that the experts of the Peace Delegations worked out their proposals for the Polish frontier on the basis of pre-war *German* official statistics, and not on the statistical material supplied by the Poles, and in the same way their proposals for the Hungarian frontiers on pre-war *Hungarian* official statistics (in this case there was no serious alternative). On the former point see Lord Howard's public statements, on the latter Mr Harold Nicolson's *Peace-Making*.

It is not immaterial to add that the political theories upon which the present regime in Germany rests logically preclude it from pressing home, as the democrats were entitled to do, the various arguments relating to evasion or non-fulfilment of Wilsonian doctrine. Moreover, the agreement reached between Germany and Poland, which has resulted in a political truce, and in the abandonment of the pre-Nazi propaganda against the Poles, despite a steady deterioration in the status of the German minority in Poland, illustrates the extent to which these problems rest on political advantage or calculation, rather than on true national theory or moral claims.

Signor Mussolini, not long after his accession to power, made a very pertinent criticism of the Treaty when he said that we neither made a peace of the sword, by occupying Berlin, Vienna and Budapest, nor a peace of approximate justice.

Lest, however, this quotation should seem to deflect the balance unduly in one direction, it may be well to close this chapter with the words of Mr T. W. Lamont, the American member of the Reparations Commission in Paris: "When German fortunes were on the top of the wave, her people were acclaiming with glee the thought that they would be able to impose an indemnity upon the Allies of not less than $500,000,000,000. The final judgment on the degree of vindictiveness of the warring nations must be reserved to the historians who shall obtain access to the hitherto jealously guarded terms of peace of the German Government, of which Brest-Litovsk and Bucarest were merely the foretaste."[1]

---

[1] *What Really Happened at Paris*, ed. House and Seymour, p. 288.

V

FROM VERSAILLES TO LOCARNO
AND BEYOND

"It is hard to be patient with men who point to the economic dissolution
War has brought, and say, 'There are the fruits of your peace'."
ALLYN A. YOUNG.

IT was essential at the very outset to analyse the main lines
of the Peace Settlement and its bearing upon the question
of responsibility for the war. For not merely had public indifference and shallow sentimentalism in this country permitted
the growth of a very mischievous myth which aims at actually in-
verting the responsibility; but at the same time, thanks in no small
measure to our indifference to the problem, German opinion has
been inoculated with a belief in complete innocence, and now
that it is in the grip of the totalitarian gospellers, and there is no
longer a free press in Germany, it is too late to obtain a hearing
there for our point of view. This is all the more regrettable,
since our experience of the "Encirclement Myth" should have
shown us the danger of neglecting propagandist theories which
are capable of influencing a nation's whole spiritual evolution.

While, however, it is useless to cry over spilt milk, it is not too
late to clear our own ideas as to the causes of the present situation
in Europe, to realise the moral issues involved for the future,
and so to be able to make public and fearless confession of our
faults, while holding no less resolutely to the many good features
of the settlement and giving fair warning of the points at which
we cannot yield. Personally, I should like to see our statesmen
explicitly repudiate the doctrine "My country, right or wrong",
of which we are (quite falsely) supposed to be the inventors
and chief exponents, and which in my opinion is not merely
immoral, but unpatriotic and very shortsighted. Certainly it is
not a doctrine which will be acted upon in the present survey.

If on the one hand the harsh attitude of the victorious Powers made of "Versailles" a positive obsession in the German mind, it may be doubted whether under the circumstances of 1919 any conceivable settlement would have been accepted by Germany as "just". The contrast between four years of victory and of extravagant dreams of conquest and the sudden and overwhelming defeat and downfall that followed—this was the underlying and psychological cause of all subsequent troubles, and disturbed the mental balance of the nation. That the victors also were not quite normal, is illustrated by the Khaki Election, and the "Hang the Kaiser" agitation, and by the extravagantly vindictive projects which fear led a section of French opinion to advocate. It is quite true that Britain, being a little further removed from the main scenes of devastation, began to awake from her frenzy a little sooner: but Mr Lloyd George, who voiced this return to sanity, had already unfortunately put himself out of court by his election speeches and by his Prinkipo policy. The result was, during the six months of the Paris Conference, a growing divergence of view between the two principal Allies, which—from a realist though not from a moral standpoint—is the only valid excuse for the policy of excluding the enemy Powers from all discussions. The French, remembering the skill with which, a century earlier, their own spokesman, Talleyrand, had insinuated himself into the counsels of the Allies at Vienna and thus achieved what was, in effect, a re-grouping of the Powers, can hardly be blamed for fearing something much more dangerous and more chaotic from the lightning twists and improvisations of Lloyd Georgian policy. Today every one recognises the part played by German resentment and bitterness in the post-war situation: but the real key to an understanding of that situation lies in the further fact that not only Germany but France also (and for yet other reasons Italy) was gravely dissatisfied, and that in the first instance the only really satisfied Powers were Britain and America, who had simultaneously eliminated Germany overseas and secured acceptance for their own conceptions of a League of Nations, and some of the smaller states, which had achieved or regained liberty and nationhood. Then came the withdrawal of America from Europe, and Britain, true to her hybrid position—"one foot in sea and one on shore"—continued to make the League the basis of her policy, yet shrank back on more than one decisive occasion from commitments which followed logically from this. In the words of Dr Gooch, "The League was above all an Anglo-American creation": and if there were many who always doubted whether it would stand the strain of a major crisis, it was above all America's withdrawal and Britain's half-heartedness that inspired their scepticism.

AMERICA AND THE PEACE

The divergence of views between France and Britain was naturally accentuated by America's withdrawal—an event as fateful as her original entry into the war. France had only been induced to renounce the separation of the Rhineland and the annexation of the Saar by an explicit pledge of military support from Britain and America in the event of renewed German aggression. This Treaty of Triple Guarantee was signed on the same day as the Treaty of Versailles (20 June 1919). But when the American Senate repudiated President Wilson, we found in the fact that the guarantee was not single but collective, an excellent technical pretext for repudiating in our turn. This was the second fatal blunder from which our present troubles spring. By not upholding our pledge at all costs, we created in France that sense of grievance and insecurity which has never left her since that day, and indeed robbed ourselves of that restraining influence over Paris which we might have asserted to good purpose.[1] For we were in effect withholding payment for goods already delivered: and in the name of "Security" France looked elsewhere and set herself to build up

[1] In the spring of 1936 we were not very far from committing the same blunder in respect of Locarno. A very vocal section of the press, when Germany repudiated Locarno, clamoured that we should regard her action as invalidating the whole arrangement. Had this grossly dishonourable suggestion been adopted, not merely would the nickname of "Perfide Albion" have been amply merited, but we should today be truly isolated in a world of foes, and should richly deserve our fate.

a system of alliances in Eastern and South-Eastern Europe, as counterweights to the possibility, always foreseen, of a revival of German power in the centre of the Continent. And we— the nation whom William Pitt galvanised during twenty years of war by this very catchword of "Security"—were unable to see that France's reactions were determined almost equally by a deep-seated instinct of self-preservation and by our own half-hearted attitude. In passing, we may contrast the sanity of a policy that sent General Weygand to save Warsaw from the Bolsheviks and the unwisdom of a policy that encouraged Greece in an Asiatic adventure for which her strength was inadequate and of which she was left alone to bear the cruel consequences.

In one respect, it is true, our policy of the middle way was highly sympathetic. Refusing France's "penny wise, pound foolish" method of seeking to extract the uttermost farthing from Germany, and undeterred by America's fatal rejection of the Covenant together with the rest of the Treaty, Britain sought to make a reality of the League, as a kind of middle way between an impossible isolation and a renewal of world-wide war. In Mr Steed's phrase, the League became for many of our people "an object of semi-religious fervour", though the old unsolved problem of the "Freedom of the Seas" still haunted the background of the stage. There can be little doubt that in President Wilson's own conception of the League which he was creating there was no room for "neutrals" or "neutrality" and that therefore freedom of the seas in its pre-war sense would disappear:[1] but in view of his disavowal by the dominant section of American public opinion there were many who feared a reversion of America to the pre-war interpretation, in which case there would probably be a straight fight between "Freedom of the Seas" and the new League idea of collective League action against an aggressor, and of this Britain would, from the nature of things, have to bear the brunt. In other words, the British Government's reserve was heightened by one of the most praiseworthy features of its general policy,

[1] See Stannard Baker, *Woodrow Wilson*, II, p. 319, and Steed, *Vital Peace*, p. 213.

namely the earnest desire to remain in closest accord with America. So far indeed did it go in this direction, that it accepted Naval Parity with the United States (recognising, it is true, that if it ever came to naval competition *à outrance* between the two countries, America's vast resources were bound to win) and in further deference to American opinion allowed the Japanese Alliance to lapse.

It is not too much to affirm that, just as America's intervention turned the scale of war, and prevented a drawn peace, so her withdrawal destroyed the real hope of European consolidation, by depriving Geneva of one of the two chief exponents of Genevan doctrine. An inexorable consequence of this withdrawal was to strengthen that detached and hesitant outlook on the part of Britain which is inherent in her geographical situation—with the result that public opinion immersed itself in Genevan illusions and brought up the new generation on the assumption that pacifism had triumphed and that the reign of law had superseded brute force, while all the time the corresponding generation in most Continental countries was being deliberately trained to believe in force alone and to reject liberty and peace as a degenerate dream. Perhaps the most serious criticism against British Governments of the post-war era is that they were afraid to warn the public as to grim realities and followed, rather than led, until Abyssinia brought a rude awakening. On foreign Governments the effect of all this was to create an impression of insincerity and weakness, since they took it for granted that Britain's leaders could not be ignorant of the hard facts of the situation and must therefore be engaged upon some extremely subtle manœuvre. Once more the superficial, but plausible, theory of "Perfide Albion" emerged.

ANGLO-FRENCH FRICTION

By 1920 the Franco-British alliance was at an end, to be succeeded by close co-operation tempered by constant friction. This was doubtless due in the first instance to the great difference in the temperaments of the two peoples, one of which is almost always blowing hot while the other blows cold (a fact already notorious during the Crimean War, but one of the major calamities of the post-war period 1919–36). The personal factor also played its part, and in 1921, when Briand, who was negotiating quite seriously for a renewal of the British pledge of 1919 without America as partner, was replaced by the rigid Poincaré, not merely did the discussions languish, but the two nations rapidly fell apart. Radical disagreement as to reparations led to a long series of abortive conferences—the most important being that of Cannes in January 1922—and was the main cause of the steady decline of German credit. Anglo-French friction reached its height in 1923 when Poincaré, accusing Germany of defaulting on reparations, ordered the occupation of the Ruhr, and the Bonar Law Cabinet declined to co-operate. The modern Shylock, like his prototype, was immune to reason, and his failure was inevitable. Germany, in the recklessness of despair, resorted to evasive practices, and while the result brought ruin upon her once flourishing middle class by reducing their savings and investments to waste paper, it did at least offer some hope for the future, by ridding Germany at one stroke of her crushing internal debt. The British attitude towards French policy on the Rhine is reflected in the famous Clive Report,[1] published by an indiscretion: and while inclined to question the legality of the Ruhr experiment in terms of the Treaty, it made not the slightest concealment of its disapproval of the use of coloured troops in the army of occupation, and of the shady separatist experiment in the Rhineland. The obstinacy of Poincaré brought disaster upon all Europe: France did not obtain the payments at which she aimed, the franc itself was adversely affected, and in Dr Gooch's words, the Weimar regime became "still further identified with humiliation and suffering", and a further step had been taken towards the coming of a dictator, though for some years first Stresemann and then Brüning fought a gallant losing fight. The Dawes Plan (concocted in April and adopted in August 1924) was a makeshift to meet an altogether impossible financial situation: but the defeat of the "Bloc National"

[1] See *Survey for 1924*, pp. 312–13.

in Paris facilitated its task, and ended the first fatal phase of coercion and recrimination. The advent to power of Herriot and Briand brought France and Britain nearer to each other once more: and a new note was struck when Briand insisted that statesmen "must learn to speak European".

In this first period Britain found herself exercising a decisive influence at Geneva, but in a League which, in Mr Balfour's words, "in its present shape is not the League designed by the makers of the Covenant".[1] The United States refused to acknowledge paternity: Russia was still convulsed by revolution and civil war, still eager to confer those blessings upon all other countries, and consequently not wanted by anyone at Geneva: Germany seemed not yet to have qualified for admission, and was still doubtful whether she ought not to hold aloof entirely: Italy, after passing convulsions, due largely to government incompetence, was the first Power to answer Moscow by establishing a dictatorship of the Right, though in many respects following Moscow models. She was also the first Great Power to defy League principles by her attitude in the Corfu incident, and thus the first to test the League's powers of resistance to aggression. In a word, the League was far from including all the Powers, and then, as now, three Great Powers were absent from its councils: yet no one drew from this the conclusion that it should be abandoned as useless, as some of its more superficial critics do today in a similar situation.

THE DRAFT TREATY AND THE GENEVA PROTOCOL

The year 1924 brought a change of atmosphere. For the first time since the war German statesmen met their French and British colleagues on terms of equality, to discuss a *détente* in Europe. Germany, it is true, had in April 1922 at Rapallo taken a first hesitant step towards the renewal of her old alliance with Russia, and for over a decade to come certain military and economic contacts were to survive every political vicissitude.

[1] A. E. Zimmern, *League of Nations and Rule of Law*, pp. 303–4.

But Stresemann realised that, though re-insurance had its advantages for Germany, any real hope for the future lay in a western orientation, and that he might purchase on honourable terms her entry into the League and her consequent acceptance of the new international order.

The search for a compromise such as would also satisfy France's insistence upon Security preceding Disarmament—an insistence which (we can see today) has alone saved both France and Britain from disaster—centred round the devising of unmistakable means of defining aggression and identifying the aggressor. Much valuable preliminary work was expended upon the Draft Treaty of Mutual Assistance, but as Mr Gathorne Hardy has pointed out more clearly and succinctly than most writers on the subject, the attempt to combine "a general guarantee and a local system of alliances" failed, mainly owing to the peculiar position of the British group of nations. "The apportionment of liability on Continental lines cut fatally across the structure of the British Commonwealth with its world-wide responsibilities. Either some parts of the Empire would be at war while others remained at peace—a situation regarded at that date as intolerable" (this well illustrates the speed at which international relationships inside and outside the Empire are changing) "or Great Britain and her Dominions would have to assume a wholly disproportionate share of the burden of resisting aggression in all parts of the world. In any case no Continental exemption could apply to the British Navy, and the arrangements contemplated seemed likely to raise in an acute form the difficult question of constitutional relationships between the nations in the British Commonwealth."[1]

Though the Draft Treaty soon had to be abandoned, the need for a settlement was imperative, the discussions continued, and on 2 October 1924 their concrete result, the so-called Geneva Protocol, was unanimously commended to the various Governments by the Assembly of the League. No fewer than seventeen states gave their signatures almost at once, and Czechoslovakia, whose Foreign Minister M. Beneš was, with Mr Ramsay

[1] *Short History of International Affairs* p. 59.

Macdonald and M. Herriot, one of the chief initiators of the Protocol, went the length of ratification. The Protocol proclaimed "the solidarity of the members of the international community" and referred to a war of aggression as "a violation of this solidarity and an international crime": and it went on to propose the amendment of the Covenant, with a view to rendering really efficacious Article VIII, which prescribes "the reduction of national armaments to the lowest point consistent with national safety and the enforcement by common action of international obligations". The means by which this aim was to be attained have been summarised as follows: (1) Not to resort to war against other nations observing the Protocol, whether members of the League or not; (2) To recognise as compulsory the jurisdiction of the Court of International Justice in certain specified matters; (3) To refer political quarrels to the League or to arbitral bodies; (4) Not to mobilise armed forces during the course of arbitration of a dispute; (5) To consider as an aggressor any power resorting to war in defiance of the agreement; (6) To consent that aggressor states should pay the costs of war to the limit of their ability, but that war indemnities should not include cessions of territory; and (7) To take part in an international Conference on the reduction of armaments, as a preliminary to rendering the Protocol operative. "A state engaging in hostilities should be presumed to be an aggressor unless an unanimous decision of the League Council should declare otherwise."[1]

If the Protocol was "a brave and consistent attempt to bring down to earth the ideal of Peace through Law"—"the culmination of five years' hard work"[2]—it was also unhappily open to the objection that it was better adapted to the needs of Europe than to those of other Continents. In particular, it aroused misgivings in all the British Dominions, though their main reaction seems to have been towards those problems of immigration and coloured labour which mean so much to them and

[1] P. W. Slesson, *Europe since 1870*, p. 506; Steed, *Vital Peace*, pp. 152-3; A. E. Zimmern, *op. cit.* pp. 345-7.

[2] A. E. Zimmern, *op. cit.* p. 350.

so little to the European drafters of the scheme.[1] The situation was further fatally complicated by the fall of the Macdonald Government and the advent to power of the Conservatives: and the question had to be considered in the thoroughly unfavourable atmosphere created by the Zinoviev letter and the murder of the Sirdar. The Baldwin Government found itself unable to sponsor a project condemned on all hands with varying degrees of thoroughness: and after Lord Balfour had turned the scales against a policy of amendment, the Foreign Secretary, Austen Chamberlain, was sent to Geneva to announce on 12 March 1925 that, despite the sympathy felt for "any effort to improve the international machinery for maintaining the peace of the world", Britain saw "insuperable objections" to the Protocol "in its present shape". France remained, in Briand's phrase, "attached to the Protocol", but saw that Britain's action rendered it stillborn.

Rejection, however, did but add to the gravity of the problem, and the work expended upon the Protocol proved not to have been wasted, when Herr Stresemann made his famous proposal for a Western Pact resting on the principles of mutual guarantee. It may well be that his mind was coloured by the overpowering desire to free German soil from enemy occupation, as the essential preliminary to all progress: he certainly saw clearly that without explicit territorial renunciation on the West this aim was unobtainable, and that Germany would strengthen, not weaken, her position by entering the League. It may be presumed that he also saw that a Russian alliance was not at that stage a possible alternative, and that it was with the Western Powers that he must deal. Moreover, he openly proclaimed his conviction that, failing any reciprocal arrangement, Britain would logically and inevitably be drawn back to something very like the Convention of June 1919—to something not far removed

---

[1] A curious analogy is supplied by the international Eastern crisis of 1875–6, when Disraeli and Derby opposed the proposed reforms not on their merits, but (privately) for fear of creating an awkward precedent for land reform in Ireland. See my *Disraeli, Gladstone and the Eastern Question*, p. 22; Buckle, *Life of Disraeli*, VI, p. 13.

from an Anglo-French alliance. If this was his view, the events following Hitler's violation of Locarno are a proof of his perspicacity.

LOCARNO

With the long negotiations which led up to the Locarno Conference in October 1925 and ended in the signature of the Locarno Pact on 1 December, this book is not concerned: it must suffice to indicate the main trends of European policy and Britain's reactions to them. The central document was the Pact of Western Security between Germany, France, Britain, Italy and Belgium, guaranteeing *"jointly and severally"* the western frontiers as created by the Treaty, and also the Rhineland demilitarised zone. Germany, France and Belgium bind themselves not to resort to war save in resisting an unprovoked breach of the Pact and the Rhineland clauses of Versailles, or in fulfilment of Article XVI of the Covenant, against a declared aggressor. They are also pledged to arbitration of disputes by the World Court and to prompt reference to the League Council. To the main document were appended a series of arbitration conventions between Germany on the one hand, and Belgium, France, Poland and Czechoslovakia on the other, and two treaties of mutual assistance between France and the two last Powers for the event of German aggression. The essential factors in the background were Britain's firm resolve to limit her obligations to the West, France's insistence that the question of Rhineland evacuation should be kept clear of the Pact, and that Germany should promise to enter the League without reservations, and Germany's insistence that the Pact should not be allowed to interfere with her recent Treaty with Soviet Russia at Rapallo, and that in respect of obligations under the Covenant she should be granted an interim solution of Article XVI, pending general disarmament.

Locarno seemed to mark at long last the abandonment of dictation in favour of free and equal negotiation (and it is important to remember that this was explicitly recognised by Hitler in his speech of 21 May 1935), and therefore offered reasonable hope that Germany on her side would throw off the inferiority complex in which defeat had confirmed her. The price to be paid was voluntary renunciation in the West, and entry into the League system on equal terms. While France linked herself with Poland and Czechoslovakia for purposes of mutual assistance, Britain resolutely declined to commit herself to any Eastern guarantee of frontiers, while the Dominions and India were expressly excluded from commitments. Thus the idea of regional agreements asserted itself against the more general guarantee of the Geneva Protocol.

If Locarno limited our commitments in one direction, it certainly may be said to have gone further than any previous undertaking ever assumed by Britain: and yet it was generally felt that as the absence of a treaty could in no way guarantee us against the necessity of intervening for the defence of France or Belgium, *as vital British interests*, it was better to accept definition and thereby avoid the general uncertainty of 1914 as to our probable attitude. Under the circumstances of 1914 it was quite impossible to commit ourselves beforehand, though the knowledge that we would join in would almost certainly have averted war. With such an example before our eyes, we found it easier to realise that definition serves as a deterrent, while vagueness encourages a gambler's throw.

In Germany there was keen opposition to the Locarno Pact, and Stresemann had only a slender margin in his favour, even after President von Hindenburg—who had succeeded Ebert in April 1925—threw the weight of his prestige into the scales. There was indeed a curious passing co-operation between the two extreme groups most hostile to an arrangement with the West—the Russian Communists and the German nationalists and militarists—whose point of contact lay in their joint denunciation of the League as capitalist, predatory and Machiavellian.[1] Not without reason could it be said of the Treaty of Rapallo (16 April 1922) that it had effectually prevented a *rapprochement* between Germany and the Western Powers: and now it did not at all suit the Soviets—still at the very height

[1] For a full account see Toynbee, *Survey for 1925*, pp. 1–63.

of their subversive revolutionary propaganda throughout the world—that Briand should be able to declare, "In the light of these treaties we are Europeans only", and that Stresemann should present the fruits of his policy as "an European idea".

The settlement was followed by a wave of sentimental confidence which events were unhappily not to justify. No other than Austen Chamberlain himself spoke of it as "the real dividing line between the years of war and the years of peace". It had followed logically from the failure of the Ruhr adventure, and had seemed to mark a definite return of Europe as a whole to what the Americans, conveniently if cacophonously, call "normalcy". The military evacuation of the first zone of German territory and Germany's entrance into the League— momentarily marred by Poland's foolish insistence upon the status of a Great Power—were the outward and visible signs of a *détente*. For the next four years there seemed every prospect of finding a reasonable compromise between the old national and the new international ideals. The fetish of absolute state sovereignty began to yield to the Genevan ideals of automatic co-operation against aggression, in place of alliances, of renunciation of war as an instrument of policy, and of arbitration as a substitute for ultimatums. In particular the Western Security Pact precluded—and this had of course been one of Stresemann's chief aims—any return to an Anglo-French alliance. The way was now open to a serious discussion of the three great unsolved problems of disarmament, evacuation and revision of reparations.

In the ensuing period, it is important to bear in mind, the main obstacle to disarmament lay, not in France, as is too often asserted by facile controversialists, but in Russia: for so long as a state of such magnitude pursued a policy of open hostility towards the whole existing "capitalist" order and at the same time was steadily engaged in creating the Red Army as an instrument of future policy, it was not at all obvious how states farther West could seriously disarm without exposing all Europe to acute dangers from the East. If the French, with their clear and logical minds, showed special hesitation in this respect, such an attitude cannot lightly be dismissed as merely prompted by a desire for hegemony in Europe, or by illegitimate alliances for the encirclement of Germany. The true answer is that throughout that period France was perturbed by fears for the survival of Poland, whom she had from the very first—and not without reason—regarded as one of the two main foundation-stones of the post-war settlement (the independence of Austria and Czechoslovakia being the other). And to those Germans who are disposed to lay the whole blame upon France two pertinent reminders may be addressed: (1) We now know that Stresemann, despite Locarno, aimed at the recovery of Danzig, the Corridor and at least part of Silesia from Poland,[1] and hoped to secure them by German neutrality in the fresh war which he expected to break out between Poland and Russia. (2) We also know that from the Treaty of Rapallo onwards there remained close ties between the German and Soviet General Staffs, and that much of the constructive work in the Red Army was the work of German experts, who were thus able to continue their technical experiments and even build up useful stocks, at a safe distance from all inter-Allied control. And it should be unnecessary to add that the maintenance of these contacts was not the work of the politicians of the now derided Weimar Republic, but of the responsible chiefs of the Prussian military machine.

DISARMAMENT AND THE KELLOGG PACT

During the two years following Locarno a Preparatory Commission tried to pave the way for a Disarmament Conference, but was handicapped by much obscure thinking and even deliberate obstruction: and the atmosphere was rendered still less favourable by the failure of the Three-Power Naval Conference at Geneva in June 1927—the first of a series of conferences which were allowed to meet without adequate political preparation beforehand.

A fresh and gallant effort to check the dry-rot was made in

[1] See his letter of 7 September 1923 to the German Crown Prince.

April 1928 by the American Secretary of State, Mr Kellogg: and in the following August the so-called Kellogg Pact was signed in Paris, by fifteen nations in the first instance, and eventually by almost every nation in the world (including the United States and Soviet Russia). But though their signature involved the most solemn renunciation of war "as an instrument of national policy" and pledged them never to seek a solution of any disputes whatsoever "except by pacific means", and though public opinion throughout the world greeted the Pact with overwhelming approval, security remained almost as much a phantom as before. "C'est magnifique, mais ce n'est pas la paix", it might very fairly have been remarked: it was a magnificent gesture, but sanctions were conspicuous by their absence. Mr Kellogg himself, in his eagerness to overcome objections, made it clear that the Pact only applied to aggressive war, and that its signatories remained free to defend themselves against unprovoked attacks: and as no attempt was made to provide machinery for a prompt definition of aggression, the old dilemma of rival interpretations persisted unabated, and worst of all, there was nothing to indicate what action, if any, other signatories should take if faced by aggression—even when proved—on the part of one of them. In particular the attitude of extreme *désintéressement* in the affairs of Europe adopted by the United States, the chief sponsor of the Pact, increased the scepticism which descended upon most students of foreign affairs after the first sentimental impression had evaporated. It may indeed be affirmed that the only practical result of the Kellogg Pact was the attitude of Soviet Russia, which from the moment of signing the Pact began to renounce its negative, not to say hostile, attitude in international affairs. In December 1928 M. Litvinov proposed an additional protocol, to be signed, on a regional basis, by Soviet Russia with her immediate neighbours: and in February 1929 this was actually concluded between Russia, Poland, Roumania and the three small Baltic States. Meanwhile Britain, in accepting, did so "on the distinct understanding" that it did not "prejudice her freedom of action in respect of certain regions of the world, the welfare and integrity of which constitute a special and vital interest for our peace and prosperity".[1]

Theoretical as it may be, the Kellogg Pact has, on paper, performed a memorable function as (in Sir Alfred Zimmern's phrase) "the most farreaching engagement so far entered upon by the sovereign states of the world": it is "irrevocable" and cannot be renounced with honour, and it "undermines the traditional doctrine of sovereignty",[2] thus creating a precedent which cannot be wiped out. But at the same time it is essentially negative and shrinks back from the logical sequel of erecting the Hue and Cry theory of English common law into a general principle of international law. Unless Europe returns to the backwoods, the day will come when theory will be followed by practice: a precedent has been created, which no amount of bad faith and cynicism on the part of individual governments can permanently extinguish.

THE YOUNG PLAN

Despite certain ominous rumblings, the impetus of public opinion seemed sufficient during 1929 to ensure further progress towards the goal of international appeasement and equality to which every Government paid lip service. A new Committee was set up under the American financier, Mr Owen D. Young, to explore the possibility of a final regulation of the reparations problem: and its report, issued in June 1929, did at last fix a reduced scale of payments which, though still very formidable, bore some relation to Germany's capacity to pay and was adjustable according to the extent of economic recovery. The collection of the actual sums was assigned to a non-political "Bank for International Settlements", with its headquarters at Basel. Before the Young Plan was adopted in a final form, there were somewhat heated discussions in Paris and London, where Snowden was now Chancellor of the Exchequer; and two further Reparations Conferences were held at The Hague. But when at last in May 1930 the new Plan was ratified, and

[1] See *Survey for* 1928, p. 21.   [2] *Op. cit.* p. 392.

bound up with it was the decision for an immediate evacuation of the Second Rhineland Zone by Allied troops, there were obvious signs that the French attitude was moderating. Already in the autumn of 1929 at Geneva Aristide Briand had aired his noble, if premature, idea of an European federation or "United States of Europe": and if at this time the main objection raised to it sprang from the fear lest anything should be done to weaken the existing League and its prestige, there was a general consensus of opinion that the scheme might first of all be profitably explored in the economic field.

Unfortunately Stresemann, who in an eloquent speech before the Assembly had firmly refused to reject the scheme as impracticable and had also rejected all idea of "an economic autarchy of Europe", died on 3 October and left a blank among the constructive statesmen of Europe which remained unfilled. Before the end of the year Austen Chamberlain had fallen from power, and Briand remained alone, little more than the ghost of his former self. Unhappily also, before ever the Young Plan could be made fully operative, the first mutterings of a world economic crisis made themselves heard: and it became all too soon clear that the Young Committee, like all its predecessors, had erred on the side of optimism in fixing the German capacity to pay, or at least the Allied capacity to extract payment. As the crisis turned into a veritable blizzard, which threatened to smother even America herself, increasingly drastic measures had to be adopted by one country after another. The failure of the Austrian Kredit-Anstalt, with its repercussions in Austria and Germany (May 1931), the Hoover Moratorium (July), the Standstill Agreement which forced itself, rather than was forced, upon the International Bankers' Committee in August, the renewed disagreements between London and Paris as to the amount of relief to be accorded to Germany—all this was completely dwarfed by the financial crisis in Britain, her abandonment of the gold standard, and their political consequences, the *débâcle* of the Labour Party and the election of a National Government by majorities hitherto unrecorded in British history.

THE SLUMP

The calm, energy and promptitude with which all classes responded to the strain imposed upon them undoubtedly impressed the outside world and saved those two inseparable and imponderable factors, our prestige and our credit. But in the interval before our recovery could be regarded as assured, certain events had occurred which nothing could make good. For in the first place Germany declared herself unable to continue reparation annuities, and though it came to renewed disagreement between London and Paris as to the tactics to be adopted towards Germany, there was in the end no alternative to the abolition of reparations, and the decisions taken at Lausanne in June 1932 no less inevitably linked together once more the problems of reparations and war-debts, thereby complicating the already delicate relations of Europe and America.[1] Secondly, Japan took advantage of the general preoccupation to seize Manchuria and to carry her aggression into China itself: and thanks to the deplorable weakness of the British Government and its failure to agree upon joint action with America, Japanese defiance of Genevan principles was completely successful and gravely undermined the prestige of the League, since the paper fulminations of the Lytton Report were not followed up by the application of sanctions.

Worst of all, however, was the general *malaise* created by economic conditions for which there was no precedent—starvation amid plenty; trade restrictions seemingly increased in proportion to the unemployment which they had provoked; simultaneous demands for a rigid system of autarchy and for a redistribution of raw materials. In most of Europe it followed logically that the tide of democracy ebbed rapidly, and counsels of despair and violence gained the upper hand. So long as the only exponents of autocracy among the Great Powers were Russia, still relatively remote from Europe, and Italy, in Pro-

[1] For an unusually lucid survey of the economic crisis, see Chapter XVII of Mr Gathorne Hardy's *Short History of International Affairs*.

fessor Toynbee's apt phrase, only the greatest of the "Would-be-Greats", the danger was not so acute, despite the many propagandist possibilities: and the various brands of hybrid dictatorship evolved by Spain, Poland, Jugoslavia and Greece were neither durable nor suited for export. But in proportion as Germany in her turn began to abandon the path of democracy while it was still only very imperfectly trodden in, and to develop a peculiarly virulent type of dictatorial regime, the repercussions were all the more grave because of her central geographical position. But the most disquieting feature of all—a fact which must be constantly borne in mind in all that follows—was that the adoption of the Young Plan, the Briand plan of federation and the final evacuation of the Rhineland—three events which were greeted in the West as outward and visible signs of appeasement and a change of heart among the nations—did not have a corresponding sedative effect in Germany, but were followed almost immediately by the emergence of National Socialism, no longer as a faction but as a great and all-compelling national movement, antagonistic not only to the Weimar regime at home, but to the whole Genevan structure abroad. In other words, at the very moment when the worst features of the post-war system seemed to have been removed, when the tendency to treat Germany as a pariah had been abandoned, and when the two intimately connected problems of disarmament and equality had come to occupy the very front of the European stage—it was at this moment that German opinion turned decisively away from the "policy of fulfilment" associated with the name of Stresemann, and allowed itself to be lashed to frenzy by the unbalanced eloquence of Adolf Hitler and a small group of resolute and reckless fanatics.

With his political creed, as expounded in *Mein Kampf* and in a long series of speeches, we shall have to deal more fully later. For the moment our main emphasis must rest upon the incontestable fact that concession, moderation and readiness for fulfilment on the part of her former enemies only served to whet the appetite and stiffen the demands of German opinion and, worst of all, to strengthen the conviction that an appeal to force was more effective than an appeal to justice. It is possible to argue that the former Allies had by their long delays and prevarications so exasperated the German people and Government as to reduce them to a pathological state in which reason and peaceful discussion were losing their effect. It is, moreover, but just to make allowance for the dire results of a renewed crisis on a nation which had graven on its memory the devastation wrought by the downfall of the Mark. But we are left with the unanswered question whether the German mind, at least as it has evolved in the last two decades, has not learned to respond more readily to force than to discussion and is not disposed to regard concession as a sign of weakness.

BRÜNING AND THE DISARMAMENT CONFERENCE

The Brüning Government already found itself between two fires before ever the Disarmament Conference could open on 8 February 1932. It is no exaggeration to speak of a growing "national panic" due to the failure of the politicians in the brief period of optimism between Locarno and the Slump.[1] It was in no small degree the anxiety due to this position and the hope of regaining its waning popularity by a rapid success in the sphere of foreign policy, that prompted the maladroit project of an Austro-German Customs Union put forward by Curtius and Schober. The surreptitious methods employed not merely killed the project at birth, but sowed fresh suspicion among the Powers and undermined Chancellor Brüning's influence in two directions, even though his own personal good intentions were freely recognised by his critics. A veto was successfully imposed upon the "Anschluss", and the result was "a terrible diplomatic reverse to Germany": "her impotence to conduct even the shadow of an independent foreign policy was exposed to the world".[2] And meanwhile French suspicions were not diminished by the knowledge that Germany had long been engaged in evasion of the military clauses of the Treaty

[1] See R. T. Clark, *The Fall of the German Republic*, pp. 315-18.
[2] *Ibid.* p. 319.

and in secret rearmament, and (to take but a single illustration) had established chemical and gas factories in Russia as part of the practical co-operation between the German and Soviet General Staffs.[1]

In the first stage of the Disarmament Conference Dr Brüning pushed the German claim for equality, while privately endeavouring to disarm opposition by the argument that Germany's financial and economic position rendered increased expenditure on armaments difficult (it was left to his National Socialist successors to evolve the idea that such expenditure could be used to solve, at least temporarily, the problem of unemployment). Unfortunately, the British Government adopted a vacillating attitude in face of the French plan of an international force, which was obviously inacceptable in its original form, but not necessarily incapable of amendment, and it showed no signs of a constructive policy of its own: while successive German Governments (first Herr von Papen in June 1932, then General von Schleicher in November, had replaced Brüning) hinted more and more plainly that a recognition of equality of rights was the sole condition on which Germany could continue to collaborate. On 11 December 1932 a formula was found between the four Powers and the United States in favour of "equality of rights in a system which would provide security for all nations": but each state upheld its own interpretation, and in other directions no real progress was achieved. By the autumn the psychological moment had passed, and the cause of disarmament began to lose ground steadily.[2]

THE HITLER REGIME

The advent of Herr Hitler to power in Germany on 30 January 1933, and Japan's skilfully calculated withdrawal from the League on 24 February, still further reduced the prospect of success. The new Plan laid before the Conference on 16 March

[1] Toynbee, *Survey for 1932.*

[2] One of the most authoritative accounts of the events leading to the Hitler regime will be found in J. W. Wheeler-Bennett's *Hindenburg: the Wooden Titan* (1936).

by Mr Ramsay Macdonald did, it is true, include concrete suggestions for limitation of effectives, control and inspection, and a ban on chemical warfare: but it was not pushed home and its British sponsors too easily allowed themselves to be diverted by Signor Mussolini's proposal for a Four-Power Pact. This equally sinister and futile plan was a scarcely veiled attempt to complete the undermining of League prestige, to eliminate the lesser Powers from their increasing importance in the counsels of Europe, and to establish a sort of directorate of four, in which France, deprived of her Eastern alliances, and with Russia strictly excluded, would be in a minority of one, while Britain's chronic vacillation would make of Italy the finger on the balance of European power. Not unnaturally France and her allies were entirely opposed to the plan, Britain as usual took up an intermediate position, and before it could be signed in July 1933 it had to be altered out of all recognition and was henceforth of very little interest to anyone. But it had served its purpose as a diversion from the main business at Geneva, and had a most unsettling effect in more than one direction. On 14 October Germany, entirely disregarding the fresh proposals outlined that very morning at Geneva by Sir John Simon, announced her withdrawal from the Disarmament Conference and her impending resignation from the League.[1] In face of this open flouting of the League the other Powers seemed helpless and disunited; the Conference continued until the summer of 1934 to meet and talk "in a state of suspended animation":[2] but from this moment it was really dead, and the two Western Powers had been driven on to the defensive.

Hitler now announced his terms for a resumption of negotiations—a conscript army of 300,000 men, unrestricted in its

[1] Already on 15 September Baron Neurath had uttered the ominous phrase: "if the highly armed countries continued to evade their obligations to disarm, the German Government would have the right and duty to provide for the equality and security of its own people according to its own judgment and without any hesitation or false scruple": cit. Toynbee, *Survey for 1933*, p. 297.

[2] Gathorne Hardy, *op. cit.* p. 322.

choice of weapons, and exclusive of the various semi-military
formations which owed allegiance to the Nazi Party: and the
conciliatory phrases which he addressed to France could not
conceal the patent fact that unilateral action and *re*-armament
were being substituted for international co-operation and *dis*-
armament. Mussolini again drew nearer to Hitler and prompted
the Fascist Grand Council to demand a radical reform of the
League as a condition of Italian collaboration. The unsettling
effect of all these developments upon the lesser Powers was
exemplified by the Pact of non-aggression concluded in January
1934 between Poland and Germany, by which Marshal Pilsudski,
by forcing the pace with a still unready Germany, adroitly
secured a ten-years' respite for a country which, after a decade
of unnatural armed superiority over two disarmed giants, was
inevitably doomed to a lower level of strength and security
when once the giants were rearmed. Hitler's right hand in
foreign policy, Herr Rosenberg, had in 1927 declared "the
sweeping away of the Polish State to be the very first requirement of Germany", and a common German-Russian frontier
to be a necessity—whether as a step towards territorial conquest
both in Southern Russia and on the Baltic, or towards the
overthrow of Bolshevism and the revival of the Russo-German
alliance, is not entirely clear.

Another no less curious feature of the changing situation
in Europe since the advent of Hitler was the abandonment
by Soviet Russia of her policy of aloofness, based upon militant
propaganda and pride in the role of pariah. Her new policy
was determined on the one hand by an internal evolution upon
which it would be very rash to put any too precise political
or even economic labels, and on the other by a recognition
of the vital need for peace, as the only condition under which
the Russian experiment can succeed, by the knowledge of
Hitler's avowedly aggressive designs upon Russian territory,
and by a very natural desire to escape from isolation in view of
the possibility of a German-Japanese alliance. In a word, events
were forcing Russia, without renouncing her revolutionary
and autocratic basis at home, to adopt an increasingly conser-

vative and pacific foreign policy, to oppose any radical alteration in the *status quo*, to welcome co-operation on the Genevan basis and to improve her relations with America. The natural reluctance of the Western Powers to enter into close relations with the Bolshevist State could not conceal the existence of parallel interests in the supreme question of World Peace, and it was also counterbalanced by the sinister events of 30 June and 25 July 1934,[1] when the Leader of the Third Reich replaced the great traditions of German law by midnight execution and hip-pocket justice, and then seemed to connive at assassination as a means for the achievement of German Unity.

In this situation it cannot be denied that Britain pursued a weak and hesitating policy. The best plea that can be put forward on her behalf was the double fact that, by a perversity of fate, French and British opinion, not once but repeatedly in these years, blew alternately hot and cold in such a way as to render uniform action by London and Paris very difficult, and again that apart from France Britain's search for possible allies led her to a mere choice of evils. While repudiating the view that a community of political ideals is the necessary basis of alliance or understanding between two nations (and in so doing I have the explicit authority of practically every holder of the office of British Foreign Secretary), I feel that it would be no less futile to hope for intimate friendship or collaboration between a nation whose policy rests on "consent of the governed" and free public opinion and a nation organised on extreme totalitarian and dictatorial lines. Today this definition is of course equally true of Russia, Germany and Italy, so far as *internal* policy is concerned: but there is this curious difference between them, that Russia, since her entry into the League, has in her *foreign* policy faithfully observed her international treaty obligations, and stands for an extension of the Genevan order on a basis of right, discussion and arbitration, whereas

---

[1] For (1) the *coup* in which Röhm, Schleicher, Strasser and many others met their deaths and (2) the attack by Nazi conspirators on the Chancellor's office and Radio Headquarters and their cold-blooded murder of Dr Dollfuss, see *infra*, pp. 223 and 228.

Germany, and still more Italy, have violated one pledge after another, and not only such as had been imposed on them by *force majeure*, but many to which they had freely given their signatures. How far this distinction is one of tactics rather than conviction, as also the question whether the value of signatures to public treaties has not been entirely undermined by recent events, must be reserved for discussion in later chapters. For the moment there can be no doubt as to which Powers stand for "the European Anarchy" and which for the collective system.

As a general proposition it has to be admitted that since 1934 Europe, under the triple menace of Bolshevism, Fascism and National Socialism, has moved steadily backwards towards the abyss from which she had seemed to have escaped. In particular, Germany, while throwing off the shackles of the first post-war period, is trying to have it both ways. She denounces the Peace Settlement as Carthaginian, treating its alleged non-fulfilment by the Allies as an excuse for unrestricted repudiation, and in the very same breath denounces as decadent and objectionable the twin principles of Democracy and Internationalism on which President Wilson built up those very Fourteen Points to which she is constantly appealing.

VI

BRITAIN AND THE DICTATORS. (A) RUSSIA

MORE than once in her history Britain has dislocated the calculations of friend and foe alike by withdrawing from policies which she had been pursuing with a vast expenditure of effort, and assuming an attitude of detachment, and almost of indifference, towards problems which she had herself helped to shape. This tendency reasserted itself to a marked degree after the signatures of the Peace Treaties in 1919–20. Her interest in the area lying between the Rhine and the Narrow Seas was too overwhelming to be relinquished, and it was almost equally impossible to escape from a series of commitments in the Middle East (Palestine, Irak, Egypt). But in all that lay between these two extremes, and especially in that Danubian and Balkan region in which the transformation wrought by the war had been the greatest, she reverted to an attitude of *désintéressement* which may or may not have been justified, but which certainly accentuated the political and economic deadlock in that part of Europe. Throughout the period hurriedly surveyed in the last chapter, the two main trends that inevitably determined our policy, even when it was most vacillating, were on the one side the international movement in support of the League of Nations and a new World Order based upon Peace, Law and Arbitration, and on the other side the violent oscillations of opinion in many Continental countries, due largely to economic dislocation and shattered nerves, which suddenly arrested the democratic tide and brought a series of dictators into power.

By degrees, though not in the first instance, it became apparent that the two trends were incompatible, and that if the new autocracies could entrench themselves permanently and secure control over the education of the rising generation, the whole structure of international relations, and in particular the Genevan experiment, would be endangered. Hence, before it is possible to bring our survey up to date and to discuss British policy as it presents itself since the summer of 1937, it is necessary to examine our relations with the three principal dictatorships of Europe, bearing always in mind that ever since the war, and today more than ever, all other problems have centred round the German problem, as the crux of the whole European situation. If the triangular relations of London, Paris and Berlin can be placed on a satisfactory and more or less permanent footing, the Continent will have peace for a long period, and all other problems will fall into their proper places. If not, Mr Baldwin's prophecy will be realised, and European civilisation will fall in ruins. Any attempt to bring two of these Powers together at the expense of the third, or to introduce a fourth or fifth into the main discussions, will only make confusion worse confounded and will inevitably end in failure. It will, I trust, soon be apparent from my whole line of argument, that this is in no way intended as an abandonment of League principles on the one hand or as an attempt to eliminate Russia or Italy from the final settlement: for it is obvious that unless a basis can be found for a rehabilitation of the League, and unless both Russian and Italian (and it must at once and most emphatically be added, American) interests can be duly safeguarded, no settlement reached by the three Powers would be permanent. It is none the less certain that as things are at present in Europe, the triangular approach offers the best, perhaps the only, chance of a solution.

THE TSARIST AND PROVISIONAL GOVERNMENTS

Let us in the first instance consider our past relations with Russia and see whether they provide any clues for our present guidance.

Russia has always been a country of extremes—in the political sphere, of violent oscillation from Right to Left, in the literary, of incalculable and ungovernable changes of feeling. From Ivan the Terrible through Peter, Catherine and Nicholas, to

Lenin and Stalin, there has been the same tendency to solve all problems by dictatorial methods, by brute force, brooking no delay and riding roughshod over the lives and hopes of the individual man and citizen. Yet on the other hand Russia had preserved certain very ancient institutions, popular in character and resting upon healthy local idiosyncrasies—the "mir" or self-governing commune, the "zemstvo" or essentially co-operative community. It is only in our own day that the tidal wave of revolution has overwhelmed these things, and it is still too soon to predict whether they will again sprout from a new alluvial soil after the great flood has subsided. It may, however, safely be affirmed that the peculiar development of Russian political life since the war is due to a strange lack of balance in the national character, such as may be observed in most of the great Russian writers, and especially in Dostoyevsky, whose very abnormality is accepted by almost all Russians as typically Russian.

It was the supreme tragedy of a nation to which psychology and history, geography and climate, have all imparted a bias towards extremes, that the Revolution, which folly had long since made inevitable, should have coincided with a gigantic war which imposed a strain far in excess of the country's utmost physical powers of endurance. That thousands of men were sent into the field without rifles in their hands and suffered casualties out of all proportion to those of properly equipped nations, is only a single crass illustration out of many. In the end rage and demoralisation supervened upon war-weariness: and the old Tsarist regime collapsed even more suddenly and completely than the most subversive elements had expected.

Even in the light of all that has followed it is difficult to feel any very keen regret for the old system, which fell by reason of its inward rottenness. To this there is one very important qualification: for land reform had not remained stationary after Alexander II's great act of emancipation in 1861, and had received a notable stimulus from the measures of Stolypin. But the figure of Stolypin may well stand as a symbol of the abnormality of the pre-war regime: for if it is but bare justice to that statesman to stress his enlightened outlook towards the peasantry, the really incredible circumstances of his assassination in 1911— as a victim of double-dyed treachery both inside the police and in the revolutionary ranks—show how deep the canker of corruption had penetrated the Tsarist system. Even the scandals connected with the name of the rascally pseudo-monk Rasputin—which were to the Russian, what the affair of Marie Antoinette's necklace was to the French, Revolution—did not surpass the earlier affair of Azev the police spy: they were merely the culmination of a long process.

The Provisional Government, which took the helm from the nerveless hands of the old regime in March 1917, has never received the sympathy and recognition which it deserved for a gallant attempt to achieve the impossible. Indeed, so persistent has been the propaganda of its successors, and so superficial the reactions of Western opinion, that today one constantly hears it assumed by the devotees of the Extreme Left, that Bolshevism freed Russia from the enormities of Tsarist rule. Never was there a greater travesty of the facts. The Provisional Government, with all its faults and weaknesses—and of these the most decisive was the fact that Russia was too exhausted and nerve-racked to support War and Revolution simultaneously, and that the new regime's loyalty to the Allies was ruthlessly exploited against it by its enemies at home and abroad—stood for all the political ideas for which the West daily declared itself to be fighting, and made a genuine attempt to put them into practice. Representative and parliamentary government, universal secret suffrage, freedom of religion, the press, association and assembly, land for the peasants, free education, federation and minority rights for the non-Russian races—such were the main foundations on which the new Russian Republic was to be built. War-weariness, the breakdown of military discipline, a skilful propaganda assisted by the Germans, the overpowering desire of peasant-soldiers to reach home in time to share in the partition of the land—all this led to political anarchy and economic crisis: and after a reconstruction in a more radical sense, which left Kerensky—eloquent and upright, but unpractised in administration—in supreme control, power was wrested from the hands of the Provisional Government by the determined onslaught of the Bolsheviks.

It should be unnecessary to point out that the charges of "pro-Germanism" and "treachery" levelled at the time against Lenin and Trotsky are grotesquely irrelevant: such words meant nothing to men who repudiated the very foundations of the social and political order of their day, and who, in the hope of establishing a base of operations in Russia from which they could organise the World Revolution, did not hesitate to accept help wherever they could obtain it, without thereby for one moment accepting any obligations. The decision of the German General Staff to despatch Lenin and his friends to Russia in the famous "sealed carriages" will long remain in history as a symbol and a warning. For while it served only too well their immediate purpose by hastening the disintegration of what still remained of the Russian army, it must surely have often caused its authors bitter regret and concern in view of the infection thus spread not merely in Russia but throughout the centre and south of Europe. Just so may "the next war" be reserving for the inventors of poison gas and bacteriological war the just fate of being "hoist with their own petard".

THE SECOND REVOLUTION

It can never be too strongly emphasised that the immediate effect of the Second, or Bolshevik, Revolution of November 1917 was not to establish, but to annihilate, liberty in Russia— that it overthrew not the already vanished Tsarist regime, but an advanced democratic regime of the Left, which despite its all too manifest defects had all that was really vocal in Russia behind it. The elections for a Constituent Assembly, which were already pending, could no longer be cancelled, and took place before the close of the year, on surprisingly representative lines, considering the chaos into which the country was rapidly drifting. But the Bolsheviks, failing to obtain a majority in this Assembly, applied to it the tactics of the terrorist Jacobins of the French Revolution. Many of its leading members were thrown into prison, the galleries were packed with a howling mob, the entrances guarded by revolutionary sailors fresh from the massacre of their officers: and when the deputies in the teeth of arbitrary Bolshevik decrees still gallantly tried to assert their control over legislation, the Assembly was dissolved after a day and never again allowed to meet. The leaders of all parties save the Bolshevik[1] were scattered to the winds; Shingarev, the noted Liberal leader, whose whole life had been devoted to the service of the people, was brutally murdered in a prison hospital; the same anathema was placed upon the Social Revolutionaries of Kerensky as upon the Cadets of Milyukov or the Octobrists of Guchkov; such veteran exponents of extreme Socialist doctrine as Plekhanov, Kropotkin or Breshkovskaya were ruthlessly swept aside when it became apparent that they placed liberty above party. If the First Revolution had been comparatively bloodless and free from reprisals (though, it must be added, marked by serious agrarian outrage on some of the large estates), the Second Revolution degenerated almost at once into wholesale butchery and prolonged civil war, aggravated in the end by privation and famine. The exact number of victims, and of those who escaped into exile, will never be known. For our present purpose it is sufficient to note that whereas the victims of the French Terror did not exceed 20,000, those of its Russian namesake cannot have been less than 2,000,000, while the two famines of 1921 and 1933 accounted for several millions more. And just as today even the most ignorant knows—if only from the pages of Charles Dickens—that sempstress and peasant and petit bourgeois also shared the fate of many a guilty, and innocent, aristocrat, so it is time that public opinion accepted as an axiom the incontestable fact that the victims of the Russian Revolution were not merely so-called "Whites"—an impudent and superficial label, intended to confuse the true issues—but men and women

---

[1] A further exception is provided by the Maximalists (the extreme Left of the Social Revolutionaries), who were also thrown over a few months later.

belonging to every social stratum from the Right to the Left, merchants, priests, tradesmen, artisans and above all peasants, no less than aristocrats or officers.

This bare statement provides the essential perspective for any understanding of the new autocratic regime in Europe. Russia, always abnormal in her reactions and in her social processes, spent years of torture upon the rack and infected all Europe, unconsciously even more than consciously, with her agony. The fear of a repetition of these appalling horrors in countries outside the Russian frontiers weighed upon the corresponding sections of society there and warped and distorted their own political institutions at a moment of maximum strain. We shall see later that what may fairly be described as "inverted Bolshevism" has also played its part in the undermining of Democracy in Europe, and that though the wholesale bloodshed into which the Russian Revolution eventually degenerated has so far been averted in the other dictatorial states, and though unmeasured denunciation of Bolshevism forms one of the main planks in their programme, there has been on their part a growing tendency to adopt methods of compulsion against the individual, alike in the economic, the financial, the intellectual and the religious spheres, such as were first applied in Soviet Russia. Imitation and vituperation often go hand in hand.

THE ALLIES AND "INTERVENTION"

Another misconception, scarcely less fatal, runs through much of the comment about Russia since 1917 and relates to that ominous word "intervention": and here too it is well to explode deliberately misleading catchwords. During the summer of 1917 we continued to be the allies of Russia in a war already waged in common for three years: and the abdication of the Tsar and his brother left the supreme power in the hands of men who loyally recognised the alliance, desired to fulfil its obligations wherever possible and earned much unpopularity by that very loyalty. So far as foreign relations were concerned, they were the loyal successors of the old regime. With the coming of the Bolshevists all this changed: Russia's new rulers repudiated all connection with her allies and made no concealment of their desire to overthrow the whole social order in the West as they had already done at home. Their haste in concluding peace with the Germans is of course to be explained by a genuine inability to continue the struggle: but the prime cause of this inability was their own subversive propaganda within the Russian army. Once more, however, we should be using misleading language if we called their attitude in making peace "defeatist" or "unpatriotic": their aim was an altogether transformed and reconstituted Europe, in which the territories "lost" by Russia would soon recover their former contacts as units of a new World Order. And meanwhile Lenin was not afraid to argue: "Let us give way in peace, but gain time."[1]

From the Allied point of view, then, the Second Revolution was a blow dealt at an ally in distress still feebly trying to uphold the common cause—a blow all the more deadly because the Treaty of Brest-Litovsk released German divisions for war in the West and replenished German stores of grain and oil. The idea that even if we betrayed our friends we could come to terms with the Bolsheviks in their first flush of elation and hatred could only be entertained by those whose intelligence was as scanty as their sense of honour: while the knowledge of what happened in the Russian Constituent Assembly justified Western statesmen in assuming that the usurpers of power did not represent a majority of the nation. The confusion was still further confounded by the breakdown of diplomatic relations between Russia and the Allies, by the occupation of Riga, Kiev and Odessa by German troops, by the rise of the small Baltic states (as also of three ephemeral Caucasian states) and by the formation of provisional anti-Red Governments under Admiral Kolchak in Siberia, under Colonel Semenov in the Far East, under the Socialist Chaykovsky in Archangel, and under General Denikin on the Don and Dniepr.

In face of this kaleidoscopic situation it is not surprising that

[1] Quoted by Trotsky in his article on Lenin in the third edition of the *Encyclopaedia Britannica*.

Allied policy towards Russia should have been negative and fluctuating: but if it was also lacking in unity, this merely reflected the warring tendencies among the Russians themselves. Huge sums of money continued to be expended in support of anti-Red campaigns, but without any real system or effect.

Meanwhile the attitude of the Peace Conference towards Russian problems was even more open to criticism. By the act of her Government in concluding a separate peace she had automatically excluded herself from a share in its deliberations: but it cannot be denied that there were powerful circles in Paris which found Russia's absence highly convenient, and which also, in their alarm at the Bolshevik danger, desired to see her western frontiers pushed as far eastwards as possible, and thus encouraged what amounted in effect to partition. It was resentment at this whole outlook, scarcely less than the mistaken belief that a few resolute blows would carry the Bolshevik cause in triumph across Poland into Germany, that prompted the great Russian drive against Warsaw in 1920, while the eastern frontiers of Poland still remained unsettled, but when the successive failures of the Denikin and Kolchak Governments had already made it clear that the anti-Red forces were not far from collapse. The victory of Pilsudski and Weygand destroyed the Bolshevik hopes, and Poland yielded to the fatal temptation of extending her boundaries far beyond the "Curzon Line" or the linguistic frontier into White Russian and Ukrainian territory. This marked the height of Soviet Russia's isolation and ostracism in Europe.

LENIN AND THE N.E.P.

Throughout all this critical period it was personality that weighed most in the scales. None of the leaders of the older parties, none of the soldiers whom fate drove into politics, showed such qualities of statesmanship as might have achieved a unified front. On the other hand the Bolsheviks had the supreme advantage of possessing in Lenin a leader of rare energy and constructive qualities, devoid of all scruple or hesitation, reckless of life, and above all not afraid to compromise or retrace his steps when tactical necessities arose. In establishing his autocracy he was never much disturbed by charges of inconsistency or opportunism: his writings laid down the pure doctrine, but first of all, before this could be put into practice, the counter-revolutionary and the bourgeois must be fought and exterminated, and then all else would follow. All that is now summed up in "the totalitarian principle" under the other dictatorships of Europe is but a faint reflection of the system established by Lenin. In place of party government, based upon free and direct election, there was a packed assembly formed by a process of indirect "election", which was so tempered by wire-pulling and intimidation as not to be election at all in any sense of the word, and which in any case (in its ostensible aim of a "dictatorship of the proletariat") eliminated all save workmen and peasants and assigned to the former class five times the voting value possessed by the latter. Of debate or legislative control nothing was left: the addresses of a few leaders were accepted by acclamation, and the delegates were mere registering automats, subject to iron discipline. The status of the German Reichstag under Hitler is an exact copy of the totalitarian methods long current in Soviet Russia.

Meanwhile the press was completely controlled: the right of association nominally subsisted, but it sufficed to apply the label "counter-revolutionary" to any attempt at criticism, in order to nip it in the bud. After the first terror began to subside, the average Russian's natural need for outspoken statement reasserted itself, and travellers in Russia have constantly been struck by the frank, and at times even abusive, comment levelled by individuals against existing institutions. But it would be a complete mistake, at any rate during the first fifteen years, to interpret this as a sign of liberty: it was simply a safety valve which the authorities quite wisely but nonchalantly left open. "Popular Courts" were substituted for professional judges. Education was, it is true, very widely extended and imparted for the first time in all the languages of the former Empire:

but it was rigidly confined to the now privileged proletariat and twisted in every sphere into an instrument of extreme Marxist doctrine—religion in all its forms (Buddhist, Moslem and Jewish no less than Christian) being not merely proscribed, but held up to scurrilous ridicule by state-aided militant atheist organisations. "We have to proceed towards freedom", wrote the Bolshevik Commissar Bobrinsky, "through the iron yoke of proletarian dictatorship, towards equality through rationing according to class, towards fraternity through civil war. Political science becomes in practice a weapon in the struggle for power and economic existence. Science becomes politics...."[1] History was taught on narrow materialist and Marxian lines, and all other factors dogmatically dismissed into the background.

The attempt to create a new world out of the most backward of all European countries—handicapped by huge distances and faulty communications, though also enjoying the inaccessibility of remoteness—absorbed all the efforts of Lenin and his colleagues. Poland's victory in 1920 drew in effect a political, no less than a sanitary, cordon along Russia's western frontiers. Fortunately for Poland, Germany was still too prostrate to join Russia in action which might have led to a new partition: she was more concerned with the possible social reactions at home. The Bolshevik Government, however, had been entirely wrong in its sanguine calculations of World Revolution: and though the "Comintern" (which no human skill has as yet convincingly disentangled from the Moscow Government) continued its propagandist intrigue in all parts of the world, for a time Russia may be said to have "gone clean out of Europe" and to be absorbed in matters of life and death at home. The "New Economic Policy" was a compromise with bourgeois and capitalist principles such as strained even Lenin's immense prestige, while testifying to his realistic statesmanship: and even it could not avail to avert a dreadful famine. The Union of Soviet Socialist Republics was organised on a federal basis and recognised the national and linguistic individuality of the non-Russian

[1] *The October Upheaval and the Dictatorship of the Proletariat*, p. 163: cit. *Encyclopaedia Britannica*, vol. XXXII (1922).

races to an extent undreamt of under the Tsar: but in all essentials centralisation remained, and indeed has quite recently reasserted itself more strongly than ever, in particular at the expense of the Ukrainians.

STALIN AND HIS ASSOCIATES

Lenin died in 1924, leaving political power in the hands of a small group of party leaders, of whom Trotsky was best known as the Russian Carnot, organiser of the Red Army, Zinoviev as President of the Third International, and Stalin as party manager. Whatever else may be said of them, it is clear that for a long time they resolved to avoid the internecine feuds of the French Revolution, realising that he who sends his colleagues to the guillotine sooner or later follows them himself: and it was not till the second half of the 'thirties that Russia in her turn provided proof that Revolution does indeed devour its children. The trial of strength which resulted in Stalin's expulsion of Trotsky and his growing ascendancy over all rivals may be said to have centred above all round a difference of tactics in foreign policy. To Zinoviev and his friends the achievement of World Revolution was the supreme aim, while Stalin, with Chicherin and with his much more astute and flexible, but also much more constructive, successor Litvinov, realised the absolute need for compromise if Russia was to pierce the iron ring of European ostracism and re-establish certain indispensable trade relations. It is true that their ideas as to the ultimate goal did not very greatly differ, but a recognition that World Revolution was distant and not immediate in itself involved increasing opportunism, which events were to accentuate. While steadily building up his personal dictatorship, Stalin laid more and more weight upon securing a breathing-space in which to stabilise the new regime at home: and this involved at least tolerable relations with the outside world. The recognition of Soviet Russia by the British Labour Government in February 1924 was the first notable step towards the resumption of normal diplomatic relations with Europe, and was followed by lengthy financial and commercial negotiations in London. Constant violation of the terms laid down for a trade agreement rendered British parliamentary sanction impossible: and the scandal of the Zinoviev letter—whose authenticity has never been proved, but which was completely in keeping with similar missives which even Zinoviev himself never challenged—contributed very materially to the defeat of Labour at the general election. It seems, however, probable that in the end the incident reacted against Zinoviev in Russia itself and prepared the way for less intransigeant (some would merely say more insidious) diplomatic methods.

For some years after this relations between Moscow and London remained thoroughly bad: and for this the main blame rests upon the extremists of the Comintern, which the British Government was amply justified in treating as a mere façade behind which the Soviet Government pursued its own ends. Its ill-judged interference in the General Strike of 1926, and its subversive propaganda in India increased the friction, and in 1927 it came to the clumsy raid upon "Arcos" (a trade organisation controlled by the Soviet Trade Delegation in London) and to the cancelling of the Trade Agreement of 1921. Later in the year there followed the expulsion of Zinoviev and Trotsky from the central committee of the Communist Party, and then from the Party itself: and if this was as yet regarded in England as the merest camouflage, we can today see in the light of subsequent events that it marked a real parting of the ways.

MOSCOW AND BERLIN

Long before this, however, the Russian problem—the existence of a Great Power organised on lines directly antagonistic to all previous conceptions of the State—had filled the background of more than one international conference, and Mr Lloyd George at Cannes had committed himself to the view that there could be no recovery for Western Europe save in conjunction with Eastern Europe. But Bolshevik repudiation of Tsarist debts long remained a fatal obstacle to normal relations, and traders naturally enough hesitated to deal with Russia save on a basis of cash on delivery. It must at once be added that as far as commercial transactions were concerned the Soviet Government pursued a policy of punctilious fulfilment of obligations—this being, the cynic rejoins, its only hope of establishing credit or satisfying really urgent needs. The rigid attitude of the Allies at the Conference of Genoa in April 1922 had meanwhile brought the two pariahs of Europe together: and to the general indignation Russia and Germany concluded the Treaty of Rapallo, which laid the basis, for more than a decade to come, of more normal relations than those enjoyed by Russia with any other country. There were indeed at this time many in both countries who for quite different reasons favoured a definite alliance—on the one side as the surest means of preventing a united front against Bolshevism, on the other as a step towards Germany's recovery of her old Russian market, and as a protection against undue pressure from the West.[1] It is interesting to note that Moscow did all in its power to prevent Germany from entering the League of Nations, Chicherin warning her that for either Power to enter would mean a loss of independence and a probable breach between them. When Locarno was concluded, Chicherin visited Berlin in the hope of setting it off by some extension of the Rapallo arrangement, and publicly repudiated all idea of Russia entering the League and acting "as tame domestic animals in the yard of the great ones of the earth". He could not prevent Locarno, or Germany's adhesion to the League, but he did obtain a neutrality treaty (24 April 1926), which greatly promoted German-Soviet trade and opened the road to Russia for thousands of German engineers and expert artisans. The movement was reciprocal, for if Germany supplied Russia with much necessary machinery, her General Staff was in search of safe

[1] On 12 October 1925 long-term credits were arranged between Moscow and Berlin, and the "Russland-Ausschuss der deutschen Wirtschaft" had its own monthly, *Die Ostwirtschaft*. In the banking consortium founded to promote this trade were the Deutsche Bank, the Dresdner Bank, and fourteen other of the biggest German banks.

centres where, out of reach of all Allied control, large stocks of military material could be built up and the necessary experiments in chemistry and aeronautics carried out.

THE CHANGE IN SOVIET POLICY

The year 1928 marked a definite change in general Soviet policy, which had again its origin in foreign affairs. The adoption of the Five Year Plan for the industrialisation of Russia—to be pursued by Stalin with the same ruthless haste that had once characterised Peter the Great's or Joseph II's reforms—made Soviet Russia more than ever dependent upon peace. The Red Army was steadily developed, in the Far East no less than in Europe, and increased attention was paid to problems of the air: but it was conceived above all as a defensive force, behind whose shelter the greatest of all experiments could at all costs be pushed forward. War, it was obvious, would fatally dislocate the whole plan, not merely by draining and diverting the vast financial resources, but by decimating the stalwarts of the regime and mobilising all sorts of doubtful elements.

The Plan was grandiose, but utterly inhuman in conception. Its idealist side was the resolve that all citizens of the Union should suffer temporary privation in order to bring a new world to birth, such as would exercise an irresistible attraction upon all outside Russia. Its basic idea of "national planning" could only appeal to minds warped by autocratic and materialist theories, but for this very reason it found ready imitators in Fascist Italy and Nazi Germany. What rendered it so odious was its wholesale and drastic liquidation of the Kulak or yeoman class and the attempt to collectivise the whole agricultural system of Russia. With an utter disregard for human life and suffering, the cream of the Russian peasantry were deprived of their holdings and driven by the hundred thousand into the labour camps of the White Sea and the penal settlements of Siberia. As in 1921, production was utterly disorganised, and as Bolshevik policy had at all costs to provide the most necessary means of subsistence for the great urban centres upon which they most depended politically, famine was the inevitable result, and famine in its worst form in those very districts of Ukraine, the Volga and Northern Caucasus, which in other days had produced some of the finest wheat in Europe. It reached its height in 1933, when for political reasons it suited Moscow to conceal the gravity of the situation and even to prevent the sending of relief from the outside. In the Ukraine famine killed two birds with one stone: it weakened what was left of the most democratically minded peasantry in all the former Empire, and it weakened the Ukrainian separatist national movement, which was not confined to the inarticulate masses, but was permeating even the ranks of the Communist bureau-cracy of Kiev.

Much as we may deplore these horrors and the perverse policy which provoked them, it will at once be apparent that the speeding up of the first and second Plans and the chaos thus created rendered a pacific foreign policy more imperative than ever. It has also been pointed out that the Kellogg Pact was accepted by Litvinov and that he soon afterwards took the initiative in concluding an Eastern Pact with all Russia's im-mediate neighbours, including Roumania, which had hitherto avoided all relations with Moscow. At the same time there was a gradual tendency on the part of the Soviet Government to co-operate with Geneva, and it took part in the preparatory work of the Disarmament Conference. In 1929 a Russo-German arbitration convention was concluded and in 1931 there were further negotiations with Berlin. At this period Russo-Japanese relations rapidly deteriorated, owing to Japan's aggression in Manchuria, and this made Soviet Russia more conscious of her uncomfortable isolation. In 1932, therefore, pacts of non-aggression were signed with France and Poland, and in July 1933 conventions were concluded with Czechoslovakia and Roumania, with a view to definition of an "aggressor". Even the advent of Hitler to power did not immediately affect Russo-German relations, and indeed the Führer himself, on 23 March 1933, publicly expressed his desire "to cultivate friendly relations, profitable to both countries", while defining the struggle against Communism in Germany as "our internal affair, in which we shall never tolerate interference from outside". Late in the same year Litvinov also expressed the desire to be on the best terms with Germany, adding the two-edged comment that Russia was "capable of keeping on good terms with capitalist countries, under whatever political regime they may be". In May the Berlin treaty was ratified, and the Soviet Union received a further credit of 200 million Marks from the German banks. It is to be added that in 1934 Russia exported to Germany bullion double in amount to the entire gold holding of the Reichsbank; that as late as April 1935 a further bank credit of 200 million Marks was set up for five years, under the Schacht Plan, Germany's object being to acquire mineral rights, manganese ore, platinum, flax and hemp, in return for machinery and rolling stock: and that for the first three years of his regime Hitler publicly insisted that close economic relations were both feasible and desirable, despite the political abyss.[1] But indeed as late as 21 July 1937 Hitler and the Soviet Ambassador, Yurenyev, exchanged cordial speeches in favour of normal relations between U.S.S.R. and the Reich.

GERMAN-SOVIET RELATIONS

In the light of these facts the rapid deterioration in German-Russian relations after 1934 cannot be explained by rigid doctrinal views on either side, but far rather by the fact that Russia's emergence from isolation and gradual acceptance of the Genevan system (and with it no doubt the main lines of the *status quo*) offered an unexpected obstacle to German designs of predominance in Central, or aggression in Eastern, Europe. In particular Russia's new foreign policy of peace, arbitration and international co-operation ran counter to the ideas of Herr Alfred Rosenberg, the official mouthpiece of the Führer in foreign policy, and the chief exponent of German colonisation at the expense of Russia and Ukraine. It is quite true that

[1] For details, see W. Höffding, "German Trade with the Soviet Union" (*Slavonic Review*, January 1936).

the sufferings of the once flourishing German colonies of South Russia during the famine aroused keen and legitimate concern in Germany, and that autarkist tendencies in Russian industry were upsetting German calculations (and incidentally hoisting Germany with her own petard). But the prime factor has always been strategic. While Germany was exhausted and imperfectly armed, and Russia eliminated from Europe, France, with her eastern satellites, naturally played the leading part in Europe, with a somnolent Britain and a restless Italy providing certain correctives of balance. If Germany could rearm, and at the same time keep Russia in isolation, a German hegemony in Central and South-eastern Europe would automatically follow, Italy would have to move in the orbit of Berlin, and France and Britain combined would be reduced to a most precarious defensive. But if Russia re-entered Europe and threw her vast weight into the scales of peaceful development, the Western alliance would retain the allegiance of all the secondary states, and such a balance of forces would be established as would render a policy of adventure and aggression extremely dangerous for either side. Whether such a balance would merely degenerate into a bad imitation of the pre-war Balance of Power (which rested on Power Politics, but preserved peace for a whole generation), or whether it could be made the foundation of a revived Genevan system, depends in the first instance upon the vision and staying powers of British and foreign statesmen and on their co-operation with America. But it also depends upon the evolution inside Russia and upon whether or not she remains steadfast to the foreign policy pursued for some years past by Litvinov, with Stalin's express approval. And it may be added that every move in favour of German-Japanese co-operation increases Russia's need for alliances upon which to fall back, as a second line of defence, if that international peace and co-operation which she so urgently needs for home purposes should prove impracticable. But the extreme delicacy of the situation will only become apparent if it be realised that behind the scenes both of Moscow and of Berlin a third alternative has been pursued—that of a reversion to the traditional policy of Russo-German friendship. We shall soon see that this is not entirely chimerical, though for the present it has failed.

During 1931–33, then, the danger of war with Japan stimulated Russia's efforts to establish stable relations with all her Western neighbours, and also with France (29 November 1932) and Italy (2 September 1933), by treaties of neutrality and non-aggression: and the last of these was followed on 16 November 1933 by America's epoch-making recognition of the Soviet Union.

The position during 1934 was determined by the fact that the two Powers most hostile to Russia—Japan and Germany—were the very two which were seceding from the League and making vast increases in their armaments.[1] It therefore almost equally suited Russia to abandon her former hostility to the League and the three Western Powers to arrange that she should be invited to join: and under the stimulus of the 30th June in Germany and of the 25th July in Austria, this actually took place at Geneva in September 1934. M. Litvinov, in accepting the invitation, defined the common aim of Russia and other members of the League as "the organisation of peace": in effect the defence of Russia was to be promoted through the collective system and to take precedence over active work in favour of World Revolution.[2]

THE IDEA OF AN EASTERN PACT

During this critical year M. Barthou was French Foreign Minister and had already laid the foundation of an Eastern Pact of Mutual Guarantee, on Locarno lines, to which Russia, Poland, the Baltic States, Czechoslovakia *and Germany* were to become parties, with the benevolent approval, though without the participation, of Britain and Italy. Henceforth, with every successive stage in the Hitlerian repudiation of the Versailles system, the need for Russo-French co-operation grew stronger. On the one hand Britain, quite logically and inevitably, adhered to her refusal to undertake liabilities in Eastern Europe

[1] Cf. *Survey for* 1934, p. 390. [2] *Ibid.* p. 403.

at all analogous to her Western commitments under Locarno, while on the other hand Nazi designs of territorial expansion eastwards—as preached by Hitler in his new revelation *Mein Kampf* and by Alfred Rosenberg as the chief official mouthpiece of Nazi foreign policy—impelled Russia, France and her smaller allies at all costs to fill the gap of Eastern security. Early in 1935, then, the Eastern Pact took definite shape, on the lines of a mutual guarantee against aggression. As, however, it was fairly obvious that France and Russia were far more interested in the *status quo* than Germany could ever be, and not at all obvious whether Germany could rely on the active help of France against a Russian attack, Germany held back and ended by not merely refusing to adhere, but by violently attacking the whole idea of such a Pact as a hostile manœuvre. On 2 May 1935, therefore, the Franco-Soviet Pact was signed without Germany, but only after the text had obtained the approval of the British Government. It followed strictly defensive lines, within the framework of the League Covenant. Sir John Simon had told the House of Commons that "if Russia is prepared to offer the same guarantee to Germany as she has now offered to France, and if France is prepared to offer to Germany the same guarantee as she has offered to Russia", no objection could be raised to the scheme as a whole: indeed he was implying that the aim was not an anti-German front, but a system of mutual security on equal terms. In March 1935 he tried to obtain from Herr Hitler German adhesion to an Eastern Pact, but without success: and it soon transpired that Poland also preferred to hold aloof and to rely upon her new arrangement with Germany. This naturally led to a certain coolness between Poland and France, but it stimulated Russia's defensive tactics of seeking to surround herself with a network of non-aggression treaties.

There has been so much misapprehension—often deliberate—as to the defensive character of this Pact that it may be well to emphasise two important features. First, it leaves in full operation the Pact of Non-Aggression of 29 November 1932, by which the signatories undertake, not to interfere in each other's internal affairs by propaganda, intervention or any subversive action: and this would obviously be extended to any third signatory also. Clearly, then, Germany, if she had joined in, would have benefited in exactly the same way as France herself, whose Communists have for some years past been restrained by Moscow, instead of being incited to sedition as in the great days of Trotsky. Second, the Pact expressly includes the statement that France and Russia "continue to regard as desirable" the signature of a Treaty of Assistance between Germany and themselves. Thus it was, and still is, at any moment within Germany's own power to put an end to her alleged "encirclement".

The Franco-Soviet Pact was so worded as to exclude any French obligations in the Far East: but an interpretation was added that in the event of the question of aggression being referred to the League Council, and of its making no recommendation or failing to reach a unanimous decision, "effect shall nevertheless be given to the obligation to render assistance". It was to this that Germany took very special objection. On the other hand, the two Governments expressly left it open to other Eastern European Powers (and therefore in the first instance to Germany) to adhere on equal terms to the Pact, adding that they "continue to regard as desirable" such adhesion.[1] On 16 May a similar Pact was signed between Czechoslovakia and Soviet Russia, the obligation being, however, limited to cases in which France had already come to the aid of the attacked country under her treaties with Moscow or Prague. The absolutely defensive character of both Pacts and their faithful reflection of the Genevan spirit, cannot reasonably be denied: but it is none the less no exaggeration to say with Professor Carr[2] that "the result of the Nazi Revolution had been to reconstitute the pre-war Franco-Russian Alliance". That Germany by her own action had thus restored the situation created by the "Franco-Russe" of 1894, did not make it any the less galling: Herr Hitler, in his Reichstag speech of 21 May 1935, violently attacked Russia and denounced the Pact as a military alliance

---

[1] *Survey for 1935*, II, p. 82.   [2] *International Relations*, p. 204.

which meant "the introduction of the new East European Asiatic factor, the military extent of which is incalculable, into the European Balance of Power". He even went so far as to treat the Bolshevisation of France as a possibility, in which case, he argued, France and Russia would be controlled "from one headquarters in Moscow".[1]

This was a most convenient theory, for it enabled Herr Hitler to shake off one of the last remaining checks upon unilateral action by Germany. In repudiating Versailles in March 1935 he had reaffirmed his loyalty to Locarno: he now announced (7 March 1936) that France's obligations under the Soviet Pact were incompatible with Locarno and had deprived that treaty of "its inner meaning", and that consequently Germany was no longer bound by it. Needless to say, argumentation such as this strikes at the very root of all international contract.[2] Henceforward fierce abuse of the Bolshevik state was to figure in the forefront of all German propaganda, and indeed to contribute as much as any other factor to the vicious circle of European rearmament. For while the German leaders treated the growing strength of the Red Army as a direct menace to themselves, Marshal Tukhachevsky justified the Russian military and naval programme by absolutely open and public references to German war preparations, while Stalin—notably in an interview accorded to the American journalist Roy Howard[3]—spoke with a directness rarely equalled in a responsible statesman of Hitler's "symptomatic" inability to speak even of peace without threats against Russia. Nor is it possible to blame him for his suspicions

[1] Professor Toynbee (*Survey for* 1935, I, p. 86) very pertinently argues that Germany, in her criticisms of the Franco-Soviet Pact, was in reality attacking not so much it, or its compatibility with Locarno, "but Article XVI of the Covenant and the whole idea of immediate assistance to the victim of aggression".

[2] From the French side M. Sarraut effectively answered: "There is no engagement which can lead France to act as though the Covenant and the Locarno Treaty were not in force": and France for nearly a year continued to offer Germany recourse to the opinion of the Hague Court, but she had preferred to be sole judge of the case.

[3] 1 March 1936.

of the Führer, in view of the latter's openly avowed designs upon Russian and Ukrainian territory, to which we shall have to refer more fully when we come to analyse the practical bearings of Hitler's political philosophy. The Führer's indignant phrases about the Balance of Power are highly disingenuous, for if, in face of a rearmed Germany and a doubtful Italy, Russia could be completely isolated from Europe, France would obviously be in a position of extreme danger. In a word, the main aim of the Pact is to preserve that very Balance of Power in Europe which Herr Hitler professes to favour.

STALIN AND THE FIVE-YEAR PLANS

The two Five-Year Plans, so recklessly speeded up by Stalin, represent (whatever we may think of their human aspect) an immense and almost unexampled effort towards the industrialisation of Russia and its emancipation from all foreign dependence. In proportion as the Second Plan neared completion and Russian life became less abnormal and intolerable, there was a noticeable evolution alike in home and foreign policy in an essentially national sense, and away from purely Marxist theory. Stalin emerged more and more as a national leader, more was heard of a new patriotism (sovetskaya rodina) and, most striking of all, a vast majority of the Russians in exile, recognising the danger of German aggression, modified their old attitude of barren, if all too comprehensible, negation and spoke once more of "Russia first". The theory of Trotsky and Zinoviev, that World Revolution was an absolute condition of Bolshevist success inside Russia, steadily paled before Stalin's very different view that Russia must at all costs secure a period of calm in which to consolidate the new structure of the state, and that all else was secondary. "The export of Revolution", he told Howard, "is nonsense. Each country, if it so wishes, will make its own revolution, and if it does not wish it, there will be no revolution."

Another no less significant formula of Stalin is "the highest possible development of the power of the State, with the object of preparing conditions for the dying out of the State". But as a very profound critic of Russian affairs points out, "the highest possible development of the State is the practice, the dying out of the State is the theory.... The withering away of the State plays much the same role in Soviet dogma as the Second Advent in Christian theology. It occupies an essential place in every confession of faith. But since the days of the primitive Church the prospect has not been regarded as imminent, or allowed to affect day-to-day practice."[1]

Propaganda had for years been one of the main weapons of Russian Communists: its promoters now began to feel its sharp point in their own ribs, and to realise that two can play at such a game. For National Socialism in its turn made of Propaganda one of its main foundations, and of Russian Bolshevism a convenient bogey on which to concentrate abuse. Hitler himself expressed the conviction that there was "an unbridgeable gulf" between National Socialism and Bolshevism, whose "deadliest and most fanatical enemies we are".[2] All this served as an undoubted stimulus to that internal transformation of Russia since 1934 which as yet defies definition and to the foreign observer, perhaps even to ordinary citizens inside her borders, is still little more than a gigantic shadow on the screen, but of which abundant evidence is accumulating. As in other great movements, the leaders who have so long imparted drive and directive, now find themselves driven hither and thither like corks on the current of a mighty stream. In some cases the old catchwords receive the same, or even added, emphasis but the whole trend of action has altered.

This at once becomes apparent from a study of recent Russian "legislation"—(admittedly a somewhat misleading word in the authoritarian states of today). In the first place collectivisation has assumed a milder form. After "nearly 30 millions of individual privately owned farms"[3] had been swept into the

---

[1] "Lenin-Stalin: a Retreat from Utopia", *The Times*, 6 July 1937.

[2] Speech of 31 May 1935 (Approved translation, p. 32).

[3] See Ivan Solonevich, "Collectivisation in Practice", p. 97 (*Slavonic Review*, No. 40, July 1935).

new system, there is now a partial return to individual rights. "The peasant may now possess his house, his garden of three acres, one or more cows, and as many pigs and poultry as he can acquire. Earnings are guaranteed as property and are heritable, and the savings banks are full. Large numbers of those who had been despatched to the timber camps have now been brought back to work. It is only the middle-man and the principle of hired labour that are still rigorously excluded".[1]

Social and educational policy is also changing. There is definite resolve to check the disastrous results of indiscipline and neglect among the children, and of the earlier marriage and divorce laws: the new laws all seek to strengthen family ties, to make divorce less easy, to prevent abortion, to provide for homeless children. In the exiled Trotsky's striking phrases, the original Bolshevik Youth policy had meant "a shaking of parental authority to its very foundation", and there is now "a sharp turn" in the other direction.[2] Even "the storming of Heaven," he laments, "like the storming of the family, is now brought to a stop". This is doubtless going too far, for

[1] Sir Bernard Pares, "The Russian Situation" (*Slavonic Review*, No. 44).

[2] Nothing is more instructive than Trotsky's evident disgust at the turn away from abortion. He himself is not ashamed to write: "You cannot abolish the family: you have to replace it" (*The Revolution Betrayed*, p. 140). Incidentally he admits the existence of terrorists among the youth of Russia, "recruited exclusively from the ranks of the Communist youth and the party, not infrequently from the offspring of the ruling stratum" (p. 159). Much of his book is an altogether futile discussion as to whether bourgeois and capitalist culture "should be replaced by a Socialist, not a proletarian, culture". He, one of the destroyers of the shortlived Russian liberty, has the effrontery to declare that "spiritual creativeness demands freedom", as though he had ever worked for "freedom". On p. 172 occurs the contradictory phrase: "The very purpose of communism is to subject nature to technique and technique to plan—to free once for all the creative forces of mankind from all pressure, limitation and humiliating dependence." But we may learn from his many admissions, that the system which he first helped to establish—"a series of contradictory zigzags" (p. 87)—has developed into an all-powerful bureaucracy, "by converting thinking Communists into machines, destroying will, character and human dignity" (p. 99). And his only remedy is a fresh revolution!

the restrictions upon religious practice have not as yet been removed, but they are no longer applied with the old vigour, and the era of direct persecution would seem to be over. The Universities are no longer to be "close" preserves for the children of proletarian parents, the elaborate revision of text-books shows that propaganda is yielding first place to learning.[1]

Mr Yaroslavsky, the President of the "Union of Militant Godless" in Russia—in other words, the organiser of the anti-religious campaign—issued new instructions for "religious propaganda" in May 1937, complaining bitterly of the failure of the Union to eradicate religion, and giving numerous examples of "the penetration of religion into public institutions". He laments the fact that though huge new cities have sprung up since the Revolution, without a single church, it is quite a mistake to suppose that "where there are no churches there are no believers, or only a very few". "Some console themselves", he says, "with the thought that a great number of churches have been closed, which they think means that religion is finished. This is a profound delusion." In a word, the whole circular is a proof that Lunacharsky was right in 1928 when he compared Russian religion to a nail: "the harder you hit it, the deeper it goes into the wood".[2]

History and geography are no longer taught on purely materialist and Marxist lines, and there is an open warning against "the over-burdening of the child mind with civic and political training". Highly symptomatic of the new mentality was the extraordinary series of celebrations organised through-out Russia at the centenary of Pushkin,[3] of whom it is true to say that no poet was ever less Bolshevik in mentality or less suited by his writings to be commended to the new generation,

[1] A striking confirmation of this is the circular issued to directors of secondary schools, and sternly reminding them that there is no other road to the University than that of examination.

[2] See "Yaroslavsky and Religion", by Sir Bernard Pares, in *Slavonic Review*, No. 47 (January 1938).

[3] Never was any poet honoured on such a scale; for full details see "The Pushkin Centenary" in the *Slavonic Review*, No. 44 (January 1937), pp. 309–27.

whereas he appeals strongly to nationalist and romantic sentiment. Nor is his vogue an isolated fact. Peter and Catherine
are again coming into their own, the former in Alexis Tolstoy's
great novel: Napoleon's defeat at Borodino is widely cele-
brated, the painters and musicians of the Tsarist period are
again in favour.

THE NEW SOVIET CONSTITUTION

Even these changes are a mere prelude to those of the new
Russian Constitution, due entirely to the initiative of Stalin
himself, and presented by him in November 1936 to the
All-Union Congress. It establishes a Supreme Council, con-
sisting of two chambers (the Council of the Union and the
Council of Nationalities), based upon direct elections and a
secret ballot (instead of a show of hands!): and this Council,
in which resides the supreme source of sovereignty, has legislative initiative (§ 38) and appoints ministers and higher officials,
and its members enjoy immunity and the right of interpellation
(52). The number of federal units is increased from seven to
eleven, each with its own Council and sphere of influence.
Further, the Constitution lays down the right to work, to
rest (a seven-hour day), to security in old age, sickness or
disablement, and to education; the equality of women; equal
rights for all "irrespective of nationality or race, in all fields
of economic, state, cultural, social and political life"; freedom
of conscience and religious rites; freedom of speech, of the
press and of meetings; inviolability of the person and the home
(118–128). Judges are declared to be "independent and subject
only to the law" (112); but they and public prosecutors are
elected for a period of five years, in the supreme court by the
Supreme Council, in the individual federal courts by the federal
assembly, in the people's courts by all citizens of the district,
in each case, it is true, under universal suffrage. Universal
service is established, defence being "a sacred duty of all",
and treason, desertion and espionage are punished as most
"heinous crimes" (132–133).

All these provisions, except the judicial, may be said to follow fairly closely the main lines of pre-war liberal constitutionalism in Europe: the really distinctive features are contained in the first twelve paragraphs, which declare all power in Russia to belong to "the toilers of the town and village in the form of soviets of toilers' deputies" (3), "as a result of the overthrow of the power of the landlords and capitalists and the conquests of the dictatorship of the proletariat" (2). "The abolition of private ownership of the instruments and means of production and the abolition of exploitation of man by man" (4), are treated as accomplished facts, not mere aims: and a distinction is drawn between Socialist ownership (through the State or through co-operative and collective farms and associations) and "personal ownership by citizens of their income from work and savings", of "objects of domestic and household economy and of personal use and comfort". The whole theory of the Communist state is summed up in Article XII in the two principles, "He who does not work, shall not eat", and "From each according to his ability, to each according to his work".[1]

Nothing could be more dangerously naïve than to accept this Constitution, as yet merely on paper, as a reality, still less as a democratic reality: and indeed the bare summary given above shows it to be a very composite production, in which rival tendencies are contending. In some quarters it was all too rashly greeted as an abandonment of Soviet ideals, whereas its advocates dismiss this as "a fundamental misunderstanding of Bolshevist aims and ideals"[2] and claim that the supersession of such temporary measures as indirect elections and open voting is a sign of strength and growing maturity. The most that can be safely affirmed is that the leaven of free election and free speech, if once allowed to work, cannot fail to transform the lump, and that the attempts now being made to popularise such a Constitution and explain it to the masses are likely to work in a "liberal" and anti-totalitarian sense among the rising

[1] Cf. Communist Manifesto.
[2] *The New Soviet Constitution* (Anglo-Russian Parliamentary Committee), p. 11.

generation. Sooner or later it must become apparent, even to the most uncritical, that the fundamental "liberties" of the modern world are irreconcilable with the totalitarian One-Party system—and that a party numbering two million members out of a population of 170 millions is a crude form of oligarchy.

The alarm of the older generation of Bolshevik stalwarts is reflected in the high-pitched denunciations of the regime by Trotsky, who from a safe exile was able to say outright what those at home could only whisper. He quoted as more valid than ever the earlier dictum of Rakovsky: "The ruling circles have succeeded in converting themselves into an irremoveable and inviolate oligarchy, which replaces the class and the party."[1] But the conflict of opinion was still more crassly revealed in the series of arrests and treason trials which began in August 1936 and which constituted a frontal attack of Stalin against all the heads of his own oligarchy. Now with unexampled fury the Russian Revolution has indeed begun to devour its own infants, and we are left speculating as to whether Robespierre has killed not only Danton, and Chaumette and St Just, but also Bonaparte and even Barras.

THE TERROR

The murder of the High Commissar Kirov at Leningrad in December 1934 was the first unmistakable sign to the outside world that dissensions within the higher Bolshevist ranks had again reached an acute stage, despite a series of earlier purges: it was followed by a number of arrests, degradations and executions. Mr Chamberlin very pertinently points out that when Tsar Alexander was murdered in 1881, five men proved to be implicated were executed, whereas after Kirov's murder 117 persons were "liquidated", only thirteen of whom were even accused of complicity.[2] The principle "Pour encourager les autres" remains one of the foundations of Soviet rule.

A fresh sign of crisis was the dissolution of the notorious "Ogpu" and the transference of its functions to the Com-

[1] Cit. Trotsky, p. 99.
[2] W. H. Chamberlin, *A False Utopia*, p. 6.

missariat of the Interior,[1] in July 1935. But the climax *seemed* to have been reached in the summer of 1936, when Zinoviev and Kamenev, Stalin's two colleagues in the triumvirate of 1922–5, and over a dozen other party hierarchs were first arrested on charges of treason, conspiracy and designs on the life of Stalin, then induced to make public confessions so abject as to be almost incredible, and finally shot like dogs, without chance of appeal. A few months later there followed the trial of seventeen equally prominent "Old Bolsheviks"—notably Pyatakov, the organiser of Russian industry, Radek, the most brilliant journalist of the Soviet era, and such diplomats as Sokolnikov and Karakhan.[2] Once more there was abject and unqualified confession, and this time some victims were allowed to crawl away into obscurity. Tomsky, the former leader of the Russian Trade Unions, escaped a similar fate through suicide, while Rykov, the former Chairman of the Council of Commissars, was acquitted but disgraced.

That persons with the blood-stained past and moral standards of these men should have plotted murder against their chief and resorted to wholesale sabotage of a regime with which they no longer agreed, need cause no great surprise: but the charges of intimate collaboration between them and their exiled colleague Trotsky and the German political police, and the specific 'allegation that Trotsky was ready to surrender vast territories both in Europe and in the Far East to Germany and Japan[3] in return for help in overthrowing the Stalin regime, took away the breath of most foreign observers, and was at first dismissed as altogether incredible. Yet as time passed, the charge became steadily less incredible, while it became possible to detect a

[1] Thus placing it in an analogous position to Scotland Yard, which is administratively a department of the Home Office. This is probably the sole resemblance.

[2] In actual fact Karakhan was not among the first victims, but fell into disgrace and was eventually executed in December 1937.

[3] Trotsky is alleged to have written a letter to Radek treating as inevitable the cession of the Ukraine, the Maritime Province and the Amur Territory, and acceptance of German conquests on the Danube. But this letter cannot be produced, if Radek's statement that he burned it be true.

striking analogy between the situation of 1936 and that of Brest-Litovsk in 1918. A comparison of these two situations will serve to explain that acute divergence alike of views and of tactics, between Trotsky and Stalin, round which the whole development of Russia has come to revolve. At Brest-Litovsk Trotsky carried the day, the more opportunist Lenin hesitating to risk a conflict with his ablest colleague at a moment when the Revolution was still in extreme danger. But Trotsky's view that nothing mattered save World Revolution, and that if that were once achieved Russia would speedily recover all that she had lost and more beside, remained an unrealised theory, especially after the Bolshevik failure before Warsaw. Lenin, then, in his later years, while duly appreciating Trotsky's great achievements in the role of Carnot, saw that he had miscalculated in the international field, and he himself was above all concerned with the internal consolidation of a new Russia. Stalin inherited, and accentuated, this outlook of Lenin: and in him it has taken a definitely nationalistic turn, while personal antipathies no doubt also played their part. More and more the conflict has centred round foreign policy—Trotsky and his friends still harking after World Revolution, fanning every subversive movement in Europe, chafing at Stalin's growing indifference to external events, treating his and Litvinov's *rapprochement* with Geneva as treason to the Communist cause, and not least of all, combating Stalin's thesis that Nazi Germany is the chief danger to European peace. As the evolution of Russia proceeded apace, Trotsky's criticisms grew shriller: and in his eagerness to overthrow Stalin and check what he looked on as a fatal perversion of the revolutionary creed, he was ready to accept allies wherever he could find them. In answering Stalin's much quoted interview to Roy Howard in April 1936, Trotsky declared that "an unfavourable situation may force us to cede various 'bits' of land, as we did in the treaty of Brest".[1]

Clearly the words "defeatist" or "treasonable" have a special

[1] Cit. Balticus, "The Russian Mystery" (*Foreign Affairs*), October 1937, p. 56.

connotation in the case of such a man. Once more, as at Brest, he calculates that territorial concessions may be worth while as the price of German or Japanese help against his rival: once obtain a firm grasp of power, and the leaven of revolution can be made to ferment in the passive but fertilising dough of many countries, and thus the lost lands will soon be recovered. In this miscalculation Trotsky had in 1918 made an ignominious peace: in 1923, during the Ruhr occupation, he and Zinoviev and Pyatokov had co-operated with the German nationalists and industrialists, each of course with entirely different objectives. And it must never be forgotten that in the years that followed, those German circles which cultivated most eagerly relations with Soviet Russia and sent thousands of experts to study and to work there, were not so much the men of the Weimar regime as the generals, the heavy industries and their exponents in the Right press. Their motives and aims remained the same—the future exploitation of a vast and helpless Russia: and to them the Trotskyites, as they grew more embittered, were ideal allies of the moment. Indeed Trotsky's gift for truculent indiscretion and his personal incorruptibility served as a blind to what was happening behind the scenes; for they seemed to render his alliance with German reaction impossible. But they were offset by other qualities—his colossal vanity and his utter bondage to theory—which gave him the belief that he could successfully play with fire. Great was his miscalculation, for on the one hand the Germans had a second string to their bow—in high military circles: while on the other Stalin had a less doctrinaire but even more ruthless belief in "Power Politics" and a firm resolve to maintain his personal absolutism, combined with a belief in the future of a Russia where a social programme would be the foundation for a transformed and invincible nationalism. For a score of reasons Stalin needed peace, whereas World War and renewed revolution were essential for a realisation of Trotsky's aims. The conflict between the nationalist, who understood the parallel interests of the new Russia and the Western democracies, and the international theorist, to whom there was little to choose between this or that form of "bourgeois capitalist" state, went very deep, and indeed became the pivot of Russian home and foreign policy, in proportion as the Nazi regime entrenched itself in Germany.

There is reason to believe that as late as 1934 Stalin was still urging upon some of his former colleagues that the leaders of the Russian Revolution must continue to eschew that frenzy of "mutual extermination" by which the French Revolution at last wore itself out. It was only when the proofs accumulated that the Trotsky faction was bent on killing, and that it was a choice of his head or theirs, that Stalin began to strike with all the ruthlessness of his Georgian nature.

Stalin's methods are truly barbarous and Asiatic, in the sense that Zinghis Khan, not Buddha or Confucius, stands for Asia (and it is doubtful if we Europeans have the right to use such a phrase of implied superiority). But those who know something of internal Russian opinion appear to be convinced that it recognises the knife of a surgeon, and feels that what has been removed was the most dangerous portion of the body politic. Surely this outlook is characteristic of the hateful and degenerate age in which we live.

THE ARMY PURGE

The executions of the summer and winter of 1936–7 cut deep into the flesh of the regime, and caused widespread dismay and disillusionment. The Russian public was now asked, or rather commanded, to believe that a majority of the men who had ruled Russia since the death of Lenin, were not prophets of a new World Order, but "counter-revolutionary" traitors, wholesale wreckers, and despicable cowards to boot. Moreover, throughout the winter a steady purge continued among the chiefs of the central and provincial bureaucracy: and incidentally, in view of Hitler's attempt to identify Bolshevism and the Jews, it is instructive to note that, with the one very important exception of the diplomatic service, the purge has nowhere been more thorough than among the Jews. At the party congress in March 1937 Stalin and Molotov initiated an amazing campaign against the holders of key positions in industry as Trotskyists—in so many words as "a frantic and unprincipled gang of wreckers, diversionists, spies and murderers".[1]

In June 1937, however, all previous phases of the Terror were thrown into the shade by the lightning arrest, secret court martial and execution of eight of the highest Army Chiefs, including Marshal Tukhachevsky (one of the organisers of the Red Army and formerly Commissar of Defence), General Oborevich (the victor against Denikin and Wrangel), General Kork (Director of the War College at Moscow) and General Putna (late Military Attaché in London).[2] In the decree issued by Voroshilov to the Red Army[3] these men are denounced as "a band of counter-revolutionary spies" whose aim it was "to destroy the Soviet power and restore the yoke of the landlords and manufacturers", and who "tried to undermine the Army and prepare its defeat in any future war" by the wrecking of war material and the sale of military secrets. Despite the floods of abuse let loose by order in the controlled press of Moscow, it may be doubted whether any serious person in Russia has accepted so crudely improbable an explanation. The truth is much subtler, and lies in the sphere of foreign policy. The generals, as Stalin himself very frankly pointed out in one of his rare interviews, were not traitors in the sense of being ready to cede Russian soil to the foreigner (here he drew a vital distinction between them and the civilian Trotskyists), but they

[1] Report of the Central Committee of the Communist Party in Moscow, *Manchester Guardian*, 31 March 1937.

[2] Tukhachevsky's rivalry with Marshal Voroshilov, the now triumphant Minister of Defence, had long been suspected. Less known is the fact that in 1919, when Moscow was threatened by the Whites and he commanded at Tsaritsin, he came into violent conflict with the political Commissar Djugashvili (now known as Stalin, who afterwards renamed Tsaritsin as Stalingrad): and again that in 1920, during the invasion of Poland, he was in no less acute conflict with General Budyenny and Stalin, as commissar attached to the latter's army. Budyenny was one of the judges at the trial of the Generals, and next to Voroshilov, profited most by their elimination. See "The Purge of the Eight Generals" in the *Manchester Guardian* of 18 June 1937.

[3] Printed in *The Times* of 14 June 1937.

were working for the overthrow of the Soviet system, the establishment of a military dictatorship, and the conclusion of a Russo-German alliance based upon close economic co-opera-tion: they were simply following the Germanophil tradition which in its latest form dates back to the agreement of Rapallo in 1922, but which (with the fatal interruption of the Great War) goes back to the partition of Poland and indeed far beyond.[1] This is why the natural delight of the Nazis at any blow to the prestige of the Red Army was far outweighed by the consternation of the German War Office at the downfall of its friends. In exactly the same proportion the anxiety of Paris lest the value of the Russian military machine should be impaired, was mitigated by relief at the failure of a *coup* which would have robbed France of a powerful military ally. The extremity of the danger is well illustrated by the fact that Marshal Tukhachevsky was about to leave as official delegate to the British Coronation, and that General Yakir had been appointed only a few days earlier as commander of the Leningrad garrison. They were detected only in the nick of time. All the eight had had a German military training, and had for years past been in close contact with the Reichswehr, had sent their most promising officers to Germany and had favoured the land concessions made to Krupp in Russia. Twixt cup and lip the prospect of a reorientation which would have meant a radical change in the balance of European forces was ruthlessly de-stroyed by Stalin.

THE "ELECTIONS"

The continuance of the Terror—which affects not merely those highest in the Bolshevik hierarchy, and the heads of count-less provincial departments and business undertakings, but also scores of harmless and entirely insignificant persons, of both sexes, who have never dabbled in politics—has not, strangely enough, prevented the holding of a "General Election" and the meeting

[1] For further details see the extraordinarily well-informed article by Balticus, "The Russian Mystery", in *Foreign Affairs* (N.Y.) for October 1937.

of the new Supreme Council in December 1937. But it is scarcely necessary to say that apart from lip-service to the words "Democracy" and "Election", the whole proceedings were as farcical as those which now mark "elections" to the German Reichstag. The 1143 deputies "elected" were all unopposed candidates of the official "Party and Non-Party Bloc", the "electors" having no alternative save to vote for the official candidate, to strike out his name, or to abstain: and abstention was a dangerous decision.[1] And this is the system which Mr Attlee, as leader of the British Opposition, described on the twentieth anniversary of the Bolshevik Revolution as "a new society, *based on the principle of social justice*"! It may reasonably be argued that Russia is in rapid evolution, in a forward, not a backward direction, and that the prolonged and drastic character of the "Purge" has hastened the trend towards some Russian equivalent of the great day of Thermidor, when the Paris mob reviled its former idol, and the frenzy of spy-mania and denunciation had run its course. But to foresee and hope for a time when we shall again have a more or less normal Russia to deal with, and when some of the achievements of the most terrible of all revolutions will come to be accepted as a permanent gain for humanity—this is a very different thing from prostituting the ideals of Democracy or Liberty by coupling them with the name of Stalin.

THE RUSSIAN DILEMMA

The apologists of the regime are on the horns of a dilemma. If we accept the allegations of Stalin himself and his adherents, Russia has for the past twelve years been governed by a horde of corrupt, unprincipled and incompetent traitors,[2] or in other words, the October Revolution brought the worst scum of the

[1] None the less there were a million spoilt votes.

[2] Trotsky has recently admitted that the French Revolution caused "such a physical and moral impoverishment" of the revolutionary forces of Paris, that they required three generations before a new insurrection was possible. Nevertheless, revolution still remains his ideal. *The Revolution Betrayed*, p. 81.

country to the top, to an extent to which there is no precedent in other modern revolutions. Alternately, the Russian regime is a depotism which in its unapproachable loneliness and uncontrolled power recalls the analogy of Tiberius on Capri, defies all calculation and falls under no known category of state. To call it a Socialist state is a misuse of terms. Moreover, whichever view may be the right one, it is difficult to avoid the conclusion that Stalin must be one of the worst judges of character who have ever attained to absolute power, or he could not have tolerated such persons in so many key positions.

One thing at least is certain, that the double process of corrosion and elimination is nearly complete, that the pace is now breakneck, and that the future of Russia will very soon be in the hands of entirely new men, whose evolution it is almost impossible to predict. Indeed, what is so appalling in the present situation is the extreme difficulty of knowing what Stalin's real mind is, and even whether he has a real philosophy and a clear plan of campaign, or is first and foremost bent on maintaining himself in power. To this problem probably no non-Russian can give an answer: and if there be one or two Russians who know—and even this is uncertain—they may be relied upon to keep their own counsel.

There is only one direction in which anything like normality can be detected, and that is foreign affairs. Litvinov, almost alone among Stalin's associates, has retained his post and influence: and it is clear that Stalin relies upon his adroit diplomacy to secure to Russia, in this supreme crisis of *personnel*, the external peace without which reconstruction is impossible. Hence the ironic contrast that Terror at home and the Genevan programme abroad march side by side.

It is obvious that in so abnormal and so fluid a situation there can be no question of an alliance, or of really intimate relations, between Britain and Russia. But much as we may detest the methods of Moscow, nothing can obscure the fact that at present more than ever the interests of the two countries run parallel and that it is not in the general interest of Europe that Russia should be isolated, since this might drive her either to revive the waning influence of the Comintern, or to erect some such bridge across the apparent gulf between her and the other autocratic states, as the fallen generals had dreamed of. It is as yet too soon to say whether, with the elimination of all the orthodox Marxist leaders, the Third International is also doomed. But it is obvious that its downfall would do more than anything else to reassure Western opinion.

As long ago as 1896 Lord Salisbury described as "the superstition of an antiquated diplomacy" the idea that Britain and Russia must be enemies. If he were here today he would doubtless, while exercising all his habitual caution, recognise more than ever that there are basic strategical factors in Europe which no amount of political likes and dislikes can affect. Hence the conclusion of the whole matter is on the one hand that Russia is rapidly evolving in a forward, not a backward, sense, and may shake off her nightmare sooner than the outside observer would dare to hope, and on the other hand that she is an absolutely vital factor in that balance of political forces whose overthrow might place the Western Powers at a fatal disadvantage and ruin the chances of democratic recovery in Europe. The return of Russia to Europe, to Geneva, to national consciousness, is an event of immense significance.

VII

BRITAIN AND THE DICTATORS (B) ITALY

O NE of the chief lessons of the Great War—one which may perhaps partly explain President Wilson's tragic illusion that he was making the world safe for democracy—was that the countries which were best able to resist its appalling strain and to avert a revolutionary upheaval were those hitherto conducted on democratic lines. If the first to plunge back from democracy into autocracy was Russia, this was after all in keeping with a long tradition of force, and with mental processes of which not the least marked was a certain indifference to the value of individual human lives.

In most cases defeat brought revolution in its train and, in the first instance, an increased emphasis on democratic radicalism. That it was in Italy, one of the victorious Western Powers, that the first great post-war turn of the tide towards reaction became visible, was due to certain special circumstances of that country, which must be briefly considered before her relations with Britain or with other Powers can be made clear.

UNITED ITALY

In the forefront of any survey must be placed the fact that Italy, despite all the splendid legacies of art and culture with which her cities are crowded, is essentially a poor country, "predominantly agricultural",[1] lacking many important raw materials (especially coal), overpopulated and therefore affected to an unusual degree by colonial and emigration problems. The generation in whose hands the government of Italy lay when war came in 1914 was still living upon the great memories of the Risorgimento, and every town in the Peninsula had its monuments of Victor Emmanuel II, Cavour, Garibaldi, and to

[1] Luigi Villari, *Italy*, p. 235.

a lesser degree Mazzini, those four incongruous leaders who between them solved the triple problem of independence, unity and liberty.[1] But it is necessary to remember that these memories were very recent compared with the long traditions of misgovernment, foreign rule and internal dissension that filled the previous three centuries. Liberty in particular was an aspiration rather than a fact, Piedmont's constitutional Statute of 1849 was an innovation which had the backing of the new middle class, but had also many enemies throughout the Peninsula; and parliamentarianism succeeded only very partially in making itself the mouthpiece of public opinion, not merely because of the prolonged conflict between Church and State, and the over-taxation of the masses, but also because of the fissiparous tendencies of the Chamber, its factiousness and professionalism, and the corruption by which the Liberal leaders—and notably Giolitti—maintained their influence. Dr Finer does not go too far in saying that "Italy from 1870 to 1922 had a Parliament, but no parliamentarianism".[2] It may be argued that Italy's assumption of the role of a Great Power— necessary though it was for far more valid reasons than mere prestige—imposed an intolerable strain upon so poor a country, and created a gulf of suspicion between the masses and successive governments, or in Signor Mussolini's unduly *simpliste* restatement of the problem, between the Nation and the State. Certain it is that the revolutionary outbreak of 1898 and the less known "Red Week" of June 1914 were the outcome of

---

[1] Mussolini's challenge to the widespread view that the Risorgimento was an achievement of Liberalism is much less questionable than many of us would like to think. It is quite true that Mazzini, Garibaldi, the Bandiera brothers, and Pisacane, were anything but Liberal in a conventional sense (24 March 1924, *Scritti e Discorsi*, IV, p. 76): and Cavour, seemingly the Liberal *par excellence*, was not merely none too particular in his choice of methods, but on certain critical occasions committed actions as unconstitutional as those of Bismarck in his great quarrel with the Prussian Diet. This, and not his quite genuine admiration for the British Constitution, explains the high praise lavished upon him by Treitschke (*Aufsätze*, II, "Cavour").

[2] *Mussolini's Italy*, p. 62.

a system which scarcely deserved the name of Liberal, and were quelled by far from Liberal methods. These events, and still more the divorce between Parliament and people in the spring of 1915, provide precedents for what was to happen in 1922.

The widespread sympathies felt for the Italian cause in Britain during the last century—which have left a permanent mark upon many of our greatest poets and novelists—have obscured the very important fact that the movements for independence from foreign rule, for free institutions at home, and for national unity, were in no way identical and sometimes even antagonistic. For instance, it is not generally realised that Lord John Russell and Lord Palmerston, while eager that the Austrians should leave Italy (it is only fair to add, in the interests, as they conceived them, of Austria no less than of Italy), had no desire to see the Peninsula united under a single head. Indeed Russell as late as February 1861—that is, eighteen months after the Peace of Villafranca and nine months after Garibaldi's entry into Naples—publicly expressed in the House of Commons his preference for "the establishment of *two Kingdoms of Italy*" and the restoration of the petty sovereigns. This does not detract from the great and even decisive services rendered by the British Government to the Italian cause, but it shows how little London saw ahead during the most critical decade of European history between Waterloo and the Marne.

The hesitations of Napoleon III, strategic considerations on the Rhine, and French Catholic support for the Temporal Power, combined to undermine Italian gratitude to France, who was unquestionably the chief promoter of Italian Unity. During the 'sixties Italy threw her weight, for what it was worth, into the Prussian rather than the French scale: and this was an important contributory fact towards Britain's negative attitude in 1866 and 1870. But after 1870, when Rome at last became the capital, Italy was in a position of uncomfortable isolation, and though accepted at the Congress of Berlin as one of the six Great Powers, she left it "with empty hands" and with the knowledge that her growing interests in North Africa

were increasingly endangered. Her adhesion to the Triple
Alliance in 1882 was the direct result of France's annexation of
Tunis, cleverly exploited by Bismarck in two directions: but
for the first two decades she occupied, as Signor Villari neatly
puts it, the status of a poor relation. It suited Germany
admirably that Italy and France should be on bad terms, and
this continued till well on in the new century: but the French
isolation which it was also intended to promote ceased when
the clumsiness of Bismarck's successors allowed the German-
Russian Reinsurance Treaty to lapse and brought Paris and
St Petersburg together. At the same time Italy profited by the
Alliance: for quite apart from enhanced prestige, it meant immunity from any French attack, while the recognition of her
two allies that she could not be expected to take part in a naval
war against Britain made her position definitely easier. Nothing
permanent, it is true, came of the somewhat tentative Mediterranean agreements of 1887: but the various negotiations seemed
to confirm the traditional belief on both sides in a permanent
community of interests between Italy and Britain. Crispi, the
only Italian statesman of this period who can be said to have
approached greatness, enjoyed the confidence of Bismarck and
Salisbury: but the disasters of the Abyssinian War in 1896 drove
him finally from power and postponed the dream of Italian
colonial expansion. For the rest of the nineteenth and for the
first decade of the twentieth century, Italian policy was mainly
negative—periodic renewals of the Triple Alliance, tempered
by an occasional "Extra-Tour" with Marianne in the ball-
room of the European Concert, and, as a consequence, periodic
concessions on the part of Germany and Austria-Hungary,
notably the pledge of 1909, ensuring to Italy compensation for
any change in the Balkan *status quo*.

In 1911, however, Italy abandoned her passivity, and by the
Tripolitan War set in motion forces that led inevitably to the
Balkan Wars, and to radical changes in the *status quo* throughout
the Near East. It is of course true that she had a real grievance
in the French seizure of Tunis, so dependent on Italian settlers
and strategically so close to Sicily: and Tripoli was her last

hope in North Africa, with Britain in control of Egypt, France extending her sway over Morocco, and frustrated Germany as a possible rival who might be forestalled before it was too late. If Italy declared her occupation of the Dodecanese to be a mere temporary war measure and definitely broke the pledge, she was able to point to precedents provided by Britain's occupation of Egypt and her repeated postponement of evacuation. Certainly Italy's attitude in 1914, under the wise guidance of San Giuliano, was entirely correct: for Austria-Hungary's action against Serbia was a violation of the *status quo* (under Article VII of the renewed Triple Alliance) and as it was taken without previous agreement with Rome, the *casus foederis* did not arise. Behind this was the basic geographical fact that the Italy of 1914 could not risk war with the two Sea Powers of the West.

THE SECRET TREATY OF LONDON

The neutrality observed by Italy for the first nine months of the World War was felt, even by her most timorous politicians, to be something provisional which could not be permanently maintained. Baron Sonnino, who succeeded San Giuliano as Foreign Minister in October 1914, was governed by those same promptings of "sacred egoism" which the Premier Salandra publicly proclaimed: and throughout the winter and spring he conducted parallel, and extremely secret, negotiations with the two rival belligerent groups. In the end he extracted greater concessions from the Entente, whose military advisers fondly imagined that Italy's entry would decide the war: and the Secret Treaty of London (26 April 1915) was the result.

This treaty was of capital importance for the whole future settlement: for on the one hand it violated those rights and interests of Small Nations to which the Allied statesmen had paid repeated and emphatic lip-service, while on the other hand it tied their hands towards Italy, and when in due course events made exact fulfilment impossible, gave her an obvious grievance and a strong legal case. Moreover, its extreme secrecy reacted in two directions. Its terms only became known after the second Russian Revolution, when the Bolsheviks published all secret treaties with the object of discrediting the "Imperialist" and "capitalist" states: and long ere this America had become an Associate Power, exercising a decisive influence upon war, finance, and peace terms, and in this capacity flatly declined to recognise the Treaty of London as in any way binding. No one, indeed, could read the text of the Treaty without realising that it was quite irreconcilable with the public definition of peace terms issued by the Allies in answer to President Wilson's inquiries in December 1916. At the same time it is important to note that the real motive force of Italy's entry into the war was not the tortuous diplomacy of Sonnino, playing off allies of thirty years' standing against their enemies in the field, but the spontaneous outburst of popular feeling in Italy, voiced by three such different figures as D'Annunzio, Bissolati and Mussolini (who had shaken off his Socialist and Syndicalist antecedents and was making of the *Popolo d'Italia* the organ of ultra-radical opinion). But this made it all the more deplorable that, behind the back of opinion in all countries, a discreditable bargain should have been concluded which was never legally annulled, and which, at a moment when national hysteria and territorial greed were throwing their shadow over the high professions of idealism at the Peace Congress, could be represented as Italy's hardly earned reward and just rights, of which unscrupulous allies were seeking to rob her.

The treaty, then, assigned to Italy South Tirol to the Brenner (including the purely German districts of Bozen and Meran), Trieste, Gorizia, Istria and northern Dalmatia (with not less than 700,000 Jugoslavs), the Dodecanese Islands, a special position in Albania in the event of a partition of Asia Minor, the province of Adalia, and in the event of France and Britain acquiring German colonies in Africa, the right of territorial compensation along the borders of the three Italian colonies of Eritrea, Somaliland and Libya. In May 1916 another secret treaty, generally known as the Sykes-Picot Agreement, provided for the partition of Asia Minor between France, Britain and Russia:[1] and when this too became known through Bolshevik revelations, a redivision on paper was agreed upon between the Allied Premiers at St Jean de Maurienne in April 1917. By this convention, if possible even more reprehensible than that of London, Italy was to receive not only Adalia, which her forgetful allies had already conceded by the Treaty of London, but also the vilayet of Smyrna. The result was that her claims came into direct conflict with both Jugoslav and Greek aspirations towards national unity. The grave reverse of Caporetto had produced a more reasonable frame of mind in Italy and the Congress of Oppressed Nationalities which was held on the Roman Capitol in April 1918, and played so notable a part in preparing the downfall of Austria-Hungary, was based above all upon a friendly reconciliation of Jugoslav and Italian national claims along the coast, expressed in terms clearly incompatible with the secret treaty. But for reasons which cannot be particularised here, the precise terms of the agreement had not yet been worked out when peace came: and intoxicated by victory and angered at what she felt to be inadequate Allied recognition of her contribution to the final result, Italy reverted to a demand for the exact fulfilment of the Treaty of London; a lively propaganda for the Adriatic as "Mare Nostro" and for the seizure of all Dalmatia (in which less than 20,000 out of 650,000 inhabitants were Italian) was set on foot in Rome: and D'Annunzio and his filibusters raided and held the port of Fiume, which even the Treaty of London had expressly reserved for Croatia.

THE ADRIATIC DISPUTE

The Adriatic dispute was one of the thorniest incidents of the whole Peace Conference and led to Italy's temporary withdrawal. President Wilson remained adamant against Italy's claim to Dalmatia, but in the end she retained possession of

[1] The only conceivable excuse for omitting Italy would be that she had not yet fully implemented her own treaty, which pledged her to declare war on Germany (this she did not actually do till 28 August 1916).

territory including Fiume, the whole of Istria and over 600,000
Slavs whom, after an all too brief interlude of liberal promise,
she proceeded to Italianise by the most ruthless methods. She
also obtained from Wilson the wholly illogical concession of
the Brenner frontier, with a similar sacrifice of 200,000
"Germans of the Germans". Her temporary absence from the
Conference was skilfully exploited by the Greeks, who won
over the Allies to accept their own superior claim to Smyrna:
but here an unexpected turn of fortune's wheel enabled the
Turks to evict the Greeks and keep the Italians at arm's length,
at the price of the final surrender of the Dodecanese.

On a pure basis of nationality and self-determination, Italy
had no case whatever against either Jugoslavia or Greece: and
the Treaty of London was in many respects the most nakedly
Imperialistic of the whole bunch of secret conventions. But for
this the Allies were equally, if not more, to blame: they had
undertaken commitments which could not be reconciled with
their public pledges, yet they were not prepared to take the
only honourable course, namely to provide the compensation
to which Italy was legally entitled out of their own property,
instead of that of others. If we sum up the resultant situation,
as it affected Italy, we find that she was deprived of Dalmatia
(except Zara) but consoled herself by seizing and holding on
to Fiume until Wilson's term of office ended and Jugoslavia
had to come to terms; that Wilson, without consulting the
Allies, promised the Brenner frontier to Italy, in direct contra-
vention of his own Point Nine; that she had to renounce her
designs upon Asia Minor, while rendering her occupation of
the Dodecanese permanent;[1] that the Allies skilfully took advantage of her absence from the Conference to pass her over in
the assignment of the various colonial mandates: and that, at
any rate for the time being, nothing was heard of territorial

---

[1] One day after the Treaty of Versailles Italy signed a direct treaty with
Greece, by which, in return for Greek support in other directions, she agreed
to cede the islands, retaining Rhodes for fifteen years and then ceding it also
if Britain ceded Cyprus. But if she did not receive satisfaction in Asia
Minor, she could resume "full liberty of action", and this is what occurred.

compensation in Africa by the sated and victorious Powers. Her statesmen may have struck too high a note in threatening "the complete isolation of Italy" from her allies: but even those who, like the present writer, felt and still feel most strongly the injustice done to the Jugoslavs by the Adriatic settlement, must surely admit that no amount of inept and selfish statesmanship on the part of Sonnino and Orlando could justify the "raw deal" to which her allies subjected Italy.

Thus the Italian people emerged from the Great War in a mood of cynical disillusionment and scarcely less exhausted than the beaten foe. The more they tended to exaggerate the decisive character of Vittorio Veneto,[1] the more inevitably they were driven to criticise the futility and barrenness of a war which cost infinitely more in blood and treasure, and brought in infinitely less, than their unification in the previous century. Malcontent opinion turned in two directions—the "patriots" demanding a drastic reform of the whole governmental system on strongly nationalist lines, while the "defeatists", throwing the whole blame upon "capitalist Imperialism", turned towards no less drastic social and international experiments, and in particular exalted Soviet Russia as the paradise of the worker. It is worth noting that the Fascist party at its birth declared its opposition to "the imperialism of other peoples at Italy's expense, and of Italy at the expense of others", but qualified this by declaring that "Imperialism is the foundation of life for every people which tends towards economic and spiritual expansion".[2]

[1] A complete legend has been encouraged in Italy, to the effect that Vittorio Veneto decided the World War. In reality Austria-Hungary was already in full disintegration, and quite apart from wholesale surrender of the non-German and non-Magyar troops for nationalist reasons, the Austro-Hungarian High Command thought expedient to encourage surrender, from the fear that if the troops poured back in too great numbers to the half-starving capital, there might be famine and revolution. A vivid account will be found in Karl Friedrich Nowak, *Chaos*.

[2] Mussolini, *Scritti e Discorsi*, I, pp. 372–4: 23 March 1919.

THE RISE OF FASCISM

There can be no doubt that Italy's discomfiture in the field of foreign policy increased the neurasthenia from which the masses were suffering, as the result of so gigantic an effort: and the fatal weakness of successive Governments—under Orlando, Nitti, Giolitti, Bonomi, Facta—provoked a situation which did not very materially differ from civil war. It directly encouraged communist and subversive efforts, which culminated in the occupation of many factories and in the astonishing decree by which Nitti legalised such action. Parliamentary government seemed in real danger of breaking down: some indeed would say that it never recovered from the fatal eclipse of May 1915, when war was forced upon the Government by the insistence of "the Street" (la Piazza), in the teeth of a strong majority among the deputies. Mussolini, who on the earlier occasion had declared "unintelligent statesmen" to be "a prerogative of the Third Italy",[1] and had denounced Parliament as "the bubonic plague which is poisoning the nation's blood, and needs to be extirpated",[2] now set himself to organise a movement in every village and at every street corner that would meet violence with violence, a revolt from the Left by a revolution from the Right—but this a revolution based upon rigid discipline and upon the assumption that Democracy and Liberalism are played out and must be replaced by some new and more abiding political force.

The victory of Fascism in Italy is the classic proof of what can be done with the amorphous masses by one man of ruthless and irrepressible dynamic force against leaders who lack the power to lead or to govern. With a bare 100 comrades Mussolini founded in March 1919 the Fasci di Combattimento (Groups of Conflict): at the election of the same year he only obtained 4064 votes (out of 346,000) in Milan itself: but two years later the Fascist Congress had 248,000 members.[3] His supporters

[1] 25 January 1915, *Scritti e Discorsi*, I, p. 26 (references throughout are to this).

[2] 15 May 1915, I, p. 36.　　[3] See his speech of 24 March 1924, IV, pp. 64–6.

were drawn from many different quarters—extreme nationalists, the romanticists of art and literature, wild spirits whom the war had finally unsettled, many ex-Socialists who resented defeatism or Russian Bolshevist doctrine, genuine seekers after a rival political idealism and adventurers who hitched their waggon to a new star. But all were united in recognising that the machine of state was breaking down, thanks to an inability to govern on the part of the governing clique (the word "clique" must be used, for there was no "governing class" in any true sense of the term). What made the situation still more serious was that those very sections of the community which in most countries impart a steadying influence, namely the bureaucracy, the army and the Church, became possessed of a deep-seated unrest and lack of confidence. Indeed the Church, thanks to its unregulated status in United Italy, had always been "a disturbing, dividing" rather than a "stabilising element",[1] and the new post-war Partito Popolare, despite its genuine desire to atone for long abstention, came too late and only added to the confusion. In a word, it is inaccurate to treat Italy's experience as an illustration of the failure of the parliamentary system: for this had never been genuinely applied.

The artificial system of cliques and bosses proved unequal to the stress of post-war conditions compounded of economic stress and war-hysteria: the propertied class not unnaturally took alarm at the orgy of strikes and unpunished acts of violence: the Socialists were too doctrinaire and too divided to wrest the power into their own hands: the Russian programme of their extremists raised antagonism on all sides, which Mussolini skilfully exploited for the Fascist movement, openly offering to accept the arbitrament of civil war, if the Socialists demanded it,[2] and with a magnificent demagogic assurance bidding his followers "stand up to demagogy with courage and impetus"[3] and not believe in "the Asiatic Utopias that

[1] Finer, *Mussolini's Italy*, p. 76.
[2] 22 November 1920, II, p. 116.
[3] 20 September 1920, II, p. 106.

come to us from Russia".[1] The period of anarchy may be said
to have reached its height with the murder by the Socialists of
the ex-officer Giordani in the municipality of Bologna: and this
served as a pretext for a full-fledged counter-offensive by the
Fascists, conducted with infinitely greater energy and ruthlessness. In 1921 the Socialists were in full retreat and ready to
bargain with Giolitti for a division of power: but that ultra-
astute politician, still living upon pre-war calculations, had
failed to reckon with the new force of Fascism, subject to iron
discipline within its own ranks, but rejecting all discipline save
brute force in dealing with its opponents. Already on 23 March
1921, on the second anniversary of the movement, Mussolini
openly declared it to be his aim "to govern the nation":[2]
another of his watch-words was "against the return of the
triumphant beast".[3]

At the elections of that summer he was returned to Parliament, and in his maiden speech breathed open scorn and
defiance upon the Government's "lachrymose" policy, declaring that he would be "more or less (*non so quanto*) parliamentary in form, but flatly anti-democratic and anti-Socialist
in substance".[4] He was not afraid to take responsibility for a
Fascist bomb, and spoke of violence as "not for us a system, still
less a sport, but a dire necessity". That winter he stated his
political theory even more frankly. "The humanitarian dream
(*d' umanità*) rests on Utopia, not on reality. Nothing authorises
us to affirm that the millennium of universal brotherhood is
imminent." "It is said that we must conquer the masses: some
say that history is made by the heroes, others that it is made by
the masses. The truth lies halfway. What could the mass do if
it had not its own interpreter, expressed by the Spirit of the
People?" "In me", he went on, "two Mussolinis are contending—one who does not love the masses, and is individualist,
the other absolutely disciplined. . . . I prefer the work of the

[1] 7 January 1923, III, p. 45.
[2] II, p. 152.
[3] 3 April 1921, II, p. 158.
[4] 21 June 1921, II, pp. 166, 187.

surgeon who plunges the gleaming knife in the gangrenous flesh to the homoeopathic method which puts off action."[1]

It is often affirmed that the Fascist victory alone saved Italy from Bolshevism: but this is to overlook two capital facts, that the experiment of factory seizure had already failed by the end of 1920, and that by 1921—in other words, under the old Liberal regime—Italian finances were already markedly re-covering.[2] It was not till 7 November 1921 that Mussolini, overcoming no little hesitation among his adherents, trans-formed what had till then been a "movement" into the "Fascist Party", and henceforth set himself to overcome what he called "the bestiality of Red demagogy"[3] by counter-action no less drastic and energetic. Some years later he spoke of 1921 as decisive for Fascism, because in it was completed "the armed organisation of the Squadre or Blackshirt gangs", the establishment of syndicalism and the change from "move-ment" to "party".[4]

His political doctrines are clearly foreshadowed in an article of *Gerarchia* in February 1922: "The democratic war *par excellence*,... which was to realise the immortal principles, is ushering in the century of anti-democracy. 'All' is the word that filled the nineteenth century. It is time to say 'Few and elect'. Democracy is everywhere in agony, in Russia it has been killed. War had liquidated in streams of blood the century of democracy, of numbers, of majorities, of quantity. The orgy of indiscipline has ceased."[5]

[1] 21 November 1921, at the Augusteo, II, pp. 201–6.

[2] On 20 September 1920 Signor Mussolini wrote in *Popolo d'Italia*: "What has happened in Italy in the September that is now ending has been a phase of the revolution started, *by us*, in May 1915." On 31 December 1920 the same paper wrote: "The Italian domestic situation is improving daily." Again in *Popolo d'Italia* of 1/2 July 1921 Mussolini wrote: "To say that a Bolshevik danger still exists in Italy, means taking base fears for reality. Bolshevism is overthrown." In his big speech of 24 May 1925 (the tenth anniversary of the war) he spoke of "the failure of the occupation of the factories in Italy towards the close of 1920".

[3] 19 June 1923, III, p. 175.   [4] 24 May 1925, V, p. 87.

[5] V, pp. 259–65.

Here be it added in parenthesis, that while the many outrages on the Left were, as Mussolini quite correctly saw, the
result of indiscipline and of doctrinaire theory run riot, the rival
outrages organised by Fascism were the result of a deliberate
technique of violence and reprisals, forming an integral part of
an increasingly iron discipline. Already in June 1922 Mussolini
openly declared that Fascism and the State were undoubtedly
ere long destined to become identical,[1] and in his last speech in
the old Parliament[2] he warned it that "no Government can
rule in Italy, if it has in its programme machine-guns against
Fascism. To reaction we shall reply by insurrection." Only a
month before the final crisis, while defending violence as "most
moral when it solves a gangrenous situation", and again insisting on "rigid discipline", he boldly declared, "Our programme is to govern Italy. It is not programmes that are
wanting for the salvation of Italy, but men and will-power."[3]

If from the very first Mussolini insisted on the revolutionary
character of his movement, he really secured power at the
supreme crisis by a process not altogether dissimilar from that
which brought Italy into war in 1915. Government and
Parliament were paralysed and isolated, the extreme Left was
already routed and on the defensive, while the three most
vital forces in the country were by his audacious tactics won
for benevolent neutrality or even something more. In more
than one pronouncement he shook off the last shreds of his
former republicanism and virtually offered an alliance with
the dynasty:[4] while high compliments reassured the Army,
which had hitherto held aloof from politics, but was naturally
enough perturbed by the post-war anarchy and indiscipline
and resented the insults directed against it by the extreme Left.
The bureaucracy were tired to death of parliamentary in-
stability and interference with the machine of state, while the
big industrialists and the banks had not recovered from their
panic in 1920. The Church took note with relief that Fascism,

---

[1] v, p. 297.   [2] 19 July, v, p. 303.
[3] 20 September, at Udine, v, pp. 309–15.
[4] v, p. 219; 24 October, at Naples, v, pp. 340–6.

in contrast to the extreme Left, proclaimed its respect for religion. Only a few here and there remembered the age-old precedent of the scorpions that followed the whips. But the crux of the situation was that power was in old and nerveless hands, and that other hands, strong and young and resolute (*un' Italia gonfia di vita*, to use one of the Duce's many eloquent phrases), were ready to snatch it from them.

After the March on Rome Mussolini suddenly found himself in the position of a constitutionally appointed Premier, and many thought that he would soon tone down in office: it is true that he included several non-Fascists in his first Cabinet, but he kept the key positions for himself and he warned Parliament, which he all along treated with such scant courtesy, to be "under no illusions as to the briefness of our passage to power".[1] Over and over again he was to insist that it was "grotesque to look upon his Revolution as a mere ministerial crisis",[2] or Fascism as something transitory. The new regime was "not an episode, but an epoch".[3] Yet for a certain time he denied the intention of "governing against Parliament", though it in its turn must realise "its perilous position, which may entail dissolution in two days or two years": and after six months he still denied the desire to "abolish Parliament".[4] But meantime he set up a rival—what he called a "duplicate"— in the Fascist Grand Council, which together with the Fascist Militia he quite accurately, at a later stage, described as "fixing the irrevocable elements of Fascist success".[5] And he further entrenched himself by forcing through the Electoral Law of 1923, which ensured to the parties with the largest number of votes in the whole country two-thirds of all the seats of the Chamber. His speech on the bill was still partially defensive: he repudiated the name of "liberticide" for his Government and was entitled to argue that "advocates of the Russian regime

[1] 16 November, 1922, IV, p. 17.
[2] E.g. 24 March 1924, IV, pp. 67, 70.
[3] 10 February 1926, reply to Stresemann, V, p. 276.
[4] 16 November 1922, IV, pp. 1–16; 8 June 1923, IV, p. 150.
[5] "Elementi di Storia", in *Gerarchia* for October 1923, V, p. 175.

have no right to protest against a regime like mine, which can't even remotely be compared with that of Bolshevism". Fascism favoured elections (*é elezionista*): it was still possible to reconcile Parliament and country, though tomorrow it would be too late. And near the end there slipped out the ominous phrase, that he did not want Fascism "to become wise too soon —not till all are resigned to the accomplished fact".[1]

The elections held under the new law (April 1924) were the most lawless of modern Italy, and outrages on all sides were frequent; but the parliamentary system, ostensibly at least, still survived when the Socialist leader Matteotti arraigned the Government on 30 May. Mussolini himself replied with one of his frequent catalogues of anti-Fascist outrage, and then offered the Socialists a choice of co-operation or insurrection, in which case "in 24 hours or 24 minutes all would be over". Three days after this speech Matteotti was spirited away and foully murdered under circumstances which will probably never be fully cleared up, but which clearly implicated "some of the highest figures in the Fascist ranks".[2]

THE MATTEOTTI AFFAIR

The effect of this crime was to set all Italy in uproar, and for a short time the Duce found himself forced on to the defensive. He not merely disavowed "this abominable outrage" which was not only a crime, but a blunder: but he took action against some of the wilder "squadrists", and admitted "vast repercussions" and "a profound moral oscillation in the mass of the Italian people".[3] Declaring it to be "no longer a question of Matteotti, but of the regime", he even went so far as to say, "*We are still disposed to make Parliament function regularly, to make Fascism return to legality, to purify the Party, to follow a policy of national conciliation*"[4]—thereby inferring that none of

---

[1] 15 July 1923, IV, pp. 196–203.
[2] Finer, *Mussolini's Italy*, p. 234.
[3] 24 June 1924, in the Senate, IV, p. 198; 25 June, p. 201; 22 July, p. 218.
[4] IV, p. 209.

these aims had been followed hitherto. But "the regime would not allow itself to be indicted, save by history", and the abdication of Fascism was too high a price for normalisation.[1]

Whether, if the old leaders had been more masterful, Parliament could at this stage have reasserted its authority, and enforced some sort of compromise upon the Fascists, may well be doubted. Certain it is that the secession of the Opposition to the Aventine, and the new co-operation between Liberals and Communists, made the gulf unbridgeable, and were fatal tactical blunders: Mussolini could hardly have asked anything better, as he once hinted to Emil Ludwig. He soon resumed the offensive, proclaiming Nietzsche's "Live dangerously" as the motto of his whole movement, treating "Head of the Party and Head of the Government" as "two aspects of the same phenomenon", and in one of his frequent soliloquies on the history of the Risorgimento making a most ominous reference to its complex character. "There is everything in it (*c' è di tutto*)— the bombs of Orsini at the Paris Opera were one ingredient, and it was singular that he should be so much honoured in the Italy of today!"[2] By the close of 1924 he had turned the tables on the Opposition, and was soon denouncing "this Aventine sedition" as "anti-constitutional and flatly revolutionary",[3] as though he himself had never boasted of Fascism's revolutionary character and origins. "I assume alone", he said, "the political, moral and historical responsibility for all that has happened." There must be "subordination of all to the will of a Chief".[4]

Thus by June 1925 he was more uncompromising than ever; for he felt that the Opposition was vanquished: with the double outrage upon Amendola—committed by Fascist bands, while the gendarmes looked on—the last hope of a young and constructive constitutional leader was conveniently removed. The Duce's address at the Fascist Congress pleaded for "absolute intransigeance, ideal and practical". "For me violence is perfectly moral, more moral than compromise or bargaining",

[1] IV, p. 214.   [2] 3 January 1925, in the Chamber, V, pp. 11–13.
[3] 24 August 1924, to the National Council, IV, pp. 225–9.
[4] 15 May 1925, V, p. 65.

and he stopped to boast that he had never read a line of Benedetto Croce. "Today Fascism is a party, a militia, a corporation. That is not enough: it must become a manner of life. There must be the Italians of Fascism, as there are the Italians of the Renaissance, and the Italians of Latinism". Sometimes strategic retreats were necessary: "but the goal is there—Empire!" "It took England over two centuries before she secured the fundamental keys of her Empire. But Italy must resolutely abandon the whole Liberal phraseology and mentality." This time it was war upon Parliament. "I presented myself to Parliament, but in order to humiliate that cowardly (*imbelle*) Chamber by pronouncing the most anti-parliamentary speech recorded in history." He had obtained full powers from it, "which meant reducing the power and function of Parliament to a minimum": and these full powers were backed by the 300,000 bayonets of the Fascist militia. And he laid a brutal emphasis on "the anti-parliamentary, anti-democratic, anti-liberal character" of his regime.[1] The pretence of "electionism" was at an end. "All the world feels", he argued, "that the parliamentary system has had its usefulness"[2] and the Aventinians, before they could be allowed to return even to the Chamber which was already being recognised as entirely secondary to the Fascist Grand Council, "must recognise the accomplished fact of the Fascist Revolution, which has profoundly changed the constitution of the Italian State, for which a preconceived opposition is politically useless, historically absurd and only comprehensible for those living outside the limits of the state". They must admit the bankruptcy of their "infamous campaign" and repudiate the foreign critics of Fascism. Otherwise, said the autocrat, they will never return at all.[3] On the fourth anniversary of the March on Rome he declared that during the past year "we have buried the old democratic, liberal, agnostic and paralytic state—buried it with a third-class funeral!!"[4] and there was no one to stand up and answer his crude insults.

[1] At the Augusteo, 22 June 1925, V, pp. 118, 121.
[2] 18 November 1925, V, p. 203.   [3] 17 January 1926, V, p. 242.
[4] 28 Oct. 1926, VI, p. 440.

MUSSOLINI'S TYRANNY

During 1925–6, then, the bulwarks of Italian liberty were one by one overthrown. Party Government became impossible, municipal self-government was replaced by government through the Podestà, or nominated party boss. The Premier was expressly made independent of any parliamentary majority, and responsible to the Crown alone—in the Duce's own words, "a profound innovation in our public law".[1] A series of laws and decrees subjected the press to more and more stringent rules: soon nothing could escape the combined pressure and control of the police, the Ministry of the Interior and the Prefects. The Liberal *Corriere della Sera*, once one of the foremost organs of European opinion, was unable to continue the unequal struggle, and was acquired by one of its successful rivals, while the organs of the Left met with much shorter shrift.

Education also became a mere handmaid of the regime. The Duce demanded that "the school should be inspired by the idealities of Fascism": it must not adopt a "detached (*estraneo*)" or "agnostic" attitude.[2] From this it soon followed logically that all teachers are state servants, liable to dismissal "if they put themselves in situations of incompatibility with the general political principles of the Government", and compelled to belong to the Fascist party and to take an oath of active loyalty to the regime.[3] School and university textbooks are of course a state monopoly. Radio and cinema have become instruments of all-pervading propaganda. By every means youth must be captured for the regime, before it has time to think for itself, and subjected to military training from its earliest years, in the hope that the identification of State and Party may become more complete and obedience to authority more unquestioning.

[1] 19 August 1931, on the Centenary of the Council of State, VII, p. 311.
[2] 3 December 1925, Parole ai Docenti, V, p. 220.
[3] See Finer, *Mussolini's Italy*, pp. 468–85.

The Law of Public Security and the establishment of a special tribunal for the defence of the State reduced almost to a minimum the possibility of criticism or opposition. A drastic regime of "confinement" in the islands or "supervision" at home crushed the few intellectuals who tried to hold out, while special legislation made it possible to deprive Italian exiles abroad of their citizenship and to confiscate their property. No one need weep for the suppression of secret societies (Mussolini has overcome the Mafia, which had defied every statesman of United Italy), nor even of Italian Freemasonry, with its rabid atheism and its strange subservience to the "Grand Orient" of Paris. But since their downfall the spy and the informer have been more than ever in evidence, and a far-reaching system of intimidation has been established. "Opposition", the Duce declared, "is foolish and superfluous in a totalitarian regime."[1] Education, too, must be totalitarian, and "since the contemporary world is that world of savage wolves which we know", it must be warlike, and avowedly so.[2]

Meanwhile Mussolini, ex-syndicalist and pupil of Georges Sorel, was evolving the theory of a corporate state in which "the syndicalist movement was to be guided by Fascists and directed towards the ideas of Fascism".[3] "Fascist Syndicalism" —so much better, as he claimed, than Red Syndicalism, with its class war[4]—was to consist of "syndicates" and "confederations" ostensibly based upon an adaptation of the medieval guild. Strikes and lock-outs both became illegal, negotiations between employers and employees became compulsory and all the competent bodies were under the absolute control of the state. In the words of an American historian, "the old syndicalism preached by Sorel, whom Mussolini had carefully studied and much admired, was a proposal for the capture of industry by large workmen's guilds or syndicates, independent of the state: as 'tamed' by Mussolini, it became a method of subordinating labour organisations (and capitalist organisations as well) to

[1] 26 May 1927, Discorso nell' Ascensione, VI, p. 62.
[2] 25 May 1928, in the Senate, VII, p. 108.
[3] May 1925, IV, p. 87.   [4] IV, p. 256.

the supreme authority of the state."[1] On 26 May 1927 he solemnly declared: "We have created the Corporate State.... Today we solemnly bury the lie of universal democratic suffrage."[2] But it was not till 1930 that the National Council of Corporations was created, and as then constituted it was merely advisory, without legislative powers: nominations to it had to be ratified by the Duce, who was in no way bound to follow its advice. All major issues remained with the Grand Council, which in its turn was entirely subservient to the Duce. In 1930 Mussolini placed renewed emphasis upon his "formula of 1925—all power to Fascism and exclusively to Fascism".[3] But though "the Party is the capillary organisation of the regime", under the revised Constitution of 1932 admission to the Party is restricted and hedged in, a distinction is drawn[4] between "Fascists of the first hour" and later comers, and the passing of time automatically favours the growth of an oligarchy. But internal jealousies and dissensions are dwarfed and dominated by the iron will of the Duce.

Hence any survey of tendencies in modern Italy leads logically to the figure of the all-powerful Duce, consumed with a belief in force as a solution of most problems and in his own monopoly of power as the basis of the whole regime. "It was I who decided the March and cut short all delays", he has publicly declared.[5] "Power does not soften me."[6] "I am the Chief, the creator, and must be the defender, of this Revolution."[7] "I created two institutions [the Militia and the Grand Council] which provoked an irreparable rupture between the old democratic-liberal world and the new Fascist world." In his reports to the party he would allude to "decisions which

[1] Slosson, *Europe since 1870*, p. 653.

[2] Finer, *Mussolini's Italy*, p. 257. An interesting, but quite unconvincing, theoretical study of *The Corporate State*, by Harold Goad, will be found in *International Affairs*, vol. XII, No. 6 (December 1933).

[3] Message for the ninth Year 18 October 1930, VII, p. 225.

[4] Speech of 14 September 1929.

[5] 24 March 1924, IV, p. 66.

[6] 1 February 1924, IV, p. 52.

[7] 26 May 1930, VII, p. 208.

I alone mature", and of which the King alone was "informed"[1] (*informed* rather than consulted or participant). "There is no question of whether the party should exist or not, because if it were not in existence, I would invent it." To a foreign student of affairs whom he once received, he declared that he meant his Ministers to realise "that they are but dust and ashes, and that the flame of life issues from, and is extinguished by, him".[2] "I am your Chief and am always ready to assume all responsibility."[3] In May 1927 he told the world: "All Ministers are soldiers! They go where their chief tells them, and they stay if I tell them to stay",[4] and this he has ruthlessly applied to men like Balbo, Grandi, de Bono, Farinacci, Starace. Almost at the outset he asked of his Blackshirts "the mysticism of obedience":[5] and it would be absurd to deny that Mussolini possesses to the highest degree that personal magnetism which inspires such service. In the words of an ardent exponent of the Fascist doctrine, "religious dogmas are never discussed, because they are verities revealed by God. Fascist principles are not to be discussed, because they issue from the mind of a Genius— Benito Mussolini."[6]

Yet the Duce, following that writer who has most deeply influenced his political thought, Machiavelli, is a pessimist as to human nature, and tells us that he endorses with new emphasis the Florentine's "fundamentally negative view on men".[7] And so quite logically he approves the cynical phrase: "Hence it comes that all armed prophets conquer and the disarmed are ruined." After one attack on his life he repeated his motto, "Live dangerously", adding, "If I advance, follow me; if I retreat, kill me; if I die, avenge me". In the same breath he disclaimed all optimism, yet gloried in the "splendid fact that a Revolution should have a whole old world against it".[8] This

[1] 14 September 1929, cit. Finer, p. 287.
[2] 17 October 1932, VIII, p. 120.   [3] Finer, p. 252.
[4] Finer, p. 252.   [5] 27 November 1922.
[6] Valerio Campogrande, *Cultura Fascista*, cit. Finer, p. 477.
[7] "Preludio al Machiavelli", April 1924, IV, pp. 106–10.
[8] 7 April 1926, V, pp. 307–12.

gives the clue to his more abstract theories. The idea that power is "an emanation of the free will of the People" is "an illusion". Popular sovereignty is "a tragic joke".[1] Political equality is "an absurd constitutional lie".[2] "The individual exists for Society: the State is the supreme expression of power. Public order ranks higher than liberty."[3]

With the years Mussolini grew more and more domineering, the star that outshone all others in the firmament. His ways are not our ways, but we should commit an act of folly not to recognise his many high qualities. For of all the dictators he has the highest sense of realities, the deepest knowledge of human nature, the widest general culture (won by wide reading of the best literature, and an artistic sense such as doubtless comes easily to an Italian). He is a master of tactics and advertisement; though he loves parade and pomp on great occasions he lives simply and is not self-seeking, and though he insists on absolute obedience, he is not afraid of awkward truths from those whom he trusts.[4] It would be unjust to deny his sense of duty, though it blends insensibly with soaring ambition. It would be simply absurd to deny his intensity, will-power and initiative, his capacity for hard work in a score of different directions. What vitiates it all is his blind belief in brute force as a solution, his low opinion of human nature (this he shares with Stalin and Hitler), his intolerance of all other opinions save his own, his deliberate concentration of power in his own person. A really great orator, he has destroyed freedom of speech: a journalist of high quality, he cannot tolerate a free press.[5] He is the key-

[1] April 1924, IV, p. 109.

[2] 1932, "La Dottrina del Fascismo", VIII, p. 79.

[3] Cf. Villari, *Italy*, p. 188.

[4] Cf speech to Carabinieri Officers, 18 February 1928, VI, p. 135.

[5] One of his most revealing utterances is that on "Journalism as a Mission" (10 October 1928, VI, pp. 249–55), in which in the same breath he asserted that "in a totalitarian regime the press must be in its service", yet claimed that the Italian press was "the freest in the whole world"—free because "it serves only one cause and one regime, and because within the ambit of the regime and its laws it can exercise functions of control, criticism and propulsion". Here words simply lose their meaning.

stone of the arch, and everything goes to suggest that he is
irreplaceable. He has multiplied to the *n*th degree the problem
that faces all dictators—how to secure an adequate succession
to the all-powerful leader in whom every control is concentrated. This is the spectre which haunts the Duce himself
and compels him to live dangerously and at high tension: and
no man can tell how long he will stand the strain.

MUSSOLINI'S FOREIGN POLICY

No apology should be needed for the numerous extracts
given in the above survey; for it is quite impossible to understand the trend and outlook of Fascist Italy today without
carefully studying the mentality and utterancesof its all-powerful
and ever-alert dictator. Moreover, they alone provide the key
to Italian foreign policy, which has been from the outset, and is
now more than ever, under his direct personal control. That
foreign policy must rest on brute force, expressed in an omnipotent and all-pervading State, and a ruthless national egoism—
as to this he has never left either his admirers or his dupes under
the slightest illusion. "Imperialism", he laid down at the
foundation of Fascism, "is the basis of life for every people
which tends to expand economically and spiritually."[1] Under
the motto "Navigare Necesse"—intended not so much literally
as allegorically—he declared, "We do not believe in programmes, schemes, saints, apostles: above all we do not believe
in happiness, salvation, the promised land. We do not believe
in a single solution....Let us return to the individual":[2] but
this was perhaps the first and last occasion on which he failed to
subordinate the individual to the State or to the Leader.
Already eighteen months before seizing power he made it
quite clear that "Fascism does not believe in the vitality and
principles which inspire the so-called Society of Nations. In
it the nations are not at all on a footing of equality. It is a kind
of Holy Alliance of the plutocratic nations of the Franco-

[1] 23 March 1919, I, p. 374.
[2] 1 January 1920, II, p. 51.

Anglo-Saxon group, to guarantee to themselves, despite the inevitable conflicts of interest, the exploitation of the greater part of the world". He therefore demanded the revision of treaties,[1] emancipation from the West, a *rapprochement* with the former enemy, friendship with the peoples of the East (including the Soviets), colonial development and further colonial claims. "It is destined that the Mediterranean should become ours", that Rome should be "the directing city of civilisation in the whole West of Europe": and he quoted "Imperium oceano, famam qui terminet astris".[2] The discipline which he preached in home policy, he commended for the further reason that "without it Italy cannot become the Mediterranean and World-Nation of our dreams".[3] In his last great speech before the March on Rome, he regretted that the Italian army had not marched along the Ringstrasse and the streets of Budapest, and he insisted that democracy may have suited the nineteenth century, but in the twentieth there was "some other political form which will knit national society together more closely".[4]

Miss Curry in no way exaggerates when she declares that "with the coming of Fascism the entire rhythm of Italian foreign policy was changed".[5] Mussolini affirmed his loyalty to the Peace Treaties and to the Allies—to "a policy of peace, not of suicide"—but while pleading for an examination of "the realities of the situation", put forward the two revealing mottoes of "Do ut des" and "Nothing for Nothing". To the Senate he spoke of "an Italy bursting with life, preparing to assume a style of serenity and beauty, an Italy which does not live on income from the past, like a parasite, but which intends to establish its future fortunes by its own forces, its own intimate

[1] On 1 December 1921 he put forward the dilemma, "either a new war, or revision of frontiers", II, p. 226.

[2] 6 February 1921, at Trieste, II, pp. 148–50.

[3] 3 April 1921, at Bologna, II, p. 163.

[4] "Che potenzî di più la comunione della società nazionale" is hardly translatable: 24 October 1922, at Naples, II, p. 341.

[5] *Italian Foreign Policy*, p. 75.

labour, its martyrdom and passion".[1] He as yet spoke with a studied moderation, pegging out Italy's interests and indicating, as he was fully entitled to do, her right to share in all European decisions, her desire and need for a speedy return to normal conditions. In particular, while regretting the previous Government's treaty with Jugoslavia, he considered himself bound to respect it, since the sole alternative was to throw the whole Adriatic settlement back into the melting-pot. But he contrasted the method of the Liberal and the Fascist State: "Fascism does not merely defend itself, but attacks."[2] " *What is the state?*" he asked, in his parliamentary defence against the charge of "liberticide". "*It is the gendarme* [carabiniere]. All your codices and doctrines and laws are worthless without him."[3] And in the new Fascist review *Gerarchia* he explained that liberalism was not the last word in the art of governing, and that "in Russia and in Italy it has been proved that one can govern outside, above, and against, the whole Liberal ideology". Communism and Fascism, he added, are outside Liberalism, and liberty is not an end, but a means.[4]

Already in 1923 the murder of General Tellini and of other Italian members of the commission for fixing the Greco-Albanian frontier revealed to all Europe the new rhythm of Italian policy. Mussolini gave Greece twenty-four hours to accept his stringent ultimatum, and then, when Athens made reservations and appealed to the League, he sent the Italian fleet to bombard and occupy Corfu, flatly denied Geneva's competence to intervene, and even threatened to resist its rulings and to withdraw altogether. The League's condonation of Poland's lawless action in the seizure of Eastern Galicia and Vilna now came home to roost: now for the first time it saw itself openly defied by a Great Power. Public indignation ran specially high in Britain: it resented this reversion to the crude method of ultimatum by which Austria-Hungary had envenomed the situation in 1914: but still more it resented the

[1] 27 November 1922, III, p. 33.
[2] 16 February 1923, p. 60.
[3] 15 July 1923, III, p. 198.   [4] March 1923, III, p. 78.

Fascist leader's brutal contempt for the new international machinery provided by the Covenant and his obvious desire to enhance his prestige at home at Geneva's expense,[1] and at the same time to establish Italian control of Albania and the entrance to the Adriatic. It also keenly resented the weakness of the Powers in withdrawing the dispute from the League and referring it to the Council of Ambassadors. Indeed, today it seems reasonable to regret that the inevitable trial of strength between Liberal and Fascist conceptions of the new order was weakly shirked, at a moment when Italian intransigeance would probably have met with a reverse, and was postponed till both Italy's internal and international position were to render defiance so much easier.

The Duce on his side openly expressed profound disappointment at the British attitude, all the deeper, he claimed, because he had always believed in Italo-British friendship. Characteristically enough, in an interview with a British sympathiser, he assumed that Britain's sole motive was to support Greece as a useful ally in the Mediterranean, and argued that Italy occupied a similar position and could be much more useful.[2] It does not seem to have occurred to him that the British Government might be genuinely concerned for the fate of the new Genevan system and indignant at his attempt to revert to the crudest of pre-war methods. Some of the phrases with which he justified himself to the Senate after the settlement are too revealing to be omitted. At Geneva, he assumed, "all the shady world of 'Socialistoid' and plutocratic democracy was furious" because Italy had a Fascist Government. The Corfu incident was in his view "of capital importance in Italian history, because it posed the question of the League before Italian opinion, which till then had never been excessively interested in the League, thinking it to be a dead, academic thing, without any importance". Italy, he frankly admitted, could not leave the League without breaking the

[1] On 16 November he admitted that it was his deliberate aim to increase Italy's prestige.
[2] Curry, p. 111.

treaties, but she could not remain in conditions of ignominious inferiority.[1] Isolation was not possible for Italy: she was too vitally concerned with both Balkan and Mediterranean problems. It is interesting that Mussolini should have chosen this moment to establish close relations with Soviet Russia— still the pariah of Europe, save for the German-Russian bargain at Rapallo. In advance he asked that recognition should be regarded "in the light of frank, I might say brutal, national utility",[2] and afterwards he publicly boasted of Fascist Italy's initiative in bringing Russia "back to the political and diplomatic circulation of Western Europe",[3] and in the Senate insisted on the "political utility" of recognition,[4] especially in view of the growing tendency of the Moscow Government and the Third International to draw apart—a tendency, be it added, which did really exist, but which scarcely anyone in Europe save Mussolini was perspicacious enough to detect.

FROM THE BRENNER TO THE "ROMAN LAKE"

The plan of this volume does not permit a detailed narrative of Italian foreign policy, and must be confined to main tendencies and directives. Speaking broadly, it may be said that for seven or eight years after Corfu Mussolini's attitude was one of reserve and cautious realism. He sought to allay foreign misapprehensions by declaring that Italy needed "a long period of peace and respect for treaties".[5] He made no concealment of the grave difficulties due to her lack of raw materials and growing population—difficulties aggravated by the American Immigration Bill: but he absolutely repudiated birth control, and declared it "not allowable to think of acquiring colonial territory by war",[6] and he indicated no clear line of escape from the dilemma. At the same time he treated foreign policy

[1] 16 November 1923, in the Senate, IV, pp. 268–9.
[2] 30 November 1923, III, p. 283.   [3] 4 October 1924, IV, p. 289.
[4] 20 May 1925, V, p. 75.
[5] 15 November 1924, IV, p. 382.
[6] Curry, p. 143.

as closely linked with the internal regime[1] and never lost an opportunity of denouncing Liberalism as effete and proclaiming the twentieth century as "the century of our power".[2] No less characteristic was his view that "we have no right to believe in humanitarian and pacific ideologies, beautiful as they may be in theory". "The reality of facts warns us to be very vigilant and to consider the *terrain* of foreign policy as one of maximum mobility."[3]

As regards the major problems, he supported every action which could genuinely be described as collective, and favoured the return of Germany, and also of Russia, to the comity of nations, reminding the world that the time must come "when Germany will return effectively to the game of European politics", and when "Russia will recover from her wounds and her excesses". He would have signed the Geneva Protocol, if everyone else had done so. In the same way he took a moderate line in the Dawes negotiations; insisting that reparations and debts were interdependent. Again in the disarmament question he insisted on the interdependence of every kind of arm—land, sea and air—and demanded parity between Italy's own armaments and those of "the most highly armed *Continental* nation".[4] He fell in with the arrangements of Locarno only when it became clear that the other Powers had come to terms, and announced quite openly that his motives were to prevent Italy from being isolated, and "to put Italy on an equality with England".[5] He would have liked the Brenner frontier to be included in a Western Guarantee, but wisely did not press the point, and explained that he had not done so, because "we are able to defend it by ourselves". He had already made it quite clear that "Italy could never tolerate such a violation of treaties as Austria's annexation by Germany", for it would "frustrate Italy's victory" and would make Germany more

[1] "I invite those who wish to vote against my home policy to begin by voting against my foreign policy." Cit. Curry, p. 140.

[2] E.g. 28 October 1925.

[3] 24 March 1924, IV, p. 73.

[4] 5 June 1928, VI, p. 215.   [5] 11 December 1924.

powerful than before. On the other hand, he was already reversing with a strong hand the liberal concessions made to the Germans of South Tirol ("Alto Adige"), under earlier Governments, yet he repelled with vehemence the protests of the Bavarian Premier Held, the German Foreign Secretary Stresemann and the Austrian Chancellor Mgr. Seipel.[1] Italy, he said, would make towards her own subjects "a policy of *italianità*", otherwise she would have a state within a state. "In a few years", he warned Vienna, "such elements of German descent as are left will be proud to be citizens of the great Fascist Fatherland, and will only be recognisable by the sound of their names, if they have retained them." None the less he insisted that Italian Imperialism "does not exist in an aggressive, explosive sense: it is not preparing war";[2] but he expressed his dislike of "high-sounding phrases about international solidarity", when all the time no nation was pursuing such an aim, but each was protecting itself behind high walls, economic and political. Disarmament must be total, or it was merely "a bad joke". Nor might anything be given to any other country "until Italy's legitimate demands are satisfied". The Italian Empire, he said on another occasion, "does not mean a determination to conquer new territories, but an attitude of mind, a line of conduct, strong, resolute, combative".[3] In the light of his later Abyssinian and Spanish policies this phrase too reads like "a bad joke".

"Italy's legitimate demands" were not as yet specified. In 1923 he had negotiated with Britain the cession of Jubaland, as compensation under the Treaty of London, and had secured from Turkey the final renunciation of the Dodecanese: in 1924 agreement was reached with Jugoslavia, on terms which

[1] It was in one of these three speeches that he drew the comparison between Walter von der Vogelweide and Dante, as between "the Pincian and the Himalaya". 20 May 1925, V, p. 78; 6 February 1926, V, p. 265; 3 March 1928, VI, p. 150.

[2] 29 May 1926. Cf. 5 December 1928, when he declared that "our Imperialism is not a menace to other nations. What we need is peaceful expansion, which all must respect, because it is a sign and a law of life".

[3] Curry, p. 161.

allowed Italy to annex the Free City of Fiume. The treaty with Switzerland was proclaimed as a proof of unaggressive aims, and as a means of maintaining a bulwark against reviving Pangermanism. The commercial treaty concluded with Albania in the same year led to the much more important Treaty of Tirana (27 November 1926), which laid the foundations of Italian influence, economic, political and military, over the otherwise bankrupt Albania and *per contra* destroyed for nearly a decade the tender plant of Italo-Jugoslav friendship which, it must be admitted, the Duce in his earliest phase had watered with some care.

The central fact of this period, however, was the chronic friction between Italy and France, compounded of a whole series of factors—rival theories of government, the activities of numerous anti-Fascist refugees in Paris and their periodic attempts on the Duce's life, the unregulated position of the Italians in Tunis (forming an actual majority of the white population), Italy's increasingly revisionist aims and her attempt to counter French influence on the Danube.

From 1926 onwards a more arrogant tone is noticeable in the Duce's pronouncements—an insistence, during his African visit, upon Italy's Mediterranean and seafaring mission,[1] an exaltation of Ancient Rome, above all for its conquest of Carthage and its domination over "the Roman Lake",[2] a resolve "to defend the lira to the last breath, to blood" and to brazen out the blunder of having pegged it far above its proper figure,[3] a prophecy that between 1935 and 1940 Europe was to reach "a crucial point in its history" and that by then Italy must be able to mobilise five million men.[4]

Between 1926 and 1930—the period aptly described by Professor Carr as "the zenith of the League"—the Duce played his full part in international discussions, and while refusing to

---

[1] 8 April 1926, v, p. 315.

[2] 5 October 1926, "Roma Antica sul Mare", v, p. 403.

[3] The Pesaro speech of 18 August 1926 (v, p. 386), reaffirmed on 21 December 1927 (vi, p. 124).

[4] 26 May 1927, vi, p. 72.

"attribute to the League mythological virtues", admitted its "utility", and while differing keenly from Paris on the question of naval parity, took the initiative in favour of a naval holiday and proclaimed Italy's readiness *a priori* to "accept and adopt as limitation of armaments whatever figure, no matter how low, is not less than that of any other Continental European Power".[1] This was, however, a skilful tactical position to cover up demands which, as the French pointed out, would in the name of equality actually have reduced them to a position of inferiority in the Mediterranean. Meanwhile he continued to pursue the policy of "Divide et Impera" on the Danube, rousing the hopes of Hungary by his pronouncements in favour of revision.

In one direction, however, the Duce showed high constructive statesmanship; namely in his settlement of the Roman Question (February 1927): many have criticised it from the angle of the Church, but few have challenged it from that of the State.

"EITHER WE OR THEY"

From 1930 onwards the Great Depression wrought kaleidoscopic changes everywhere. The Duce's mentality readily responded to the universal need for drastic and exceptional measures. "Live dangerously" became more than ever his motto, and aggression, which he had employed with such effect against his internal enemies, seemed to him more possible in foreign policy, in proportion as the Locarno spirit "evaporated" and deep-lying dissensions among the Powers diminished the efficacy of the League. In April 1930 Italy announced a large naval building programme, and the Duce himself, in his speech at Florence on 17 May, added the warning that it would be realised "ton by ton", in order that the Italians "should not remain prisoners in the Roman Sea". Then amid his Blackshirts he burst out into the phrases—"Words are a very fine thing, but rifles, machine-guns, warships, aeroplanes and cannon are still finer things. They are finer because right without

---

[1] 19 November 1929, VI, p. 215; Curry, p. 275.

might is an empty word."[1] About the same time he denied any desire for "precipitate adventures"; "but if anyone threatened our independence or our future, I do not know to what temperature I should bring the whole Italian people".[2]

In 1925 he had assumed that it was not possible to copy Fascism abroad, though it did contain "ferments of life of universal character" and though "round an Italian idea the World divides, for and against":[3] in 1928 he still treated Fascism as not being an article of export.[4] But now, after warning foreign opinion not to take for reaction what was in reality a revolution,[5] he opened the ninth year of his regime by a fighting speech, hitting out in all directions. On former occasions he had contrasted the mildness of the Fascist Revolution with the violence of the French,[6] or had expressed satisfaction at not having a long array of executions,[7] but now, "the Revolution which spared its enemies in 1922, will put them tomorrow against the wall". With a lightning turn of phrase he was insisting that *his* Revolution was "unitary", and that "Jacobins, Girondins, Thermidorians, Right or Left, are terms unknown in the Fascist regime". And then back again to denounce "the moral state of war against the regime", "the universal Vendée, Socialist, Liberal, Democratic, Masonic, which fears for its fetishes and sees its altars falling. We are fighting against a world in decline, but still powerful, because it represents an enormous crystallisation of interests." Italy, he went on, was "arming because all arm: she will disarm if all disarm. I repeat, as long as there are cannon, they will be more beautiful

[1] 17 May 1930, at Florence, Toynbee, *Survey for* 1931, p. 261.

[2] 9 May 1930, at Livorno, VII, p. 200.   [3] 18 November 1925, V, p. 203.

[4] 3 March 1928, VI, p. 151. Cf. Finer, *op. cit.* p. 60.

[5] 26 May 1930, at Milan, VII, p. 208.

[6] "It has another style", 31 October 1925, V, p. 175. None the less on the tenth anniversary of the decision to march (17 October 1932) he declared: "Our insurrection was of all modern ones the most sanguinary. The Russian cost only a few dozen lives: ours a vast sacrifice of young blood" (VIII, p. 120). For once his meaning is quite obscure.

[7] Though if necessary to defend the Revolution, they would have done so, 24 March 1924, IV, p. 68.

than beautiful, but often vain, words. When the 'Word' (*Verbo*) alone shall suffice to regulate relations among the peoples, then I shall call the word (*parola*) divine. But let it be clear, that we are arming materially and spiritually to defend ourselves, not for attack. *Fascist Italy will never take the initiative of war.*"[1] The policy of revision, he added, aimed at avoiding war in the general European interest. The real breakers of the Covenant were those who sought to perpetuate the two categories of armed and unarmed states.

His mind turned to the future. Italy was developing every inch of her soil, but her population was growing. "In 1950 Europe will be wrinkled and decrepit. The sole country of young men will be Italy. It is only towards the East that our pacific expansion can be directed: this explains our friendships and alliances. But my Florentine dilemma remains—'harsh to our enemies, we shall march to the end with our friends'...The struggle between the two worlds does not allow of compromises. *Either we or they. Either our ideas or theirs. Either our State or theirs.* The new cycle is of greater severity: whoever has interpreted it otherwise has fallen into a grave error of incomprehension or of faith."

"The phrase that Fascism is not an article of export is not mine: it is too banal.[2] Today I affirm that Fascism, as regards idea, doctrine, realisation, is universal.... *One can foresee a Fascist Europe, a Europe which draws inspiration for its institutions from the doctrines and practice of Fascism*—a Europe which solves in a Fascist sense the problem of the modern State, of the twentieth century, very different from the States which existed before 1789 or were formed afterwards." "We have to crush and pulverise, in the character and mentality of the Italians, the sediment deposited by those terrible centuries of political, military and moral decadence, which came from 1600 till the

[1] 18 October 1930, VII, p. 227. This phrase was to be often repeated till the very eve of the attack on Abyssinia. Cf. 1 January 1931, Message to America, VII, p. 278.

[2] In his speech of 3 March 1928, in answer to Mgr Seipel, he had said: "Il Fascismo non è un' articolo di esportazione", VI, p. 151.

rise of Napoleon." "Above all, the legend that the Italians are not fighters must be dispelled: for yesterday as today, the prestige of nations is determined almost absolutely by their military glories and their armed power." Finally he quoted a foreign writer who had compared Italy to "an immense camp", and went on approvingly: "Exactly, Fascist Italy is an immense legion which marches under the lictorian symbols towards a greater morrow, and no one can stop it."

This series of aggressive speeches was, in his own phrase, intended "to tear the mask from the face of this hypocritical Europe which babbles of peace at Geneva and everywhere else prepares for war". It was also deliberately planned in contrast to the project for a federal Europe, advanced by Briand that summer at Geneva. That there were many insincerities in the Genevan situation, no serious student of affairs could deny, and the Duce's realism might have become a valuable constructive element if only it had not been accompanied by the most cynical belief in brute force and intolerance as the true foundations, by the advancement of specious proposals which deliberately reversed the relations between security and disarmament, and by an accentuation of intrigue in the Balkans and on the Danube.

During the winter of 1930–31 the economic blizzard overwhelmed one country after another and assumed hitherto unknown proportions throughout the world. The downfall of the Austrian Kredit-Anstalt was merely the danger signal: the Hoover moratorium, Britain's precipitate abandonment of the gold standard, Japan's skilful exploitation of the world crisis, the final collapse of the whole reparation and debt structure—all this created a situation in which the Duce found ample opportunity for living tensely and dangerously. It was no longer possible to conceal the fact that the lira had been pegged far too high, yet he found himself debarred from any kind of deflation by the resounding pledge of his Pesaro speech.[1] The

[1] "I will not inflict on this marvellous people of Italy, who for four years works like a hero and suffers like a saint, the moral shame and economic disaster of the collapse of the lira....I will defend the lira to the last breath, to the last drop of blood", 18 August 1926, v, p. 386.

only alternative was the gradual introduction of exchange control, which by 1934 could no longer be camouflaged, but which
was more and more rigidly upheld, until the abandonment of
the gold standard by France, Holland and Switzerland in
September 1936 left Italy no alternative save that devaluation
against which the Duce had declaimed.

Throughout these years, however, his mind was reacting in
the sphere of international affairs very much as it did at home:
he was coming to regard collective action and peaceful bargaining with the same aversion as he showed to liberal and representative government. "If he who says 'liberalism' says
'individual', he who says 'Fascism' says 'State'."[1] And now,
"the twentieth century will be the century of Fascism, of
Italian power, the century during which Italy will for the
third time direct human civilisation.... Within ten years,
Europe will be modified, and will be Fascist or Fascised. The
antithesis by which contemporary culture is enchained can only
be overcome in one way, by the doctrine and wisdom of
Rome."[2]

CONTEMPT FOR THE LEAGUE

More realist and more outspoken than many contemporary
statesmen, he understood, sooner than most, the fatal reactions
of economic distress, and of such desperate remedies as autarky,
upon the political framework of Europe: and in the light of
subsequent events it is impossible to doubt that his increasingly
critical attitude to the League, to the Disarmament Conference,
and to the various French plans for a *détente*, was the façade
behind which he was already laying his own plans for Italian
expansion. His distrust of any "super-governmental mechanism" was natural enough: but he also challenged the formula
"security, arbitration, disarmament" which was the bedrock
of the French case, and put forward the rival formula "disarmament, then arbitration, and thereafter security", which, if
at first sight plausible, never had a chance of adoption. To the

[1] "La Dottrina del Fascismo", October 1932, VIII, p. 86.
[2] 25 October 1932, at Milan, VIII, p. 131.

Briand federation scheme he opposed the doctrines of national sovereignty in its extreme form (tempered by territorial "revisionism" in certain selected cases, but not in others), and of social revolution as against "the economic liberalism which to-day we are burying". Simultaneously he proclaimed his contempt for League principles—"it has lost all that could give it political significance"—and his desire for "integral revolutionary corporatism", resting on the basis of "a single party and of the totalitarian state". But he added significantly, "this is not enough; we must live a period of highest ideal tension".[1]

The coming of Hitler to power and the failure of the London Economic Conference powerfully affected the Duce, who already on 29 July 1933 expressed his open conviction that with the latter "the system of conferences is finished", and denounced "the eternal fiction or conventional lie, by which incense must be burnt to democratic equalitarianism, which does not exist in nature and never existed in history".[2] It would be far better to eliminate the lesser states and restrict discussions to the eight or ten states with world interests: for the former "have legitimate but limited interests, which can only be safeguarded if the great states which have greater responsibilities and more inhabitants, agree among themselves". Nay, it would be well to impose "an embargo on conferences," to recognise that popular sovereignty is an illusion and that "democracy can only talk".[3] This view, pronounced in respect of an ill-prepared general conference, was unmistakably directed against the whole Genevan system, which under a "Four Power Pact" such as the Duce advocated, would have been superseded by a Directorate of Four, in which Britain would waver between France and Germany and Italy would be the finger on the balance, while Russia would be relegated to the steppes of Asia. Never was the lack of directive in British policy so strikingly in evidence as at the moment when Mr Ramsay Macdonald and Sir John Simon consented to discuss these thinly veiled designs

[1] 14 November 1933, "Per lo Stato Corporativo", VIII, pp. 260, 271-3.
[2] Cf. 7 May 1928, "Nature is the realm of inequality", VI, p. 162.
[3] "Dopo Londra", VIII, pp. 223-5.

of sabotage in Rome itself. Needless to say, they speedily found that France was in no way disposed to accept the virtual isolation which would have followed her abandonment of the Little Entente and the elimination of the Russian factor at the very moment when it was swimming back into the ken of Europe. Hence the Pact, in the revised form acceptable to Paris and her allies, had little or no value in the eyes of Mussolini, who henceforth reckoned that London was blind and nerveless alike in Europe and in the Far East, and as yet unlikely to reach a common basis with Paris; that Washington would talk, but not act; and that the hope of Fascist Italy lay in co-operation with the rising star of Nazi Germany.

He was thus deliberately allying himself with the chief enemy of the Genevan system, but true to his motto of living danger-ously, hoped at one and the same time to hold back Germany from swallowing Austria, to drive a wedge between victors and vanquished in the Danubian area, and to maintain yet awhile a free option between Mediterranean, Balkan and colonial expansion. It may be freely admitted that he saved Austria by his resolute action after the Dollfuss murder in July 1934, and that this for a time clouded Italo-German rela-tions, undoing the effect of his meeting with the Führer at Venice a few weeks earlier.

It was almost certainly the nebulous and negative attitude of Britain during this succession of crises, and her increasing divergence from the tortuous Laval Cabinet in France, that finally decided him to concentrate his main effort upon a bid for sea-power and a colonial empire. We know now—what we ought to have known all the time, for it followed logically from a long series of actions and utterances—that he was con-sciously training the nation for war, and intended to throw his weight where most could be secured with the least resistance. "War", he declared only a few weeks after he had incited his dupes to destroy Socialism in Austria by the February *coup*, "war is to man as maternity is to woman. I do not believe in perpetual peace." And a month after his intervention in favour of the murdered Dollfuss's successors, he announced, "We are becoming, and shall always approach nearer to being, a military nation. Since we are not afraid of words, let us add militarist, war-like, that is, endowed more and more with the virtues of obedience, sacrifice and devotion to the Fatherland." In a contribution to the *Enciclopedia Italiana* in 1932, the Duce was even more explicit. "Above all, Fascism...believes neither in the possibility nor the *utility* of perpetual peace. It thus repudiates pacifism, born of a renunciation of the struggle and an act of cowardice in the face of sacrifice. War alone brings up to its highest tension all human energy and puts the stamp of nobility upon the people who have the courage to meet it."

ITALY AND RUSSIA

It is important to note in passing that (unlike Hitler after his first year of office) he still kept the door open towards Russia, taking open pride in the fact that Italy had been the first Western Power to resume relations with the Soviet State in 1924 and was now concluding the first Western Pact of non-aggression with it. His line of argument on this occasion deserves special attention in view of the later tactics of the dictatorial states. "It is true," he said, "that between two nations erected on analogous political systems and ideas social and cultural exchanges and sympathies are more easily established: but it has also been proved that such sympathies and elective affinities must not guide in a dominant, still less exclusive, fashion the foreign political and international relations of great peoples."[1] In political theory there was a deep gulf between them, but "we cannot ignore Russian political strength", and an agreement with Russia was not an act of hostility towards any nation. Here, then, we have an absolute and unanswerable precedent, from the mouth of Hitler's chief ally, for that Franco-Soviet Pact to which the rival dictators take such exception. Moreover, not once but repeatedly, Mussolini has admitted that "our tactics were Russian", and by 1937 it must be fairly obvious—even to those who espoused

[1] 30 September 1933, VIII, p. 240.

his cause in the fond belief that he would save them from Bolshevism—that his whole regime leads logically and inevitably to a kind of "inverted Bolshevism" in which the so-called "propertied classes" will gradually be squeezed dry, to meet the requirements of a soaring Imperialism which neither they nor the Italian masses really desire.

ITALY AND THE BALKANS

The Duce's short-lived effort to establish a European Directorate of Four, in which he himself might hope to exercise the casting vote, naturally caused acute alarm throughout the Near East, where Italy ever since the war had followed the pre-war Austrian policy of "Divide et Impera". His aim had been to prevent a definitive settlement in the Danubian area, by maintaining the division into two groups of states (the two vanquished and curtailed, Austria and Hungary, and the three victorious and aggrandised, Czechoslovakia, Jugoslavia and Roumania) and at the same time to play off the Balkan states against each other, and in particular to prevent the reconciliation of Serb and Bulgar (as also of Serb and Croat), or of Bulgar and Greek. In view of the political and social upheaval following upon revolution, land reform, and all too drastic frontier readjustments, feeling ran high, many crying injustices were committed on all sides, and it was only too easy to fan the flames. In so doing, Italy took full advantage of the changed position of the Great Powers in relation to the Near East. The result of the war had eliminated the two Powers whose rivalry in pre-war years had overshadowed the whole Balkan Peninsula; Austria-Hungary had ceased to exist, Russia was driven back and for nearly a decade and a half absorbed in other problems. Germany, after the failure of the "Berlin-Bagdad" programme, was also for the time being out of the picture, though already planning in an entirely legitimate manner the revival of her lost economic influence. Britain since 1920 followed a policy of virtual *désintéressement* on the Danube and in the Balkans, greatly to the regret of all the Balkan States, who realised that she at least could not nourish territorial ambitions at their expense. Thus only two of the Great Powers can be said to have had an active Balkan policy in the post-war years. France, it may be admitted, was unduly concerned with building up alliances in Eastern Europe and thus ensuring that Germany should not reach by some new path the lost goal of Central European hegemony. But though only too apt to view Danubian and Balkan problems from the standpoint of her own fancied interests rather than on their own merits, France could at least claim to have always pushed her smaller allies in the direction of Geneva and to have thrown her whole weight into the scale of Balkan and Danubian co-operation and unity.

Any criticism of Italy's very different attitude must of course in common justice begin with the admission that she had certain legitimate interests in that area and certain grounds for anxiety. She could not wish to see Jugoslavia as a mere satellite of France, nor could she allow either Jugoslavia or Greece to secure control of Albania: in either case her eastern coast would be exposed to attack, and the elimination of the Austro-Hungarian fleet would have been in vain. It is true, on the other hand, that her wartime understanding with the Jugoslavs, if upheld, might have proved a first step towards Italian commercial (and perhaps partially political) supremacy in the Balkans: it was her reversion to the baneful policy of the Treaty of London, her annexation of 600,000 Croats and Slovenes in Istria and Venezia Giulia, her further designs on Dalmatia, D'Annunzio's filibustering raid upon Fiume, that so completely alienated Jugoslav opinion and provoked the famous Adriatic conflict with President Wilson, from which, thanks largely to the shuffling attitude of Great Britain, she in the end emerged as *beatus possidens*. A certain *détente* was reached by the Treaty of Rapallo (12 November 1920), concluded under the saner influence of Count Sforza, and Mussolini, on attaining to power, showed studied moderation in accepting the accomplished fact. But the two Treaties of Tirana (November 1926 and November 1927), establishing something very like an Italian protectorate over Albania, were all the more resented by

Jugoslavia because she had had her own guilty designs of penetration.[1] Thus Italy and Jugoslavia again fell rapidly apart, and
for eight or nine years their relations were dangerously strained.
At one time or another Italy supported the Montenegrin exiles,
the Macedonian and Croat terrorists, and sent periodical supplies
of war material to Hungary (the St Gotthard incident of
January 1926 and the Hirtenberg incident of January 1934
achieved notoriety, but did not stand alone).

The Little Entente, founded originally in 1920-1 with the
double purpose of maintaining the new *status quo* on the Danube,
preventing territorial revision in favour of Hungary and Habsburg restoration in either Austria or Hungary, was also openly
based on the "Genevan system", to which all its leading
statesmen—Beneš, Take Ionescu, Titulescu, Ninčić, Marin-
ković—stood irrevocably pledged. But there was a growing
tendency in all three countries to supplement their political
accords by others of an economic nature and to extend this to
Austria and Hungary also. The most serious of the various
projects put forward in this sense was the Tardieu Plan (March
1932) which aimed at a political truce as a preliminary to
economic collaboration. But while Russia and Britain, for
utterly different reasons, followed a passive policy in the
Balkans and on the Danube; and France reckoned above all in
terms of isolating Germany; Italy and Germany, though not
seeing eye to eye on the Austrian question, were united in
fearing a challenge to their perfectly legitimate economic
interests in the Danubian basin, and put periodical spokes in the
wheel. Italy in particular had convinced herself not only that
the Little Entente was an artificial organism which could be
coerced into drastic concessions, but that Jugoslavia and Czechoslovakia in particular were doomed to disintegrate, thanks to
Croat discontent and Slovak autonomist tendencies. Italian
support for the cause of Hungarian "revisionism" was admirably
calculated to maintain discord on the Danube, both by fostering
illusions at Budapest and by stiffening, in a more nationalist
sense, opinion among the Slovaks, the Transylvanian Rou-

[1] For a fairly detailed summary, see H. Fish Armstrong, *The New Balkans*.

manians, and the Serbs and Croats of the Banat, Bačka and Croatia.

The Little Entente, on its side, was keenly alive to such dangers, and, spurred on by Hitler's advent to power, by the weakening of the League and by the failure of disarmament, its three Foreign Ministers MM. Beneš, Titulescu and Jevtić, on 16 February 1933 signed a new Pact of Organisation, establishing a common organ at Geneva and providing for the complete unification of their foreign policy. This attempt of the three states to attain the united status of a Great Power was peculiarly distasteful to Mussolini and indeed was one of the main targets at which the Four Power Pact was aimed. It was above all the vigorous resistance of the Little Entente which led France to insist upon the emasculation of that Pact. Dr Beneš, speaking in the Parliament of Prague, summed up the main objectives of Italian policy as (1) a special status for the Great Powers, especially as against the lesser states of Central and South-Eastern Europe; (2) a new balance of power aimed at the military weakening of France and her friends; (3) treaty revision on such lines as would weaken the Little Entente and Poland; and (4) colonial concessions to Italy. He made it abundantly clear that frontier adjustments could not be imposed upon any state, save by war, and could only be considered at all, in an absence of external pressure, by direct and free negotiations between the parties concerned, on a basis of mutual compensation, and in an atmosphere of calm such as unhappily did not then prevail in Europe. The Pact, when adopted in its modified form on 7 June 1933, omitted the points most objectionable to the Little Entente, but these were also some of the very points to which the Duce had attached most value. Incidentally, while for this reason the Little Entente was able to accept the compromise with a fairly good grace, Poland intensely resented being left out, and hence the Pact may be regarded as an important contributory cause of the German-Polish Pact of January 1934.

For the next few years we see blow and counter-blow following each other in rapid succession. Every major event in

Europe served as an incentive towards a united front, and the exploratory work of four unofficial Balkan Conferences between 1930 and 1934 had not been wasted. On 4 February 1934, then, it came to the conclusion of a Balkan Pact between Jugoslavia, Roumania, Greece and Turkey, based on a mutual guarantee of frontiers against outside aggression. There was the important qualification that this was not binding against a Great Power—an indirect way of saying that Greece was not bound to help Jugoslavia if attacked by Italy. But the Pact had the effect of adding the weight of Turkey and Greece to that of Jugoslavia and Roumania in the case of the Hungarian frontiers, and of ringing round Bulgaria in such a way as to render aggression quite hopeless. The Gladstonian principle of "the Balkans for the Balkan Peoples" seemed at last to be coming into its own. Moreover, the tide of terror and recrimination in Macedonia had at last turned, and public opinion both in Bulgaria and Jugoslavia, steadily encouraged by Kings Alexander and Boris, favoured fraternisation between the hostile brothers.

Within a few weeks the Duce countered, first by pushing the Heimwehr extremists into the armed suppression of Viennese Socialism, and then by extracting from the Austrian Chancellor Dr Dollfuss and the Hungarian Premier General Gömbös, the so-called "Rome Protocols"—a first step towards converting Austria and Hungary into vassals of Italy and thus preventing Danubian union save on Italy's terms. The summer of 1934 witnessed parallel terrorist campaigns—one for the "Gleichschaltung" or Nazification of Austria, organised and financed by the Brown House in Munich and the Austrian Legion, the other for the separation of Croatia from Jugoslavia, organised by a group of Croat exiles in Italy, well supplied with money, rifles and explosives and enabled to maintain training camps for young terrorists. These two movements culminated in the murder of Dollfuss on 25 July, which led Mussolini to mass troops on the Brenner for the defence of Austria, and in the murder of King Alexander at Marseilles on 9 October by emissaries of the Croat terrorist leader Pavelić, who has to this day continued to enjoy asylum on Italian soil. When the Schuschnigg regime showed itself able to suppress the *Putsch* in Austria, the Third Reich called off the Terror and substituted those more subtle methods of sapping and mining in which the new envoy in Vienna, Herr von Papen, had proved himself such an adept as German Military Attaché in Washington. On the other hand, when Jugoslavia, so far from breaking up after the royal Dictator's death, rallied round the Regency, the Duce abandoned his stubborn belief in Croat separatism and began to feel his way towards a *détente* with Belgrade.

M. Barthou's tenure of office of the French Foreign Ministry and his sensational visits to the capitals of South-East Europe seemed to mark the zenith of French support to the new Double Entente. But after Barthou's death at the hands of the Marseilles assassin, his successor M. Laval adopted a dangerous game of balancing, which culminated in the Franco-Italian agreement of 7 January 1935. During 1935 France steadily lost influence among the Danubian and Balkan states, and for a time at least Germany profited by their disorientation to push her trade throughout the Near East. It is, however, essential to remember that throughout the conflict between Mussolini and the League—with which we shall deal in Chapter XI— the Little and Balkan Ententes unreservedly supported the Covenant, the League system and the policy first put forward, but then abandoned, by the British Government. They did so, because they realised very clearly the dangers to which the small Powers would be exposed as a result of unrestricted competition in armaments and of the hegemony of a few Great Powers who cared nothing for their plighted word. They also supported it because their interests lay in maintaining the *status quo*, and because the chief offender against the Covenant and the Kellogg Pact was also the chief advocate of revisionism and the chief opponent of Jugoslav Unity and of Bulgaro-Jugoslav friendship. And they also supported it because they were greatly alarmed at the Duce's talk of an "Impero Romano", of "Mare Nostro" and the "Sea of Rome" and feared for themselves if Italy were predominant in the Mediterranean.

While therefore welcoming the leadership assumed by Britain at Geneva in face of Italian aggression in Abyssinia, they were correspondingly discouraged when that aggression was crowned by complete victory and followed by Britain's ignominious retreat. Thrown back on their own resources, the statesmen of the Double Entente set themselves to strengthen its machinery still further, and King Carol's state visit to Prague in October 1936 was a notable demonstration of solidarity. It was almost at once countered by the Duce's Milan speech of 2 November, in which he held out to Hungary the prospect that revision would be achieved in the near future, and soon afterwards the Regent Horthy paid a state visit to Rome and Naples, and even reviewed an Italian fleet including many units formerly under his command as Admiral of the old Austrian fleet. On the other hand the Jugoslav Premier was ostentatiously welcomed at Angora by the Turkish Dictator and on his return journey home entered upon negotiations which led to the Bulgaro-Jugoslav Pact of 23 January 1937. The Austro-German Agreement of 11 July 1936, and finally the Italo-Jugoslav Pact of January 1937, illustrate still further the kaleidoscopic changes of Danubian and Balkan policy under the stress of competition among the Great Powers. For the moment the question whether the Double Entente deserves the title of a sixth Great Power or is doomed to disintegrate in the face of German or Italian expansion to the South-East, must remain unanswered. But some brief indication of warring forces was necessary in order to bring home to the British reader the extent to which the Danubian and Balkan problem as a whole is interlocked with the Mediterranean question, as modified by Italian Fascist ambitions. To this we shall have to return in connection with the situation created by Italy's conquest of Abyssinia and her military intervention in Spain.

A STRAIGHT ISSUE

Our survey of Italian post-war policy and aims leads to certain general conclusions. In the first place, in dealing with Italy and above all with Mussolini we must dismiss from our minds every spark of sentiment, every historical analogy from the long-vanished era of the Risorgimento, and must study attentively Machiavelli, and the despots and condottieri of the Italian Renaissance. Secondly, we must realise that the Duce has long had a poor opinion of British statesmanship, an opinion confirmed by the ease with which he has deceived a long series of distinguished Foreign Ministers and Ambassadors. He is now convinced that the British nation is emasculated by pacifist doctrine and excessive comfort, and threatened by a catastrophic decline in man-power. He believes that the British Empire is disintegrating, and deliberately aspires to take its place, at any rate in the Mediterranean, in Africa and in the Middle East. Thirdly, we must remember that in this he is inspired not merely by ambition, but by a far-reaching political theory which shapes his every action. He is equally hostile to the whole system of free and representative institutions on which the British and American Commonwealths are built up, to the ideas of individual right and popular sovereignty, and to the new Genevan system of collective action, renunciation of war and equality of great and small states. He has defined the issue beyond all possibility of misunderstanding by declaring that "Either We or They" must go under—either the new totalitarian dispensation or the (in his view) pernicious liberties won by our fathers in the liberal era. Either the Power Politics of the dictatorial states, or "the false Gods of Geneva".[1] It is high time for us to realise what Mussolini has realised long ago, that Britain is the main obstacle to every section of his total design, and that it is useless to hug illusions as to his friendship or to trust his word. With Russia under Stalin our interests need not collide: with Germany under Hitler a compromise is

[1] He has even gone so far as to couple Geneva and Moscow.

difficult but by no means impossible: with Italy under Mussolini there can be nothing better than armed neutrality and perpetual vigilance. The "European Anarchy" of 1931–4—the flabbiness of Britain, the constant disagreements between Paris and London, Japan's triumph and immunity, above all Germany's deliberate withdrawal from the comity of nations—tempted him to believe that a situation had arisen in which he could conquer an African Empire in the teeth of European opinion. No sooner was Abyssinia at his mercy, than he tried a fresh adventure in Spain, which represents a far more direct and deadly challenge to British interests: and those who talk glibly of recapturing his friendship only increase the danger by convincing him of British gullibility.

VIII

BRITAIN AND THE DICTATORS:
(C) GERMANY

"L'EUROPE sentira de plus en plus que la France de 1830, libre, ardente, regorgeant de force et d'activité, ne peut être traitée comme la France de 1815." So wrote the *Journal des Débats* in 1831, fifteen years after the Peace Settlement of 1815. A century later Europe found herself confronted by a similar revival on the part of Germany—so full of force and ardour, so resentful of her treatment, that she was ready to sacrifice her liberty in the cause of self-esteem.

During the fifteen years following the War the two main challenges to free institutions came from Russia and from Italy: with the various minor dictatorships which arose in Spain, in Turkey, in Poland, in Jugoslavia, in Portugal, in Greece, we need not concern ourselves here, for each was determined by special local circumstances, and exercised little or no influence beyond its own frontiers. In the case of Russia, it is true, distance lent enchantment to the view, and the very vastness of the social experiment upon which she had embarked aroused an ill-grounded enthusiasm both among the proletarian revolutionaries of other countries and among a certain set of intellectual doctrinaires. But her remoteness and vast spaces, her extremes of temperament and social standards stood in the way of closer contacts and left her almost as much isolated as in the days of Ivan the Terrible. In the case of Italy the transition from liberty to autocracy was less drastic and more gradual, and made a less immediate and vivid appeal to foreign opinion. In Britain in particular Fascism remained an exotic creed, and it was only at quite a late stage that even the Duce himself began to regard it seriously as "an article of export". Geographically, Fascism remained isolated: it encouraged kindred bodies in other countries, but without much effect, and indeed it could not even exert any very great influence over its nearest analogy, the Latin dictatorship erected in Spain by Primo de Rivera.

With the coming to power of Hitler in Germany this situation was radically transformed. Autocratic government now came to occupy the key position in Central Europe, democratic and international tendencies were everywhere driven on to the defensive. Incidentally, the strategic position of Fascism was greatly strengthened, and its possible value as an ally slowly emerged, whereas the abnormality and isolation of Russia received added emphasis. It is from this angle that we must examine the Third Reich and its prospects of converting the world to its political ideas.

NATIONAL SOCIALISM

The National Socialist movement owed its success to a combination of causes. The abrupt transition from four years of victory to utter downfall had upset the mental balance of the German nation, and this pathological factor was still further accentuated by the harsh unwisdom of the Allies, by the collapse of credit that inevitably followed, and by the financial and moral devastation wrought among the most cultured sections of the population. If the Peace Conference of 1919 had treated Germany with the same minimum of consideration which was shown to France at the Congress of Vienna, if Wilson had had as his colleagues Castlereagh and Wellington, instead of Poincaré, Clemenceau and Lloyd George, then the in any case unpopular tasks incumbent upon the German Republic might have been accepted by German public opinion as a necessity of war, and the attempt of the extremists to represent the new rulers as traitors and as the veritable scum of the earth would have gradually exhausted itself. But the fatal refusal to draw any distinction between Potsdam and Weimar—between William and Ebert—in the end proved fatal to the survival of the Republic, and provided those who preached a reversion to "Power Politics" with a whole armoury of arguments. For fifteen years the vicious circle was upheld, France and Britain alternately blowing hot and cold, and each in turn disagreeing with the concessions or reprisals alternately proposed by the other, with the result that any real concessions either came too late or were interpreted as signs of weakness. Nothing ever quite atoned for Poincaré's fatal blunders in the Ruhr, and though Locarno brought a revival of confidence in the new Genevan system, an infinity of time was wasted in the next six or seven years in the discussion of disarmament and debts, while all the time public opinion in Germany grew more bitter and restive, and water flowed to the extremist mills. The World Depression, coming as it did while both problems still remained unsolved, increased the difficulty of solution, in that it multiplied tenfold the unrest inside every country, forced unwilling governments on to the fatal path of autarky and restrictions, swelled the number of ruined and unemployed persons and, especially in Central Europe, of the so-called "intellectual proletariat". Once again, the course both of internal and external policy played straight into the hands of the extremist parties in Germany.

Moreover, without in any way attempting to minimise Allied blunders, it is necessary to insist that the period between 1920 and 1933 had brought a number of very real mitigations of Germany's lot. First had come the Dawes Plan, then Locarno, then admission to the League: in 1930 evacuation had been completed, perhaps too late, but still four and a half years earlier than provided for by the Treaty: in 1932 reparations ended, doubtless because their enforcement was ceasing to be possible, but in any case before the cognate question of Allied debts had been settled: while the disarmament question, though admittedly delayed, evaded, unsolved, had none the less filled the stage ever since 1925 and was destined to do so until Germany, by her own deliberate action, drove it into the background. It is vital to remember that just as the Dawes Plan and the Pact of Locarno had led to a recrudescence of nationalist agitation in Germany, so evacuation was not followed by an appeasement of public opinion, but by the first great advance of Nazism (whose deputies increased in 1930 from 12 to 107).

And it must be added that some of the hesitation of the Allies was due to the knowledge that behind the façade of the Weimar system there had for years been steady evasion of all the military clauses of the Treaty, and secret German rearmament through the connivance of Soviet Russia.

It is far from my purpose to describe the rise of National Socialism, nor would it be profitable (since the facts would defy scientific analysis), to examine the relative effects of the World Crisis and its financial and trade reactions inside the Reich, the weakness of successive German Cabinets and the "Hide and Seek" of the French and British Governments at Geneva. It has already been pointed out how the Brüning Cabinet sought to revive its flagging reputation by the unwise *coup* of an Austro-German Customs Union: and the very natural opposition of the Western Powers was not the least of the causes leading to Brüning's fall, and the circumstances under which Herr von Papen succeeded him as Chancellor almost compelled him to adopt a less conciliatory attitude. In this he was further encouraged by the powerlessness of the League in the face of Japanese aggression in Manchuria and its fatal effects upon the Disarmament Conference. Indeed, this whole complex of events was a direct incentive to the Nationalist and National Socialist exponents of a return to "Power Politics" in the foreign sphere. Papen in his turn was followed for a brief term as Chancellor by General von Schleicher, who after a vain attempt to pose as "the People's General", was thrown by President von Hindenburg to the Nazi wolves. Yet to the last there were many serious observers in every party who declined to take the "Nazi" agitation too seriously, and who noted that its phenomenal increase of votes in 1930 from 12 to 107, and in July 1932 from 107 to 230, had been followed in November of the same year by a decline from 230 to 196. Certainly the original idea of Hindenburg was a Coalition Cabinet, in which Adolf Hitler, as Chancellor, was to be the prisoner of the Nationalist Right, under Papen and Hugenberg: but the calculation was utterly false, for at the elections of March 1933 the Nazis held 340 seats out of 647, and within a few months were so completely in control that Hugenberg had to resign, his party being shelved almost as effectually as those of the Left, while Seldte and his "Steel Helmets" were forced into the background by Hitler's own formation the S.A. (Sturm-Abteilungen).

Shock now followed shock in rapid succession. On 30 January 1933 Hitler had become Chancellor. Within less than a month the burning of the Reichstag, under circumstances of the utmost suspicion—a suspicion only deepened by the farcical trial of Van der Lubbe, Dimitrov and others—was exploited by the new regime as the excuse for a frontal attack upon Communism. Captain Göring, the newly appointed Prussian Premier, relying not so much upon the police authorities as upon irregular Brownshirt formations, arrested all the Communist deputies and ordered a thorough round-up of all alleged sympathisers (28 February). This was followed in May by the dissolution of the Trade Unions and the confiscation of their funds, the prohibition of the Social Democrat party, the liquidation of the Centre, and the shelving of the older nationalist groups. Political resistance was met in thousands of cases by the methods of the concentration camp and the oxhide whip.

Parallel with this abrupt overthrow of the parliamentary and representative system and the conversion of the Reichstag into a mere totalitarian vote-adding machine, went the "Gleich-schaltung" of the administration, first in Prussia and the Rhineland, then in all the lesser states of the Reich, even Bavaria. The ease with which this victory of an iron centralism was effected boded ill for resistance in any quarter. Under Dr Goebbels as head of a new Reich Ministry of Propaganda the whole German press[1] and publishing trade were speedily placed in the straightjacket of an all-powerful and all-pervading censorship, which paid the same minute attention to radio and to cinema activities. The essentially Bolshevist-Fascist principle (for such indeed it is) that the State can only tolerate a single

[1] By April 1934 a thousand newspapers had been suppressed, and "a further 350 had ceased publication voluntarily" (cf. Roberts, *House that Hitler Built*, pp. 247–52).

party, in this case the National Socialist, was strictly applied, and specially repressive measures were directed against all international or pacifist organisations or tendencies. Education became a monopoly of the Party, as co-terminous with the State: and the academic world was convulsed by the wholesale expulsion of all savants, however distinguished, who were identified with liberal principles or whose pedigree to the third and fourth generation did not meet the standards of "racial purity" now arbitrarily established from above. The Jews, in particular, became the most convenient scapegoats of a movement which (in the teeth of science, and especially of anthropology) preached a virulent form of "Racialism", based on entirely bogus theories of "Aryan" blood. The very natural reactions of Jewry abroad against the brutal persecution of their kith and kin and the scurrilous abuse levelled at every section of the race—reactions which sometimes expressed themselves in the demand for a Jewish boycott of everything German—only roused the Nazi leaders to yet more violent reprisals.

It was moreover only a question of time that the fanatical promoters of such a movement should come up against the Christian Churches, which could not accept the new racialism without denying the very foundations of Christianity itself. "There is no distinction between Jew and Greek"[1] comes to us not merely with the authority of St Paul, but is reinforced by eighteen centuries of the Church's teaching: its repudiation would mean the abandonment of the Church's claim to be a World Religion. At first the Holy See sought to avert an open breach with Berlin, and by the Concordat of 8 July 1933 made the substantial concession that priests should no longer be allowed to belong to political parties. But this could not deter the Nazis from claiming the exclusive control of the youth of Germany or their extreme wing from propagating ideas of aggressive Paganism as the ideal of future generations. It was at first assumed that indifferentism had made such strides

[1] Romans x, 12; "There cannot be Greek and Jew, circumcision and uncircumcision, barbarian, Scythian, bondman, freeman: but Christ is all, and in all", Colossians iii, 11 (R.V.).

in German Protestant circles that less resistance need be antici-
pated from them: but fortunately the activities of the so-called
"German Christians", and notably the attempt to apply the
"Aryan Paragraph" to the Protestant pastors and to propagate
a version of the Psalms reframed to suit the modern Berserker
mood, kindled something of the old Reformers' spirit. It may
well be that in the end Germany's return to sanity may be
achieved by common action of the two main religious bodies,
whose disunion was one of the main causes of Germany's
political weakness in former centuries.

The profound innovations thus briefly summarised were to
change the face of Germany out of all recognition, and to
intensify the differences of outlook and aim between her and
most of her neighbours. Foremost in ·the Nazi creed was
a direct challenge to the whole Versailles settlement—a flat
denial of war-guilt and defeat in the field, a refusal to be bound
by a peace which had been dictated, not negotiated, and whose
terms, it was contended, had not been observed by the other
side. From the first it was clear that this challenge was certain
to find expression in the field of foreign policy and greatly
to complicate the position of the League. But only the actual
course of events revealed the extent to which, under the Hitler
regime, home and foreign policy were bound up together and
reacted upon each other. For our present inquiry it follows
that we shall not be able to understand Hitlerian foreign policy
without a previous study of the political ideas and aims of the
Führer and his chief lieutenants.

ADOLF HITLER AND *MEIN KAMPF*

The mind of Mussolini is reflected in the eight volumes of
his collected speeches and writings from which our quotations
are drawn: for the mind of Hitler we have a much more
authoritative source in his famous book *Mein Kampf*. First let
us be clear as to its contents, and then we can compare it with
the successive pronouncements of his four years in office.

It is frequently objected that this book was written in a

disgruntled mood during the period of arrest which followed Hitler's unsuccessful *coup* at Munich, and also at a time when the French occupation of the Ruhr rendered strong language excusable, but that it has long ceased to represent his real mind. In actual fact, the first volume was written in 1924, but the second—in which the most contentious references to foreign policy occur—not till 1927, in other words, more than a year after Locarno, when there was still hope for the "policy of fulfilment". But of course the real answer to those who seek to detract from the book's importance lies in the double fact that year by year it continues to circulate unaltered in the original German, in gigantic editions,[1] whereas all attempts to secure permission for unabridged editions in France and England have been prevented by the holders of the copyright.[2] As it is commended by all political and municipal authorities in Germany, and prescribed for the younger generation, we must conclude that its author wishes the objectionable passages to be read by his own compatriots, but does *not* wish them to be known to the foreign public.

Three examples of the German official attitude towards *Mein Kampf* should suffice for the information of the reader. (1) On the occasion of the Oxford religious conference in July 1937, a brochure entitled "Positive Christianity in the Third Reich", by Dr C. Fabricius, was widely distributed in England; and this contains the statement that "the only official book on National Socialism is Adolf Hitler's *Mein Kampf*". (2) In a learned treatise on the reform of German penal law (*Das neue Strafrecht*) published in 1937 by two eminent jurists, with an introduction by the Minister of Justice, Dr Gürtner, extracts from *Mein Kampf* bulk prominently, and that book itself is described as the "guiding star" (*Leitstern*). (3) In the negotiations between the German and Austrian Governments last

---

[1] When I bought my copy in 1933, at the price of 8 Marks, the sales had already reached 1,040,000, and they now exceed 3,000,000. If we were to reckon the author's royalties at the very modest sum of 6*d*. a copy, they would represent a minimum of £75,000.

[2] The English edition contains 80,000 of the original 230,000 words.

summer for an extension of the Agreement of 26 July 1936, a point to which the German delegates attached special importance was the demand that the sale of *Mein Kampf* in Austria should be allowed.

Mein Kampf is not the first book in history to exercise enormous influence upon the contemporary world, in defiance of many glaring literary defects, great diffuseness and lack of arrangement. Only the pedant will stop to pick holes in its style or its grammar: what matters is that it has been *lived* by its author and expresses all the varying moods of an intense, daemonic nature. As a key to one of the most enigmatic characters in history, its importance can hardly be exaggerated: and as his personality is capable of rousing to white heat large sections of the younger generation of his countrymen, it cannot be too closely examined.

We must not be diverted from our main study by the extreme violence of mood and phrase which constantly meets us in its pages. Let us merely note in passing, that it is the violence of a mind very imperfectly educated and utterly lacking in self-discipline. Time after time we read of Marxists as "vermin" (186),[1] "bloodsucking spiders" (212), "parasites" (99), or "a gang of street-thieves, deserters, party bonzes and Jew literateurs" (413). All through the book there is a rain of phrases against "the rotten and craven bourgeois world" (409). The bourgeois press is "partly pitiable, partly *gemein* as ever" (617). The Jewish press "has the habit of spilling the muck-pail of meanest calumnies over a clean dress" (93). Of parliamentary democracy we read that "only the Jew can praise an institution which is as dirty and untrue as he himself" (99). "There is no principle which, objectively regarded, is so wrong as the parliamentary" (92). "I utterly hated the whole gang of these miserable deceiving party curs" (218). The German Revolution is for him "the bandit blow of autumn 1918" (378). Its Ministers deserve the names of "*Schuft, Schurke, Lump und Verbrecher*" (302). Eisner's Government at Munich is a "pig-stye" (235). "It is one of the most shameless impudences of

[1] All page references are to *Mein Kampf*, edition of 1933.

the present regime" (i.e. in 1927) "to speak of 'free citizens'"
(640). The Terror of Socialism will always be successful, "until
met by an equally great terror" (46).

These few examples out of many (to which ought to be
added the most frantic outbursts against the Jews) show a lack of
balance, an intolerance, which permeates the whole Nazi system
alike in its home and in its foreign policy. We need not go to
Mein Kampf for historical accuracy: but we may learn from it
what an Austrian of his low culture in pre-war days was
capable of swallowing and believing, and what he has been
able to "put across" the post-war public of the Reich as true
statements about Austria. And this is worth dwelling on: for
on the one hand it is quite clear that Hitler *really believes* his
own fantastic travesty of the Austrian situation, and that it
already found credence in the Reich at a time when serious
criticism of it was still a possibility. Two examples must suffice.
He roundly asserts that the Arch-House of Habsburg "Czechised
wherever possible", and that Francis Ferdinand was the patron
of the Slavisation of Austria! (13, 101, 118), and again he lays
stress on the hostility of the Jewish press of Austria towards
Germany (58, 61). Now to every serious student of Austrian
affairs in the decade preceding the Great War two things were
especially apparent—first, the fact that what Herr Hitler calls
the "world-press" of Vienna, and notably its two greatest
organs, *Neue Freie Presse* and *Neues Wiener Tagblatt*, were year
in, year out, working as the exponents of the Wilhelmstrasse
and of the Triple Alliance: and second, that Francis Joseph was
essentially anti-Slav and especially anti-Czech in outlook, while
Francis Ferdinand, though obsessed with the need for the reform
of the Dual Monarchy on federalist lines, was no less German in
feeling, loyal to the alliance with Berlin, and at most eager to
reconstruct the traditional League of Germany and Austria
with Russia. Those who did not know these two facts had
a very distorted view of the old Austria.

A third instance of crass inaccuracy might be cited—his
belief in that notorious forgery, "The Protocols of the Elders
of Zion" (337): but this of course falls into a different category

of error, namely his frenzied hatred and denunciation of every-thing Jewish. It is indeed impossible to omit from this survey Hitler's attitude to the Jewish question, for it is the classic proof of his lack of balance. But I do not intend to dwell upon it with any wealth of detail, lest I should seem to be stressing what, however important it may be, is only a symptom or an illustration, and not the central argument.

Let it then suffice to say that throughout his book the Jew is treated as a mere parasite on the body of other peoples (334), as "the great master in lying" (335–86), as essentially "de-structive" (387) and lacking alike in self-sacrifice, idealism and creative qualities (331–2). The Jew, we are told, "never possessed a culture of his own" (330), and, as intolerance is a typically Jewish quality, Christianity was "the first spiritual Terror"—"in the much freer antique world" (507). Moreover, it is the aim of the Jew to undermine the importance of the person and to substitute that of the mass (498), and Bolshevism is "the Jewish bid for world-power" (751). Democracy, parliamen-tarianism, trade unionism and an uncontrolled press are all, in his idea, exploited by the Jew (347, 356), who is "working syste-matically for political and economic revolution" (357), in accordance with "his whole inmost plunder-loving brutality" (354). "The Jew is the real enemy" (628), "the pestilence in our blood" (629). This must suffice, but there are pages and pages of this: the Jew remains "King Charles's Head" through-out the long homily.

The two main tenets of the Hitlerian creed are "Race" and "Force": they are a strange amalgam, on the one hand from the writings of those two gifted national renegades, Count Gobineau and Houston Stewart Chamberlain,[1] and on the other from the philosophy of Hegel and Nietzsche, supplemented by Richard Wagner. Gobineau's main work, *The Inequality*

---

[1] The best summary of these ideas is to be found in Mr H. W. Steed's two illuminating little books: *Hitler; Whence and Whither?* (1934) and *The Meaning of Hitlerism* (2nd edition 1937), which also contains extracts from the almost incredible correspondence between Chamberlain and William II (*Briefe*, II, Munich 1928).

of Human Races, written in the 'fifties of last century, and
Chamberlain's *The Foundations of the Nineteenth Century*, first
published in 1899, both rest on a theory of racial purity such
as runs counter to the views of all serious anthropologists
throughout the world, and of the superiority of a more or less
imaginary "Aryan" race, of which the "Nordic" Teutons are
the backbone. Chamberlain established a contrast between the
Teuton and the Jew, the latter legalist, intolerant, incapable
of mystic or romantic ideas; and proceeded to depict (though
without providing anything that would pass as evidence) a
struggle inside the bosom of Christianity between the mummi-
fied Jewish beliefs and the Indo-Germanic conception of religion.
Our Lord Himself was represented as of Aramaic, non-Semitic
blood, coming as He did from the more or less Gentile country
of Galilee. Chamberlain had some remnants of restraint and
sanity, but the door was now open for more reckless theorists,
who would fain dismiss the whole Pauline theology as a Jewish
excrescence on the teachings of an Aryan Christ.

In Hitler the illusion of racial purity—in a Europe where the
facts of far-reaching racial intermixture in every country cannot
seriously be gainsaid—was linked up with the need for a scapegoat, and this was found in the Jew, as a parasite and essentially
alien element which must be eradicated from the body politic
before the process of pollution could spread any further. Once
accept this obsession, and no method of enforcement could
be too drastic. Meanwhile it is easy to see how the initial
obsession led on quite logically to two others. On the one hand
the Jew was blamed for the pacific trends of thought noticeable
in Christianity, while at the same time he is identified with
democratic, liberal and parliamentary institutions (347) and
Marxism is adduced as a proof of this. "The bourgeois world
is Marxist, but believes in the possibility of the rule of definite
bourgeois groups, while Marxism is itself planning to bring
the world into the hands of the Jews" (420).

Crossbreeding between two strains which are not entirely
equal, Hitler contends, is "contrary to the will of nature":
not a blend between higher and lower is the right solution,

but the complete victory of the former. "The stronger has to rule, and not to blend with the weaker and thus sacrifice his own greatness" (312). History, we are told, shows that every intermixture of Aryans with inferior peoples was fatal to the "Kulturträger" (313). "What is not good race in this world, is chaff" (324). "The sin against blood and race is the hereditary sin of this world, and the end of a humanity that surrenders to it" (272). The idea that man can overcome nature is "Jewish nonsense" (314). "Anyone who desired the victory of the pacifist idea in this world must aim at the conquest of the world by the Germans: for if the opposite happened, it might easily happen that with the last German the last pacifist would also die" (315). Less crude, perhaps, and certainly more convincing, is that other passage in which he advocates "a peace resting not on the palmbranches of tearful pacifist women, but on the victorious sword of a master-nation (*Herrenvolk*) which takes the world into the service of a higher culture" (438).

The *völkisch* outlook, as proclaimed by Hitler, starts from a denial of equality between races, and treats the State as merely the means to an end, but sees "the meaning of mankind in its original racial elements" (420–1) and claims that "culture and civilisation" on this planet are "inseparably bound up with the existence of the Aryan". In another passage he starts from a rejection of "the democratic mass-idea", and aims at winning the world for "the best nation, that is the highest men, and inside that nation establishing the aristocratic principle and building on the idea of personality, not of majority" (493). He denounces "the democracy of the West" as "the forerunner of Marxism, which would be unthinkable without it": its external form is "the absurd" institution of parliamentarism (85)—"an abortion of filth and fire"! "There is no principle which objectively regarded, is so wrong as the parliamentary" (92): it is "one of the gravest signs of human decay" (379), its influence is "baleful" (498), it is "madness" (661), and must be opposed with the utmost sharpness (659), and it stands in direct conflict with that truly Germanic, democratic conception, the idea of a freely elected leader, upon whom the full responsibility of action and inaction falls (99). His authority must be unrestricted: "Only the hero is qualified for the task" (379). "To be leader means to be able to move the masses" (650). It is one of the many contradictions of *Mein Kampf* that with all this, and despite his clear recognition of England as "the land of classic democracy" (81), his general tone towards England is frank and cordial, pouring scorn upon the false German pre-war estimates of this country. England, it is clear, remains an enigma to him: for at one time he writes of the Jew "still dictating in England" (721, 724), at another treats hatred against England as "the work of the Jewish press" (704).

If, then, the *völkisch* State is to be won "by a will of steel", through a unitary movement, the basis of its authority must be a combination of "popularity, force and tradition" (579). And it is to propaganda that Hitler attaches a capital importance: to him it is "a real art", capable of achieving "immense results" (193). Nothing could be more cynical, and at the same time more naïve, than the grounds on which he criticises German war propaganda. He is quite right in thinking that it showed a great lack of psychology (199), but he also seems to think that the essence of the problem is simply to obtain an absolute monopoly of news and distribution. "It would be best to lay war-guilt exclusively on the enemy, even if this did not correspond so entirely to the truth" (200); and again, "Propaganda is to be fitted to the masses, and its rightness is to be judged exclusively by its real effect" (376). And again, "By skilful and sustained use of propaganda one can make a people see even Heaven as Hell, or the most wretched life as paradise" (302). The aim of propaganda is, in his view, "to *force* a doctrine upon a whole people" (652) and "to break up the existing order and replace it by the new teaching" (654).

It is highly instructive to compare with this the contemporary view of Dr Goebbels, who regards "the people" as above all an instrument to be used and played upon. He writes of "the mystical consciousness of a mission and the inability of the people to comprehend this mission, much more to fulfil it".[1] "Propaganda", he maintained, "should not be in the least respectable (*soll gar nicht anständig sein*): nor should it be mild or humble: *it should be successful*."[2] "The question for propaganda is not whether it is on the right level, but whether it attains its end." "If a movement has the strength to conquer the state, then it also has the strength to reshape the state. Without propaganda the idea could never conquer the state." The secret of great ideas is that "they eat through like fire: if a movement has conquered political power, it can achieve something positive".[3] In other words, a series of skilful variations of the well-worn theme that the End justifies the Means: this is common ground for Hitler and Goebbels. One who knew the Führer intimately in former days assures me that his admiration for Machiavelli, which nothing could shake, rested above all on that poor opinion of human nature which is fundamental to them both, and which is found also in Mussolini.[4] Here is a powerful bond of union.

It is always dangerous to assume that what is good propaganda for one nation is necessarily so for another also; and it may be that on the one hand German opinion is so gullible, and on the other Dr Goebbels' propagandist efforts so all-pervading, that Abraham Lincoln's famous maxim "You can fool some people all the time, and most people some of the time, but not all the people all the time", has lost its validity for Germany. My personal experience in the Department of Enemy Propaganda under Lord Northcliffe, and that of all my colleagues, was that though a momentary effect could doubtless be obtained by misrepresentation, in the long run nothing was more destructive of the public confidence, and that what made British propaganda so successful during the summer of 1918 was that it was at last possible to publish the facts and let them speak for themselves. Today we have every few months abundant and glaring evidence of the complete indifference of the German Ministry of Propaganda to accuracy or consistency of statement

[1] *Signale der Neuen Zeit*, p. 14.
[2] *Ibid.* p. 29: 9 January 1928.   [3] *Ibid.* pp. 48, 39, 34.
[4] See *supra*, p. 164.

(the lying campaigns against Czechoslovakia as a Bolshevist state, the periodic intimidation of Austria, the suppression of the facts about Guernica or the Italian "volunteers", are only the most outstanding examples). But whether the German public has yet reached the stage when it believes nothing that it sees in print, or whether in the event of war it would accept all that was laid before it, are questions which are better left unanswered.

Certain it is that whatever view may be taken of the Treaty of Versailles, Hitler came to power on the basis of persistent and rabid misrepresentation of the post-war facts. Only a public opinion which had altogether lost its mental balance could have accepted such extravagant allegations as that the Weimar Republic aimed "not at Order, but plunder"; that the real organiser of the revolution was "the international Jew" and its supporters consisted of "thieves, burglars, deserters and profiteers" (584); that the new State "unconditionally crept to the Cross before Marxism" (599); or again to write of "the international Slave State" or "the present Jewish democratic Reich" (642), or to describe it as a Jewish interest "that the *völkisch* movement should bleed away in a religious struggle" (632). As today press freedom is non-existent save for the adherents of the regime, all these and similar theories circulate unchecked: and their chief propagator is the Führer himself, in the three million copies of his book. It is at this stage that we may quote his illuminating phrase: "The aim of a political reform movement is never attained by educational work or by influencing the ruling forces, *but only by acquiring political power*" (377).

HITLER ON FOREIGN POLICY

Let us turn to Hitler's ideas of foreign policy, as laid down in *Mein Kampf*. He started by assuming great confusion in the conduct of German policy, and dismisses the masses as a mere "herd of stupid sheep".[1] Germany's aim must be to recover her freedom and to further her own nationhood (*Volkstum*)

---

[1] *Die grosse stupide Hammelherde unseres schafsgeduldigen Volkes* (689).

and she must realise that oppressed people cannot be set free, or provinces recovered, by flaming protests or by the wish of those concerned, but only by power (*Machtmittel*) and by "a strong sword". "To forge this sword is the task of a people's leaders at home: to assure the work of forging and to seek comrades in arms, is the task of foreign policy" (689).

Looking back upon pre-war Germany, he considers her to have had a choice of four policies. The first was to avert over-population by artificial restrictions, and this he rejects as contrary to nature, and ruinous to Germany's future. The second was to concentrate on "internal colonisation": this again he rejects on the ground that "Nature knows no political frontiers" (147), and that "mankind grew great in eternal conflict, in eternal peace it perishes" (149). The other two courses were to acquire fresh land for the surplus millions of the population, or to develop industry and trade for others' needs and to live upon the profits—in other words, a land policy (*Bodenpolitik*) or a colonial and trade policy. In throwing his weight in favour of the third of these, he makes it quite clear that Germany cannot find the additional land which she requires, "in the Cameroons, but today almost exclusively in Europe" (152). Moreover, if one wanted land (*Grund und Boden*) in Europe, this could, on the whole, only be done at the expense of Russia, and the new Reich "must again march along the road of the former Teutonic Knights, in order to win with the German sword soil for the German plough, and for the nation its daily bread" (154). This aim, he argues, was only attainable before the war through an alliance with England, based on a renunciation of world trade, colonies and war-fleet: to win her over "no sacrifice was too great". If Germany had taken the place of Japan in 1904, there would have been no world war, the fatal alliance with that "mummy of a state", Austria, would have been avoided, and Germany's position in the world would be very different. If, on the other hand, a colonial and world policy were decided upon, then Russia's alliance against England was essential, and Austria should have been thrown over as quickly as possible (157).

This conception figures early in Hitler's first volume, written in 1924: in the second volume, written five years later, it has been elaborated still further. The Second Reich is condemned as having chosen "the worst of four courses": and a sound European land policy (*Bodenpolitik*) is enunciated as the true goal of that Third Reich of which he already dreams. That a community should subordinate all other tasks to "the preparation of a coming war for the subsequent safeguarding of the state", is a situation for which he finds analogies in the Persian and Punic Wars, and in the military policy of Frederick the Great's father.[1] And Germany must "never tolerate the rise of two Continental Powers in Europe", and must "by all means prevent the establishment of a second military Power on her frontiers" (754).

The main problem, then, is how to find allies: and here we note the Hitlerian definition, that "an alliance whose aim does not comprise the intention of a war, is senseless and worthless" (749). France he at once rules out: she "is, and remains, the irreconcilable arch-enemy of the German people", whether under Bourbon, Jacobin, Napoleonic, Republican or Bolshevik rule (699). She wants to split up Germany: "her intentions towards us will never change" (765). But she is slowly dying out (766), and falling more and more a prey to "negroising" (*Vernegerung*)[2] and Jewish world aims (704, 730). In the long run Germany must aim at "a final reckoning with France"—"somehow or other" (*so oder so*)—and to this end the arch-enemy must be isolated (755, 757). But the annihila-

---

[1] In passing, he finds no hope of this among "the fathers of our democratic parliamentary nonsense, of Jewish brand" (690).

[2] Compare with this a passage in Alfred Rosenberg's *Der Mythus des XX. Jahrhunderts*, p. 103: "Whole districts in the South [of France] are altogether dead and are already drawing Africans to them as Rome once did. Toulon and Marseilles send fresh seeds of bastardization into the country. Round Notre Dame de Paris floats a population in ever-increasing decay. Negroes and mulattos go on the arm of white women, a purely Jewish quarter is rising, with new synagogues. Revolting hybrid upstarts poison the race of still beautiful women which are being beguiled to Paris from all France", etc. etc.

tion of France is only a means towards ensuring the possibility of expansion in another direction (766). Here his views would seem to coincide with that school of military thought which considers that a full-fledged adventure in Eastern Europe can only be risked with any safety, *after* French power has been crushed in the West.

Where, then, can Germany find allies? Not in such "decaying state corpses" as those to whom she was allied in the last war (756), but in Britain and Italy, two healthy and expanding organisms, neither of whom desire a French hegemony in Europe (697, 705). Such an alliance, which could not be prevented by France, would free Germany from her present awkward strategic position, and enable her to pursue "the most sacred right in this world, the right to soil" (754). "Sufficient space" (*Raum*), "more land" (*Grund und Boden*)— these must be the aims of National Socialism. "State frontiers are made by men, and altered by men." The true solution lies, not in colonies, but exclusively in acquiring a colonial territory "such as will enlarge the area of the motherland" (741). In other words, the Germans are to abandon their pre-war policy and not to trouble too much about the old haphazard frontiers of 1914, which "mean nothing for the future of Germany" (738). Far rather, "We are to start again where we ended six centuries ago. We stop the eternal trail (*Germanenzug*) to the South and West of Europe, and turn our glances to the land in the East. We at last end the colonial and trade policy of the pre-war era, and take up the land policy of the future. But if today in Europe we talk of new land" (*Grund und Boden* is the constant phrase), "we can in the first instance think only of Russia and the border states subject to her.... Our mission is in the industrious work of the German plough, to which the sword only has to give the soil" (742–3). "Ostpolitik", then, means "the acquisition of the necessary soil for our German people", and so the out-distancing of France and the final reckoning with her (757, 766). For "today we have 80,000,000 Germans in Europe", but within a century there must be "250,000,000 Germans on this Continent, not cooped up like factory coolies, but as peasants and workmen, assuring each others' existence by their mutual work" (767). A state, so runs his conclusion, which in the era of race poisoning devotes itself to cultivating its best racial elements, "must one day become master of the earth" (782).

"WE COME AS ENEMIES"

That *Mein Kampf* was the repository of Adolf Hitler's whole political creed at the moment of his access to power, and that his followers, in voting for him in 1932–3, accepted that creed, cannot seriously be denied: and the Nazis themselves openly proclaim it as being still the most authoritative statement of Nazi policy. That a nation till recently the most cultured in the world should be unable, or unwilling, or afraid, to criticise a book so full of crude overstatement, and inflammatory violence, is the best proof of its own unbalanced state.

It remains for us to consider whether five years of responsibility have led the Führer to modify any of the views expressed in *Mein Kampf*, to compare them with his later public utterances, and so to reach clarity as to the main aims of his foreign policy and his true attitude towards Britain and other Powers.

The year 1933 saw the downfall of the Weimar regime, and the rapid transformation of Germany into a centralised, totalitarian and increasingly anti-Christian state. Hitler's success was due to a combination of many causes—an inferiority complex on the part of large numbers of Germans (and of this he himself was the supreme expression, even when he was most insistent upon Germany's renewed self-confidence); the effects of the long, unbridled agitation against the Treaties and the West's foolish refusal to take this fundamental question seriously; the alternate intransigeance and yieldingness of the Allies, and their constant disagreements among themselves; the grave economic crisis, acting with treble force upon classes already reduced to ruin or penury by the collapse of the Mark; the inevitably abrupt termination of those foreign loans by which alone Germany had financed herself for some years past; and last, but not least, a number of personal factors, such as the extreme age and political inexperience of the President von Hindenburg and his entourage, and the rival intrigues of the "Bureau-General" von Schleicher and of Herr von Papen, once the organiser of German war espionage and sabotage in America, but latterly the political champion of German Catholicism. One further indispensable ingredient must be added to the salad: it is well known that enormous sums were placed at the disposal of National Socialism by many of the great industrialists of the Rhine and elsewhere, who saw in the new movement a convenient counter at once to Communism and to the reparation settlement, but were too shortsighted to realise that it would one day dragoon them no less effectually than the trade unions, and that events would drive the regime of their choice ever more and more in the direction of the "inverted Bolshevism" which follows logically wherever the individual is made a mere pawn of the all-powerful State. It will probably never be known what practical form the assistance of men like Kirdorf, Thyssen, Hugenberg, Vogler assumed, and how far it contributed to the Nazi triumph: still less likely is it that the persistent allegations of foreign financial help will ever be clearly established. If, however, all these varied threads be woven together, it might doubtless be argued that they form a vast pattern in the web of fate and are far from being merely accidental.

The short-sighted folly of those who helped the National Socialists into power can hardly be exaggerated. They had abundant warnings: for no one at any rate can say that Hitler and his immediate entourage lacked the courage of their opinions. They were outspoken to the last degree, as may best be seen from their fighting organ *Der Angriff*, which Dr Goebbels, when he came to power, judged worthy of reproduction in book form, lest there should be any doubt upon the matter. Here week by week the leaders of the Nazi movement preached Revolution and proclaimed that they came "not to uphold what is falling, but to give a further shove", to produce "a new spiritual and political attitude tending in other directions". "We are an anti-parliamentary party, rejecting the Weimar Constitution and its republican institutions, we are opponents of a sham democracy which treats the clever and foolish alike, we see in the present system of majority votes and organised irresponsibility the main cause of our steadily growing decay.... We enter Parliament in order to supply ourselves, in the arsenal of democracy, with its own weapons, to paralyse the Weimar sentiment with its own assistance. If democracy is so stupid as to give us free tickets and salaries for this purpose, that is its affair.... *We come as enemies. As the wolf bursts into the flock, so we come.*" And in particular he repudiated "the Young-Slavery", which "Black-Red-Yellow Marxists" accepted, and he declined all share in the "catastrophe which is approaching with uncanny certainty". To him and to the fanatics around him "the magic of Hitler's word breaks down all resistance: he divides the hot from the cold, but the luke-warm he spues out of his mouth".[1]

The fierce intolerant *élan* of the Nazi regime as it swung itself into the saddle caused acute alarm on every frontier, and nowhere more than in Soviet Russia. As we saw, there was no immediate break between Berlin and Moscow; for a time trade actually increased, and the cryptic relations of the two Staffs continued. But friction grew very rapidly, owing to the repression of the Communist Party in Germany. Dimitrov, the Bulgarian communist who was accused of a share in the burning of the Reichstag, owed his release mainly to Moscow's efforts, was appointed to a post in the Comintern headquarters and became an active centre of anti-German propaganda all over Europe. Quite apart from this, however, Moscow took very seriously the Führer's openly avowed designs upon Russian territory, and was naturally confirmed in this view when he appointed the Baltic German Dr Alfred Rosenberg—an equally rabid enemy of Russia and of Jewry, and author of that extraordinary outburst of Nordic heathenism *The Myth of the Twentieth Century*—as Chief of the Foreign Department of the Nazi Party. Russia was swift to draw the natural conclusions,

[1] *Der Angriff*, pp. 96, 47, 71, 141, 217.

and to escape from the isolation which she had hitherto courted, by damping down her propaganda abroad and making common cause with France.

If the advent of Hitler had the effect of bringing Russia back to Europe (especially to Paris and Geneva), it also gravely affected the position of Poland. Polish policy since the liberation had rested upon three points—a resolve to correct as far as possible the fatal handicap of open frontiers both on east and west, to maintain her access to the sea, and to prevent Polish territory from again becoming a theatre of war between foreign Powers. Since 1920 Poland had fancied herself to be a Great Power between two unarmed giants, but with every year it was now becoming painfully evident that she was only a medium Power between two giants engaged upon rearmament on a scale beyond her strength. Marshal Pilsudski in 1933 was still in a position to call a halt to Nazi designs on Danzig and to confront Herr Hitler with a choice between war and peace. The Führer "could not afford to fight, so he offered a treaty of non-aggression instead". Poland thus obtained a respite of ten years against German propaganda, and reduced her dependance upon French aid, while at the same time avenging what to her had seemed to be French disregard for Polish interests both in the Pact of Locarno and in the Four Power Pact. The Polish-German Pact of 26 January 1934 was quite insincere on both sides, yet Poland cannot be blamed for an experiment which at worst would postpone the final struggle, and at best might enable mutual animosities to calm down. She skilfully extracted, as the price of her support for Russia's admission to the League, a pledge not to support at Geneva the claims of the minorities inside Poland: but she also made the capital blunder of withdrawing her recognition of the League's right to deal with Polish minority questions. She was thus adding to her previous defiance of the League in the questions of Eastern Galicia and Wilna a gross violation of her Minorities Treaty, and creating a highly dangerous precedent. Nothing, however, can alter for Poland the fundamental necessity of maintaining a balance between Germany and Russia.

Compared with this, her attitude towards Geneva is entirely secondary.[1]

At this early stage the Führer's eyes were especially directed towards his own country of origin, Austria, where a militant, and often openly terrorist, form of National Socialism was vigorously financed from the Reich and encouraged in the press and on the wireless. An already dangerous situation was still further complicated by the attitude of Mussolini, who did not wish to see the Germans on the Brenner, and supported the Heimwehr (the private army of the Austrian Clericals) as the best focus of resistance to Nazi penetration. But his general antipathy to Socialism blinded him to the peculiar triangular character of Austrian politics, in which the pre-war division of Christian Socialist, Social Democrat and Pan-German still survived in the almost equally balanced forces of Clerical, Socialist and Nazi, with the result that some kind of working alliance between the first two was the most obvious and safest means of preventing the Anschluss. The forcible and illegal overthrow of Viennese Socialism in February 1934 by the Heimwehr acting under the direct inspiration of Mussolini rendered any such alliance for the time being impossible, left his ally Chancellor Dollfuss in a very dangerous minority, and plunged the Austrian working classes into a mood of bitter negation. This directly encouraged the Nazis of the Reich, working under two refugees from Austria, Habicht and Frauenfeld, and their well-armed "Austrian Legion", to further efforts: and the Putsch of 25 July 1934, in which Dr Dollfuss was brutally murdered, came within an ace of success. It is true that the ring-leaders in Vienna showed themselves as inept as they were brutal, and that the revolt in Styria fizzled out miserably: it is true also that while Europe expressed its horror in conversation, Mussolini massed troops on the Brenner. But it may be doubted whether, if the coup had succeeded, and if the traitor Rintelen had carried out the "Gleichschaltung" of

[1] See two important articles on "The Foreign Policy of Poland", by "Argus" in the *Slavonic Review*, No. 44 (January 1937), and by M. Smogorzewski, *ibid.* No. 48 (April 1938).

Austria, and perhaps even staged a triumphal entry of Hitler into Vienna, Italy would have been able to reverse the accomplished fact. If war had come under those circumstances, Jugoslavia would almost certainly have been involved on the opposite side from Italy, and no one can estimate the complications that might have ensued. Fortunately those forces in Germany to whom the double initiative of Thirtieth June and Twenty-fifth July may be traced, had for the moment shot their bolt; it seemed advisable to humour the outraged opinion of Europe: the crisis of President Hindenburg's last illness absorbed Hitler's attention: the paramount task was to consolidate and entrench the Führer's position. Austria was put back into cold storage and left to experiment with the "Christian Corporate State": what external impulsion had failed to achieve would come a little later by spontaneous action from within.

It was indeed high time that an attempt should be made to convince Europe that the violence of the internal regime did not of necessity mean a breach of European peace. From the first moment of taking power, it is but fair to say, Hitler had struck a more moderate note in his references to foreign policy. His opening broadcast had announced a double Four-Year Plan, to restore the German peasant to prosperity and to solve the question of unemployment: after four years "the nation can do what it likes with me—crucify me if it will". His first press statement declared that it was no mere change of government, but of regime, and defined as its first task the extermination of Communism: and the means adopted were the arrest of all Communist deputies and a decree of 28 February suspending freedom of the person, press and assembly, and inviolability of post, telegraph and domicile. Goebbels, on his appointment as Minister for Propaganda, spoke of the third estate as a piano on which the Ministry can play: while Göring, who supplied the S.A. formations with arms, and refused official protection to the Jews, announced that the spirit of Potsdam had overcome the spirit of Weimar. But Hitler, in his speech of 23 March, was distinctly conciliatory. It was his sincere desire to refrain from increased armaments if foreign countries were willing to carry out their obligations to disarm. Three things, in his opinion, were needed to solve the world crisis—a political regime of unchallengeable authority in Germany, a long-term consolidation of peace by agreement between "the really great national Powers", and the victory of reason in economic relations, combined with relief from reparations and debts. He was "ready to hold out the hand in a spirit of sincere under-standing to every nation which is prepared to wipe the slate clean from the sad past": and incidentally he also desired friendly relations with Russia, on the basis that the fight against Com-munism was a purely internal affair. Such phrases were in themselves reassuring, but to alarmed foreign opinion they could not outweigh the daily practice of Nazi intolerance in suppressing all political and cultural liberties. Early in April, for instance, Dr Goebbels, in announcing a twenty-four hours' boycott of Jewish shops, added the warning that if the campaign against Germany abroad were not stopped, and if the boycott had therefore to be resumed, it would be done "in a manner calculated to destroy German Jewry". And meanwhile the new "German Christian" movement in the Protestant Church began to demand the abolition of the Old Testament and the substitution of German sagas and legends, while its leaders insisted that Christ was not a Jew and that Christianity was born of a struggle against Judaism. Sir Austen Chamberlain voiced a widespread feeling in Britain, when he spoke of recent official utterances in Germany as revealing "a spirit which we hoped had departed from this world". "Germany", he told the House of Commons on 13 April, "is afflicted by this narrow, exclusive, aggressive spirit, where it is a crime to be in favour of peace, and a crime to be a Jew. This is not a Germany to which we can afford to make concessions." When Hitler on 23 April affirmed "a policy of peace...but not as a second class nation", British opinion accepted this as reasonable, and showed critical impatience at the deadlock at Geneva in the question of dis-armament. On the other hand, the Foreign Minister, Baron Neurath's warning on 11 May that Germany would rearm if no agreement were reached, and Vice-Chancellor von Papen's declaration that "Germany on 30 January 1933 struck the word pacifism from its vocabulary", seemed to confirm all the worst misgivings.

HITLER'S FIRST REICHSTAG SPEECH

It was with a view to arresting Germany's complete isolation in Europe, that Herr Hitler made his first big speech on foreign policy in the Reichstag. It opened with a measured denunciation of Versailles as a shortsighted settlement and of reparation policy as suicide: "the international economic crisis is absolute proof of the correctness of this assertion". "The treaty is no solution of the world's problems, but *nevertheless no German Government will of its own accord break an arrangement without being able first to supplant it by a better one.*" Germany demanded general disarmament, but asked nothing that she was not prepared to give to others: yet the equality promised to her had not been realised. "No fresh European war is capable of substituting something better for the unsatisfactory conditions of today:... new wars and sacrifices, new uncertainties and economic distress would be the result. The outbreak of such madness would lead to the collapse of the existing social order in Europe."

He then argued that general disarmament rested on right and commonsense, and was laid down in the Peace Treaty. Germany as well as France was entitled to security, after assuming all the obligations of Versailles, the Kellogg Pact and arbitration agreements: but she was "at any time ready to assume further international security obligations, if all nations are prepared to do so", and if not, she must at least claim equality. She would accept a *general* control of armaments, and even "prohibition of weapons" if others favoured it, and here the Chancellor endorsed President Roosevelt's view that "*without a solution of the disarmament problem, no permanent economic recuperation was possible*". The one great task was "to assure the peace of the world", and Germany desired a peaceful settlement of all difficult questions. But she would never "be forced into any kind of signature which would signify the perpetuation of her degradation....As a permanently defamed people, it would be very difficult for us to continue to belong to the League of Nations." After quoting the 224,000 German suicides of the post-war period as "accusers against the spirit of the Peace Treaty", he ended by declaring that *"Germany will tread no other path than that laid down by the Peace Treaties"*, and has *"no thought of invading any country"*.

There can be no doubt that this speech for a time greatly eased the tenseness of the European situation. With many anxious listeners its unexpected tone of sweet reasonableness and moderation outweighed the contrast between its words and the grim realities of the internal situation, and they were eager, only too eager, to believe that these words were as real and as seriously meant, as the parallel process of German rearmament, on which French eyes were steadily set. But in view of what has happened since—the unilateral repudiation of one pledge after another, of voluntary pledges in speeches no less than of what might be called the involuntary pledges of Versailles and Locarno—the reader is invited to keep carefully in mind our quotations, for comparison with German *action* between 1933 and 1937.

HITLER LEAVES THE LEAGUE

For the four summer months there was comparative calm, and then on 14 October 1933 Germany withdrew both from the Disarmament Conference and from the League itself. This step was taken on the very day when Sir John Simon, as British Foreign Secretary, made an important statement at Geneva, intended to promote a compromise between the divergent French and German points of view: and it is difficult to avoid the conclusion that the discourtesy was deliberate, since it was aimed at the very Power which had made the greatest efforts for an escape from the deadlock. Herr Hitler on the radio renewed his attack on Versailles, but appealed for an end to the long feud with France, insisting that there were no grounds for a territorial conflict, and that only a madman would think of a Franco-German war when once the Saar had been restored. Baron Neurath made very blunt allusions to Sir John Simon's "impossible plan" and to the inaccuracy of his assertions, and "energetically" rejected "any attempt to shift on to us a responsibility which rests on others".[1] Simon quite effectively replied that Britain, at any rate, had reduced her armaments "to the edge of risk", and refused to accept the reasons given for Germany's withdrawal. On 8 November Hitler made a short radio speech declaring that "the League will never see us again till the last vestige of discrimination is removed", but that the Germans were not crazy enough to want war, but "work, peace and happiness". When, he asked, had the German people ever broken its word? Versailles rested on the two false theses that the victors were always in the right, and that the worse things were for one nation, the better they were for another. As regards "differential rights", there was no real difference between the theories of class warfare and of international warfare.

Hitler was now completely isolated in Europe, and hence the suggestion of a Pact with Poland was much more welcome to him than might have been expected. It is true that it was virtually imposed upon him by Marshal Pilsudski at a time when Poland was as yet more heavily armed, but both men realised the political value of a ten years' truce. Which of the two would gain most in the end could not be foreseen, but nothing was actually renounced on either side, and meanwhile each could look elsewhere, Poland scanning the eastern horizon, Hitler dreaming of an entry into Linz and Vienna. For Hitler it was the first of a long series of theatrical *coups* in foreign policy, calculated to assure German public opinion of his resolve to uphold the Reich's prestige abroad. In his Reichstag speech of 30 January 1934 he claimed it as proving his pacific aims. It was for every nation to choose its own form of State, and he desired friendly relations with everyone—Russia also: here we see that he had not yet abandoned what may be called the

[1] See *Survey of International Affairs* for 1933, pp. 307-9, *Manchester Guardian*, 17 October 1933.

Rapallo phase of Russo-German relations, and is still far from the unmeasured denunciations of his later career.

This speech also contains two interesting references to Austria and to France. With the first he frankly admits bad relations, while denying that the blame lies with Germany. "An idea which has stirred the German people to its depths, could not stop at the frontiers of a country which was for centuries an integral part of the Empire." To France he addressed yet another appeal. If France feared for her security, no one in Germany wished to threaten it, and he was ready to do everything to prove that the Saar question was the only territorial question still open between the two nations. Once it was settled, *Germany would accept not only the letter, but above all the spirit of Locarno.* In the light of the events following the Saar settlement in 1935, it is essential to keep this phrase clearly in our minds.

With the complicated disarmament negotiations of the winter of 1933–4 it is quite impossible to deal within our present limits. Certain it is that deep divergences of view between London and Paris were the main cause of the virtual deadlock that ensued. During Mr Eden's visit to Berlin in February Germany offered to waive her claim to all "offensive weapons", to accept control of the S.A. and S.S. as well as of the regular army, and to accept any limit for the latter which was also accepted for the French, Italian and Polish armies: but she insisted upon an air force at least half as strong as that of France. To London, as so much the least intransigeant of the Western Powers, there presented itself, in a form that could not long be evaded even by the weakest Minister, an uncomfortable dilemma between the rigid French protest against "the legalisation of German rearmament" and Germany's more and more open threat of repudiation, on the approved lines of the Nordic hero,

Und gehst du nicht willig, so brauch' ich Gewalt.

In passing, however, it is important to note that Germany, in her answer of 18 March to the French Memorandum, stated that she had *never questioned the validity of Locarno.*

GERMANY REARMS

At the end of March two events occurred which destroyed the last chance of the all too rigid Barthou adopting a more accommodating attitude. Herr Hitler, speaking at Munich, said that the German boundaries had always fluctuated and would continue to change until all German peoples were united— a confusion of the conceptions of "state" and "nation" of which the world was to hear more and more in the ambiguous form of the doctrine of *Volkstum*.[1] The full significance of this pronouncement passed almost unnoticed at the time among the slow-thinking British, but profoundly alarmed the more vigilant and suspicious French. Much more serious were the German Budget figures, which became known only a few days later (in parenthesis be it said that since 1934 the German dictatorship has withheld the facts of German expenditure from the nation and from the world at large). These showed an increase of 357,000,000 Reichsmark in armament estimates: and the curt explanatory Note sent from Berlin on 11 April, in answer to London's request for information, "did nothing to allay apprehensions",[2] and indeed set French public opinion still further on edge. For, while accepting international control of the S.A. and S.S. and the postponement for five years of the actual disarmament of other Powers (this seemed a real concession), Germany insisted on a short-term army of 300,000 men, and flatly refused to wait two years for a defensive air-force. The essence of the German argument was that further money was needed for "the conversion of the Reichswehr into a short-service army": and an instructive commentary was provided by Herr Hitler's categorical statement of 29 March to the Associated Press: "I have no intention of accepting an army of 250,000 men, and in no circumstances shall I submit to the orders of anybody." Not even the most ostrich-like temperament could now fail to realise that the process of German rearmament was already in full swing, following upon that

---

[1] See *infra*, p. 384.   [2] *Survey for 1935*, p. 26.

"remarkable intensification and improvement in the methods of forming, disciplining, controlling, uniforming and organising man-power since National Socialism came into power", on which the Berlin Correspondent of *The Times* laid suitable stress.[1] On 17 April, then, France broke off the discussion: the Disarmament Conference, though it might still meet at intervals, was really at an end, and Europe was in the throes of a new armament race which was utterly to eclipse all precedents. In Professor Carr's words, "the vicious circle which the statesmen of 1919 had hoped to break was once more complete. The return to Power Politics which had first declared itself in 1931 in the Far East, spread in 1933 over all the world."[2]

Baron Neurath's unconciliatory statement of 9 April is a fitting close to this section. Germany, he claimed, had fulfilled the Treaties to the letter, but the corresponding obligation of general disarmament had not been fulfilled. "*Germany had never aimed at unilateral decisions*": she was still ready to agree, but there must be an end to ultimata and dictation. He hoped that other Governments would still avail themselves of "the great chance" offered to them.

THE THIRTIETH JUNE

During the first eighteen months of the National Socialist regime, which we have very briefly surveyed from the angle of foreign policy, there was inside Germany a growing trial of strength between the two very divergent groups which had brought it to power. As we saw, Hindenburg and his entourage, in calling Hitler to office, had done so on a coalition basis, calculating that he would supply a certain fanatical driving force and demagogic enthusiasm to the Nationalist cause, but that he would soon become the more or less willing prisoner of the Right. In this they misjudged alike the power of the available brakes, their own power to apply them and above all Hitler's passion for power, his complete ruthlessness towards

[1] "The Arming of Germany, I," 23 January 1934.
[2] *International Relations*, p. 190.

former friends and his real genius as a political tactician, living by periodic *coups* and always on the watch for the right moment at which to launch them. Within six months the Nationalists, instead of dominating the Cabinet, had been relegated to the background: Hugenberg and other ladders by which Hitler had climbed to power were kicked from under him, and Papen found himself on the defensive. But the struggle for power went on, the real issue, apart from personalities, being whether the main stress should be laid on "Nationalist" or on "Socialist" in the programme of the regime. Men like Röhm, the S.A. leader, and Gregor Strasser, the real organiser of Nazism in North Germany, put forward the view that Hitler's advent to power was merely the first stage in a revolutionary process, rendered acute by vast unemployment, parallel rise of prices and fall of wages, and the growing shortage of raw materials, and to the very last they seem to have believed that they would carry the Führer with them. Otto Strasser, on the other hand, whose demand was a simultaneous assault upon "bourgeois capitalism" and "international Marxism", had as early as 1930 broken with Hitler, because he realised him to be essentially reactionary, wedded to the old regime and without any belief in the progress or reformability of mankind.[1] Already on 1 July 1933 Hitler, in a speech at Reichenhall, declared that the first three stages of the Revolution (preparation, seizure of power and totalitarianism) were now past, that order was now the chief requisite, and that the idea of a Second Revolution, or a "revolution in permanence", could not be tolerated. But the Left of the Party continued its agitation, Hitler balancing between them and those two new planets, Goebbels and Göring, the organisers of propaganda and terror respectively. The quarrel between the rival factions may be said to have culminated in Röhm's speech of 18 April 1934, before the diplomatic corps and foreign journalists, in which he declared that the movement was "not a nationalist, but a National

[1] One of the most interesting documents of the Nazi Revolution is Appendix III of Otto Strasser's *Aufbau des deutschen Sozialismus*, entitled "Meine Aussprache mit Hitler" (21–22 May 1930), pp. 116–36.

Socialist revolution, with special stress on the word 'Socialist'....
There are still men in official positions today who have not the
least idea of the spirit of the revolution. We shall ruthlessly
get rid of them, if they dare to put their reactionary ideas into
practice."

The challenge was speedily taken up from two different
sides. Hitler, with the approval of Hindenburg, sent Röhm
on leave on 7 June, and thus took the first step towards the dissolution of the powerful S.A., which in Röhm's mind already
figured as a more radical military force, destined to force the
hands of the Conservative Reichswehr. Then, encouraged by
this, and believing that his connections with the President would
enable him to turn the scale, Herr von Papen made a speech
at Marburg on 17 June. Here he emphasised the new regime's
alliance with "the Conservative forces", the need for clearing
away "the refuse" (*Schacken*) that remained as the revolutionary
enthusiasm died down, and also for "silencing doctrinaire
fanatics", and the doubt whether the rule of a single party
could be more than a transitional feature. "For", he went on,
"no people can achieve permanent insurrection from below....
The time must come when the movement ends and a solid
social structure...is created. Dynamics cannot be permanent.
Germany must not become a march into the blue, of which
no one knows when it is to stop." And again, the idea of
a second revolution "might easily produce a third, and those
who threaten with the guillotine are the first to fall under the
axe".

To the very last Hitler played off these two rival tendencies
against each other, and then on the memorable Thirtieth of June
he struck. Once more, it would lead far beyond our present
purpose to attempt a narrative of that event: it must suffice to
concentrate upon certain salient features.

I. The number of victims will probably never be known.
At first stringent attempts were made to conceal certain names,
and some very distinguished names have never been published
in the German press. On 7 July an official statement put the
total at under 50; on 13 July the Führer himself in the Reichstag

admitted 77;[1] Herr Otto Strasser has published a list of 109 names (with 11 additional queries);[2] and there is reason to believe that a list running into four figures exists in Berlin.

II. The known victims fall into four main categories: (a) 59 S.A. and S.S. leaders, notably their Chief of Staff, Ernst Röhm, Heines, Ernst and Heydebreck; (b) political opponents—notably the ex-Chancellor General von Schleicher and his wife, and Gregor Strasser, either of whom was a possible candidate for the Chancellorship; (c) leading Bavarian politicians—notably the ex-Premier von Kahr, an old man of seventy-three, Dr Hein, founder of the People's Party, and two ex-Ministers; (d) leading German Catholics, notably Dr Klausener and Dr Beck, heads of the "Katholische Aktion" in Berlin and Munich; the Franciscan Father Stempfle; Probst, the head of the Catholic Youth movement in the Rhineland; Huber, the leader of the Catholic Students; Baron Guttenberg, the Bavarian Monarchist leader, and von Bose and von der Decken, the two Chefs de Cabinet of Herr von Papen himself. Schleicher was shot from behind as he sat at his desk and his wife shared his fate: Klausener was shot down in a Government office as he reached for his hat, and was not allowed by his murderers to see a priest, and the false story was officially published in Germany that he had committed suicide (which as a Catholic he could not have done): von Kahr and others were spirited away by car and murdered on a moor near Dachau: Strasser's death first became known to his family when his ashes were delivered in a parcel at the door: Willi Schmidt, a Munich musical critic, was murdered in mistake for another man of the same name. The practice of cremating the victims made many awkward enquiries impossible. Other significant details were the removal of the

---

[1] His own account is: 19 higher S.A. leaders, 31 other leaders and members; 3 S.S. men; 13 who resisted, 2 who committed suicide; 5 persons not belonging to either organisation; and 3 S.S. leaders, for gross ill-treatment of prisoners.

[2] *Die Deutsche Bartolomäusnacht*, pp. 237–41. This book, by the founder of the so-called "Black Front", a brother of Gregor Strasser, is much the most vivid and detailed account of The Thirtieth of June, resting as it does on first-hand secret information.

family lawyers of both Strasser and Röhm, and therefore of their private *dossiers* also, and again of the proprietor and two head-waiters of the Munich restaurant where Hitler, Goebbels, and other Nazi leaders used to confer in a private room. Only a fortunate accident saved ex-Chancellor Brüning and Herr Treviranus from a similar fate, and it gradually became known that even Herr von Papen's life was for a time in danger.[1]

III. The indictment against them, as brought by Hitler himself in his Reichstag defence, was to the effect that the "conspirators" looked on the existing system as untenable, and considered it necessary to bring the Army and other military formations under one hand, and to replace the reactionary Papen by the "progressive" Schleicher. No one could call this treasonable, even on the Nazi showing: and it is quite impossible to fit such charges to persons so utterly different and so out of touch with each other as Röhm, Kahr, Hein, Bredow, Bose and still more the Catholic victims. Not an atom of evidence was ever produced, either by Hitler or by anyone else, to prove that Hitler's life was in danger: and indeed most of the scanty information available points towards a pathetic last-moment belief on the part of men like Röhm or Ernst, that Hitler was on their side and was being duped by his and their enemies. Göring, who openly assured the public that he had "not worn mittens", and who had a free hand in Berlin while Hitler was busy at Munich headquarters, made a concrete charge of treason against Schleicher, who was, however, over a year later publicly rehabilitated by Field Marshal von Mackensen in presence of many high generals. Before the Reichstag, however, Hitler had taken the high and utterly unreasonable line, "If three traitors in Germany" (here he begs the question) "have a meeting with a foreign statesman,

[1] A terrifying document, throwing light upon the "rounding-up" methods employed on 30 June, will be found in Nos. 16 and 17 of *Die deutsche Revolution* (the organ of the "Black Front" of Otto Strasser). It is entitled "Geständnisse eines Gestapo-Mörders" and contains the detailed confession of a certain Erasmus Reichel, an Austrian by birth, who joined the S.S. but eventually fled from Germany.

which they conceal from me, then I have such men shot, even if it be true that they only talked of the weather, old caps and so on". Here spoke the omnipotent dictator, whose contempt for all law and precedent culminated in the terrifying sentence: *"In those twenty-four hours the Supreme Court of the German people was I."* After this it causes no surprise that he should have protested against the suggestion "that only legal proceedings could have produced a just estimate of guilt and atonement....I have not to investigate whether and which of these conspirators, agitators, destroyers and well-poisoners of German public opinion met too harsh a fate: I only have to watch that the fate of Germany can be borne."[1] Here is the same straight issue as in an oft-quoted conversation between Hitler and Otto Strasser, when the former claimed that "with us Leader and Idea are one, and every member of the Party has to do what the Leader commands", and the latter answered in the words of Luther, "Here I stand: I can no other". And the reader, remembering that Luther is truer to the German type than Hitler, must also bear constantly in mind the extent to which Hitler is dominated by the personal conviction that he is a law unto himself. This will again and again provide the key to unilateral action in German foreign policy.

IV. Not the least repulsive detail in the whole affair was the attempt to discredit the dead S.A. leaders—Röhm and Heines—by concrete charges of luxury, extravagance, drunkenness and above all filthy homosexual practices. These charges were first launched on the wireless by Dr Goebbels, who on 10 July went so far as to describe his dead comrades as "a little clique of saboteurs and arrivistes". Of this aspect of the affair the less said the better: but it is essential to note that these scandals were no secret in Germany, since no other than Ludendorff had denounced them, and it had come to an open trial for libel in 1932. Hitler had appointed Heines as Chief of Police at Breslau, knowing him to be accused of homosexuality, perjury

---

[1] *"Dass das Los Deutschlands getragen werden kann."* To the *New York Herald* Hitler declared that there was no alternative in order to save Germany from the tragedy of civil war.

and murder! Heines' and Röhm's propensities had long been known to him, but had not prevented him from appointing them to high office, defending them "as rough fighters" in a great cause, not to be judged "by drawing-room standards",[1] or from thanking Röhm, in the second person singular, for his "imperishable services" and thanking Fate for giving him "such men as friends and comrades".[2] And now, he had shot first, according to the most approved Chicago method. "By the executions of Thirtieth June he not only broke the back of the S.A. before they could as much as protest, he also shifted the accusation of treachery from himself to the S.A. leaders."

In all Germany there was no one to protest: a sympathetic telegram came from Neudeck in the name of the dying President, and on 1 July General von Blomberg, the head of the Reichswehr, issued a decree to his troops praising the Führer's "soldierly resolution and exemplary courage" and incidentally revealing the fact that emergency orders (*Alarmzustand*) had been issued on 30 June. Germany was in the hands of gunmen.

THE DOLLFUSS MURDER

"*Und gehst du nicht willig, so brauch' ich Gewalt.*"

All Europe was still gasping under the impression of these events when a no less criminal outbreak occurred in Austria. The long terrorist campaign waged in Austria by the Nazis since the middle of 1933 culminated in the *coup* of Twenty-fifth

[1] "Why Hitler Struck" in the *Morning Post* of 3 July 1934. The article makes other pertinent comment. "It is a further consecration of political murder in a country in which large circles of the Right are not shocked by the idea. Particularly in Röhm's circles the murder of 'November criminals' was a virtue." And again, "Millions of Germans...will sigh with relief to know that Herr Heines is dead. It is another question whether on reflection they will think better of Herr Hitler for having turned upon his friends and suddenly denounced them to the nation for weaknesses with which he has been familiar for years".

[2] Letter to Stabschef Röhm, 30 June 1933—exactly one year earlier! Cf. General Göring's statement in "The Rebirth of Germany, III" (*Morning Post*, 31 January 1934): "It is one of Hitler's qualities as a leader that he knows how to put the right men in the right places." Shades of Röhm and Heines!

of July, in which a detachment of desperadoes, acting on orders from Munich, seized the Vienna Foreign Office and murdered the Chancellor Dollfuss, deliberately refusing his requests for either a doctor or a priest. But for a fortunate accident the whole Cabinet would have been caught in the same trap, Vienna might have fallen into the hands of the rebels, and the "Austrian Legion", which was concentrated on the Bavarian frontier, might have given the necessary stiffening to the sporadic risings which broke out in Styria and Upper Austria. Why the two chief plotters, Habicht and Frauenfeld, countermanded at the very last moment their aeroplane for Vienna: why the "Austrian Legion" was recalled and partially disbanded: what exactly were the relations of Dr Rintelen with the Brown House and whether, if he had succeeded in proclaiming himself as Chancellor, he would at once have carried out the "Gleichschaltung" of Austria, are questions which as yet remain only half answered. But the message issued by the conspirators during their brief control of the radio headquarters in Vienna, the premature reports of the Putsch published in certain Reich newspapers, and the material captured from Nazi agents and *only partly* given to the world in the Austrian Brown Book,[1] amply suffice to prove the complicity of the Reich. Fortunately the situation was saved, in the first instance by the crass bungling of the gunmen to whose hands the plot had been entrusted, and probably by the restraining influence of the Wilhelmstrasse and the Reichswehr chiefs. Since July 1934 milder methods have been adopted towards Austria. Herr von Papen, with his American reputation for sapping and mining and his strange, unmerited, prestige in high Catholic circles, was sent as Minister to Vienna, to promote a process of irresistible peaceful penetration. Time alone can show whether Nazism will triumph over the supremely non-Nazi mentality of Austria and over those three powerful elements, all equally inimical to the Nazi system, but incapable of combining—the Catholic Church, the Socialists and the Jews.

[1] *Beiträge zur Vorgeschichte und Geschichte der Julirevolte* (official, Vienna, 1934).

There were two further urgent reasons why the Führer "called off" terrorist methods in Austria—the first, the massing of Italian troops on the Brenner, which showed that the Duce (quite apart from any indignation at the murder of his personal friend Dollfuss) was not at that time prepared to accept the forcible annexation of Austria: and the second, the fact that in the week following the Twenty-fifth of July he was absorbed by the final stage in the consolidation of his own regime. On 2 August 1934 President von Hindenburg died at his country house: and within half an hour a decree had been issued unifying the offices of President and Chancellor in the person of Adolf Hitler. Henceforth the dividing lines between the State and the Party were indeed indistinguishable.

The argument that this step was "constitutionally valid" is an unwarranted use of plain legal terms. If the external forms were preserved, that simply means that they had been reduced to negligible proportions by the most drastic paring. In effect, Hitler assumed all that he did not as yet possess of supreme power, because there no longer existed any machinery to stop him. The change was confirmed on 19 August by a referendum, in which 38 million votes were recorded in his favour.[1]

On the previous 20 July Göring, speaking at Halle, had uttered phrases which provide an equally apt comment upon Hitler's absolutism at home and his attitude to the Austrian Putsch: "For Hitler the supreme law is justice.... We are what we are from and through the Führer alone. Herr Hitler is German—a leader just and ineffably kind, but hard as iron." Hitler himself, in a radio speech on the eve of the Referendum (17 August), declared that criticism was not a vital function of a nation, which had no right of fault-finding, but only of better achievement. The Nazi Party, he declared, was the sole bearer of the Reich's political will, just as the Reichswehr was the sole bearer of its arms. [The inward meaning of this phrase is that the dissolution of the S.A. was the price for the Reichswehr's condonement of gangster methods.] Discipline and

[1] There were 4,200,000 hostile votes, 872,000 spoilt papers and 2,000,000 abstentions.

order were what most mattered. "I will not have ignorant, misled, insignificant people shot. But I will in all such cases crush to earth the really responsible."

DEADLOCK IN EUROPE

During the remainder of 1934 the European deadlock continued, and the nervous tension was still further heightened by the assassination of King Alexander and M. Barthou on 9 October at Marseilles. Yet it seemed as though at the last moment every Government shrank from the arbitrament of war: and the League of Nations could still congratulate itself upon two notable successes—the acceptance of Genevan arbitration between Jugoslavia and Hungary (with the sinister figure of Italy behind her, as the real inspirer of Croat terrorism), and, even more important, the peaceful execution of the Saar plebiscite. At the New Year both Hess and Goebbels declared that the Saar might become a bridge between Germany and France, and though French opinion was by no means responsive, the Führer himself, on learning the result of the plebiscite, declared that he had no more territorial claims on the West, that the time had come for appeasement and reconciliation, and that he had a deep desire to preserve peace. In face of all this there was a brief revival of optimism in Europe: and today (despite all the naked violence and repudiation that was to follow) we are still left speculating whether Hitler's peaceful professions can have been sincerely meant, whether his action in March 1935 was the improvisation of an emotional and unrestrained autocrat, roused to sudden anger by his own interpretation of the course of European diplomacy, or whether all his reassuring utterances were not a mere blind to conceal his capacity for swift panther-like action after long bouts of indecision and evasion.

Parallel with these events there were in Europe two other tendencies to which the Führer could not possibly remain indifferent. On the one hand Russia, abandoning the policy which she had pursued since the Second Revolution, entered the League and pushed on by several stages the idea of a regional pact of non-aggression in the East, while Germany, obsessed by the Hitler-Rosenberg dream of eastern expansion, steadily refused to enter the trammels of an Eastern Pact, in whatever form. On the other hand, Barthou's successor as French Foreign Minister, M. Laval, sought to meet the growing danger from Germany by an Italo-French *rapprochement*, and British statesmen naïvely welcomed this, without realising its fatal implications. From this event dates the final resolve of Mussolini to crown "the Crucial Year" 1935 with an onslaught upon Abyssinia. Whether Laval gave private pledges to the Duce cannot positively be affirmed: but he gave public assurances as to the territorial integrity of Abyssinia, which lulled the Negus in a false security and encouraged the Duce in his warlike preparations. (In passing, we may note that the agreement roused acute alarm in the Little and Balkan Ententes, and led to a tightening of the ties that bound them together, while French influence for a time sank almost to zero.) Obviously the removal of friction between Paris and Rome was a good thing in itself, but the immediate effect of the Pact was to heighten the impression of German isolation and so increase the susceptibilities of Berlin, while at the same time unsettling Warsaw, Prague, Bucarest and Belgrade.

This impression was not removed by the joint Franco-British statement published in London on 3 February 1935 after conversations between M. Laval and Sir John Simon. It declared in favour of "a general settlement freely negotiated between Germany and the other Powers" and invited "the direct and effective co-operation of Germany". It foreshadowed (*a*) "the organisation of security in Europe", especially by pacts of mutual assistance in East and Central Europe, (*b*) "agreements regarding armaments generally", to replace the restrictive military provisions of the Treaty of Versailles, and (*c*) an air convention, in the first instance between the five Western Powers: and it also assumed that, as "part of the general settlement", Germany would "resume her place in the League of Nations". After twelve days' deliberation Herr Hitler expressed his readiness to examine any means for preventing an armament race, and to discuss the London proposals as an integral whole, but argued that instead of a conference there should be separate conversations, "to clarify a number of preliminary questions of principle". To this end he invited British statesmen to Berlin. A week later, at a party anniversary in Munich, the Führer declared that there would be no pact till full equality of armaments had been granted, but that then *"our Yes will remain Yes and our No No"* (24 February).

The course seemed set fair towards conciliation, and the heavy squall that so swiftly followed has usually been ascribed to the tactless publication on 4 March of the British "Statement relating to Defence" and the just offence which it caused in Berlin. Yet it is quite impossible to read the document— especially in the light of events from 1935 to 1937—without admitting its entire accuracy: for the root cause of British rearmament (which the Government was trying to explain to a far from enthusiastic House of Commons), and indeed the only valid excuse which could be adduced for it, was "the unabated and uncontrolled" rearmament of Germany and "the general feeling of insecurity" which it had called forth throughout Europe. Mr Baldwin was quite right in refusing to stand in a white sheet. The whole incident is a classic illustration of the German contention that Germany may call a spade a bloody shovel, but other nations may not even call it an agricultural implement. It is almost impossible to escape the conclusion that Herr Hitler and his military advisers were searching for a convenient pretext to break the thread of interminable discussion and to act according to their own sweet will. For the other explanation of German anger—the French parliamentary discussions on military service—is even less valid. None knew better than the Germans that France had reached "the lean years" in which the catastrophic fall in her birthrate during the Great War[1] would make itself most acutely felt, and that if

---

[1] While in Britain the birthrate had fallen from 24·3 (1911–14) to 20·8 (1915–19), and in Germany from 27·4 to 16·5, it had in France fallen from 18·8 to 11·3! See *Survey for* 1935, I, p. 136 and R. R. Kuczynski, *The Balance of Births and Deaths.*

no steps were taken to redress the balance, "her annual contingent would stand at only about 120,000 instead of about 240,000",[1] at the very moment when Germany was trying in every way to lessen the gap between the military status of the two countries. Doubtless it was annoying for Berlin to find that the French could not after all, like the British, be taken off their guard: but of provocation there could be no question, for the Bill to prevent a fall in French effectives by a temporary prolongation of the period of service was caused *solely* by German action, and was naturally most unpopular in France, though accepted as quite inevitable.

GERMANY RESTORES CONSCRIPTION

Berlin's action came in a series of explosions. On 10 March General Göring announced the existence of a German Air Force, thereby revealing the fact that Germany had broken her word while negotiations were still pending. On the 13th the German contingent offer to renounce the use of bombing machines was explicitly withdrawn. On the 16th a decree was issued re-establishing conscription, on the basis of a peace footing of 12 corps and 36 divisions—in other words, about 550,000 men, or very nearly double the figure round which the disarmament negotiations had latterly revolved, and be it added, a figure which the German Staff knew perfectly well to be unattainable by France, "even by drafting every available Frenchman into the ranks and retaining him with the colours for two years". Germany was thus "deliberately planning to possess an army not merely equal to the biggest in non-Russian Europe, but larger than any other".[2]

It was sought to justify this step by the argument that Germany had fulfilled her treaty obligations, while others had evaded the reciprocity undertaken at Versailles; that she could not be expected to practise unilateral disarmament in perpetuity, and that as she, in contrast to others, had now discharged her

[1] *Survey*, p. 137.
[2] *The Times*, leader of 18 March 1935.

temporary obligation, it was her right and duty to rearm forthwith. After this crude attempt to conceal German unilateral repudiation under counter-charges of non-fulfilment, the Note closed on a more conciliatory tone, by assuring the world that Germany had no desire to "fashion any offensive military instrument, but only, and exclusively, an instrument of defence". Next day the War Minister publicly expressed belief in "the possibility of establishing a new order in Europe by peaceful means", adding that "Europe has become too small to be the battlefield of a second World War".[1] Baron Neurath for his part took the line that the ex-Allies had been the first to violate the Peace Treaty, and that the German decision had cleared the air: "we shall now be talking realities instead of phrases".

Representative British opinion was voiced by Sir Austen Chamberlain, who refused to admit that "dilatory action" in disarmament could ever be pleaded as "justification for the unilateral breach of a treaty". "You cannot build peace in Europe, if that is the mood of any great nation." In the House of Commons he did not hesitate to call the situation in Europe "graver than at any time since 1914".

Sir John Simon at once protested against action so contrary to "the general settlement freely negotiated" which was to have been the subject of discussion in Berlin: and it was at once obvious that negotiations had been rendered infinitely more difficult. None the less, as neither Britain nor France was prepared to hold Germany to her word by force of arms (a fact as to which Germany had already formed a shrewd guess), it was very wisely decided that the British Foreign Secretary and his colleague in League affairs, Mr Eden, should pay their intended visit to Berlin, supplementing it by visits to several Eastern capitals. Their conversations with Herr Hitler had an entirely negative result. He refused to consider an Eastern Pact, and showed his dislike for the idea of "mutual assistance": he insisted upon an army of 550,000 men, on air parity between Britain, France and Germany, and on a German fleet equal to 35 per cent of the British Navy. He accepted

[1] *Survey*, pp. 142–3.

supervision of armaments if limitation could first be agreed upon: but he declined to take any part in the League of Nations, so long as Germany remained "a country of inferior right". Mr Eden went on to Moscow, Warsaw and Prague: but there was little or nothing to show for the four visits, and the deadlock in Europe was complete. Opinion in London was not reassured when it became known that the Führer had given away to Sir John Simon—whether deliberately or unwittingly is not clear—the fact that the German Air Force was at that moment equal, if not superior, to that of Britain! In the light of this even the ostriches began to muse upon the value of German official assurances. On the other hand German opinion appears to have been surprised and hurt at finding that Sir John Simon, after visiting Berlin, took a lead in proposing a vote of censure upon Germany.

The Conference of Stresa, held by the three Western Powers on 11–14 April 1935, and the extraordinary session of the League which immediately followed, only served to emphasise still further the helplessness of Europe. The former criticised Germany's "method of unilateral repudiation...at a moment when steps were being taken to promote a freely agreed settlement of the question of armaments" and argued that this "had undermined public confidence in the security of a peaceful order": while the latter urged "measures to render the Covenant more effective in the organisation of collective security, and to define in particular the economic and financial measures which might be applied, should in the future a state, whether a member of the League or not, endanger peace by the unilateral repudiation of its international obligations". The farcical nature of these phrases only became obvious at a later date: but what was already in the mind of Mussolini may be gathered from one of his periodical anonymous articles in the *Popolo d'Italia* on the opening day of Stresa, which after stressing "the indecision" of the Powers and the "flux" of the Eastern situation, alluded to a practical Italian contribution towards guaranteeing the peace of Europe—namely, the maintenance "until the horizon has thoroughly cleared, of a force of 600,000 men perpetually under arms", and the speedy increase of the Italian Navy and Air Force!¹ The plain fact is that the Duce was laughing in his sleeve: at Stresa and Geneva Italy endorsed the solemn phrases about unilateral repudiation, but meanwhile he was preparing a similar *coup* on so grand and effective a scale that, he calculated, France and Britain would again be left talking and the League would therefore not function. Already Germany and Italy, without having identical interests in the ultimate position of Central Europe, found it increasingly convenient to take in each other's washing in the diplomatic field: and each was able to serve the other's turn by an attitude which acted as a strong deterrent to any collective action. There can be no doubt whatever that in the Duce's calculation the hesitating attitude of Britain and France in face of Germany, and their fear of fresh complications, increased the prospect of his "getting away with" a colonial adventure.

Moreover, the imperfect character of their co-operation was rendered still more apparent by two instances of separate action—M. Laval's conclusion of the Franco-Soviet Pact (2 May), which lay quite outside the British conception of possible commitments and, far more flagrant, the conclusion of an Anglo-German Naval Convention, without previous consultation with Paris.

HITLER'S SPEECH OF 21 MAY 1935

Before, however, this latter step was taken, the Führer had delivered on 21 May the most important of all his pronouncements on foreign policy, which still deserves the reader's careful consideration. The opening passages are devoted to an entirely unconvincing claim that Germany "also" has a "democratic" constitution, a far more convincing criticism of the shortsightedness of the statesmen who imposed economic impossibilities upon Germany, and a sketch of the planned economy, based on the destruction of trade unions and political parties, on the control of prices and wages, by which the new Germany is emancipating herself alike from "bourgeois jingoism" and

¹ *Survey*, p. 137.

"Marxian internationalism". This brings him to a statement of racial theory which is, up to a point, definitely reassuring. "National Socialism", he declares, "dogmatically rejects the idea of national assimilation", and regards "every war for the domination of an alien people" as bound sooner or later to "change and weaken the victor internally and eventually bring about his defeat". "In no future war will the national states of Europe be able to achieve... more than petty adjustments of national frontiers, of no consequence in comparison with the sacrifices made.... The blood shed on the European Continent in the last 300 years bears no proportion to the natural result of events. In the end France has remained France, Germany Germany, Poland Poland, and Italy Italy." This doctrine fits in quite logically with Hitler's chimerical belief in "purity of race", but is not necessarily incompatible with the idea of conquering a fresh patrimony in the East for the cramped German race of today—an idea to be achieved not by assimilation or conquest of another race, but by its ejection to make way for the Germans.

Forgetting what he had written of the coveted Russian borderlands, he proclaims Nazi Germany's desire for peace, first from conviction, secondly because it realises "the simple, primitive fact that no war would be likely essentially to alter the distress in Europe". The assurance he had given to France at the time of the Saar plebiscite was, he contended, and not without reason, a far greater contribution to peace "than many a signature under many a pact". But peace must rest not on unilateral rights, but on general equality and universal justice. In considerable detail he tried to show that Germany had fulfilled her disarmament obligations on a vast scale, until "in her completely defenceless and unarmed condition she was anything but a danger for the other states". "It was not Germany who broke a contractual obligation": the revival of conscription was "nothing else than the restoration to Germany of a status of equal right which threatens nobody but guarantees Germany security". Germany was "in any case not prepared to be treated for all time as a second class nation, or one with inferior rights".

After claiming that the final renunciation of Alsace-Lorraine and the Polish-German Pact were valuable contributions to European peace, he launched a frontal attack upon Bolshevism—quoting a long list of plots and outrages engineered from Moscow—and claimed that National Socialism had "saved Germany, and perhaps the rest of Europe, from the most frightful catastrophe of all times". He declined to enter any pact of mutual assistance with Soviet Russia and condemned such pacts as in no way differing "from the old type of military alliances". The Franco-Soviet "alliance" had introduced "an element of legal insecurity into the Locarno Pact". He therefore asked for "an authentic interpretation" of the effects of the Pact upon Locarno obligations. In passing he denied any desire to "annex Austria or conclude an 'Anschluss'", but hinted pretty plainly that "no regime not resting on public consent can continue permanently".

In conclusion he summed up German policy under thirteen points:

I. In answer to the Geneva resolution of 17 April he contended that the Treaty had been violated not by Germany but by the Powers who had failed to disarm in their turn: and she could not return to Geneva save on a basis of real equality, and after the Treaty, with its classification into victors and vanquished, had been separated from the Covenant.

II. Germany was breaking away from the clauses of the Treaty which involved "a moral and material discrimination" against her, but not those others which concern the mutual relations of nations, such as the territorial clauses.

III. Germany will sign no treaty "which seems to them incapable of fulfilment, *but will scrupulously maintain every treaty voluntarily signed*", and in particular all the obligations of Locarno. *In respecting the demilitarised zone, she is making "a contribution to the appeasement of Europe"*.

IV. Germany is ready to share in a system of collective co-operation, but must keep the way open for treaty revision, in accordance with "the law of perpetual evolution".

V. "The reconstruction of European collaboration cannot be achieved by imposing conditions unilaterally."

VI. Germany is ready in principle to conclude pacts of non-aggression with her neighbours, and to supplement them with provisions aimed at isolating the war-maker and localising the area of war.

VII. She is ready to add an Air Pact to the Locarno Treaty.

VIII. She has announced the extent of the expansion of the new Defence Force, and "will in no circumstances depart from this". She accepts limitation of armaments—in the air, on a basis of parity with the Western Powers, on sea at a rate of 35 per cent of the British Navy. "*For Germany this demand is final and abiding.*" She renounces naval rivalry and "recognises the overpowering vital importance, and therefore justification, of a dominating protection for the British Empire on sea" as for Germany on land, and desires to prevent "for all time" a repetition of the Anglo-German conflict.

IX. She is ready for a practical limitation of armaments, on the basis of the Geneva Red Cross Convention. If bombing could once be "branded as an illegal barbarity, the construction of bombing aeroplanes would soon be abandoned as superfluous".

X, XI. She is ready for limitation of aggressive weapons, especially heavy artillery and large tanks, and again of the size of warships, and also complete abolition of submarines. Such renunciation, he hinted, might make the new French frontier fortifications impregnable.

XII. She favours steps to prevent the poisoning of public opinion "by irresponsible elements orally or in writing, through theatre and cinema".

XIII. She is ready for "an international agreement to prevent outside interference in the affairs of other states", and as a first step, for "a precise international definition" of what is meant by interference.

He ended "by repeating our confession of faith in peace". "Whoever lights the torch of war in Europe can wish for nothing but chaos": but he believed "not in the decline, but in the renaissance of the West".

Once more the striking difference between drastic action and conciliatory phrases produced a certain *détente* in public opinion, especially among the many who were searching eagerly for any excuse for inaction. Even Mr Baldwin, while admitting that he had been "completely wrong" in his estimate of future German air strength, and hardly going beyond the cautious phrase that he saw "some light", also confessed that he had torn up the peroration of his Commons speech. With a wise caution, the Foreign Office on 24 March addressed to Berlin a number of questions intended to elucidate the many obscurities that lurked behind the Führer's eloquent phrases. What, for instance, was still necessary in order to establish that "truly juridical equality of all the parties" without which Germany would not return to the League?

No written answer was ever vouchsafed, and the impression was thus left upon London that Berlin preferred the river bank of eloquence to exploratory movements upon the thin ice of fact. But on one vitally important point Sir Eric Phipps did obtain satisfaction from Baron Neurath. It was made clear that the unconditional undertaking to respect the still remaining clauses of Versailles *did include the clauses relating to the demilitarised zone.*[1]

THE ANGLO-GERMAN NAVAL CONVENTION

Meanwhile there were clear signs of a very dangerous tendency to regard the Continental position as irremediable, and hence to concentrate upon British interests rather than upon British commitments. The highly concrete form given by the Führer to his eighth Point, following upon a preliminary feeler during the Hitler-Simon conversations, served as a bait to the British Foreign Secretary, who had returned from Berlin with an empty basket. Conversations began in London early in June, and speedily resulted in an Anglo-German Naval Convention, by which Germany definitely accepted a ratio of 35 : 100, to be applied by categories, and "not to be affected

[1] *Survey*, p. 176.

by the construction of other Powers". This agreement was heralded as a realistic acceptance of the situation, and contrasted with the "all or nothing" attitude of Paris in the military question: due (or it may be, undue) stress was laid on the desire that the Convention should prove the first step to a world-wide naval agreement: and the Führer was (with justice) given full credit for his desire to avoid William II's blunder of alienating Britain as well as Russia. All this was good enough for the readers of the *Daily Chit-Chat*; but it overlooked two vital criticisms, which swiftly forced themselves to the front. The Convention had been concluded behind the back of France and Italy: and though Mr Baldwin might deny "any deviation from wholehearted co-operation" with the Stresa Powers, and point out that it in no way hurt their interests, the fact remained that it was greeted with deep dismay in Paris and cynical anger in Rome. Moreover, it knocked the bottom out of one of the main criticisms of Germany's treaty repudiation: for the very Government which condemned her for breaking the military clauses of Versailles now concluded, within two months, a separate bargain which involved a breach of the naval clauses of the same treaty. If, then, it was a proof of our practical commonsense, it was also a proof of our inconsiderate egotism. Moreover, there were many who shook their heads over the news that the German Government, as an encouragement to discussions, had on 26 April notified London that it proposed assembling twelve submarines "*manufactured during the previous winter on the pattern of designs which had been drawn during the previous year*". What, it was asked, was the use of signing any convention with a Government which employed such methods?

It was found necessary to despatch Mr Eden to Paris and to Rome, to assuage the very prevalent and very natural fear that Britain was planning to abandon the whole collective system and to add a bilateral Air Pact to a bilateral Sea Pact. Small wonder that the Duce, with his Machiavellian standards, should have been confirmed in his view that Albion, when not perfidious, is profoundly stupid. Fortunately it proved more possible to reassure the French, doubtless because the vital necessity for France and Britain holding together at all costs had already forced itself upon the meanest intelligence south of the Channel: but the shock to M. Laval's system was great, and it is probably not going too far if we assume that the whole incident explains the reserved attitude adopted by France when Britain six months later became involved in acute conflict with Italy in the Mediterranean. The shadows of the Abyssinian crisis already hung over the landscape of Geneva and threw into high relief the madness of those who were ready to play for their own hands, instead of always seeking the highest common factor of Anglo-French confidence and agreement. Meanwhile British neglect of French susceptibilities (and far more than mere susceptibilities were at stake) encouraged both Rome and Berlin in a forward policy, in the belief that Anglo-French solidarity might very largely be discounted.

SIR SAMUEL HOARE AT THE FOREIGN OFFICE

The decision in favour of naval discussions had been Sir John Simon's last serious act as Foreign Secretary: on 7 June, the day on which agreement was reached on all save the mere technical details, the National Government was reconstructed under Mr Baldwin, and Sir John was succeeded by Sir Samuel Hoare. The new Minister found it advisable to inaugurate his term of office by a frank and comprehensive survey of foreign policy, and at the outset argued that the Naval Pact was "in no sense a selfish agreement": though it was recommended by British naval experts "as a safe agreement for the British Empire", it also greatly improved France's naval position by comparison with the pre-war period. He went on to argue very convincingly that peace was indivisible, especially in the air, that Britain, while avoiding further commitments, could not be indifferent to either an Eastern or a Danubian Pact, and that if these were based on the principle of "non-aggression", as was the French intention, they need not form a stumbling-block to Germany either. The rest of the speech was an appeal on behalf of the League, as the best instrument of collective security, pointing out that the only alternative was a return to the old system of alliances. There could be no wedges driven between Britain and France, with whom we shared "a common theory and vast common interests": and he had many conciliatory things to say of Italy, explanatory of the abortive Zeila offer, and deprecating both hostility and any idea of sanctions.

By midsummer 1935 the Abyssinian question and Italy's defiance of the League dominated the whole European situation, and Germany was, as it were, able to sit back in her chair and watch with *Schadenfreude* the rapid disintegration of the Stresa front. For the remainder of the year German efforts are concentrated upon internal consolidation: and this took the form of feverish military preparations (rearmament being used to reduce unemployment), a further extension of the anti-Jewish campaign, the adoption of repressive measures against the Catholic Church and its organisations, and not least of all, the initial steps towards a planned economic autarky. The Jews were formally excluded from full German citizenship, placed in an inferior category and not allowed to marry "Aryans". The Minister for Propaganda, Dr Goebbels, struck the true note of Nazi culture in relation to the Jews. Replying to the "worn-out phrase" that even the Jew was after all a human being and must be treated as such, he reminded his audience that "a flea is also an animal, but that does not make it by any means a pleasant animal".[1] Another notable feature of the new Germany was the destruction of that academic freedom which had once been her greatest pride, and the removal from the Universities of all who had a reputation for liberal principles.

Such negotiations as took place during this critical period centred round the idea of an Air Pact, but no progress was made, because the French insisted upon bilateral arrangements inside the wider Pact, whereas the Germans as strongly opposed the idea. In a conversation between the British Ambassador and the Führer on 16 December 1935, a complete deadlock was

[1] In this connection a reference is necessary to *Der Stürmer*, the anti-Semite review, edited by the Führer's intimate friend, Herr Streicher, Gauleiter of Nuremberg. This must be seen, to be believed!

reached, the latter going so far as to say that "the Franco-Soviet 'military alliance', directed against Germany, rendered any Air Pact out of the question: for the bringing of Russia into the picture had completely upset the balance of power in Europe".[1] In January 1936, when the new Foreign Secretary Mr Eden pointed out that Germany had never taken this line till the conversation of 16 December, Baron Neurath drew back a little, and interpreted the Führer as meaning "that the Franco-Soviet Treaty had rendered an air *limitation* agreement impossible for the present, but that he was ready in principle to conclude an Air Pact between the Locarno Powers".[2] It seems reasonable to suppose that Germany was not averse to dilatory tactics during the winter of 1935–6, for meanwhile the Abyssinian campaign was in full swing, and even in Europe much must depend upon its success or failure, upon the efficacy of sanctions and upon the attitude of America towards them. German military opinion seems to have shared the scepticism of other military experts as to the speed with which Italy could overrun Abyssinia: but the substitution of Badoglio for the incompetent De Bono, the use of poison gas, and the extreme ineptitude of Abyssinian military strategy, combined to transform the situation: and in proportion as it became obvious that Italy would after all triumph before sanctions became effective, Germany's attitude stiffened, and Hitler, realising his tactical advantage in a deeply divided Europe, prepared for a new *coup de théâtre*.

The events of that autumn are better treated in connection with the Abyssinian question (*infra*, Chapter X). Here it will suffice to remind the reader that Sir Samuel Hoare's great Geneva speech of 11 September seemed to rally most of Europe behind Britain as the champion of a policy of sanctions, and that the resounding electoral victory won by the National Government under Mr Baldwin on 14 November was in no small measure due to the country's satisfaction at the lead thereby given in Europe. Correspondingly great was the general public's dismay at the Hoare-Laval proposals of 8 December,

[1] *Survey for 1935*, p. 201.   [2] *Ibid.* p. 202.

and its prompt and wrathful uprising. Rarely in our history has there been a more striking, never a swifter, reaction of opinion to errors in foreign policy: and if the full facts had been made known, not the Foreign Secretary, but the Government as a whole, would have been overthrown within a few weeks of its resounding victory. But as this would have been contrary to the most vital interests of the home situation, a scapegoat had to be found, and while strongly differing from Sir Samuel Hoare's proposed solution for the Abyssinian crisis, we may admire the gallantry with which he assumed the scapegoat's task.

German observers have not always been happy in their reading of a British situation: but this time their diagnosis was not far wrong: the Coalition (like a famous predecessor on the eve of the Crimean War) proved to be not one of the strongest, but one of the weakest, Governments of modern times, while public opinion was more than usually fickle and wavering, for the excellent reason that the Government had for some years past paid lip service to Opinion as the master of Policy, but steadfastly refrained from giving it the necessary lead or the relevant information. Moreover, the coolness which the Hoare-Laval incident had generated between Paris and London seemed likely to condemn them both to inaction: whereas the probable success of the French Left at the impending elections might well lead to a renewal of amity. From the German point of view the moment seemed ripe for action with a prospect of impunity. And meanwhile the high tension of the internal situation was shown by the resounding speech of Dr Goebbels on 16 January 1936, in which he declared that "we can do without butter, but not without guns", and that "we must become a nation of martyrs, because we have certain tasks to fulfil in the world". In these phrases are reflected the blended idealism and inferiority complex which are so characteristic of the Nazi official outlook.

GERMANY REPUDIATES LOCARNO

On 7 March, then, the Führer struck again, with all his habitual suddenness and force. Speaking in the Reichstag, he announced Germany's denunciation of the Locarno Treaty and the simultaneous reoccupation of the demilitarised Rhineland zone by German troops. This action he tried to justify by the argument that the Franco-Soviet Pact was a violation of the Locarno agreement, which had "thereby lost its significance and practically ceased to be. Germany regards herself as no longer bound by this extinct Pact." He treated as "indisputable" the view that the Pact was "directed exclusively against Germany", that it contained obligations far in excess of any commitments under the Covenant, that France "claims the right to decide at her own discretion who is the aggressor", and might therefore "in practice...act as though neither the Covenant nor the Locarno Pact were still valid".

The speech itself alternated between pathos and abuse, between aggression and conciliation. Attacks upon "the unholy treaty" as "a fatal encumbrance for Europe", and on the foreign press for its obvious delight at Germany's difficulties, were followed by a friendly recognition of Poland's vital need for access to the sea, and by keen expressions of regret that his three years of endeavour to reach an understanding with France had not been crowned with success. He had made, he said, "a whole series of proposals" with a view to lessening tension—first, the limitation of the German army to 200,000 men, then to 300,000 men; then limitation of arms; then an Air Pact: thanks to British realism a naval ratio had been agreed upon, but on the French side the sole result of all these offers was "the introduction of the new Eastern European Asiatic factor into the European balance of power". Soviet Russia, he claimed, stood for World Revolution, and he had to reckon with the possibility of the triumph of that philosophy in France also, in which case Germany would find herself between two states controlled from a single headquarters in Moscow. "The intro-

duction into Central Europe of this mighty military factor",
with a peace footing of 1,350,000 men and the largest air force
and tank force in the world, "destroys any real European
balance of power, and makes defence impossible."

In order to lessen the effect of repudiation, he closed by
affirming his desire for an understanding with the Western
nations, and declaring that "after three years I can regard the
struggle for German equality as concluded today", and that
"we have no territorial demands to make in Europe". He then
put forward seven suggestions for "a system of European
security":

I. The establishment of "a bilateral demilitarised zone" by
agreement between Germany, France and Belgium.

II. A non-aggression Pact between the three states, for
twenty-five years, "to assure the inviolability and integrity of
the frontiers in the West".

III. Adhesion of Britain and Italy as guarantor Powers.

IV. Inclusion of Holland "in this treaty system", if it and
other Powers approve.

V. Air Pact with the Western Powers.

VI. Non-aggression Pacts between Germany and her Eastern
neighbours, "similar to that concluded with Poland".

VII. Germany, having "eliminated" the chief reason for
her withdrawal, "is prepared to re-enter the League of Nations,
but expects" the problem of colonial equality of rights, as
well as of the separation of the Covenant from its Versailes
Treaty base "to be clarified in the course of friendly negotiations".

This skilful attempt to divide Western opinion at a moment
when strong action was more than usually difficult was supplemented by formal assurances to the British and French Ambassadors in Berlin, that the occupation was merely "symbolical"—
a patent design to gain time, whose insincerity was speedily
proved by the thoroughness of remilitarisation and frontier
fortification. Equally specious was the offer to establish a double
demilitarised zone along both sides of the Franco-German and
Franco-Belgian frontiers; for this was glaringly inacceptable

to the French, who in that case "would have to scrap the chain of fortresses on which they had spent £35,000,000 in the last few years and rebuild them further back".[1] Indeed, from the purely strategic standpoint, successful reoccupation meant for Germany the double gain of "making herself impregnable in the west and of achieving her maximum offensive power in the west also".[2]

The advantages which Germany stood to gain were enormous: the only real question was whether the other side, realising this, would be forced to intervene. We know now that the Reichswehr considered the risk to be too great, and therefore advised against the *coup*, and that it had been arranged that if the French mobilised or marched in, the "symbolical" troops were at once to withdraw again beyond the Rhine—in which case the latent conflict in Hitler's entourage might have come suddenly to a head and produced dangerous political reactions. But events proved the wilder spirits right, and hence, for some time to come, the influence of the Reichswehr over the Führer was considerably weakened, the more so as its chiefs were also proved wrong in the Abyssinian campaign.

In two directions the Führer's strategy was brilliantly successful. The bait of German re-entry into the League bewildered sentimental British opinion, which, after demanding the uttermost farthing from Italy, was illogically ready to condone unilateral action on the part of Germany. Obviously those French critics who drew this contrast were forgetting that Germany's action, at its worst, related to German, not foreign, territory, and that her action was not an open war of conquest like Italy's. But the decisive fact remained that in the two crises of December 1935 and of March 1936 French opinion grew cold whenever British opinion grew hot, and vice versa.

Secondly, a moment had been selected for action when the League was wellnigh paralysed. The Council now had to decide whether a breach of Articles XLII and XLIII of Versailles and of Article II of Locarno had occurred: and as unanimity

[1] *Daily Telegraph*, leader of 9 March 1936.
[2] *Manchester Guardian*, "Implications of Hitler's Move", 9 March 1936.

was required, Italy's position was a strong one. If the Committee of Thirteen, then on the point of considering the replies of Italy and Abyssinia to the proposal for negotiation, were not to play weakly for time, but to take a strong line in accordance with the obvious facts of Italy's design of complete conquest, Italy had it in her power to prevent any decision on the part of the Locarno Powers. Germany, then, by her action had done Italy a great service, and had forestalled the danger of Britain, in return for French support of oil sanctions against Italy, committing herself to sanctions against Germany in the event of action in the Rhineland. It should be unnecessary to labour still further the essential interconnection of Abyssinia and the Rhineland.

Despite the disconcerting outbreak of sentimentalism in certain sections of the press (super-pacifists joining hands with the declared sympathisers with Fascism, Power Politics and British isolationism), it was at once clear to all thinking people that a position of extreme gravity had arisen to which the late Mr Lowes Dickinson's phrase "The European Anarchy" might be applied with infinitely greater reason than to the pre-war period of rival alliances, in which at least treaties were scrupulously observed. Germany had now become, more than ever before, a law unto herself. For she had now torn up, not only a treaty which she had repeatedly denounced, and which the world was slowly growing accustomed to regard as riddled and only partially valid, but also a treaty which (by her own admission) had been freely negotiated—Locarno—and in which the Rhineland zone provisions had been included at Germany's express wish, and whose scrupulous observance Herr Hitler himself, only ten months earlier, had gone out of his way to promise. On that occasion, indeed (21 May 1935), he had boasted of German observance of the demilitarised zone "as a contribution towards the appeasement of Europe". In his Berlin conversation with Mr Eden in April 1935 the Führer had drawn a clear distinction between Versailles and Locarno, the latter being "freely signed".

HITLER AND THE EASTERN PACTS

Moreover, his argument that the French and Czechoslovak Pacts with Soviet Russia were violations of Locarno and therefore justified Germany's unilateral repudiation of the Treaty was entirely inadmissible. In the first place, the speech by which he himself reaffirmed Locarno was delivered three weeks after the signature of the Franco-Soviet Pact, so the latter could not be the sole reason for his changed attitude in March 1936: and though he had expressed his disapproval of the Pact in his talk with Mr Eden, it had not then occurred to him to denounce it as incompatible with Locarno. Secondly, if Germany held that Locarno was in danger of violation, she should have consulted the other signatories, instead of taking unilateral action, and if this led to nothing, she should have applied to the Hague Court as the competent body to decide whether the Soviet Pacts were indeed incompatible with Locarno. That she did not take this course was all the more flagrant, because Article III of Locarno provided for a reference of doubtful points to "judicial decision", and because France was at all times ready to refer rival interpretations to the Hague Court, and in the event of its ruling that modifications were necessary to bring the Pacts into line with obligations under the Covenant, was also ready to comply. Indeed, the knowledge that Germany was opposed to the Pact had led the French Government to submit its text to minute examination by many eminent international lawyers, in order that they might ensure its perfect legality and "compatibility". Moreover, the French Premier, M. Sarraut, speaking on the wireless, was able to refute the Führer's charge of French irresponsiveness to German overtures. France had in November 1935 urged the conclusion of a Western Air Pact, but Germany had declined to discuss while the Abyssinian war was in progress. On 21 February 1936 Hitler had given an interview to *Paris-Midi*, and the French Government had instantly instructed its Ambassador to call upon him with a view to discussing the basis of Franco-German friendship, but at Hitler's own special request this fact was not made public. M. Sarraut reaffirmed the readiness of France to submit the question to arbitration, but refused to accept a *fait accompli* as a substitute for international law: "We declare to Herr Hitler solemnly, that we have never wished, and never shall wish, to assail the liberty and honour of the German People." French public opinion, already affronted by Hitler's open assumption that France might become a mere annexe of Moscow, concluded that Germany's real aim was to make herself impregnable in the West before proceeding to put into effect her new Eastern policy.

The official British attitude was voiced in the House of Commons by Mr Eden, when he condemned "the unilateral repudiation of a treaty freely negotiated and freely signed" and declared that "it strikes a severe blow at that principle of sanctity of treaties which underlies the whole structure of international relations", while Mr Baldwin spoke of "a new and disturbing factor in the international situation", "a flagrant breach" and "an unfortunate and indefensible action". It was also made clear, amid general approval, that in the event of "any actual attack upon France or Belgium which would constitute a violation of Article II of Locarno", Britain would, "notwithstanding the German repudiation", regard herself "as in honour bound to come to the assistance of the country attacked". On the other hand, the Government "would examine the new German proposals clear-sightedly and objectively, with a view to finding out to what extent they represented a means by which the shaken structure of peace could again be strengthened". It is pertinent to add that from two opposite angles Sir Austen Chamberlain and Dr Dalton insisted that such examination must include a special regard for the independence of Austria.

FRANCE AND BRITAIN IN ALLIANCE

In effect, then, the two Western Governments, while indignantly protesting, and driven to ask whether under such circumstances any treaty concluded with Germany could have any value whatsoever, were not prepared to take military action, and thus left Germany in the position of *beatus possidens* on the Rhine. At the same time, however, the sudden stress of events had converted, almost in a day, the Locarno Pact into a triple defensive alliance between Britain, France and Belgium, and brought home to British opinion in unanswerable form the assertion of Mr Baldwin that "defensive requirements and foreign policy are so closely inter-related that one cannot be considered apart from the other", and that other assertion of Sir Samuel Hoare that German rearmament had become "the central factor in the European problem" and "the central problem of our defensive programme" (9 March 1936). On the other hand it was abundantly clear that neither Britain nor France, with the Italian sanctions crisis on their hands, was ready for actual war on the Rhineland issue and, in a word, that there was no one to call Hitler's bluff. In June 1934 he had proclaimed himself "for twenty-four hours the Supreme Court of the German people", without appeal: in March 1936 he advanced an exactly similar claim for decisions in the international sphere. On 14 March in Munich he declared that "God's voice is the people's voice", and that the German people "would not tolerate being sent from one international law court to another". He remained "indifferent to threats, compliments and slurs. I go my way with the assurance of a somnambulist, the way which Providence has sent me." "If I have done wrongly, then I shall ask God Almighty to strike me down."[1] Here spoke the fanatic and the fatalist, but also the despot who offers no choice. "No power in the world", he declared three days later, "can deflect Germany from her purpose. She recognises only one supreme authority—the

[1] 12 March, at Karlsruhe.

nation itself." A week earlier Dr Goebbels had already announced that "the world must accept the Führer's proposals: there is no other solution".

During March and April there were constant discussions between London and Paris, but no exit from the deadlock was found. The British Government stood pledged to consider "with an open mind" the German counter-proposals: its own avowed aims being "to maintain peace, to strengthen the League, and to uphold the sanctity of Treaties". But it had no answer to the French contention that to destroy the principle of supra-national arbitration was to cut at the very roots of the League and of collective security. In M. Sarraut's phrase, the sole alternative was "a resolute return to military alliances, rearmament and, we must admit, to war launched by the strongest at the most favourable moment". Hitler might repeat the glib phrase of "a real and actual pacification of Europe for the next twenty-five years", but how could this be achieved without effective guarantees against unilateral breach of treaty? The isolationists might urge leaving France to her "unreason" and playing a lone hand in Europe and the world: but at long last it was becoming clear, even to the most limited intelligence, that in that event it was Britain who would, in the changed circumstances of aerial warfare and the new Mediterranean strategy, be the most vulnerable of Powers—in other words, that Britain stands as much in need of French co-operation as France of British, and that the result of our refusal must sooner or later, but quite inevitably, be the formation of a Continental Bloc against Britain. The situation that preceded the Entente Cordiale of 1904 was repeating itself, in a modified form.

Such considerations doubtless loomed in the background of the special session of the League Council held in London on 14 March, which found Germany to have committed a breach of Versailles and Locarno, and of the Franco-British discussions which continued during April. Meanwhile Herr Hitler had burned his boats, ordered a general election, and delivered a series of impassioned speeches which, behind the screen of pacific professions and a desire for general reconciliation, refused all idea of arbitration (on the ground that the Hague Court was only competent to judge the legal, but not the political, aspect of the Soviet Pact dispute), refused any postponement of Rhineland fortification, and refused even the gesture of temporary and partial withdrawal, pending further negotiations, for which Mr Eden had appealed.[1] The *coup* had greatly revived confidence in the Führer, after a winter of economic discontents, and the electoral campaign ended in a 99 per cent vote in his favour— no alternative being provided, or being at that moment even possible. His position was further strengthened by the dubious attitude of Italy, who declined to associate herself with the results of the Five Power Naval Conference, and above all by the extraordinarily maladroit proposal of the Locarno Powers that as a temporary measure a mixed force, *including Italians*, should be sent into the Rhineland. This was not merely repulsive to German sentiment in its mood of exaggerated attachment to national sovereignty, but also equally to British opinion, which felt it to be nothing short of an insult to suggest that the treaty-breakers *par excellence* should be entrusted with the position of warders on the Rhine. The suggestion was of course stillborn: alarm blinded the French to the cogency of the British view that the crime of Germany in reoccupying her own territory in defiance of certain solemn and specific pledges was still as nothing to the crime of Italy in tilting against the whole fabric of international law and obligation, for the sake of a war of naked aggression and conquest. *The Times* of 20 March was right in arguing that despite the enormity of the German default and the shock thus administered to general confidence in Europe, Hitler's offer "has substance and offers a way back to action and reality. It is this which gives something much deeper than dialectical strength to the German case and promises a new foundation to the law of Europe and its observance."

If, however, London adopted a more negative attitude than Paris in the whole Rhineland affair, it did not flinch from paying

[1] The *Daily Telegraph* of 16 March summed up the whole situation in the title of its leader: "Germany's Reply: in Form an Acceptance, in Fact a Refusal".

the necessary price for holding back Paris from drastic action.
Mr Eden's speech of 26 March was one of the most realistic
delivered in recent years by a British Foreign Secretary. He
made abundantly clear what is far too often overlooked in
public controversy—that after the War the French were induced
to recede from their original demand for a separation of the
Rhineland from Germany by three promises: (1) a fifteen years'
occupation of the zone, which they and we renounced in 1930;
(2) permanent demilitarisation; and (3) a British and American
guarantee of security, which was "never forthcoming": and
that the inclusion of the Rhineland clauses in Locarno was not
due to French and Belgian clamour, but to the express demand
of Germany herself. These factors made all talk of a "Diktat"
entirely irrelevant to the question at issue. Moreover, Germany's
assumption of the right to repudiate because of the Franco-
Soviet Pact entirely ignored the position of Belgium, who had
signed no such Pact, but who was vitally affected by the change.

Mr Eden hit straight at the defeatists and isolationists when
he reminded Parliament that "we are not arbiters in this
business. We are guarantors of this Treaty, and as such have
certain very definite commitments....I am not prepared to
be the first British Foreign Secretary to go back on a British
signature." He then defended the Government's decision to
engage upon staff conversations with France and Belgium, it
being obvious that without some such technical preparation
we should not be in a position to fulfil our obligations in case
of need. He drew the necessary distinction between the conversations now undertaken and the much-canvassed military
talks between 1905 and 1914. His statement that as we had no
political commitments before 1914 the staff talks "inevitably
entailed a political commitment", elicited a few cries in the
House that clearly reflected the divergence of opinion still
prevailing in a famous pre-war controversy. He was therefore
wise to concentrate upon the current issue, pointing out that
whether the fear of commitment in the pre-war situation was
justified or not, "it cannot arise on the present occasion, because
our obligations are clearly set out by treaty already, and the

only question that can be at issue is whether or not you are prepared to make arrangements to carry out these obligations, should the need arise". Stated in this form, his argument was unanswerable, even without its cogent appeal to history to prove that "we have never been able to dissociate ourselves from events in the Low Countries". He might have added that those who objected to these staff talks in their new form had either not thought out their implications, or were in effect advocating a course which would render our obligations totally worthless. The rest of his speech was an eloquent summary of the danger of the European situation and of the Government's constant desire for "the appeasement of Europe as a whole", closing with a summons to the country not merely to feel, but "to think deeply also".

THE GERMAN "PEACE PLAN"

The great Rhineland crisis, springing full-grown as a broad river from a limestone hill, was ere long destined to lose itself in the sandy wastes of Abyssinia. The period of acute contro-versy and of active danger may be said to have ended with the German Note of 1 April 1936. It opened with a long and argumentative statement, intended to prove that the Rhineland restrictions were a breach of both armistice and peace treaty, and the Soviet Pacts an invalidation of Locarno; it went on to challenge the competence of the Hague Court to judge "the political aspects" of the conflict, all the more so as the League Council had "already taken a decision prejudicing the legal judgment of the question". It then asked the rhetorical question whether "European diplomacy" aimed at stereotyping the division of Europe into "honourable and dishonourable, free and unfree nations", or at "achieving at all costs a really constructive state of affairs", and with a view to promoting the latter course, submitted a "Peace Plan" under nineteen heads. The German Government suggested that in order to calm existing tension four months should be allowed to elapse before actual negotiations opened, and promised during this time not to reinforce the Rhineland garrisons or move them nearer to the frontier: this should be placed under guarantee of Britain, Italy and a neutral Power. They suggested immediate negotiations between Germany, France and Belgium (together with Britain and Italy as the two "guarantor Powers") for a "25-year Pact of Non-aggression": "they are ready that Holland should also be included, if she so desires": and they are ready to supplement the Agreement by an Air Pact. In order to stamp this voluntary Peace Pact as ending a quarrel of centuries between France and Germany, they suggest mutual measures to eliminate from education, the press and literature "everything calculated to poison the relationship between the two peoples, whether it be a derogatory attitude or improper interference". The agreement would be ratified by plebiscites in both countries. Germany would then be prepared to conclude Pacts of Non-aggression with her S.E. and N.E. neighbours (presumably Austria, Czechoslovakia and Lithuania), and to re-enter the League, while expressing the hope that the question of "colonial equality of rights" would be cleared up and the Covenant separated from the Peace Treaty. A new International Court of Arbitration would be set up, to guard over the various agreements; no indication was given why the Hague Tribunal was simply ignored. In conclusion, the German Government held that after "this great work of securing European peace" had been concluded, measures must be taken "to stop the unlimited competition in armaments": but, having no faith in "universal settlements", they suggested piecemeal negotiations, taking the subject of aerial warfare first. Here they were ready to prohibit gas, poison, or incendiary bombs outside the range of the fighting fronts in war, and to abolish heavy tanks and the heaviest artillery. They would at the same time be ready to exchange views on economic problems, with a view to "the recovery of confidence, trade and prosperity".

The German "Peace Plan" met with very wide acceptance from uninformed British opinion which, after judging Italy with rigid severity, was now inclined to make allowances of all sorts for Germany. The Government, however, was more realist and saw the fundamental difficulty of reaching any stable result with a country whose policy rests upon shock tactics, unilateral action, the arbitrary right to repudiate treaty obligations (voluntary no less than compulsory) and an absolute claim to be the sole judge as to the merits of the case. Moreover, it was by now becoming more and more obvious that what Germany wanted was not equality but predominance; that her objection to the Soviet Pact rested not on fear of joint Franco-Russian aggression, but on a desire to eliminate Russia from European politics, in which case a rearmed Germany would automatically place France (and even a Franco-British alliance) on the defensive. It was also only too obvious that while Germany's new rulers were rousing home opinion by denouncing the refusal of other states to disarm, the balance in Europe had already been dangerously deflected by Britain's prodigious decline in armament, and that while her rising generation was being brought up on pacifist League principles, the Empire was rapidly sinking to the rank of a second-rate Power. So long as Germany's just grievances under the Peace Treaty occupied the foreground of the picture, her ulterior aims could be overlooked: but with the introduction of conscription and the fortification of the Rhineland (to be followed, as soon as the impotence of Europe was clearly established, by the restoration of two years' military service), it was no longer possible to ignore the fact that her real aim was overwhelming military superiority. To the sceptics or innocents who failed to detect the disparity between Germany's professions and her practice, the profound alarm of all her small neighbours, south, west, north and east, was a sufficient answer.

It was in this atmosphere that on 7 May 1936 a number of inquiries were officially addressed by London to Berlin, intended to elucidate certain obscure points in the German memoranda of 7 and 24 March and 1 April, as an essential preliminary to general negotiations. The German Government affected to be hurt at the contents of the questionnaire, and a section of British opinion played into their hands by criticising the "tactlessness" of its own Government: but what really annoyed Berlin was that the questionnaire was at once made public, thus revealing to all who could still "hear and understand" the extreme lack of precision which lay behind the sympathetic phrases of the original German proposals. That this is the correct version of Berlin's attitude is confirmed by the fact that from that day to this no precise answer to these questions has ever been vouchsafed. That this was partly due to the ignominious position of Britain after the collapse of its Abyssinian and Genevan policy hardly needs to be added. Events had placed the Führer in a strong strategic position. He had defied Europe with impunity : he had regained to the full his prestige at home : he had enunciated a programme vague enough to win floating opinion to his side, yet too vague to form a basis of discussion : and he now for the first time had the prospect of ending Germany's isolation by an alliance with the other treaty-breaking Power.

UNANSWERED QUESTIONS

Without examining in detail an inquiry that led nowhere, it is essential that the reader should take note of certain fundamental questions which have remained unanswered.

(1) The German Government had drawn a distinction between treaties that were binding and such as it might be possible to conclude in the future. Did Germany regard herself as now at last in a position to conclude "genuine treaties"? For otherwise negotiations for "a binding treaty would be useless".

(2) What view did Germany take of "the continued maintenance in force of the remaining operative clauses of the Treaty of Versailles"?

(3) "Has a point been reached at which Germany can signify that she recognises and intends to respect the existing political and territorial status of Europe, except in so far as this might be subsequently modified by free negotiation and agreement?" This question, though meaningless to the man in the street, really raised the whole theory of *Volkstum* upon which the exponents of National Socialism were engaged in constructing a right of interference by the Reich in all countries inhabited

by men of German race—in other words, throughout the whole East of Europe.

(4) Was Germany ready to "accompany an Air Pact by a regional agreement for the limitation of air strength"? This question rested on the apparent contradiction between Herr Hitler's Reichstag speech of 21 May 1935 and his communication to the British Ambassador in the following December.

(5) Was Germany, in proposing pacts of non-aggression with "the States on Germany's S.E. and N.E. frontiers" (which in a strict geographical sense meant Austria, Czechoslovakia, Poland and Lithuania) ready "to interpret these words so as to cover at least also the Soviet Union, Latvia and Estonia, as well as the states actually contiguous to Germany"? And would she define the distinction between "non-aggression" and "non-interference in the affairs of other States"?

(6) Would Germany define the phrase "the separation of the Covenant from its basis in the Treaty of Versailles setting"?

It could not, and cannot, be denied that until light is thrown on these fundamental points no general settlement was possible. Yet the German Government and its chief have to this day deliberately refrained from giving any answer. This attitude inevitably gave rise to very adverse comment, not merely in Paris, but in London, and indeed to a growing doubt "as to whether Hitler wants to negotiate", and whether the Peace Plan was not "drafted merely to soften the shock which the reoccupation of the Rhineland gave, and perhaps to gain time while Germany completed her rearmament programme"? Close observers noted on the one hand Germany's "disinclination to accept a one-Power standard in the air" and on the other hand the impossibility of Britain fulfilling her obligations under a Western Air Pact, if she were "tied down to permanent inferiority in the air to one of two possible aggressors".[1] The comments of the inspired German press—the party organ *Völkische Beobachter* described the questionnaire as "a piece of cat-burglary", while the once Liberal *Frankfurter Zeitung* dismissed it as "not even honourable" because it raised "questions

[1] Diplomatic Correspondent of the *Manchester Guardian*, 9 June 1936.

of a fundamental ethical nature which cannot be answered by formal statements, but only by deeds"—this and much else showed that Nazi Germany had no use for a discussion of ethics or morals, but preferred the sphere of Power Politics.

Germany's ominous silence was a prime factor in the humiliating process of admission that the existing machinery of the League had failed, and that the policy of collective security, "as an attractive alternative to the old system of alliances and the balance of power", had "failed to prevent war, failed to stop war, failed to save the victim of aggression".[1] These admissions were followed up by Mr Eden's statement in the House, that the future of the League was the dominant issue in Europe, and that "the collaboration of Germany is indispensable to the peace of Europe":[2] but behind all the recriminations of debate there was slowly emerging the brutal fact that though Britain was not prepared to embark upon war over the Abyssinian question, she was for that very reason forced to choose between rearmament upon a gigantic scale and complete abdication of her position as a world Power, with all that this would involve for her Dominions and Colonies.

Two other motives serve to explain the unresponsive attitude of Germany. That she interpreted the failure of sanctions as a sign of the impending collapse of the whole Genevan system was suggested by her open encouragement of the Danzig Nazis in lawless defiance of the League at home and vulgar impudence at Geneva itself.[3] That she regarded the electoral victory of M. Blum and the Popular Front as a further weakening of the democratic Powers, was broadly hinted by the Deputy Leader Herr Hess on 7 June, when he declared that France was now virtually "a Bolshevist country".[4] That she was bent on solving

[1] Mr Chamberlain, at the "1900 Club", 10 June 1936.

[2] 18 June.

[3] This was the famous occasion when Captain Greiser, the fine flower of Danzig Nazism, put out his tongue and cocked a snook at the League Council (5 July).

[4] On 29 November Herr Hess argued that the Russian people had been forced by the Terror of "a Jewish clique" into the Bolshevik straitjacket. This crude nonsense could be multiplied tenfold from the pronouncements of all the leading Nazis. As it is impossible to suppose that they are so ill-

all questions of external policy on a strictly bilateral, rather than an international, basis, was shown by the conclusion of an Austro-German Agreement (11 July), by which the Reich recognised Austria's full sovereignty, and Austria declared her policy to rest upon the fact "that she recognises herself as a German state", while both were to abstain from interference in each other's internal affairs. This action seemed to substantiate a passing reference of the Führer, in a speech of 1 May, to "foreign lies" about a possible attack on Austria or Czechoslovakia.

GERMAN MILITARY SERVICE

Finally, on 24 August 1936, an abrupt end was put to negotiations on the basis of the questionnaire, by the Führer's decree (which, be it noted, revoked that of 22 May 1935) raising the period of German military service to two years. The announcement was given to the German public behind a vast smoke screen of press denunciation of Bolshevik militarism, against which German rearmament was the main bulwark, and of France for rejecting German overtures for the sake of a Russian alliance. The openly avowed aim of this campaign was to divide Europe into two camps, or, in effect, by excluding Russia from Europe, to secure to Germany the leadership of an anti-Bolshevik front, and by depriving France of the Russian alliance, to force her Eastern allies in their turn to transfer their allegiance from Paris to Berlin, and thus reduce the Western democracies to a precarious defensive. It was frankly argued that Germany was sufficiently advanced in her programme of rearmament to be able to discuss limitation, on condition that France and Czechoslovakia abandoned their pacts with Russia. Moscow, who was plotting "the most Imperialist war in history", must be "driven out of European affairs" altogether.[1] At the Nazi rally in Nuremberg further precision was given to the campaign:

informed as to believe the theory that Bolshevism and Judaism are identical' we are driven to conclude that it is still regarded as a good means of mobilising the masses against the Jewish scapegoat, and perhaps also of keeping alive the Führer's pathological obsession.

[1] *Deutsche Allgemeine Zeitung*, 31 August; *Nationalzeitung* (Göring's organ), 4 September.

in the proclamation announcing a German Four Year Plan
(imitation is the sincerest form of flattery), Moscow was denounced as "an international Jewish revolutionary centre":
and the Führer himself, perhaps prompted by his Jew-baiting
friend Julius Streicher, committed himself to the assertion that
"98 per cent of the leaders of the Bolshevik Revolution are
Jews" and that even in Spain the leaders of anarchy were Jews.
Reverting to one of the most doubtful theories of *Mein Kampf*,
he attacked European democracy as "the forerunner of anarchy.
No nation was ever created by democracy and all the great
empires were destroyed by it." After similar anti-Semite
tirades from his press lieutenant Dr Goebbels,[1] the Congress
closed on a still more frantic note of the Führer himself, refusing
all negotiation or discussion with the Bolshevik murderers,
conspirators, robbers and destroyers, and treating "Popular
Fronts" or "similarly disguised Coalition Governments" as
mere screens behind which Bolshevism could advance, until
Europe relapsed into "a sea of blood and grief". Nor was this
a mere passing mood: for on 8 November at Munich he spoke
of the Red drums beating in Europe and of the possibility that
Germany might have to defend European civilisation against
the danger from the East. This was why "for a year and a half
Germany has been forging weapons night and day"!

By this time it had been reluctantly driven home to all save
the few incorrigible isolationists and advocates of "peace at
any price", that Nazi Germany refused to be bound, not merely
by her signature to treaties, whether imposed or voluntarily
accepted, but even by her own most recent decisions: for the
new conscription decree was a flagrant departure from the
military programme proclaimed as a definitive only a year
before.[2] It was also clear that the Four Year Plan, though

---

[1] 10 September: "There can be no doubt that the Jews are the founders
of Bolshevism: it was propagated by the Jews with the object of destroying
the civilised people of Europe and setting up international Jewish domination over them."

[2] In addition to the "maximum" of 36 divisions, there were now to be
3 new armoured divisions, as a nucleus for 8 more.at an early date.

ostensibly economic, was completely dominated by military considerations, its aim being to provide Germany with those reserves of raw material without which a war can no longer be waged with safety, and to impose upon the whole nation those restrictions without which the pace of armament would have to be greatly relaxed. Enlightening comment was soon provided by Colonel Thomas, head of the Economic Staff of the German War Ministry, in the organ of the Ruhr heavy industry: "The Four Year Plan is a result of our thought along the lines of war economy, and is meant to bring us what other states have in their countries, and what every country needs in order to hold its own in the world."[1] Early in 1937 the same authority pointed out publicly that the Great War had been lost because Germany overestimated her economic resources: it had already been lost, he added, in the winter of 1916–17. This was why the German armies had to penetrate Roumania and Ukraine, in order to provide something even faintly resembling an organised food supply.[2] The obvious inference is that the Four Year Plan of General Göring (see *infra*, p. 276) was above all aimed at preventing a similar situation in the next war.

If proofs were still lacking as to the harsh realities of the European situation—in Mr Duff Cooper's phrase, "the gravest since 1914"—they were provided by the action of all Germany's smaller neighbours (Belgium, Holland, Denmark, Switzerland, Austria, Czechoslovakia and Lithuania—the last of these with a very guilty conscience) in hastily strengthening their armed forces and defences. In Britain, too, at long last, the absolute necessity of vast rearmament was reluctantly faced: and a series of debates and speeches during the winter of 1936–7 showed a firm resolve to make good the time lag which Mr Baldwin admitted as a real handicap of democracy as against a dictator.[3] The dictator could reverse his policy in a night, but a democracy had to be educated and convinced of the right of a cause.

[1] *Deutsche Bergwerkszeitung*, 17 December 1936, cit. *Bulletin*, vol. XIII, No. 14 (9 January 1937).
[2] *Frankfurter Zeitung* of 10 February 1937.
[3] At Glasgow, 18 November 1936.

MR EDEN ON BRITISH POLICY

On 24 November Mr Eden, following his chief's line, gave an equally plain *refus* to those who seek "to divide the world into democracies and dictatorships", while insisting—in the true tradition of all his predecessors since Castlereagh and Canning—that it was "neither necessary nor desirable that our likes or dislikes for foreign forms of government should prejudice our international friendships or influence the course of our foreign policy". At the same time he defined, more clearly than ever before, the purposes for which British arms might be thrown into the scale—for the defence of the British Commonwealth; for the defence of France and Belgium "against unprovoked aggression, in accordance with our existing obligations" and (in the event of a West European Settlement) for the defence of Germany against similar aggression; and for the fulfilment of our treaties with Iraq and Egypt. They "may" also be used "in bringing help to a victim of aggression in any case where in our judgment it would be proper under the provisions of the Covenant to do so": but in such case there would be "no automatic obligation to take military action". "These arms would never be used in a war of aggression, or for a purpose inconsistent with the Covenant or the Kellogg Pact." There was a sting, in more directions than one, in his claim that "attempts to uphold international law had not benefited from the comparative decline of British strength in arms".

A week later, in welcoming the Belgian Premier, M. van Zeeland, to London, Mr Eden was still more precise. Arguing that clarity was the greatest service to the cause of peace, he affirmed that "the independence and integrity of Belgium is a vital interest for this nation, and that Belgium could count upon our help, were she ever the victim of unprovoked aggression". The situation was still further clarified during the debate of 4 December in the French Chamber, when M. Delbos stated that the British pledge was reciprocal, and that "all the forces of France by sea, land and air would be spontaneously and immediately used for the defence of Great Britain against an unprovoked aggression", and that this held good for Belgium also. "The whole French nation", he said, "felt attached to Britain by the strongest bonds of reason and sentiment, and knew that Franco-British friendship was the keystone of peace in Europe." Nothing could illustrate more strikingly the immediate response on all sides to anything which suggested a return of clear thinking on the part of Britain.

Early in 1937 Mr Eden made a further series of pronounce-ments which showed him to be following his own advice of thinking deeply and seeking for the clarification of policy. He reciprocated most cordially the Führer's argument that present economic worries should serve as an incentive to reconciliation among the nations: but at the same time made it clear that "we definitely prefer butter to guns", and that rearmament was "not the road we wish to travel", yet that "no other policy was open to us in a rapidly rearming world".[1] In the House he restated the main objectives of British Policy—the negotiation of a European settlement and the strengthening of the authority of the League—and as a means to these ends, the re-equipment of the three fighting services. "Economic collaboration and political appeasement must go hand in hand.... But"—and here he flung down the glove—"we do not accept that the alternative for Europe lies between the dictatorship of the Right and of the Left. We do not accept that democracies are the breeding-ground for Communism. We regard them rather as its antidote." "Europe cannot be torn between acute national rivalries and violently opposed ideologies without bearing scars which will last for a generation. Germany has it in her power to influence a choice which will decide not only her fate, but that of Europe." But the world can only be cured by general co-operation, "by abandoning the doctrine of national exclusiveness and accepting every European state as a potential partner in a general settlement: by bringing armaments down to a level sufficient for the essential needs of defence and no more, and

[1] 12 January, at the Foreign Press Association.

by accepting such international machinery for the settlement of disputes as will make the League of Nations a benefit to all and a servitude to none". Though suave and conciliatory in form, the whole speech was a downright rejection of the doctrine of the "Two Ideologies" in Europe, of the anti-Genevan tendencies of Berlin and Rome, and of the attempt to exclude Russia from Europe and strip France of her alliances. Step by step, and with a very proper caution, the Foreign Secretary was testing the reactions of public opinion to a clearly defined policy, and doubtless seeking for himself also a clear answer to certain fundamental interconnected questions: was the country's apparent devotion to League principles only emotional and skin-deep, or was it prepared to take the supreme risks of war rather than abandon the ideal of a new international order? And in the former event, did that mean that it was not prepared to take the still vaster risks of rearmament and world-wide conflict in defence of a Commonwealth which was indeed the main obstacle to the triumph of "gangsterism" as a political form of government? Was *The Times* right in describing the policy defined by Mr Eden as "the policy not only of the British Government, but of the whole British people... the only policy consonant with our traditions"?

HITLER AND EUROPEAN PEACE

A week later, on the fourth anniversary of his access to power, the Führer delivered the third of his great "programme speeches" (30 January 1937). The announcement that "*the period of so-called surprises is now over*" seemed to suggest that the Wilhelmstrasse had succeeded in convincing him that sudden *coups* and shock tactics were less suited to diplomacy than to actual war: but in view of the frequency with which he had altered what he had himself publicly declared immutable, this new pledge did not reassure outside opinion. In the same way such phrases as "Peace is our dearest treasure" could not be taken at their face value in view of the parallel policy of super-armament, and in the light of no less positive peace pledges by

Mussolini at a time when he was planning war on a large scale. His reaffirmation of the view that there exists "no humanly conceivable subject of dispute whatsoever between Germany and France", and of the "ardent wish" for co-operation with Britain, were in the mouth of so absolute a ruler not lightly to be dismissed by any friends of peace: but their value was greatly discounted by the complete failure to respond to the extremely cordial overtures made by the French Government at Lyons only a week earlier, by the sarcastic tone[1] of his frequent references to Mr Eden's speech, and by the very marked tendency to ignore the Jewish Premier of France and appeal over the heads of Popular Front and National Government to some as yet inarticulate public opinion in the two western countries.

Other much more positive features were the offer to guarantee not only Belgium, but Holland, "for all time", the strong repudiation of any desire for isolation; the list of National Socialist agreements with other countries, e.g. Poland, Austria and Japan, cited in proof, and the hope of "similar good and hearty relations with all our neighbours"; the insistence that the permanent isolation of a Power of sixty-five millions in so central a strategic position is not possible "in a world as small as Europe today": and the announcement that Germany has only economic interests in the Mediterranean and puts forward no colonial claims save against countries which took colonies from her. The central argument is that Germany's "complete sovereignty and equality have been restored" and that she "will never again sign a treaty incompatible with the honour of the nation and Government and with Germany's vital interests, and which cannot in the long run be kept". This may perhaps be taken to mean that the fresh batch of repudiations relating to the Treaty of Versailles which he simultaneously proclaimed was to be taken as final (for the simple reason that there was little or nothing left to repudiate). The Rhine and Elbe waterways section had already been torn up in November, and now the liens established on the Railways and Reichsbank by the Dawes and Young Plans were also thrown on the ground,

[1] Very noticeable to wireless listeners, of whom I was one.

while Germany's signature to Article CCXXXI (on War Responsibility) was expressly withdrawn, with the remark that this action put an end to that part of the Treaty which was degrading to Germany.

The mentality which all this revealed was sufficiently depressing. Some arguments can be adduced for repudiating a dictated peace, lock, stock and barrel, whenever the possibility presents itself, but none for this arbitrary picking and choosing of clauses for piecemeal repudiation. It shows that Herr Hitler's whole conception of International Law is that of the Cave Man, and that he takes a positive satisfaction in flouting it. On the other hand his contention that nothing less than "the pacification of Europe" was at stake roused a sympathetic echo: but an analysis of the "Eight Ways" (strongly reminiscent of the American President-Prophet) by which it was to be achieved unfortunately revealed them as obscure and loosely worded generalisations. The need for "stable and orderly economic conditions" inside each country, or for "relations on a basis of mutual respect and equality", or for "mutual recognition of the vital interests of each", or the statement that "European problems can only be solved properly within possible limits"— such phrases do not bring us any further. The eighth "Way", indeed, seems to claim the right, in the name of national honour, to interfere in all questions of kindred minorities beyond the frontier: and here all must depend upon interpretation.

In a word, the Führer's pronouncement, despite an occasional note of conciliation, was essentially negative, and its insistence on fanatical "racialism" and on the crudest of economic autarkist theories, only served to reinforce, in all serious quarters in Britain, the need for defensive measures.

THE NEW ARMAMENT RACE

And so, on 17 February 1937, the practical proof that the British Government at any rate did not dream of craven abdication was provided by the formidable announcement of British rearmament expenditure, up to £400,000,000 in the first instance, and up to a possible limit of £1,500,000,000 in five years. This was accepted by the country with the very reverse of enthusiasm, indeed with bitter resentment and heart-searchings, but in the main with the knowledge that it had been rendered inevitable by the irresponsible and lawless action of the German Government. In Mr Neville Chamberlain's words to Parliament, it was "an unprecedented course", due to "the unprecedented conditions of the time".

With this crowning tragedy, savouring ominously of the general bankruptcy of European statesmanship, our chronological survey may close, though it will still be necessary to consider the special bearing of the Abyssinian and Spanish crises upon the general situation. It has been my endeavour to select from the vast mass of happenings which smother and stifle the average reader of the daily press, those salient incidents and pronouncements which have given shape and directive to policy. Such a survey (if I have succeeded in my desire not to omit any really essential facts) can hardly fail to reveal certain very definite tendencies in the Europe of today. But before we leave the specifically German side of the problem, it is necessary to deal briefly with the internal situation, in its military, economic, cultural and religious aspects.

Europe is today engaged upon an "armament race" such as is without precedent in history: and not only our own country, but Belgium and Holland, socialist Denmark, once neutral Switzerland, disarmed Austria, democratic Czechoslovakia, are all engaged in the same task. But while for us Italy's bid for Mediterranean power and the soaring ambitions of Japan in the Far East are contributory factors of the most vital importance, for all the others the determining factor was the fantastic rearmament of Germany. At first it was possible to accept the arguments with which the Führer mobilised home opinion—namely, Germany's absolute need for a defensive force in face of powerfully armed opponents and especially of the Red Army (nothing was said of the close military and technical co-operation between the German and Soviet Staffs ever since Rapallo). But with the Conscription Decree of

March 1935, the remilitarisation of the Rhineland a year later, and the further extension of military service in August 1936, it became obvious that Germany aimed at, and was in process of creating, the most powerful army in the world next to Russia, and one far more capable of offensive action. Foreign alarm was increased rather than diminished by the extreme difficulty of obtaining detailed figures of expenditure, and of course above all by the fact that since 1933 the last vestiges of budgetary control have disappeared in Germany.

In the first year of National Socialism the main efforts of the regime were directed towards reducing unemployment by all the speediest means that lay to hand. In 1934 the chief means of achieving that reduction was expanding armament production, which found places for the unemployed in new or enlarged factories, or in public works of a military character. Competent inquirers have reached the following estimate of German armament expenditure:[1]

1933–34	Reichsmark	3,000,000,000
1934–35	,,	5,500,000,000
1935–36	,,	10,000,000,000
1936–37	,,	12,600,000,000
Total in 4 years	,,	31,100,000,000

In view of the complicated and entirely arbitrary and artificial position of the German currency, any attempt to translate these figures into sterling is apt to be misleading,[2] but no one will deny that "fantastic" is a fitting adjective to apply. The nation's gratitude is due to Mr Winston Churchill for first drawing public attention to the immensity of German rearmament in his speeches of 10 March and 23 April 1936[3] in the House of

[1] See a series of weighty articles in *The Banker* for February 1937.

[2] At the par rate of 20 RM to £1 the figure is £1,550,000,000: at the current fixed rate of exchange of 12 to £1, it is over £2,500,000,000. A reasonable estimate could hardly fall short of £1,800,000,000.

[3] See also his article in the *Evening Standard* of 1 May 1936, his Horsham speech of 23 July 1936, and confirmatory articles in two such opposite organs as the *Morning Post* and *Daily Herald*.

Commons, and for reinforcing his figures by the most trenchant arguments in a series of subsequent speeches. From the resulting discussions it became clear that during 1935-6 Germany was spending four or five times as much on armaments as Britain, and that already before Britain was driven to pronounce the fatal sum of £1,500,000,000 as necessary for her own defence, Hitlerian Germany had actually expended something like that figure on rearmament. Most significant of all, the British Government, while veiling itself in discreet silence, pointedly refrained from challenging Mr Churchill's figures which (as was admitted on both sides) came from quite different sources, but supplemented official information.

One curious aspect of the military situation was that the Army chiefs found their wildest dreams far surpassed by what Hitler has brought them. The original aim of General von Seeckt—which had in large measure been achieved before his death—was the creation of a small professional army, highly trained and indeed specialised, and capable of serving as an irresistible spearhead in war, but merely supplemented by less trained militia forces whose duty it would be to hold down conquered country. The aim of Röhm and the Left Wing of the Party had been to assign to the S.A. the functions of such a militia, and his victory in 1934 would have given to the S.A. equal status with the Reichswehr and would almost inevitably have led to political and military dualism. Whether Hitler (who has always been devoted to the Army and only used the S.A. as a means to an end) was quick to realise this danger and was influenced by it on the Thirtieth of June, or whether his action was dominated by party considerations can hardly be determined: but it certainly seems to have weighed with the army chiefs, who sided decisively with Hitler. The downfall of the S.A. left the army without a rival, and its alliance with the Führer gave it an untrammelled position such as it had never enjoyed under William II. It was even too much of a good thing for some of the Generals, who would then have been content with a militia on something like the Swiss model. The initiative for the conscription decree of 1935 came from

Hitler himself, and the Staff were now faced by the difficult problem of converting a specialised army of 100,000 men enlisted for twelve years into a conscript army of the old style. One very great difficulty was the fact that for the past fifteen years there had been no annual conscription and that an entirely new organisation had to be created for the cadres. But it is calculated by the same acute observer that by the beginning of 1937 Germany could already place in the field "81 divisions, 3 armoured divisions, and auxiliary troops giving a total of between 1,200,000 and 1,300,000 men". Meanwhile it is in the Air Force that the most phenomenal progress has to be recorded, thanks to the ruthless, untiring energy of its chief, General Göring, the propagandist campaign in its favour and the lavish sums expended upon factory output. On the other hand, the German aeroplanes tried out in Spain are known to have shown disappointing results: while there is still a certain shortage of pilots, by comparison with Britain or with Russia. There are also signs of jealousy between the Air Force and the Reichswehr, which resents the altogether disproportionately rapid promotion of the former and, from a purely technical standpoint, criticises its often inadequate training.

GERMANY'S ECONOMIC POSITION

Only the pen of the rare few who know the innermost secrets of international finance and who would die rather than reveal them could really do justice to the lunacy of the German financial situation. My present purpose is merely to provide a few broad splashes of colour, against which the foreground of my political picture will stand out more clearly.

How German rearmament has been financed can only be learned approximately. Within the first fourteen months of the Nazi regime Germany's floating debt was almost doubled (from 2000 to 3000 millions of Reichsmark), and during the first two years, trebled:[1] while her budgetary expenditure has in four years risen from 6700 to 18,800 millions. That her

[1] *The Banker* (February 1937), pp. 110–11.

financial position is to the last degree unsound is only too obvious, for no autocracy of pre-war times ever showed such complete disregard for individual interests or such ultra-secretive methods, or such a gift for juggling with artificial values. Yet it must be assumed that the control exercised by the totalitarian state machine over the entire banking and industrial system, the investing public, and the ordinary taxpayer, is so stringent that so long as the regime can maintain its political prestige by periodic *coups*, it will be able to arrest any real danger of economic collapse for some time to come.

German currency is absurdly overvalued, and its connection with the Gold Standard bears no relation to the real facts of today, because a German gold reserve is almost non-existent. But she cannot devalue without striking a fatal blow at the prestige of the regime: for the nerves of the German public simply would not stand a repetition of the process that wiped out the savings of the middle class after the War, however confidently it might be claimed that the Mark could be pegged at a new level and its further decline prevented. As the natural road of devaluation—already followed by almost every other country, including Italy—was blocked by reasons of sentiment and psychology, there was gradually evolved, in the fertile and relentless brain of Dr Schacht, an economic system complex beyond all belief, and so abnormal that one argument and one only could serve as justification—namely, that *economically* Germany's status was one of war, not peace. The Schacht "New Plan", then, was compounded of elaborate clearing arrangements, to secure foreign credits: steady restriction of imports; a system of currency manipulations and blocked accounts; and a return to the principle of barter. The lesser states of Europe, in particular, confronted with arbitrarily "frozen credits" in Germany, had on the one hand to export large stocks of what Germany required of them (valued at such unfavourable rates that Germany was often able to resell them at an excellent profit in the world market—e.g. Hungarian wheat at Amsterdam) but on the other hand to accept payment of debts in goods or materials for which they had no very special need and whose introduction dislocated their own home market. Germany has latterly been conducting her foreign trade "in Marks devalued from 20 to 80 per cent".[1]

The fundamental economic weakness of Nazi Germany lies in the fact that her political and military aims require her to be self-sufficient (hence the periodic pronouncements of Göring, Hess, Goebbels and the Führer himself), but that autarky is rendered impossible by her lack of most of the materials most vitally essential in a modern war. Of coal and potash she has abundance, but she is short of vegetable oils, cotton, jute, flax, nickel, bauxite. She only possesses one-third of the iron she requires: and above all she must import rubber, wool and oil, unless she can produce adequate synthetic substitutes. Desperate efforts are being made to do so, and the secret is too well guarded for it to be possible to express a positive opinion as to success or failure. All that is known is that so far the experiment has proved more expensive than the resources of the Reich would seem to justify, and that the *Ersatz* material used in Spain proved much less durable and trustworthy than had been hoped. The Four Year Plan for autarky in raw materials announced at the Nuremberg Congress in 1936 aims at producing substitutes on a vast scale—staple fibre, rayon, aluminium, synthetic oil and rubber: and foreign experts are prepared to believe that as regards motor fuel Germany may eventually succeed in making herself self-supporting to 80 or 85 per cent of her requirements. But in other directions the expense is likely to be prohibitive, and the results to be inferior. The private comments of the tailoring trade in Germany on the question of substitutes are well worthy of attention.[2]

The Führer has one immense achievement to his credit: he

[1] A very clear account of "The Economics of Hitlerism" is to be found in pp. 145–8 of Professor Stephen Roberts's *The House that Hitler Built*.

[2] It is believed that in war all textile manufactures will be commandeered, the population being left with what clothing they actually possess, and again that all metals in private possession will be placed at the disposal of the military authorities.

can stand before the masses as having solved the problem of unemployment which hung as a nightmare over Germany when he came to power. If it be objected that this claim is only partially true in view of the vast dimensions of "Winter Help", it may be replied that this too stands to his credit, and is certainly not worse than "dole" methods in other countries. Even the unquestionable fact that despite all the efforts of the regime wages are slowly falling and prices slowly rising, pales before the supreme achievement of finding work for the working masses and above all for their rising generation. But of course all the resources of a totalitarian propaganda are strained to the utmost to check the silent groundswell of a popular discontent which remembers with regret the days of a free press and trade union rights, and which without knowing what *is* true, or as yet dreaming in any way of resistance, still knows that most of what it is told is *untrue*. What alone makes a continuance of this situation possible is the complete suppression of the financial facts. Already in 1934–5 there was an accumulated deficit of 2,464,000,000 Marks, and though since then the ordinary revenue has undoubtedly increased and the cost of unemployment relief has been radically reduced, yet the inevitable expenditure of an uncontrolled despotism bent on a gigantic military gamble has increased at a still greater rate. Indeed, in the first two years of the regime—that is, before the full flood of rearmament began—the public debt is admitted to have increased sevenfold.

Meanwhile, in a field to which much less attention has hitherto been paid in this country, that of agriculture, desperate efforts have been made not merely to raise standards among the peasants and to extend small holdings (though Hitler has hitherto kept his hands off the Junkers of the East), but above all to achieve *agricultural* self-sufficiency. At the back of this programme are the strange "Blood and Soil" theories (*Blut und Boden*—"Blu-Bo") of the Minister of Agriculture, Dr Darre, which make so direct an appeal to the "Racist" fanatic in whose hands power now rests. Yet despite heavy subsidies and an elaborate framework of marketing boards and technical research,

there has been in these four years a steady decline in foodstuffs
and, what is still more alarming, in livestock. The goal proclaimed had been an increase of 60 per cent in the production
of wheat, rye and potatoes, and of 40 per cent in sugar: yet in
1935 these crops barely reached the level of 1928–34 and in
1936 decreased by over 14 per cent. Home-grown fodder
has only been increased by 8–10 per cent since 1933, and as the
import of fodder has fallen enormously, German livestock has
been catastrophically reduced. This applies alike to milking
cows, to cattle, sheep, pigs and poultry, and it was calculated
early in 1937 that by the end of the year the total stock would
have declined to something like the level of 1916. The then
still unforeseen outbreak of foot and mouth disease on a large
scale may possibly have expedited the process. The margin of
essential foods has dangerously diminished during 1937 in
Germany: the catchword of "guns versus butter" has its practical impact on every household, and but for a more than
usually ample potato crop the "small man" would be feeling
the pinch still more severely. The Government has, very reasonably, devoted a special effort to keeping down the prices of
foodstuffs of the first necessity for the poor, such as bread,
sugar and potatoes: but it has not been able to keep down the
price of fruit, eggs, butter and meat, and the general standard
of nutrition is held to have fallen by about 20 per cent.[1] Worst
of all, perhaps, is the decline in the area of cultivated land by
1,100,000 hectares in four years, a fact partly accounted for by
the large amount of arable land taken over for military purposes
(almost invariably from smallholders, not big landlords). Here
lies the key to the vexed problem of autarky. The failure of the
National Socialist agricultural experiment necessitates increasing
imports of grain (to a value of 224,000,000 RM. in the first half
of 1937 as compared with 31,000,000 in the corresponding
period of 1936). And as concentration on rearmament drives
the nation ever nearer to the margin of starvation, the temptation for the propagandist to lay all the blame of "Have-Not"
misery upon the wicked "Haves" grows ever greater. It should

[1] *The Banker*, p. 143.

be added that the German trade figures for 1937[1] show that despite all the talk of self-sufficiency, imports had increased by 30 per cent in comparison with 1936—44 per cent of the total coming from overseas.

A SECRET MEMORANDUM

Foreign estimates of Germany's true economic position, however carefully arrived at, must be formed and received with great caution: for it is a vital interest of the present regime to conceal many of the essential facts, and hence there is always a danger that a general survey may be incomplete and out of focus. Hence it is of especial value to study a confidential memorandum drawn up early in 1937 by a group of influential German industrialists and business men for the special use of the Führer himself. By an indiscretion, its text found its way abroad, and it is astonishing that so little attention has been paid to its sober, yet profoundly disturbing, arguments. I make no apology for summarising them here.

The Memorandum starts by noting the three main weaknesses of the German situation. I. There is a lack of the necessary supplies of raw material—40–60 per cent below requirement: and as an increased export of German goods cannot help, the situation must be met by an increased output of *Ersatz* material at home. II. There is a lack of the necessary foodstuffs and fodder—20–25 per cent below requirement: and the regulation of prices and restriction of sales are needed to make good the poor crops of 1936 and to reduce agricultural imports. III. There is a shortage of employment in the home market: full economic output would mean the export of German goods to the value of 10–13 milliards, but at present export only reaches 4 milliards—6–8 per cent, as against 20–25 per cent at a period of general prosperity (*Hochkonjunktur*).

It then takes note that the economic activity of 1933–6 was due to public works, road construction, military armament and

---

[1] Published in Berlin on 17 February 1938. At the same time exports rose by 25 per cent, but the total excess of exports over imports declined from the equivalent of £45,833,000 to £36,916,000.

the beginnings of an *Ersatz* system, and estimates that 72 per cent of the total labour (*Arbeitskräfte*) were employed in industry. Though no exact figures exist as to the capital used to achieve this result, it estimates them at about 35–40 milliards, of which 10–15 were provided from private sources and the remainder by the State. This means that Germany is using up a considerable portion of her material resources on unproductive work.

"The first condition of an ordered economy is an ordered Budget": but exact estimates are rendered impossible by three unknown quantities. I. Rearmament rests mainly on State credit. But the final peace footing of Germany has not yet been fixed, and "*no one knows the present state of military armament, still less its necessary dimensions*". The Army's future size depends upon how far financial means can be mobilised, and how much technical material and raw materials can be acquired. II. The cost of the State administration, and especially the many new branches of "the Party-State", such as the "*German Arbeitsfront*", the *Reichsnährstand*, and the various youth organisations. Formerly it was calculated that for every twelve "productive citizens" there was one administrative official: today there is one to every eight. Exact calculations will only become possible when the new machine is complete and working normally: meanwhile, the complicated methods of currency and price control, of import and export, and the constant interference in economic life, made it necessary "to set up a ministerial dictatorship over all economic and state administrative offices", with a view to carrying out the Four Year Plan. III. The uncertainty as to the rate of interest on the public debt. Germany is faced by the alternative of converting her State debt, or of turning her unconsolidated debts into permanent low-interest Rentes.

The economic position is fluid, both as regards food supplies and raw materials. "The agrarian policy of 1933–7 has not removed the natural fluctuations of the harvest. The need for imported vital foods and fodder has been increased by three poor crops and by the exhaustion of all reserves. The normal requirement of 10 million tons of flour can be covered in a good harvest, but the deficit of roughly 1½ million tons of fodder cannot be met from our own resources. It could be met by considerably reducing livestock, but this would affect the supply of meat and fat." Germany lacks the necessary area for an increased agricultural output. "Even with the strictest economy" there must be a deficit, amounting to 20–25 per cent of the total supplies required "for man and beast", such as can only be made good by import. "It will always be impossible for Germany to attain 100 per cent self-sufficiency in grain and fodder." [1]

As regards raw materials, it may be possible in the next two or three years to meet 50 per cent of the requirements of the iron and steel works, but the maximum of home production in zinc, lead, and copper was respectively 65–70, 35–45 and 10–15 per cent of the total: while tin and nickel were unobtainable at home. The import of raw oil and benzine had risen from 2·4 million tons in 1932 to 3·8 in 1935, and in 1936, 4·5–5 millions were required: home production was rising, but imports had almost doubled. The New Plan cannot succeed without further importation of essential raw materials. Home production meets 20–25 per cent of the total requirements: at best it can be raised to 30–40 per cent.

Meanwhile the dependence of South-East Europe on the German market is diminishing, and German exports in that direction are declining. Autarky in raw materials must of necessity bring further losses in export and a deterioration of Germany's position in world-trade.

Finally, the Memorandum broached the financial problem, arguing that 25 milliard Marks had to be found. Hitherto the Reichsbank had distributed State securities and credit among the various banks, savings banks, insurance companies and

---

[1] Cf. the statement of Dr Schacht on 9 December 1936, to the effect that Germany had lost 15 per cent of her pre-war arable land, and that otherwise she would have a surplus of grain and potatoes. In *Volk und Raum*, edited by Professor Werner Sombart, it is held that Germany can only maintain a growing population within her present frontiers by increasing her livestock and her output of rye, and by returning to her ancestral practice of eating "Vollkornbrot".

industrial concerns: but this involved sinking more and more capital. The former credit of the banks was "for the most part exhausted", and replaced by book credits and claims against bills of exchange. "This process can be continued up to the limit at which the banks no longer can fulfil their obligations to their private clients": the Reichsbank could intervene in an acute crisis, but could not suddenly increase the note circulation. The extension of the Four Year Plan would use up still further reserves; it would indeed "be nothing else than the undermining of existing capital and so the immobilising of the banks".

The present system, it was argued, rests to 50–60 per cent on state contracts and short-term credits. Three factors—unproductive armament and building, expensive autarky, and export at a loss—had combined to reduce the German public's buying power by 40 per cent: and there was a further invisible rise of costs through the diminishing quality of the goods offered to the public. This could not be altered by the strictest control, or by political measures. "If prices cannot be kept down, the wage question is raised, and the currency comes into the open danger zone." There was no available alternative. For, firstly, devaluation would only be a very temporary remedy and could not safely be repeated; it was now impossible to link up the Mark with the Dollar, Pound or Franc. ("In these years it has lost its connection with foreign currencies, without any injury to them"): and there was no prospect of foreign creditors cancelling the old loans and granting a new one. "The decisive basis for a new currency is Export": but as it had already been demonstrated that export on the scale regarded as necessary was incompatible with the New Plan, a complete deadlock had been reached, and the Memorandum ended on a note of negation.

It is quite superfluous to underline the high significance of this "inside" verdict. It reveals that in her domestic, no less than in her foreign, policy Germany is on the horns of a dilemma, and that she has set her heart upon mutually irreconcilable aims. East or West, land in Europe or colonial ambitions, autarky or world trade, race-mysticism or Christianity—the conflict of ideals keeps her in a ferment.

One clear conclusion may be drawn. Three years after the conflict of June 1934 there was once more a determined tug-of-war between the "Nationalist" and the "Socialist" elements in the Party, and it would this time be mere folly to predict the final result. Instead of using my own words I prefer to quote from an unexceptionable Conservative and capitalist source. "They" (e.g. the Nazi leaders) "denounce the theory and practice of Marxist-Bolshevism with a fervour unknown in even the most orthodox countries, while their actions bear a greater resemblance every day to those carried out in Russia four to five years ago."[1] And meanwhile, by a grotesque irony, the main subject of their denunciation, Stalin, is busily engaged in rounding up and shooting by the hundred all the genuine exponents of Bolshevism in Russia.

Weighty as are the facts and arguments summarised in this memorandum, and important as are the circles responsible for their presentation to the Führer, it would be a complete error to assume that they could avail to arrest evolution inside the National Socialist Party. Their warning has been disregarded, and the fall of Dr Schacht in October 1937 was a striking proof of the diminished influence of the big industrialists upon public policy. More and more the economic situation in Germany is dominated by the lack of raw materials, and more and more private industrial concerns find themselves on the verge of disaster, owing to the constant danger of their stocks and supplies failing. But neither this nor the sullenly passive attitude of the working masses has been allowed to check the trend of the regime, not merely towards a system of autarky in which civilian interests are increasingly subordinated to military needs, but towards state control of private industries. Extremes meet, and for all their denunciation of Bolshevism, the present rulers of Germany are moving steadily in the direction of state omnipotence, behind the screen of blind obedience and personal deification.

[1] *The Banker* (February 1937), p. 133.

THE DOCTRINE OF RACE

It remains to consider—again in the merest outline—one other vital aspect of National Socialism, which is already affecting the *spiritual* development of all Europe: this is the doctrine of so-called *Volkstum*. While Mussolini goes to the opposite extreme of admitting that "there are no races: that is an intellectual illusion, a sentiment"[1], Hitler has adopted, in a raw and undigested form, the extravaganzas of "Aryan" doctrine which are the laughing-stock of all anthropologists and scientists outside the frontiers of Germany. Starting from a strange jumble of the teachings of Houston Stewart Chamberlain, Gobineau and Nietzsche, and the political symbolism which underlies Richard Wagner's romantic mythology, Hitler has evolved a theory of Aryan superiority, of a Nordic race which is the very quintessence of Aryanism and finds its highest expression in the Teutonic tribes (the "Supermen" of pagan times), of their essential racial purity and of the vital need for preventing alien, and above all Jewish, infiltration.[2]

In passing, be it noted that the Führer himself is far from being a Nordic type: he belongs to the Alpine semi-Celtic type which is common enough in his native province of Upper Austria. Dr Goebbels is also not a Nordic type: that he is a physical weakling is by no means to his discredit according to our Western standards, for he belongs to the same category as Nelson or Wolfe. But he is not an advertisement for the truly Nordic theory of the survival of the fittest. Herr Hess, again, is a more Southern type, and even General Göring, though he might pass muster as Germanic in type, cannot boast the slim figure of the true Nordic hero.

[1] Emil Ludwig, *Gespräche mit Mussolini*, p. 228.
[2] It is only fair to add that (as Mr Steed has shown in his brilliantly lucid and succinct study of *Hitler; Whence and Whither?* pp. 14–38) Chamberlain's main criticisms of Judaism are directed against the intolerance which, in his view, Ezekiel, Ezra and Nehemiah grafted upon an older religion: and that he also claims the idea of individual rights and constitutional liberty as typically Germanic and Nordic. On this showing, Hitler would seem to be Semitic rather than Aryan in two absolutely fundamental questions.

The Führer devotes many pages of *Mein Kampf* to a definition of *"völkisch"*, but after admitting at the outset that few conceptions are so variously interpreted and so lacking in precision, alike from the theoretical and from the practical angle (pp. 415–16, cf. also p. 397), he ends by leaving his readers more in the dark than ever, except that in the process he has given them the pontifical assurance that "the bourgeois world is Marxist" (p. 420) and that "human culture and civilisation on this globe are inseparably linked up with the presence of the Aryan". (p. 421). Yet it is highly characteristic of the man that he boldly declares that "the more indefinable this conception is in practice, the more comprehensive interpretations it allows, the more possible is it to take it as a basis [*sich auf ihn zu berufen*]". (p. 397). Equally obscure are the 700 pages of Alfred Rosenberg's *Myth of the Twentieth Century*, yet it starts with the idea that "a whole generation is coming to realise that values can only be created and preserved where the law of blood, consciously or unconsciously, decides the ideas and actions of man", and that the "lifeless and airless" ideals which had come to us from Syria and Asia Minor had produced spiritual degeneration and were to be rejected.

From this inchoate form, however, there has steadily developed a creed which, after making out of purity of race the foundation-stone of the nation, seeks to identify "nation" and "state". This totalitarian idea expresses itself in home politics by making the Party coterminous with the Nation: but it also has a foreign application, since every German in the world is to be claimed as belonging to the German Nation, and hence, if Nation and State be identical, the Reich Government automatically acquires the right to interfere in the affairs of all those countries where there are German minorities (and nine out of the twelve states of Europe fall under this category). In the five years of Nazi rule this view has been steadily inculcated in official quarters. As recently as 28 November 1937 the Minister of the Interior, Dr Frick, declared that "race and nationality, blood and soil, were the principles of National Socialist thought", and that "the German Nation was not composed only of the 65 millions living inside the Reich, but of the 100 million Germans distributed over the whole world". "Unification of all German peoples in a Great Germany on a basis of self-determination" was the Nazi ideal, though there were undoubtedly difficulties of frontier and of racial inter-mixture.

What specially distinguishes Nazi "racialism" is its extreme intolerance, based on rigid immutable physical facts. As Pro-fessor Toynbee has pointed out with searching eloquence, the Nazis are the first "to persecute avowedly and implacably on the ground of physical race. The Aryan paragraph penalised a *ci-devant* Jew who had become a convert to Christianity, together with his brethren who had remained members of the Jewish religious community. Under the Nazi dispensation, salvation and damnation depended neither on works nor on faith, but on physique."[1] This cuts at the very roots of morality and religion, since by its imposition of a physical disability it blasphemously challenges the craftsmanship of the Creator Himself. But it is hardly less intolerable from a more mundane point of view, since it deliberately establishes the doctrine of racial inequality before the law and excludes all Jews, on the basis of their blood, from full German citizenship.[2] Little wonder that indignation was especially deep in Britain, where Jewish enfranchisement had been regarded last century as one of the test cases of political liberty, and in America, where the Jewish element is recognised as having made a serious contribution to the national life.

It is quite true that the Jews in Germany had acquired a disproportionate influence in the press and the theatre, in medicine and, at any rate at Berlin, in the legal profession: it is also true that some Jews who had emancipated themselves from their ancient Jewish tradition were even more decadent than the corresponding class of "emancipated" Christians. But

---

[1] *Survey for* 1933, p. 158. As he points out, this far outdistances the Spanish persecution of the Jews in the fifteenth century: for when they accepted conversion they were received as full citizens.

[2] Party Programme of 25 February 1920: Law of 15 September 1935.

this cannot for one moment excuse the crass exaggerations of their persecutors; the monstrous insinuation that there is no such thing as "a good Jew"; their deliberate attempt—insulting, no doubt, but also simply idiotic to any normal brain—to identify Judaism and Marxism, or again, Judaism and the White Slave traffic; the open ill-treatment of Jewish children in school; the frequent withdrawal of police protection from their persons and property.[1] It is, moreover, necessary to insist that the frantic terms in which Hitler again and again alludes to the Jews throughout *Mein Kampf* can only be interpreted as proof of abnormality, to the point of mental obsession: and this view is strengthened by his close friendship with Julius Streicher and his constant encouragement to the foul and unprintable calumnies of the latter's paper, *Der Stürmer*. This is something in face of which it is not possible to pass by on one side of the road to Jericho. For it cannot be a matter of indifference to the outside world that a great nation, once renowned for its devotion to learning and scientific truth, and occupying a key position in Europe, should adopt "methods of barbarism" against a whole community among its own subjects, and should use the new system of totalitarian control of education, information and opinion, in order to feed the younger generation with a mass of lies which could not for twenty-four hours stand the test of criticism and discussion in a free country.

In this connection it is necessary to say very bluntly that we, on our side, while desirous to bury the past and do justice to former enemies, do quite definitely resent the grotesquely untrue theory, put about for propagandist reasons by the Nazi authorities, that Germany only lost the war because of the Jews. Alfred Rosenberg tells us that in 1918 "almost the entire

---

[1] Cf. the attitude of General Göring, as Prussian Minister of the Interior, towards the forcible boycott of Jewish shops: "I refuse to turn the police into a guard for Jewish stores" (*The Times*, 11 March 1933). Incidentally, Professor Roberts does well to point out that the German theory of intense danger from the Jew is quite incompatible with that other theory that Nazism was a spontaneous uprising of the whole German people (*The House that Hitler Built*, p. 260).

command of the state, of society, of culture, was in the hands of this race which, in common with the old parties (Social Democrat, Democrat and Centre), carried out the subjection of the German people".[1] It should suffice to point out that this utterly conflicts with the whole narrative of General Ludendorff, especially in the period from 15 July to 13 August 1918.[2]

In one aspect, this concentration of calumny against the Jews is merely a political "stunt", based on the urgent need for a scapegoat on whom to lay the blame for defeat in war. But it is also a test case in the relations between free and unfree communities. Are real intellectual intercourse, real spiritual understanding, real sympathy and co-operation, and indeed anything beyond the most perfunctory and "diplomatically correct" dealings, permanently possible between nations who preserve absolute freedom of discussion in speech and writing and the strictest constitutional control of government and bureaucracy, and nations where public opinion is absolutely muzzled, where academic freedom no longer exists, where school textbooks have been re-written in a strictly party sense, where the teaching of history has become a mere machine for inculcating German patriotism, where the entire youth movements are in the hands of party agitators, and where all religious teaching, save a glorification of pagan myths, is deliberately excluded from the training of the future leaders? This is a question which must inevitably loom large in any serious consideration of our relations with Germany. My whole thesis is built up on the geographical platitude that Germany holds the central position in more senses than the merely strategical, and on the belief that an understanding between the two Western democracies and Germany is the pivot upon which peace or ruin in Europe depends. But that understanding will not be advanced by evading or ignoring the obstacles flung in its path by militant National Socialist psychology.

[1] *Blut und Erde,* p. 342.
[2] See Ludendorff, *Meine Kriegserinnerungen,* pp. 551–3, 566, 591.

NATIONAL SOCIALISM AND EDUCATION

The National Socialist regime has not been content to apply totalitarian principles to the political sphere only: it has laid its heavy hand upon education, and from the elementary school to the University the whole curriculum is subordinated to the rigid discipline and propaganda of the Party. It is, however, its attitude to the Universities—once the glory of Germany—that is doing perhaps more than anything else to open a gulf between the intellectuals of Germany and those Western and Northern countries where learning is still free from State control. Not merely has the autonomy of which her ancient Universities were so justly proud been replaced by complete subordination to the State: not merely has the number of students been cut down by 30 per cent (this problem was already acute—and not in Germany alone—before the coming of Nazism, and there is much to be said as to the dangers of overproduction and of an intellectual proletariat): not merely have the old student organisations been ruthlessly disbanded (here too a strong case can be made out against the caste habits and snobbery which prevailed in some of them): not merely has the total teaching staff also been reduced by one-fifth. But methods that can only be described as Bolshevist (for they are an exact imitation of those till recently employed in Soviet Russia against the non-proletarian class) have been adopted both as regards admission to scholarships and as regards appointment to teaching posts. In the one case "preference is given at all stages to Nazis",[1] in the other only persons regarded as reliable from the Nazi point of view are accepted. The extent of the upheaval can best be judged by the fact that no fewer than 1684 teachers have been dismissed from various University posts under the Nazi regime: of these 313 were full professors, 493 extraordinary professors, 75 professors *honoris causa* and 322 *Privatdozenten*. In the overwhelming majority of cases the ground was purely political; the number of Jews among them is estimated at

[1] Professor Roberts, *op. cit.* p. 256.

800,[1] or slightly less than half. Thus, while the possession of a Jewish grandmother is regarded as a disqualification for teaching any subject to "Aryan" undergraduates, it is clear that "liberal" and "progressive" views are also penalised. This unexampled persecution has led to the creation of an intellectual Diaspora— not solely Jewish—to which the Universities of the entire world have endeavoured to lend a helping hand: 384 of the victims have been placed in permanent,[2] and 302 in temporary, posts. The fact that 412 were medical men and 106 physicists, as against 173 in social sciences, 132 in law and 60 in history, is in itself proof that National Socialism imports its intolerant doctrine even into pure science. "It is the task of the German Universities", so runs a decree of 24 November 1934, "to put scientific research into the clearest possible relationship with the national political needs of our people." This is fully in accord with the official attitude towards Fritz Haber, the great Jewish chemist, whose nitrogen experiments during the War were of vital assistance to the German cause, but who was expected to eject his Jewish colleagues from the Electro-Chemical Institute over which he presided, and who was dismissed when he refused. This is perhaps the crudest instance of all: but the whole outlook of National Socialism towards science, culture, academic freedom is the despair of all Western teachers who would fain still believe in that *unitas in diversitate* of European culture which, at any rate before the War, was stronger than artificial frontier barriers. Today we ask ourselves whether the Nazis have not, by their own deliberate act, fixed a great gulf between two incompatible worlds. Dr Mackail, in his presidential address to the British Academy,[3] voiced a widespread feeling when he declared that "the traditions of academic freedom" and the

---

[1] A full and reliable statement will be found in *The German Universities and National Socialism*, by E. Y. Hartshorne, especially pp. 87–102. The largest number of dismissals occurred at Berlin (242, or 32·4 per cent.), Frankfurt (108, or 32·3 per cent.), Heidelberg (60, or 24 per cent.), Breslau (68, or 21 per cent.), and Göttingen (45, or 18·9 per cent.).

[2] 96 in the United States, 77 in Britain, 40 in Turkey, 38 in Palestine.

[3] 11 July 1934.

civilisation of Europe "stands with its back to the wall", and that the supreme need was for "the clear, emphatic, uncompromising and constant upholding of a doctrine and an ideal, the doctrine and ideal of humanism".

To me, as an historian, the Nazi attitude towards historical teaching is of special interest: but I make no apology for directing the special attention of the general reader to the circular issued by the German Minister of the Interior, Dr Frick, to all educational authorities, for nothing reveals more clearly the meaning of "totalitarianism" than its application to the past.[1]

The document attempts to lay down certain "directive principles" for the teaching of history. In the first place it stresses the significance of "race" and "nationality" (*der völkische Gedanke*) "as opposed to the international idea, the creeping poison which has for the last 100 years been threatening to corrode the German soul itself". The fate of Germany's kinsmen outside her borders must always be kept in evidence, and cultural history must not be given pre-eminence "over the political history which shapes the fate of nations". "The heroic idea in its Germanic expression, associated with the idea of leadership of our own day, must penetrate historical teaching at all stages. . . . The heroic idea leads on directly to the heroic outlook on life, which specially suits us as a Germanic people." It must then be demonstrated that "the history of Europe is the work of peoples of Nordic race". The history of the Greeks, and again of Italy, must "begin in Central Europe": the decay of the Roman Empire is to be explained by the "denordicising" (*Entnordung*) of Southern Europe: the *Völkerwanderung* (what we denordicised degenerates call the "Barbarian Invasions") brought back blood into the degenerate hotch-potch (*Rassenmischmass*) of the Empire and made possible the cultural revival of the Middle Ages. "Only the fact that the German ruling class in Central, Western and Southern Europe was the bearer of medieval culture makes it possible to understand how medieval chivalry at its height exhibits everywhere such a uniform

[1] Circular No. III. 120/22. 6. The full text was published in *Nature*, 24 February 1934.

character." The Middle Ages are praised mainly because they were "a time of very great expansion of German power". But in the modern period, despite the growth of nationalist tendencies, international influences also began to penetrate, and led to "a lamentable intrusion of alien elements into German blood, speech, law, into the German conception of the state and finally into the general outlook upon the world". This must be countered by the development of German national consciousness, by renewed emphasis on "the bond of blood" and the community of the Nordic peoples. "The last twenty years of our own time must form the principal object of our study." Versailles and Potsdam are contrasted—the degradation of the former leading to the "collapse of the liberal-Marxist philosophy" and "the triumph of the National Socialist idea of freedom". In a word, history, like education, science and religion, is to become the handmaid of the all-embracing Party. From the Frick circular it is but a step to the theories of Alfred Rosenberg, that "there is no world-history in the real sense, but only the history of different races and peoples":[1] that the true heroes of medieval Germany are not Charles the Great, who led the Germans along the false track of inter- and super-national imperialism, but the rebel Widukind, Duke of the Saxons: not the Swabian and Hohenstauffen Emperors, following the will o' the wisp of Italian conquest—not even the once legendary Barbarossa—but the "rebel" Henry the Lion, who drove the Slavs back towards the East and made the rise of Prussia possible.[2]

This inroad of crude new theory is not confined to history: it has also made itself felt in the sphere of law. In a learned

[1] *Blut und Erde*, p. 258.

[2] We are indeed far from the days when Gibbon could paraphrase from the pages of Otto of Frisingen the speech in which Frederick Barbarossa apostrophised the delegates of Rome: "Are you desirous of beholding the ancient glory of Rome, the gravity of the Senate, the spirit of the Knights, the discipline of the camp, the valour of the legions? You will find them in the German Republic. It is not Empire, naked and alone; the ornaments and virtues of Empire have likewise migrated beyond the Alps to a more deserving people", *Decline and Fall*, vii, p. 234.

publication on the German penal code, written by three eminent
judges (with an introduction by the Reich Minister of Justice,
Dr Gürtner, and extracts from a Memorandum of the Prussian
Minister of Justice, Herr Kerrl),[1] it is affirmed that "penal law
may be called a mirror of the mental attitude of the people",
and that "there is need of a National Socialist Penal Code",
and that "every age has the law which corresponds to its spirit,
culture and fundamental ideas". This opinion of Dr Gürtner
is supplemented by Count Rüdiger von der Goltz, who declared
that "in the Will of the Führer party and state meet. Let the
new penal code be a witness of unified effort." It is openly
stated that the new code could not be based on the principles
which inspired the many drafts of recent decades: "on the
contrary, it could only come from one source, from the National
Socialist conception of people, popular life, popular leadership
and state". The argument is prominently reinforced by such
apodictic sayings from *Mein Kampf* as the following: "What
is not good race in this world, is chaff", and "It is not freedom
to sin at the expense of posterity, and hence of the race".

The same fantastic attitude is revealed by a pseudo-scientific
philippic against Bolshevism entitled *International Law against
Bolshevism*, by Dr Bockhoff, with an introduction by another
member of the Reich Cabinet, Dr Frank.[2] In it there occur the
following phrases: "Law is for us a special form of politics, that
is, its ordering." "The jurist must be politician, philosopher,
soldier and leader in one person, a true artist and a connoisseur."
He asserts that during the nineteenth century liberalism has
"dissolved the ethical substance of law", dismissed the conception of the Legal State as "meaningless and indeed extremely
confusing and mischievous chatter", and denounces the Liberal
intelligentsia "with its lack of moral responsibility", for talking

---

[1] *Das neue Strafrecht: Grundsätzliche Gedanken zum Geleit*, see especially
pp. 7–15 and 38. Cf. the statement of Dr Goebbels, on 20 May 1936:
"At the beginning of every Revolution stands the deed, and when the new
situation has been created, it is the task of the lawgivers to provide it with a
substructure of law."

[2] *Völkerrecht gegen Bolschevismus*, Berlin 1937, especially pp. 14–22.

of "objective research". "Objectivity towards one's out-and-out enemy (*Totalfeind*)?" he adds mockingly, and then goes on to identify "Bolshevism" and "Liberalism" as having only one foe in common, namely, "the *völkisch* National Socialism". One of his illuminating phrases is to the effect that "*Völkisch* Nationalism is today the sole true and competent defender of the right of the peoples, the only enemy whom the Red world criminals take seriously and are afraid of".[1] He has many effective extracts from Lenin and Stalin to show that the ultimate aim of both was the disappearance of the State as such, and here and there his criticism of the new Soviet Constitution condescends to be critical. But he reduces the ordinary reader to a despairing atrophy by page after page of unbalanced invective, intended to identify Bolshevism, Liberalism and the Jews in the mind of the German reader, and to suggest a world conspiracy against Germany.[2]

Still more crazy is the attempt to import National Socialism into the realm of science. As a single example may be quoted the speeches delivered at the opening of the Institute of Physics in the University of Heidelberg in December 1935. "It is very superficial to speak of science as such, as a common property of mankind, equally accessible to all peoples and classes and offering them all an equal field of work. The problems of science do not present themselves in the same way to all men. The negro or the Jew will view the same world in a different way from the German investigator." In other words, the scientific results of an Einstein or a Planck or a Haber are suspect, simply because of the race to which they belong.[3]

[1] *Völkerrecht gegen Bolschevismus*, Berlin, 1937, p. 208.

[2] Pp. 92, 99. Incidentally "the entry of the Soviet criminals into the League" is treated as destroying the latter's "last shreds of legality" (*Legitimitätssubstanz*), p. 99. Another phrase worth quoting is: "For Romain Rolland, as for all real Liberal democrats, Liberalism is not yet sufficiently anti-state, humanitarian, international, in other words, not sufficiently Nihilist", p. 159.

[3] See *Nature* of 18 January 1936, quoted by the Bishop of Durham in *The Times* of 4 February 1936. Cf. also the letter of Sir F. G. Hopkins in *The Times* of 24 February 1936.

LEADERSHIP AND CONSTITUTIONAL DOCTRINE

A word must be reserved for that extreme glorification of "Leadership" on which the whole Nazi structure is built up and which is designed to render criticism dangerous or impossible. Leadership and discipline are two of the noblest conceptions of the human mind and of the Christian religion, but, interpreted to mean an unreasoning surrender of the intellect, they lose their true balance and much of their virtue. There has always been a certain Byzantine trait in the German character: in the days of William II it was subjected to merciless attacks from three such different quarters as Count Reventlow,[1] Maximilian Harden and "Simplizissimus". Today a new object of adulation has been found and its form is cruder, because public opinion is less balanced and the vents of criticism have been tightly shut down. The attitude adopted towards Adolf Hitler borders dangerously on deification. That his portrait should be placed above the altar in some Lutheran Churches is in English eyes broadly comic as well as being blasphemous: it reveals such a basic lack of humour. But that this should be possible in a country recently renowned for its learning and culture is a danger to cultural values throughout Europe. The gulf that is opening between Germany and the West is revealed in the speech of Herr Kerrl, the Reich Minister for Church Affairs, who flatly declared that "the primary assumptions of the State as it is today, those of Race, Blood and Soil, must be sacrosanct for the Church as well. The Will of Our Father is given to us in our blood. Everything which National Socialism is now doing for the community...is doing the Will of God....The Jew is the instrument of bastardisation, as also of Communism. This tuberculous bacillus must be insulated by us. It is this which means carrying out the Will of God.... There has now arisen a new *authority as to what Christ and Christianity really are*—that is, Adolf Hitler....There will be a struggle for Christianity on the nationalist basis." This, be

[1] See his *Wilhelm der Zweite und die Byzantiner*, Munich, 1906.

it observed, is no casual opinion of some wild man of the woods, but the considered Church policy of the Reich, enunciated by its official mouthpiece with the full approval of the Führer. No Christian can give it any name save blasphemy.[1]

It is hardly too much to say that no ruler of Germany, since she first became a Reich many centuries ago, has ever possessed such unrestricted power as Adolf Hitler: but it is also true that there has never been, from the constitutional point of view, such complete chaos and obscurity. The plain fact is that the whole structure has been turned upside down, the relations between executive, legislature and judicature dislocated, or perhaps better said, the dividing lines between them blurred or effaced. And so it comes about that a serious writer on constitutional problems—Professor of Law at the University of Kiel, now one of the chief centres of Nazi "Wissenschaft"[2]— is able to argue quite seriously that the old constitution has "lost its validity", while the new one "is not a constitution in the formal sense known to the nineteenth century", and indeed that "there is no written constitution in the new Reich: but it exists as the unwritten political foundations (*Grundord-nung*)". He admits that certain provisions of Weimar have been rescinded or altered, but that the really essential fact is that "the old system as a whole has been destroyed" and that "this took place without any express proclamation, by silent disregard". "The name of Adolf Hitler is a programme, in which the deadly struggle against the Weimar system is a vital

[1] The lengths to which a perverse obsession can go are shown by Dr Goebbels' claim that the Jew is "uncreative": he "does not produce, but merely trades with products—with rags, clothes, pictures, precious stones, corn, shares, peoples and states". And again, "A Jew cannot insult a German. Jewish slanders are only scars of honour for a German Antisemite." "He who wins the approval of the Jews, is finished in advance, for a true National Socialist." See Goebbels, *Der Angriff*, pp. 329, 323, and *Vom Kaiserhof zur Reichskanzlei*, p. 155.

[2] Ernst Rudolf Huber, *Verfassung* (1937), one of the first of a large series of scientific publications, under the general heading of "Grundzüge der Rechts- und Wirtschaftswissenschaft", of which seven have already appeared and thirty more are announced.

point. When Hindenburg gave the power into the hands of
Hitler, and the people in its majority endorsed this, the Weimar
Constitution was dead."

The logical consequence, he argues, was to destroy all individual rights of liberty, alike the principles of parliamentarism,
federalism, liberalism and "the legal state" (*Rechtsstaat*). The
principle of leadership has replaced the system of the division
of powers, "the principle of movement" has replaced the
parliamentary Party State, Imperial unity has replaced federalism, the National army has replaced the professional army, the
fundamental race-idea—*Volkstum*—has replaced the formal
principle of equality. And the end of the whole matter is
that "all political power must be united in the hand of one
leader. The entire political life is determined by the unitary
and comprehensive will of the Leader." The new Racial State
(*das völkische Reich*) rests on the Leader's will—not, like democracy, on the general will. But it is not to be compared either
with absolutism or with dictatorships, which are mere temporary measures to meet a crisis. Germany is now a "Racial
Leader-State" and this is "a final and normal political order".
The Führer, not the Reichstag, is legislator for the German
people: in him, not in the Reichstag, is vested financial control.[1]
He does not hold the three offices of President, Chancellor and
Party Leader, but a new office of "Führer", in which all three
are blended. The Weimar Article 41, by which the President
is elected by the people, is no longer valid: there is no time-limit
for his post, and deposition is impossible. "Separation of executive and legislature is a thing of the past." Ministers are
responsible to him alone, and he can issue decrees in each of
their special spheres without consulting them. Law is to be
interpreted as the "Will of the Leader". "As all parliamentary

[1] Not the least amazing feature of the new regime is the status of the
Reichstag: it is filled by party nominees, who attend one session per
annum, and merely shout approval for the Führer's pronouncements. In
return they receive the equivalent of £600 a year and a free pass—in other
words, a bonus for the good boys of the Party. But why not abolish altogether an institution which has become farcical?

control has ceased, he is entirely free to decide foreign policy",
to conclude alliances and treaties, to declare war, though this
decision may be given the form of a law of the Reich. He is
also the supreme military authority, and the Army no longer
takes oath to a written constitution, but solely to him. He is
even Supreme Judge, the "old liberal distinctions between state
and law, between political decision and legal order, between
administration and justice, having become impossible in the
Racial Reich".

In short, Adolf Hitler is the source of all power: "we must
not speak of the power of the state, but of the power of the
Leader". We must face the fact that official theory is being
deliberately shaped on lines not merely unprecedented in modern
Europe, but calculated at one and the same time to widen the
gulf between Germany and the outside world and to reduce to
ruins the wonderful structure of German legal and constitutional
theory and practice.

The latest events in Germany, as this book goes to press,
provide an eloquent commentary upon these theories of omnipotence. The drastic purge of the Army and Foreign Office,
carried through with sudden energy on 4 February 1938, may
fairly be described as the last stage in the militarisation of the
Third Reich, and the blending of ultimate military and political
power in the hands of an "All-Highest" before whom the
legitimate bearers of that title pale into nothingness. Henceforward German foreign policy and German militarism are
indissoluble: the old Prussian tradition of loyalty to "God and
King" has been swallowed up in a forced allegiance to the
"Bohemian corporal". Hitler stands unchallenged and proclaims the subordination of everything to "the unitary preparation of defence of the Reich". The process has been far more
rapid, and not less thoroughgoing, than in the corresponding
cases of Stalin and Mussolini: but it is obviously far too soon
to speculate as to the completeness of its success. Of active
resistance there can be no question: but it is possible to detect
a deep-seated, if passive, psychological disquiet, opening a gulf
between the generations.

NATIONAL SOCIALISM AND CHRISTIANITY

There is one last aspect from which the totalitarian idea must be considered. The Jewish problem, deliberately envenomed by the Führer and his immediate entourage, is in itself grave enough. But it becomes still graver when we consider its relation with the future of Christianity, as challenged by National Socialism at the very moment when the "anti-God" movement is failing in Russia. For racial ostracism, consciously aimed at eventual extermination, is incompatible with the principles of a Christian state and must be repudiated by any practising Christian, whether he be Catholic or Protestant. The State is, in effect, intruding into the sphere of the Church, or of God Himself, when it tries to exclude certain categories from the free grace promised to all sinners and to hallmark them as ineligible for conversion. Cardinal Faulhaber's uncompromising claim that "not blood, but faith, is the foundation of religion", may serve as a motto for all Christians in the fight against Nazi racialism: just as all will re-echo the words of Pope Pius XI:[1] "The use of the word 'revelation' for 'suggestions' of race and blood, for the irradiations of a people's history, is mere equivocation: false coins of this sort do not deserve Christian currency." We have to reckon with the fact that the inner ring surrounding the Führer is for the most part anti-Christian, and either indifferent or actively pagan; that men like Goebbels and Himmler use their immense influence through propaganda and through the police for anti-Christian purposes; that Himmler, Frick and Rust (the Ministers of the Interior and of Education) have ostentatiously left the Church; that Baldur von Schirach, the leader of the "Hitler Youth", declared himself to be "neither Catholic nor Protestant, but National Socialist". Perhaps the most significant of all is the attitude of Alfred Rosenberg, who is not only chief of the foreign department of the National Socialist Party, but has a decisive formative influence upon educational curricula, and

[1] In his Encyclical to the German Church, 14 March 1937.

whom the Vatican has thought worthy of a place upon the Index. In his book *The Myth of the Twentieth Century*[1]— which is scarcely less deserving of attention than *Mein Kampf* itself, and even more indigestible, despite its superior literary style—Rosenberg demands that Christianity be purged of all non-Nordic elements, of all the excrescences due to "Jewish zealots like Matthew, materialistic rabbis like Paul, African jurists like Tertullian", that "the Old Testament, with its stories of pimps and cattle-dealers, be replaced by Nordic sagas and legends":[2] and he denounces the Christian doctrine of charity, while clinging to that other conception of "honour" as "foreign to Christianity". To Rosenberg St Paul is a perverter of the Gospel, characterised by "typical Jewish arrogance and intolerance":[3] and in his considered view the German Church of the future "must declare unreservedly that it subordinates the ideal of love of neighbour to the idea of national honour; that no action can be approved by a German Church which does not in the first instance serve to ensure the race (*das Volkstum*)".[4] It must gradually replace the Crucifixion by "the teaching fire-spirit, the hero in the highest sense of the word".[5]

Another exponent of the new doctrine, Professor Eibl of Vienna, writes of "a common front of Greek philosophers, Roman Senators, Nordic Vikings...against the spirit of the Bible", and argues that "in Christianity (and in Judaism) there

[1] In 1934 it had already reached its 38th edition (183,000 copies)!

[2] *Der Mythus des XXten Jahrhunderts*, p. 614.

[3] *Ibid.* p. 605. Typical of this outlook is such a sentence as the following: "A false humility combined with a side-glance at world dominion, an eager 'religious' desire (as in the case of all Orientals) to march at the head of rebels, was the Pauline perversion (*Verfälschung*) of the great figure of Christ" (p. 606). This is pure Nietzsche, who called St Paul "a slave-mind" and "this appalling imposter, pandering to the instincts of slave morality in those paltry people when he said, 'God hath chosen the foolish things of the world to confound the wise'."

[4] *Ibid.* p. 608.

[5] *Ibid.* p. 616. A curious illustration of his ideas upon heroism is the phrase: "In Bach and Gluck and Händel and Beethoven the heroic character has forced its way through, despite Church poetry" (p. 617).

is something equally repulsive to the Hellenic, Roman and Germanic nature, something that seems almost contemptible, or at least deplorable—despair at one's own sinfulness, repentance, the search for atonement...".[1]

The plain fact is that the totalitarian Moloch-State, as visualised by the National Socialist leaders, is bent upon undermining both the great Christian Churches of Germany because it cannot tolerate that even in the realm of the spirit its citizens should recognise any prior allegiance. The resultant *Kulturkampf* is far more acute than that of the 'seventies, when the German State tried to prevent what it regarded as undue interference by the Roman Church in the internal politics of Germany. Today both Churches are on the defensive, and are being steadily driven, despite a long tradition of mutual suspicion, towards a joint stand on behalf of Christian fundamentals. It is impossible here to deal with the moving history of Nazi persecution: much has been written in English on the subject, though the latest feature of the tragedy is that the German Church leaders have been driven, by an all-pervading system of espionage, to beg their friends abroad to refrain from publicity rather than to publish the details of their lone struggle against unscrupulous authority. But the manifesto read last summer from hundreds of German Protestant pulpits, boldly denouncing oppression and espionage, expulsion and imprisonment, and declaring that the Christian faith is at stake, shows that Germany still possesses men capable of echoing the words of Luther, "Here I stand; I can no other".

If it were true that, in Professor Toynbee's stinging phrase, "Western Liberalism is merely the political husk of Christianity, without its spiritual kernel", then the religious position in Germany might perhaps be dismissed as something which does not directly concern us. But indeed it is not possible to avoid the conclusion that the totalitarian principle is a creeping gas which we cannot escape by flight or by indifference: it must be met by a bold challenge and well-thought-out defensive counter-measures.

[1] *Vom Sinn der Gegenwart: ein Buch von Deutscher Sendung*, pp. 408, 421.

We have to face the fact that Nazi Germany is already after five years far more different from the Germany of William II than Mussolini's Italy is from the Italy of the Risorgimento, and that those in control of German destinies are working feverishly, day in, day out, to increase the difference. They are thereby widening the gulf between Germany and Western Europe, and consciously, deliberately, trying to train up a nation which knows next to nothing of Western institutions, or, in so far as it knows them, contemptuously rejects them. This cultural cleavage among the nations which totalitarian autocracy has brought about is perhaps the gravest of the many dangers which confront unhappy Europe. We can already see, it is true, that conscious leadership of this kind does not always produce the expected results. The human spirit is an elusive thing, and it may be that youths trained in paganism and in emotional surrender of their reason and liberty to an unrestricted authority may one day lead the return to individualism and sanity. But for the present everything possible is being done to prevent any such relapse, and we must face the facts of the situation.

To sum up, it is even now not sufficiently realised that Hitler is making a revolution and taking gigantic risks of war. Hitherto one of his assets has been that he is confronted with nations who are equally anxious to avoid war and revolution, being well aware that the margin of reserves in Europe is very scanty, and that even a war in which they were successful would probably result in a profound transformation of the whole structure of State and Society. But the changes which those in power in the West are so anxious to avert are exactly what Hitler is aiming at in Germany: while the Soviet rulers are mainly concerned to maintain what they already hold without launching into fresh adventures, and the Duce, though he still has an appetite, has an exhausted nation behind him. It follows that Hitler, who, unlike Stalin and Mussolini, is still far from his goal of German dominion, cannot be deterred by considerations such as appeal to his neighbours, and finds in the growing tension at home an incentive to fresh risks.

It is probable, then, that he will continue at intervals that policy of bluff which has already proved so successful on four occasions, until at last a point will be reached when it will no longer be possible for the other Powers to yield. Then his bluff would be called, and war might be upon us suddenly and irrevocably. The best hope of conjuring this danger is for this country to make it quite clear that there are certain things which it will not tolerate, and in particular, an attempt to alter the map of Europe by force. It is doubtless more in keeping with the traditional British policy to avoid commitments made in advance, but present circumstances are altogether exceptional, and render essential a greater clarity of aim and a courageous lead to the nation.

IX

THE PROBLEM OF SMALL STATES AND NATIONAL MINORITIES

No general survey of the post-war situation would be of much value without some consideration of the twin problems of small states and of national minorities: for the former have never played so important a part in the life of Europe as today, while the latter have acquired for the first time something like international status which, however imperfectly applied, marks a very real advance and offers much hope for the future.

It is scarcely necessary to point out that the idea of Nationality, as understood by the generation preceding the war, is something quite modern, even though national feeling in some form or other may be as old as the hills. It is no less true that today it is once more in rapid evolution in certain countries, especially Germany and Russia, and may have considerable surprises in store for us. Nationality, as we have hitherto known it, was the child of eighteenth-century Enlightenment and the spoilt darling of later Liberalism: and the profound influence of Herder and Hegel respectively upon it has not yet received the attention that is its due in our own country. For our present purpose it must suffice to consider the growing recognition accorded to the national idea in the course of the last 100 years. One of the central facts, not always recognised, is that while the Great Powers may no doubt have grown even stronger than they were before, the role of the small and medium Powers has also steadily been growing in importance.

THREE EUROPEAN CONGRESSES

At the Conference of 1815 the five Great Powers virtually ignored the others and often dictated their fate. Belgium and Holland were lumped together, not for their own sakes, but from selfish motives on the part of all who feared a French revival. The same motive underlay the Union of Norway and Sweden, which was certainly far less flagrant, but never won popular approval and also had in the end to be undone. The summary treatment of Genoa, the Ionian Islands and Cracow passed wellnigh unchallenged. Italy, then divided into eight petty states, was all directly or indirectly at the mercy of Austria; while the thirty-eight sovereign fragments of Germany which still survived the drastic carving of Napoleon were seriously overshadowed by the two great rivals Austria and Prussia. Spain and Portugal, though their well-defined frontiers saved them from any danger of partition, found themselves for a long time torn between the two rival ideologies in Europe.

When the next European Congress met at Paris in 1856, national problems were in the very forefront of all discussions on the Eastern Question; and there was much lip-service—not all of it insincere—to the rights and liberties of smaller nations. The Turkish Charter which—with all due regard to the Sultan's sovereignty—was cited in the very text of the Treaty itself, was a first step on the path towards international minority guarantees, even if the Powers failed to provide machinery for its enforcement. Moreover, in the case of Serbia, Wallachia and Moldavia, the substitution of a joint guarantee by the Great Powers for any exclusively Russian Protectorate was a very real gain for the three vassal states, and indeed the final stage towards national independence. The Concert of Europe, with its many faults, and thanks in part to mutual rivalries and ulterior motives, became the, doubtless involuntary, guardian of Balkan liberties. It is true that in 1863 the status of Poland, thanks to an ill-planned insurrection, was again altered for the worse: but in 1864 the vexed question of the Danish Duchies, so hideously bungled by Russell and Palmerston and exploited by Bismarck for his own ends, was none the less a testimony to the growing strength of national feeling: for if Schleswig was unjustly torn from its Danish kinsmen, Holstein was a German province round which centred all the genuine aspirations of South German liberalism.

By the time that a third European Congress opened at Berlin in 1878, Italy had been added to the ranks of the Great Powers, though doubtless as yet equal to the others in name rather than in fact: while Prussia had been reconstituted as the Second Reich. The achievement of German and Italian unity (neither of them, it is true, in a definitive form) had obviously transformed the whole European situation from the point of view of Nationality: for it set the tone to all other disunited races and revealed a new motive for frontier revision which had nothing in common with the dynastic manipulations of the eighteenth century. At the Congress of Berlin Europe recognised the statehood of Serbia, Roumania and Montenegro, secured to Bulgaria her first, all too inadequate, status and laid down certain paper guarantees for other nationalities, still in the birth-throes, in Macedonia, Albania and Armenia. For a brief moment the Powers even considered the possibility of admitting Greece to the magic circle where the fate of all these reviving races was being decided: in the end this was thought too drastic a concession, and the Greeks, Roumanians and Serbs were merely allowed to state their case for a brief period before the Congress and vanish once more into limbo. Yet even this was a great advance upon all previous procedure, and when the Danubian Commission came up for revision, it was felt that the two riparian states which now attained independence could no longer be excluded from membership. Even the insistence of the Congress, as a preliminary to recognition of Roumanian and Serbian independence, upon special legislation in each country in favour of the Jews (a step much resented at the time and none too tactfully carried out), may to-day be regarded as a first step in the direction of those minority guarantees which the post-war period has shown to be so necessary if inter-racial peace is to be attained.

During the forty years which separate the Congress of Berlin from a Congress ten times more complex than any of its predecessors, the latent conflict between the still unsatisfied nationalities and the Governments to which they owed allegiance grew steadily more intense, and though lacking any legal basis, forced itself increasingly upon public attention. In one of the Great Powers, Austria-Hungary, the question of Nationalities became the dominant issue, and the very difference in standards of treatment adopted in the two halves of the Dual Monarchy after 1867—a difference which grew with every succeeding decade—was a sign that the public conscience was awakening in Austria. It will always be a fascinating subject of speculation to consider what would have happened if Francis Joseph had died in 1905 and had been succeeded by Francis Ferdinand who, with all his faults, realised that the fate of his dominions depended upon a solution of the question of Nationalities, and was almost fanatically resolved to force an issue on his accession. There were other signs of progress in this period. In Prussia it is true that Bülow's anti-Polish policy, resting on expropriation of the soil and Germanisation in the school, was still obstinately pursued: but saner voices were increasingly being raised against it in Germany. In Russia, it is equally true that a policy of crude Russification was stubbornly upheld by those in authority: but the inclusion of racial statistics for the first time in the Census of 1897 was a sign that facts could no longer be defied, and in the Duma the Polish, Finnish, and even Ukrainian, questions forced themselves upon public attention. The peaceful separation effected between Norway and Sweden in 1905 was a happy omen for the future, as showing that two sister nations, nearly balanced in age, in strength and in culture, were sufficiently civilised and restrained to part company without a fratricidal struggle. At the other end of Europe, where Turkish rule had degenerated into stagnation and utter neglect of cultural values, the conflict of races not unnaturally assumed cruder forms and was complicated by foreign interference and by the appeal to rival Powers.

THE PEACE CONFERENCE OF 1919

Thus a realist survey of the nineteenth century permits us to detect a certain evolution, at the four great conferences since 1814, in respect of the relations of small and great nations. In

1815 the small were treated as mere chattels to be bartered about. In 1856 their interests were at least discussed in some detail, though the decisions remained in the hands of the Great Powers. In 1878 the small nations were already able to knock loudly at the door ("*'Rein müssen wir*"—"we want to come in" —was the title of a contemporary *German* cartoon), and were graciously listened to, before the decisions were announced to them. In 1919 the small nations were for the first time present at the council table, enjoying at least nominal equality and able to voice their wishes and objections, even though the ultimate and major decisions were still reserved by the Big Five, or Four, or Three. At the Conference of Paris the small nations occupied the foreground of the picture, if only because the Allies, sometimes from conviction, sometimes for purely tactical reasons, sometimes under the pressure of events, had publicly committed themselves to the cause of Small Nations, and because President Wilson on the one side had in all good faith adopted the slogan, while the defeated states, after giving a new interpretation to the principle of "Self-determination", first at Stockholm in 1917, then at Brest-Litovsk and Bucarest in 1918, clung to the very last to the hope that this phrase might be made a sort of camouflage behind which Germany imposed her own peace upon the border states of the fallen Russian Empire.

Hence there was never any question of denying at least nominal status, and in the end ten European states signed on the one side[1] and five on the other, out of a total of twenty-one which had been involved in war. The result of the War had been to bring a number of small states into being, not by any artificial means, but by their own volition: and as the circumstances in which the War had begun made it obviously impossible to exclude Belgium and Serbia (now the Kingdom of the Serbs, Croats and Slovenes), and as the inclusion of Roumania had been expressly promised by Treaty, it followed quite logically that Greece and the two most important of the

[1] Great Britain, France, Italy, Belgium, Greece, Poland, Portugal, Roumania, Serbs Croats and Slovenes, Czechoslovakia.

reconstituted states, Poland and Czechoslovakia, must also be included, and it is but fair to add that both received a cordial welcome, though only the Belgians and Jugoslavs among all the lesser Powers were allowed three instead of two delegates. The abnormal circumstances of the Russian Bolshevik State, which had found it necessary to make its own separate peace in the previous March, gave the Allies the legal, though not the moral, right to exclude Russia from the Conference: and it followed conveniently enough from this that the four Baltic and three Caucasian states were also not summoned. The gravest omission of all was that of the Ukraine, whose short-lived freedom could not survive the double onslaught of the devil and the deep sea, and who is reserved for the role of chief spectre at the feast when next the unsolved problems of Europe fall to be discussed. But with this disastrous exception, there is no longer any national unit in Europe *wholly* under foreign rule, and for many countries the peace settlement, with all its shortcomings, marked the beginning of an era of emancipation. In Poland, Bohemia, Slovakia, Croatia, Slovenia, Transylvania, Lithuania, Latvia, Estonia, Finland—despite many imperfections, political, economic and social, on which much might be said—the nineteen years following the War have wrought the greatest transformation in their entire history, and the process is still far from complete. Hence the idea that the War brought nothing but ruin and retrogression would be emphatically denied by the best part of 100 million people in East and South-East Europe.

In the whole post-war period no more superficial and misleading phrase was ever coined than "the Balkanisation" of Austria-Hungary: and since 1933 the wheel has come full circle with the parallel adoption of gangster methods of government in the centre of Europe and the virtual elimination of the *komitadji* and the assassin from Balkan politics. So far as it meant anything, the phrase was a protest against the substitution of a number of small and medium states for a large and powerful Empire. It suggested that the new organisms rested on a less healthy and natural basis than the heterogeneous, slow-growing, organism which they replaced. But before using any such word it is worth stopping to consider what had made the Balkans a term of reproach. Firstly, no doubt, the foul tyranny to which they were so long subjected by the Turks, and whose evil effects still remain in the victims' systems, but secondly, and not less, the perpetual interference of the Great Powers, based as a rule upon motives of the European Balance of Power, and upon a profound misreading of the local situation, and also only too often upon a cynical indifference to the fate of the countries and populations directly concerned. The new situation at last made it possible to apply the principle of "The Balkans for the Balkan Peoples", though certain of the Great Powers were far from renouncing their designs of interference in the Peninsula. Concerning the inter-necine conflict which had raged between the Balkan peoples from 1813 to 1918, the extent to which the various races were intermingled in Macedonia, Thrace and elsewhere, and the irreconcileable character of their rival ambitions, it is little short of miraculous that, after an inevitable period of effer-vescence and outrage, they should have settled down so quickly to peaceful co-operation and even alliance. Three main factors contributed—first, the emergence of several clear-sighted and constructive statesmen[1] who saw that disunited they would again become the prey of foreign intrigue, but that united they were the equivalent of a Great Power; secondly, the temporary effacement of one, and the permanent dissolution of the other, two Powers most actively concerned with Near Eastern affairs in the pre-war period, and, perhaps not least of all, the un-scrupulous efforts of a third Power, Italy, to apply in its own selfish interests the foolish old maxim of Vienna "Divide et impera".

[1] It will suffice to mention five such different men as Beneš, Take Ionescu, Titulescu, Venizelos and Mustafa Kemal.

CHANGES IN EUROPE

Let us look at the problem from a different angle and consider what has happened in the huge triangular bit of country lying between Germany, Soviet Russia, and the Mediterranean. In this area before the War there were three big political facts—in the North the hold of the Russian autocracy upon the Poles and other border races; in the Centre the double hegemony of the Germans and Magyars—less crude, but quite as real—over the Czechs, Slovaks, Roumanians, Serbs, Croats, Slovenes and Italians of Austria-Hungary and, as a result, increasing complications in foreign policy and increasing dependence of Austria-Hungary on Berlin; and then in the South, the rivalry of Austria and Russia for political hegemony in Turkey and in the Balkan States, complicated by varying degrees of intervention on the part of other Great Powers. The War broke up Austria-Hungary altogether, set the final seal upon Turkey's loss of all her European possessions west or north of Thrace, and for a long period eliminated both Russian and German political influence.

Moreover, one effect of the World War has been to destroy not merely the old Balance of Power in Europe, which so intimately concerned a country like Belgium, but also, even more drastically, the old Balance of Power in the Balkans. Before the Balkan Wars of 1912–13 the Christian states were all more or less on the same level—Roumania, Serbia, Bulgaria, Greece (apart of course from the tiny Montenegro). One of the main motives which underlay King Milan's action against Bulgaria in the short war of 1885, and again the formation of the Balkan League in 1912, and again the outbreak of the second Balkan War between the victorious allies, was either to prevent one of these States from pushing ahead of the others without compensation, or to ensure parallel all-round aggrandisement. But, for good or for evil, the Great War finally exploded any such ideal, if ideal it could be called. The two northern states now utterly outweighed the three southern—on the one hand

Jugoslavia (in 1935) with roughly fourteen millions and Roumania with nearly eighteen millions, on the other hand Bulgaria and Greece, with six millions each and Albania with little over one million: and in 1938 it is more difficult than ever to devise any permutation of the Balkan forces which would establish anything like equilibrium between the two main groups. On the whole Turkey has become part of the Middle, rather than of the Near, East, in spite of still possessing Adrianople and Thrace, and has accepted the new situation by moving her centre of gravity from the Straits to the heart of Anatolia: while Greece too has been forced by military disasters to accept a drastic racial redistribution as between herself and Turkey. Meanwhile the Balkans have been brought nearer to the West by the double fact of a partition of Hungary, and of the acquisition by the Jugoslavs of political control over their own coastline on the Eastern Adriatic. There was, moreover, a certain guarantee of stability in the fact that the great upheaval had meant in most of those countries not only the attainment of national unity and independence, but the transference of the land to the peasantry and therefore the virtual immunisation of the latter against Bolshevik seduction from the East. Thus a new situation had been created which nothing short of a new general upheaval in Europe is likely to overthrow: and even the most resolute opponent of the new order in Central Europe will admit that this would be too high a price.

It is doubtless because all this, though too little regarded by British opinion, is so obvious to the peoples of South-East Europe, that step by step they set themselves to guard against any return to the evil system of interference in their internal affairs by the Great Powers. First came the creation of the Little Entente in 1920–21,[1] resting upon two fundamental common aims—the maintenance of the new territorial *status quo* on the Danube and in the Balkans, and the prevention of Habsburg

[1] The Czechoslovak-Jugoslav Treaty of 14 August 1920, the Czechoslovak-Roumanian Treaty of 23 April 1921, and the Jugoslav-Roumanian Treaty of 8 June 1921.

restoration in any portion of the former Habsburg Monarchy. In the years that followed, every attempt to divide them only led to a tightening of the bonds between them: in particular Mussolini's persistent policy of fomenting discord between the Balkan States, even by active assistance to terrorist groups, caused a strong revulsion of feeling in favour of co-operation against foreign meddling. Finally, the Duce's determined effort to establish a kind of Five-Power Directorate in Europe and to relegate all the smaller Powers to an outer limbo, roused the Balkan and Danubian States to a sense of danger, and, as we have already seen (see pp. 182–3), led to the creation of the Balkan Entente (of Roumania, Jugoslavia, Turkey and Greece), supplementing and overlapping the older and more restricted Little Entente, and consciously aiming at the creation of a common public opinion on many vital questions of the day, as the first step towards common action in the day of supreme crisis.

GREAT AND SMALL POWERS

In view of such developments and of the deep line of division that separates the five surviving Great Powers of Europe, it may at least very plausibly be argued that the Great Powers, though in many ways stronger than they ever were before, are *relatively not* so powerful as in 1815, 1856 or 1876, and this for the double reason that Europe has to take much fuller account of three extra-European Great Powers—the United States, Japan and Russia (as a Far-Eastern Power)—and that the firmament is now studded with lesser stars. Regarded from an angle far too often ignored, the much-abused Peace Settlement has strengthened the position of the smaller states, and this on the whole makes for peace rather than disturbance, since stern necessity enjoins co-operation to preserve the *status quo*, and since there is not one among them which is ready to risk war for some new territorial adventure.

There is indeed yet another angle from which this whole problem of the Peace Settlement may profitably be regarded, and which has been obscured by a persistent smokescreen of anti-Versailles propaganda, meekly accepted by so many of our own sentimentalists, both of the Left and of the Right. It is that, apart from the *economic* provisions of the Treaty, which we are all agreed in dismissing as iniquitous and impracticable, and from its colonial clauses, which are admittedly open to discussion, its main *territorial* provisions benefited not the Great Powers, who defeated Germany, but the smaller Powers which had been the chief victims of the war or which recovered their independence as the result of the break-up of Austria-Hungary and the eclipse of Russia. The only two exceptions to this are Alsace-Lorraine, which Germany no longer claims, and South Tirol and Istria, which are the classic example of frontiers drawn on strategic lines where satisfactory ethnical frontiers could have been found. Speaking broadly, then, the Peace was on its territorial side a vindication of the principle of nationality, to an extent hitherto unknown in Europe: and this is not affected by the fact that certain races, like the Ukrainians, were excluded from its benefits, or that in certain places—notably in Hungary and in Macedonia—the intermingling of races made it impossible to draw clean-cut ethnographic frontiers.

It remains to consider for a brief moment the bearing of the changes just described upon the Genevan system. More than enough has been heard of the National Socialist theory that the League of Nations was a mere instrument, in the hands of France, for the isolation or renewed encirclement of Germany. Far too little has been made of a growing tendency at Geneva— no mere theory, but a concrete aim, steadily pursued from many different quarters—for the Small Powers to get together and make their influence felt, the dawning of a new hope that they might be able to emancipate themselves from the domination of their greater neighbours. Gradually the three enlightened Scandinavian States formed a more or less uniform group, in close contact on the one hand with their four weaker and more backward Baltic neighbours (Finland, Estonia, Latvia and Lithuania) and on the other hand with Holland and Belgium, who may have more common interests and ideas than their touchiness and passion for standing on their dignity in any mutual dealings might seem to suggest. The Little Entente and Balkan Union from the first were specially active in League affairs, and careful to register at Geneva any new contract: two such eminent Europeans as Beneš and Titulescu might be relied upon in this direction. Austria and Hungary occupied a somewhat peculiar position at Geneva, at first because of the financial and administrative assistance accorded to them by the League, without which it is doubtful whether they could have preserved their independence. In later years they again came to occupy a peculiar position at Geneva, in the equivocal sense that they were in danger of becoming the political vassals of Italy, whose aim it had become to humiliate and wreck the League. In the background were the South American states, and standing by itself Switzerland, more materialist in outlook than ever in its past history, and again Portugal, the unique example of an enlightened dictatorship, solving year by year the problem of damaged finances instead of making it irreparable. To these variegated groups must be added two intermediate Powers, neither Great nor Small nor "almost-Great"—Poland and Spain, both enjoying a strategic importance in Europe which has enabled them to pose as more powerful than they really are—the latter convulsed by civil war and well aware that Geneva is far more deeply divided over the Spanish problem than over any other problem of the day: the former regarded in many quarters as the next victim of interventionist policy under the convenient cloak of civil war, but both destined to play a vital part in European policy, not only because they are in a sense buffers between the two accursed ideologies, but also because in quite different ways their fate is linked up with the still unsolved problems of national minorities, on which the peace of Europe really depends.

It is natural enough that the chief exponents of Power Politics in Europe today should look with disfavour upon the Small Nations: but to those who believe in the ideals of international law and collective security their existence and security are one of the many hopes for the future of our troubled continent. In the words of Mr H. A. L. Fisher, "almost everything which is most precious in our civilisation has come from the small states—the Old Testament, the Homeric poems, the Attic and Elizabethan drama, the art of the Italian Renaissance, the common law of England. Nobody needs to be told what humanity owes to Athens, Florence, Geneva or Weimar....The quantitative estimate of human values, which plays so large a part in modern political history, is radically false and tends to give a vulgar instead of a liberal and elevated turn to public ambitions."[1] These are something more than eloquent phrases: they are the bedrock of the European future.

EMANCIPATION

The Small States of Europe today are those which have succeeded in resisting the process of forcible, or sometimes natural, absorption, or after a period of absorption have reasserted their independent status. But the constant fluctuation of frontiers which, either as a result of dynastic or national ambitions, or of economic greed, has marked the history of Europe for centuries, has created the further problem of racial and religious minorities, in some cases conquered or annexed and assimilated in varying degrees, and only too often inter-mingled with other races as a result of natural migration or deliberate policy, to such an extent as to render disentanglement wellnigh impossible.

In passing it is not unprofitable to note that the worst points of racial friction, and therefore the worst obstacles to European pacification, lie in the unsolved relations of the Slavs with their neighbours, and that it is in those relations that the War has brought its most radical changes. From the late Middle Ages onwards most of the Slavonic States had entered upon a period of decline, during which first Bulgaria, then Serbia, then Bohemia, and finally Poland lost their independence and only Russia maintained and extended its territorial power (notably at the expense of kindred Slavs—the Ukrainians and

---

[1] *The Value of Small States* (1915).

White Russians). The nineteenth century kindled in each of these countries a preparatory national revival, which found expression in the great upheaval of 1918–19. The only Slav nation on the vanquished side, Bulgaria, suffered severe diminution but maintained its independence, while Bohemia and Poland recovered their lost independence in a somewhat altered form, and Jugoslavia achieved the almost complete unity of three out of the four Southern Slav races. Russia, on the other hand, lost her non-Slavonic territories in Europe (but not in Asia) and a part of the spoils which she had acquired at Poland's expense, but otherwise remained untouched. Unless, then, some further cataclysm ensues, it would seem probable that we have entered a new period, in which the Slav nations are no longer to be under non-Slav rule and are each free to work out their own internal problems—immensely complicated, it is true, by the emergence of a new Russian tyranny before which the old Tsardom seems mild and ineffective.

If we compare the position before and since the War in the debatable zone lying between Germany, Russia, the Adriatic and the Black Sea, we see that with the one deadly exception of the Ukrainians, to which allusion has already been made, the racial status of most of the nationalities of Europe has been very definitely improved. Nine races—the Poles, Czechs, Slovaks, Slovenes, Croats, Letts, Lithuanians, Ests and Finns—which before the War lived entirely under foreign rule, now possess national states of their own.

In this connection it is important to lay special emphasis upon one feature of the post-war settlement which even after ten years is only very inadequately realised. It is altogether inaccurate to refer to the formation of the national states of post-war Europe as in any sense the work of the Peace Conference, or indeed of the Great Powers—except of course in the sense that the victory of the Entente provided the occasion without which such far-reaching changes could not have occurred. In order to be quite clear on this point—which materially affects the whole subsequent course of history—it will suffice to give the chronology, first as regards Austria-Hungary, and then as regards Russia.

17 October 1918	Dr Korošec in the Austrian Parliament declares the Southern Slav and Czechoslovak questions to be international, to be decided at the Conference.
18 „	Roumanian and Slovak deputies in the Hungarian Parliament deny Hungary's right to represent them at the Conference.
21 „	National Council at Prague declares for Czechoslovak independence.
22 „	German Austrian Provisional Assembly meets at Vienna.
25 „	Ukrainian National Government formed in Eastern Galicia.
28 „	Slovak National Council formed. Czechoslovak Republic proclaimed in Prague.
28 „	Polish "Liquidation Committee" at Cracow.
29 „	Independence of the Jugoslav provinces of the Dual Monarchy proclaimed at Zagreb.
31 „	Revolution in Budapest, Murder of Count Tisza.
3 November 1918	Armistice of Villa Giusti on the Italian front.
9 „	Roumania re-enters the War.
11 „	German-Austrian Republic proclaimed in Vienna. Emperor Charles renounces all share in affairs of State.
12 „	Armistice of Arad between General Franchet d'Esperey and Count Károlyi.
16 „	Formal proclamation of the Hungarian Republic.
1 December 1918	Roumanian Unity proclaimed at Alba Julia. Jugoslav Unity proclaimed in Belgrade (delegation of Zagreb National Government offers the Crown to Prince Regent Alexander).

These are the bald facts behind which lie a vast popular upheaval, a revolution social no less than political, sweeping everything before it and based upon the spontaneous action of National Councils in every province, and almost in every town and village. In a word, the essential lines of the new states had taken shape, not merely long before the Peace Conference met in Paris, but even before an armistice could be concluded on the Austro-Italian front. Indeed, General Diaz had difficulty in finding anyone duly authorised to negotiate that armistice with him, and when the Allies came to concern themselves seriously with the problem of Austria's succession, it was above all a question of ratifying accomplished facts and only here and there imposing a veto or challenging points of detail. Those who place the main responsibility for the new frontiers upon the statesmen assembled in Paris, entirely misconceive the true course of events. It is not true that the Allies *broke up* Austria-Hungary: Austria-Hungary *broke down*.

The same is true of the Russian border-states, though here the complication of enemy occupation survived the War. Finland broke away from Russia as early as 18 July 1917, when the Diet assumed supreme power. On 22 September the Lithuanian National Council was constituted, on 16 November the Lettish National Council, which on 18 January 1918 declared its independence, and on 24 February 1918 an Estonian Government was set up at Reval.[1] The Ukrainian National Rada met at Kiev on 19 April 1917, in June assumed full control of affairs, and on 20 November proclaimed a People's Republic, but soon after the Treaty of Brest-Litovsk (which its delegates concluded separately from those of Russia) it was overthrown by the Bolsheviks and gradually incorporated in the Russian State. At the moment when the War ended in the West, the Ukraine was in German military occupation, with the pseudo-dictator Hetman Skoropadski as camouflage: and the only free Ukrainian Government, the so-called "Western Ukraine" or "Eastern Galicia", was during 1919-20 ground between the upper and

---

[1] It is interesting to note that Great Britain gave recognition to Estonia on 3 May 1918, to Latvia on 11 November 1918, to Finland on 6 May 1919 and to Lithuania (where the German occupation lasted longest) on 24 September 1919.

nether millstones of Bolshevik Russia and Poland. Though, however, the situation was even more chaotic in the East than that on the Danube or in the Balkans, in each case the fundamental facts were the work of the peoples concerned, and such subsequent changes as were effected—as for instance the suppression of Ukrainian liberties and the seizure of Vilna—were due not to any decisions of the Peace Conference, but to a deliberate defiance of them, notably by Poland. It may be doubted whether Poland could have enforced her will, if the issues had been purely political: but in the end the danger of Bolshevism flooding westwards across a prostrate Poland bulked so large in the minds of all Western statesmen, especially during the Russian advance on Warsaw in the summer of 1920, that the Ukraine was reluctantly sacrificed and the Poles were left free to apply to the luckless Ukrainians all the worst methods of denationalisation from which they themselves had suffered during the previous century.

MINORITIES IN EUROPE

The post-war Question of Minorities is only the pre-war Question of Nationalities, or what remains of it, stated in a new form: and if the first axiom in any discussion of it is that the new frontiers were in the main, or in the first instance, the work of the peoples rather than the Governments, the second axiom is that in many parts of Europe a "clean cut" on ethnographic lines is a physical impossibility. This is the main, though of course not the only, reason, why there are so many national minorities on the wrong side of so many frontiers.

The most practical way of bringing home to the reader the wide bearings of the minority problem on the mutual relations of almost all the European races, is to begin with a succinct catalogue (in round figures) of post-war racial minorities (p. 322).

It is to be remembered that these figures are based on the official statistics of the countries concerned: they can only be approximate, firstly because the data vary according to the country and the year of census, and secondly because some are notoriously misleading. None the less they provide the only common factor from which deductions may be drawn. If, then, we examine these figures more closely, certain interesting results emerge. In the first place a large proportion of this formidable total consists either of widely scattered racial fragments which are doomed to occupy the position of a minority, entirely irrespective of the way in which this or that frontier may have been drawn. This of course applies to all those who for purposes of brevity are described as "others": but it also applies to the Jews in every country (and in our table there are included a total of 3,443,000 Jews), and again to a considerable number of racial islets surrounded by a sea of some other race—as, for instance, the 62,000 Wends of Germany, the 98,000 Czechoslovaks of Austria (who are mostly in Vienna itself), the 800,000 Germans and Slavs of "Rump Hungary" (who would certainly have been assigned to the Succession States if they had been less deeply embedded in the Magyar mass), the Albanians of Greece (who live mostly in Attica), the Vlachs (who could under no circumstances whatsoever be united with Roumania), the 600,000 Székelys of Transylvania (who occupy the very centre of the Roumanian ethnographic territory), or the 460,000 autonomous Ukrainians of Czechoslovakia (who could only be transferred to some other alien rule, because as yet there is no free Ukraine to which they could be consigned). In the same way it is obvious that under no circumstances could the Germans of Jugoslavia and Roumania be incorporated in the Reich, and that any change of frontier could only bring them a change of masters. Thus, though some of the minorities counted above are undoubtedly underestimated (e.g. the Ukrainians in Poland, or the Poles in Germany, or the Germans and Jugoslavs in Italy), the total figure of 32 millions is enormously in excess of the figure of those whose fate could under any conceivable circumstances be satisfactorily settled by frontier revision. (It is not easy to offer an exact estimate, but probably even 5 per cent would be an overstatement.) But it does represent the number of persons in the Europe of today (exclusive of Russia, where oppression rests on a political, social

Post-War Minorities in Europe (in round figures)

Country[1]	Date of last census available	Total population	Total minority population	Per-centage	Details
Germany	1925	62,410,000	1,198,600	1·9	406,600 Poles and "Mazurians" + 577,000 described as bi-lingual; 62,000 Wends; 30,000 Czechs; 123,000 others
Denmark	1921	3,260,000	40,000	1·2	35-45,000 Germans (estimate)
Czecho-slovakia	1925	13,600,000	4,724,900	34·7	3,250,000 Germans; 745,000 Magyars; 461,000 Ukranians; 75,000 Poles; 180,000 Jews; 13,900 Roumanians
Austria	1923	6,500,000	258,600	4·0	98,000 Czechs and Slovaks; 43,000 Slovenes; 44,700 Serbo-Croats; 25,000 Magyars; 47,900 others
Hungary	1920	7,980,000	829,000	10·4	551,000 Germans; 141,000 Slovaks; 77,000 Serbo-Croats; 23,000 Roumanians; 6000 Slovenes; 31,000 others
Italy	1921	38,700,000	549,000	1·4	199,000 Germans; 258,000 Slovenes; 92,000 Croats
Jugoslavia	1921	11,900,000	2,050,500	17·2	505,000 Germans; 467,000 Magyars; 439,000 Albanians; 231,000 Roumanians; 176,000 Slovaks and other Slavs; 12,500 Italians; 220,000 others
Roumania	1930	18,000,000	4,500,000	25·0	1,463,000 Magyars; 778,000 Jews; 713,000 Germans; 500,000 Ukrainians; 351,000 Bulgarians; 222,000 Turks and Tatars; 174,000 Russians; 133,000 Gipsies; 52,000 Serbs; 35,000 Poles; 26,000 Slovaks; 53,000 others
Greece	1928	6,200,000	1,090,000	17·6	530,000 Slavs (Serbs and Bulgarians); 200,000 Albanians; 200,000 Vlachs; 50,000 Turks; 110,000 Jews

Post-War Minorities in Europe (in round figures)

Country	Year				
Bulgaria	1926	5,470,000	877,000	16·0	580,000 Turks; 135,000 Gipsies; 70,000 Roumanians; 46,000 Jews; 10,000 Greeks; 36,000 others
Turkey	1927	13,640,000	1,712,000	12·5	115,000 Greeks; 65,000 Armenians; 82,000 Jews; 20,000 Bulgarians; 95,000 Circassians; 135,000 Arabs; 1,200,000 Kurds
Albania	(estimated)	1,000,000	90,000	9·0	50,000 Greeks; 20,000 Vlachs; 10,000 Gipsies; 10,000 others
Poland	1921	27,100,000	8,251,000	30·4	3,800,000 Ukrainians; 2,100,000 Jews; 1,059,000 Germans; 1,060,000 White Russians; 68,000 Lithuanians; 56,000 Russians; 30,000 Czechs; 78,000 others
Finland	1924	3,430,000	450,000	13·1	400,000 Swedes; 50,000 Russians
Estonia	1922	1,100,000	129,000	11·7	91,000 Russians; 18,000 Germans; 20,000 others
Latvia	1930	1,900,000	501,800	26·4	201,000 Russians; 69,800 Germans; 94,000 Jews; 36,000 White Russians; 59,000 Poles; 25,000 Lithuanians; 17,000 others
Lithuania	1923	2,028,000	317,000	15·6	153,000 Jews; 65,000 Poles; 50,000 Russians; 29,000 Germans; 14,000 Letts; 6000 others
Spain	1920	21,950,000	5,269,000	24·0	1,100,000 Basques; 4,169,000 Catalans
		246,168,000	32,837,400	13·3	

[323]

1 It will be noticed that the Jews of Germany are omitted from this table: not because I wish to minimise the gravity of this problem, but because it belongs to a category of its own. To begin with, it is not at all easy to decide whether they are a racial or a religious minority. Are they not really *both at once*?

or religious, but no longer on a *racial* basis) who are at the mercy of majorities belonging to an alien race (and sometimes religion also) and whose fate, being a matter of legitimate and vital interest to their co-nationals in neighbouring countries, must continue to envenom international relations so long as it remains in the balance.

We ought also at the outset to face the fact, of which more will be said later, that the two countries with the highest percentage of minorities are Czechoslovakia and Poland, Germany's two chief neighbours on the east, and that next to the Ukrainians, who claim a total of 40 millions, and are certainly not less than 36 millions, the race which has the largest number of co-nationals outside its own borders is the German. Let us detach from the general table the items which affect men of German race, and we have the following result:

> 6,500,000 in Austria (not of course a minority, but an independent state)
> 3,123,500 in Czechoslovakia
> 1,059,000 in Poland
> 713,000 in Roumania
> 551,000 in Hungary
> 505,000 in Jugoslavia
> 366,000 in Danzig
> 201,000 in Latvia
> 199,000 in Italy
> 59,000 in Memel
> 35,000 in Denmark
> 29,000 in Lithuania
> 18,300 in Estonia
> ———————
> 13,399,000[1]

[1] Russia is omitted from this summary because the once flourishing German settlements on the Volga and in the Caucasus appear to have been virtually wiped out by a blend of famine and Marxist policy.

SEVEN PRINCIPAL ZONES

Here, then, is yet another reason for attaching capital importance to the question of minorities in a book which treats the German problem as the key to the European problem itself (see *infra*, p. 409). There are seven principal political zones where the political and ethnographical frontiers do not coincide: let us summarise them in the briefest manner possible.

I. Austria. If purely ethnographical arguments are to predominate, then it is obvious that the case for the "Anschluss" with Germany is unanswerable. The population of Austria is overwhelmingly German, and indeed it may be added that its only non-German section, the Slovenes of Carinthia, declared themselves in favour of Austria by a perfectly genuine plebiscite. The objections to union are political, economic, social, cultural, religious, rather than ethnographic, and may be traced back to the days of Schmerling and Bismarck, of Schönerer and Lueger, when the catchwords of "Great German" and "Little German" had a very definite religious and cultural background. The virulent anti-Semitism of Hitler can of course be traced back to such Pangerman purists as Lagarde, but its Austrian affinities, as essentially the gospel of the small man, are even more important. The great transformation wrought in Germany since 1933 has, however, given the much curtailed Austria of today a new mission, as a Catholic South German corporative state; and though her present leaders have none too clear an idea as to how this is to be worked out in practice, and lay an unfortunate stress upon "authoritarian leadership", they undoubtedly have most Austrians behind them in the attempt to preserve that individuality which the Austrian State has possessed for centuries past. From the practical side there are three important sections of the population which, it is true, find it almost impossible to unite, but which have an almost equal interest in preventing the Nazification or "Gleichschaltung" of Austria—namely, the Catholics, the Socialists and the Jews.

II. Just inside the North Italian frontier there are two racial minorities: according to the official statistics 349,000 Jugoslavs (258,000 Slovenes and 92,000 Croats) in "Venezia Giulia" (i.e. the two former Austrian provinces of Gorizia, Trieste and Istria) and 199,000 Germans in South Tirol or "Venezia Tridentina".[1] There is no little irony in the fact that these two small zones are the only ones in Europe where a "clean cut" could be effected, and where, therefore, the problem could be entirely eliminated by frontier rectification, without creating some fresh minority. But the Duce, the principal advocate of revision elsewhere, has no intention of handing back minorities which should never have been assigned to Italy in the first instance, and to which he is applying a policy of denationalisation more ruthless than that of any other country. It was on strategic grounds that Italy was allowed to take the Brenner frontier: but the extensive nature of the fortifications which she has been erecting to the south of it suggest some doubts both as to military confidence in what is admittedly the most ideal of strategic frontiers,[2] and as to the intentions of Mussolini's German ally.

III. The German-Czech Frontier. The problem of Czechoslovak independence was complicated from the outset by the presence of over three millions of Germans (3,123,000 at the Census of 1921; 3,231,000 at the Census of 1930) inside the frontiers of the Crown of Bohemia. This population, which was first settled there by the Bohemian Kings in the twelfth and thirteenth centuries, and which was augmented after the fall of Bohemian Independence in 1620 (and also to some extent in the nineteenth century by Germanisation), has never formed part of Germany, except in the purely nominal sense that the King of

[1] At the last Austrian census (1910), the number of Jugoslavs in the territory now belonging to Italy was returned as 550,990 (382,346 Slovenes, 168,644 Croats)—see "The Jugoslavs of Italy" (*Slavonic Review*, No. 43, July 1936) by Fran Barbalić, who produces quite serious arguments to suggest that the present number in Italy is 650,000. See also "The Germans of South Tirol", by E. Reut-Nicolussi (*Slavonic Review*, January 1938).

[2] My point is that if the Brenner is not good enough as a strategic frontier, then the idea of strategic frontiers must be abandoned as futile.

Bohemia was one of the Electors of the Holy Roman Empire. They have never enjoyed a special autonomy, first because for the last three centuries they belonged to the dominant race in the Austrian State and therefore required no further protection, but also for the no less cogent reason that their geographical distribution was such that they could not possibly form a single unit. This is why at the Peace Conference the ancient frontiers of the Bohemian Crown (corresponding admirably to geographic and economic needs) were left untouched. For the alternative at that time would have been to detach four more or less isolated fragments from the new state[1] and unite them with Bavaria, Saxony, Austria and Prussia respectively, simultaneously carrying with them a minority of roughly 400,000 Czechs and leaving behind them another minority of roughly 800,000 Germans in the central Czech districts: and the new State, in so curtailed a form, would obviously not have been *viable*. But Czechoslovakia remained faced by an immensely difficult problem, since the German minority naturally and inevitably resented a political transformation which meant the loss of their ancient hegemony. It is true that in 1926 an important section of that minority adopted an "activist" policy, that since then there have always been two (since 1936, three) German Ministers in every Cabinet, and that an agreement concluded on 18 February 1937 pledged the Czechoslovak State to extending still further the concessions enjoyed by the Germans under the Minority Treaty of 1920. But the question of "ideology" remained and has been rendered infinitely more acute since the advent of Hitler to power, the prohibition of militant National Socialism inside Czechoslovakia and the equivocal attitude adopted by the so-called Sudeten German Party under Konrad Henlein since 1935. It is inevitable and natural that the Germans of the Reich should be keenly interested in the fate of all Germans beyond their borders, and hence in that of the unit which is numerically largest after

[1] The Eger-Karlsbad district in the north-west, the Reichenberg-Trautenau district in the north-east, the Moravian-Silesian group from Olmütz to Troppau and the strip adjoining Upper Austria to the south of Budweis.

Austria itself. But it is essential that foreign opinion should realise that of the minorities in Europe the Germans of Czechoslovakia have the fewest grievances (though their economic situation, as an over-industrialised area even under Austrian rule, has been more than usually difficult since the world depression). To take the most striking illustration in the field of education. In the year 1935 they possessed their own University, three High Schools, an Academy of Music, 80 secondary schools with 800 classes, 10 Training Colleges, 52 Agrarian schools, 447 higher and 3298 lower primary schools,[1] and 501 Kindergarten. In face of such figures the charge of Czechisation becomes simply grotesque: and, indeed, the Germans of Bohemia have always enjoyed, as a matter of course, many rights whose concession by Poland to Germany in the autumn of 1937 was trumpeted abroad as marking an epoch. None the less, the Reich press, on orders from above, and for reasons connected with European strategy rather than with national rights, has concentrated its attacks upon the Czechs, while observing silence as to the grinding oppression of South Tirol by allied Italy and the far from enviable position of the Germans in Poland.

IV. The German-Polish frontier resolves itself into four quite distinct problems:

(1) The so-called "Polish Corridor" is a mischievous misnomer, unless the question be presented as a choice between a "Polish Corridor" to connect Poland with the sea and a "German Corridor" to connect East Prussia with the main body of the Reich. On this basis we are asked to choose between depriving Poland of her only access to the sea, down the valley of a great Polish river, the Vistula, through territory which is ethnically Polish and formed part of Poland for 650 years; or leaving the Germans of East Prussia separated geographically from the Reich, but enjoying free access by sea to Germany and the outer world, and special trade and transit facilities by land, which are admittedly troublesome, but by no means unwork-

---

[1] Out of a total of 343,567 German children attending primary schools, 333,450 went to German, and only 10,117 to Czech, schools.

able. In a word, for Poland the "Corridor" is a matter of life and death, of that free access to the sea which history has shown to be essential to Polish independence.

(2) Danzig was given a special status as a Free City, under the League of Nations, because Poland's retention of the mouth of the Vistula necessarily isolated the city both from the Reich and from East Prussia. It received a constitution specially devised to safeguard its German character to all time, and it is not the fault of the League or even of the Allies if, since the coming of the Hitler regime, first Germany set herself to undermine the regime and then Poland lent herself to the plot, with results still obscure, for which she must take the consequences. In 1929 the Free City contained a population of only 29,000 Poles out of a total of 395,000.

(3) The substitution of a German Corridor connecting East Prussia with the main body of the Reich for a Polish Corridor to the sea would inevitably involve the reunion of a considerable portion of Poznania also: this could only be effected in defiance of ethnography, history and economics, the only real argument on the German side being those feelings of sentiment and prestige that have grown up since Prussia possessed herself of this territory by one of the great crimes of history. The best proof of the essentially Polish character of the disputed districts is provided by German *pre-war* statistics and by the figures of the German Reichstag elections: and the attempt to distinguish between "Polish" and "Kashubian" or "Mazurian" is as puerile as those earlier artificial distinctions drawn between "Moravian" and "Czech", between "Bosnian" and "Serb", between "Moldavian" and "Roumanian", between "Bunjevac" and "Croat".

(4) There remains the question of Upper Silesia, where German and Pole were inextricably mingled and their separation rendered tenfold more impossible by complex economic interests. The Peace Conference found it necessary to place the province under the control of a special inter-allied Commission until a plebiscite could be carried out, and when this at last took place in March 1921, the Allies were unable to agree, and the

final frontier award, partitioning Upper Silesia and establishing a provisional "Mixed Commission" for fifteen years, was made by the League of Nations in October of that year. On both sides there were determined attempts to forestall the final settlement by armed force, and Silesia remained for years the object of grave friction between Germany and Poland.

V. Poland is faced by no less grave problems on her eastern frontier, and these again fall into three groups.

(*a*) The Lithuanian-Polish dispute centres round the possession of Vilna, the ancient capital of Lithuania, the population of which is overwhemingly Polish by race, language and tradition, whereas the entire surrounding country which goes with it contains 80–85 per cent of Lithuanians and White Russians, and in no case more than 10 per cent of Poles. Since the seizure of Vilna by General Zeligowski in 1920 and its retention in open defiance of Geneva, there has been a complete deadlock in the dispute between Poland and Lithuania, with the wellnigh incredible result that the frontier between them has for years remained hermetically sealed, to the detriment not only of mutual relations, but of the pacification of the whole of the Baltic area. It has sometimes been urged that but for this regrettable feud it might have been possible to re-establish the ancient federal ties which subsisted between Lithuania and Poland under the great Jagiello dynasty, and that the consequent possession of an eastern outlet to the sea, down the Nyemen to Memel, would have greatly eased the tension in the question of Danzig and Gdynia (the new Polish port on the Baltic). In actual practice, the idea of Memel as a possible substitute has never even been open to discussion, and may in any case be regarded as shelved since the Polish-German Pact of January 1934.

It should be added that the number of Lithuanians in Poland in 1921 was 68,000, while in 1923 there were 65,000 Poles in Lithuania.

(*b*) The White Russians in Poland, according to the census of 1921, amounted to 1,060,000, but this is a notorious understatement, and the White Russians themselves, grossly exaggerating in their turn, claim to be as numerous as 2,500,000. They enjoy no special rights under Poland, but this was of course also the case under Tsarist Russia. What has given the question a new importance is the steady growth of national consciousness in the White Russian districts under Soviet rule.

(*c*) Above all, there is the thorny Ukrainian question, the largest unsolved national question in Europe, affecting a population of over 35,000,000. Of these, 4,000,000 live in Poland, mainly in Eastern Galicia, where, under the benevolent sway of Austria, the "Ruthenes" possessed a certain minimum of cultural and religious rights, in contrast to the absolute repression of Ukrainian and Uniat sentiments in Tsarist Russia. For a brief space in 1918–19 the Ukrainian National Rada ruled in Kiev and concluded a separate peace at Brest-Litovsk, while a provisional Ukrainian Government was established in Eastern Galicia; but all too soon Bolshevist Russia overpowered the one and Poland the other. The Ukraine has, it is true, formed the second most important federal unit in the Union of Soviet Republics and has enjoyed greater linguistic freedom than under the old regime. Eastern Galicia, on the other hand, was in March 1923 recognised by the Council of Ambassadors as forming part of Poland, but on the distinct condition that it should receive autonomy. Ten years have passed without this pledge being fulfilled, and the Ukrainians have lost most of the advantages which they enjoyed in Austria. Only the knowledge that conditions are still more unfavourable in the Soviet Ukraine has held in check the national discontent in Eastern Galicia. But the triangular contest between Pole, Ukrainian and Great Russian is only postponed, not in any way solved.

It should be added that the real explanation of Poland's action lies in the fact that scattered throughout Eastern Galicia is a powerful Polish minority of not less than 1,000,000, and that between 70 and 80 per cent of the population of the capital city of Lwow (Lemberg) is Polish.

VI. Hungary contests the frontier with each of her four neighbours—Austria, Czechoslovakia, Roumania and Jugoslavia; and any examination of the details at once reveals the fact that in each of the last three cases the problem falls into several quite distinct sections.

A. Austria. The so-called "Burgenland" is overwhelmingly German and ought to include the Magyarised town of Oedenburg (Sopron), where Hungary was allowed to effect a *fait accompli* in 1920 in very much the same way as Poland at Vilna, and which consequently forms a sharp and quite unnatural salient projecting into Austria. In other words, any rectification of frontier would have to be in favour of Austria rather than Hungary.

B. Czechoslovakia. Racial considerations apart, the frontier between Slovakia and Hungary was determined by Slovakia's need for access to the Danube and by the difficulties of communication from west to east of the province. (1) From the very outset Bratislava asserted itself as capital, and today there are more Germans than Magyars in it, and far more Czechs and Slovaks than Germans and Magyars combined. East of it, however, lies the rich district of Csallóköz (Žitný Ostrov), stretching as far as Komárno, which is overwhelmingly Magyar in race, but whose economic interests are bound up with the northern bank of the Danube. (2) From the mouth of the Ipel the frontier runs north-eastwards towards Košice—the natural centre for the whole of Eastern Slovakia; and owing to the mountainous nature of the terrain, it could not be very materially altered without virtually cutting all communication from west to east. It must be borne in mind that (speaking very roughly) the Slovak masses inhabit the hill country and the Magyars the plains. (3) There remains the semi-autonomous province of "Ruthenia" (Podkarpatská Rus), which still awaits the full grant of self-government promised under the treaties, but which, from being the most backward and neglected corner of pre-war Hungary, has made remarkable cultural and linguistic progress in these fourteen years—being the only section of the whole Ukrainian race which enjoys free cultural development. Here it was found essential not to separate the foothills and valleys, in which the Ruthenians mainly live, from the connecting valley of the upper Tisza, mainly inhabited by Magyars, and at the same time to retain the only railway line running from west to east (and, incidentally, the only railway connection between Czechoslovakia and Roumania).

In short, while it might be possible, by ignoring economics, to restore some 200–300,000 Magyars of Slovakia and Ruthenia without sacrificing more than 30–40,000 Slovaks, something like two-thirds of the total Magyar minority would almost inevitably remain behind.

C. Roumania. Here the problem falls into four distinct sections:

(*a*) The valley of the Szamos as far as Satu Mare (Szatmár Németi, i.e. "*German* Szatmár") is claimed by Hungary. It is, however, one of those districts which have only been Magyarised in quite modern times and in a most artificial manner; and the best proof of this is the reappearance, since the War, of a German minority of 30–40,000 which had been deprived of schools, culture and leaders, and under the influence of propaganda through the Church had entered the final stage of assimilation.

(*b*) Halfway along the Roumano-Magyar frontier the town of Oradea Mare (Nagyvárad), which is predominantly Magyar with a large admixture of Jews, was assigned to Roumania on the ground that though a more strictly linguistic frontier might be drawn ten or fifteen miles farther east, it would cut across the Transylvanian foothills and deprive Roumania of her road and railway connection from north to south.

(*c*) Arad, a predominantly Magyar and Jewish town, and the district immediately to the west of it were assigned to Roumania, on the ground that it would have formed an unnatural salient and would itself have suffered economically.

(*d*) It is probable that by rectification it would be possible to restore 200–250,000 Magyars to Hungary without sacrificing more than 40–50,000 Roumanians. But that would in no way solve the main problem, for, unfortunately, the great bulk of the Magyars in Roumania live not along the frontier, but in isolated islets and enclaves, varying greatly in size. About

100,000 are centred in the town and county of Cluj (Kolozsvár), the chief town of Transylvania. Worst of all, the Székelys, who inhabit the four counties in the south-eastern bend of the Carpathians and number about 600,000, living for the most part in solid racial blocks of 90–95 per cent, occupy what is today the exact geographical centre of "Greater Roumania"—the kernel in the fruit. The only possible way of reuniting these two main Magyar groups with their kinsmen in Hungary is to re-annex at least three-quarters, if not the whole, of Transylvania, with two to three million Roumanians.

D. Jugoslavia. Even here, though less than half a million Magyars are affected, the problem falls into three sections:

(*a*) In the Banat—the most complicated racial mosaic in all Europe (not excepting Macedonia)—the only real rectification possible would be in favour of Roumania as against Jugoslavia— the latter's frontier having been altered at Paris at the last moment in defiance of the views of many of the experts, in such a way as to block the economic outlet of Timişoara (Temesvár) to the Danube.

(*b*) In the Bačka it would be easy to draw the frontier considerably farther to the south and thereby to diminish the number of Magyars in Jugoslavia by about 200,000, were it not for the presence of a large Jugoslav element—amounting to close on 100,000—in the city of Subotica (Szabadka) near the present frontier.

(*c*) Croatia-Slavonia does not properly fall within this survey: for there could be no question of its ever returning voluntarily to union with Hungary. The only alternative to its remaining as an integral part of Jugoslavia would be that it should form an independent state in conjunction with Slovenia and Dalmatia —a highly problematical and unsatisfactory solution, which would only please Fascist Italy.

VII. Balkan Frontiers. It is not possible, within the limits of this general survey, to discuss all the many thorny minority problems still at issue in the Balkans: and indeed, after a first decade of reprisals and unrest, mutual animosities have died down to a very remarkable degree in most parts of the Peninsula. The oldest and most acute quarrel of all, that between Greece and Turkey, has been virtually eliminated, the great Greek adventure in Asia Minor having ended in a turning of the tables and in the wholesale expulsion of the Greek population on the Asiatic mainland and their settlement in Macedonia and "Old Greece". Certainly there is no precedent for other countries in this method of eliminating the minorities on both sides by a process of wholesale exchange, following upon war, extermination and terror. The case for cataclysmic solutions can doubtless be argued, on the analogy that fire and sword settled the Albigensian heresy in the thirteenth century, and with it the prospects of a separate Provençal state and culture. But it cannot seriously be put forward by anyone who accepts Genevan or Christian principles.

The second problem is that of the Macedonian Slavs, whose national origin is disputed between Serb and Bulgar, and who, after being the bone of contention in two fratricidal wars, are, it may be hoped, at last slowly coming to be the *trait d'union* which shall unite Bulgar and Serb in a higher transcending unity. Certain it is that any line drawn between them is bound to be quite arbitrary.

As between Roumania and Bulgaria there is the question of the southern Dobrogea, which was annexed after the second Balkan War in 1913 as compensation to Roumania, but which is over-whelmingly Bulgar in character, despite the regrettable attempt to redress the balance by settling Vlach emigrants from the Pindus.

As between Roumania and Jugoslavia there are two problems, old and new. The former is that of the Roumanian population in the Timok district of Serbia proper, estimated at over 100,000, and for the most part descended from immigrants from Wallachia during the Turkish era. The latter is in the Banat, where at the last moment the Peace Conference inconsiderately modified the new Roumano-Jugoslav frontier in such a way as to cut off Timişoara from its natural outlet southwards to the little Danube port of Baziaş and yet at the same time to leave the towns of Vršec and Bela Črkva as wedges driven deep into the Roumanian flesh.

As between Jugoslavia and Albania, Albania and Greece, Greece and Bulgaria, Bulgaria and Turkey, there are yet other frontier questions, too intricate to be treated here, and none of them capable of settlement on the basis of a "clean cut".

MINORITY OBLIGATIONS

We have often had occasion to point out the extent to which all international problems are interlocked: and this applies pre-eminently to the question of minorities. Indeed, to raise any one of these frontier disputes, save by direct negotiations between the parties concerned, must almost inevitably raise all the others. For almost all the states affected are simultaneously "top dogs" in one direction and "under dogs" in another, and it is inconceivable that any one of them will voluntarily surrender non-national territory to one neighbour without at least recovering its own national territory held by other neighbours. To take but a single delicate instance, is it to be supposed that Jugoslavia will ever comply with the Italian suggestion that she should cede territory to Bulgaria or Hungary, unless Italy either surrenders her own Jugoslav population or at least restores to them the most elementary political rights? But if it be true that all these frontier questions are more or less interlocked, is it not even more true that they cannot safely be discussed, much less solved, in the heated atmosphere recently engendered in Europe, and that the attempt to raise them on a large scale at the present juncture would probably turn Geneva into a bear-garden?

If it could be demonstrated that rectification would wipe out these racial conflicts, then anyone opposing it would be guilty of a crime against Europe. But on the contrary, even under the most favourable circumstances (that is, making the very large and dubious assumption that peaceful agreement could be reached regarding certain territorial changes) the major portion of almost all these problems would still remain unsolved. Hence passions would have been aroused, infinite uncertainty created, and dislocation introduced into many lives, yet without any real guarantee that the agitation which prompted the original demand would now finally die down and permanently cordial relations be established.

Something of this was implicit in the speech delivered by Dr Beneš on 25 April 1933, when he freely admitted that Article XIX of the Covenant made it possible to raise the question of revision before the international forum, but argued that territorial changes presupposed direct negotiation and free agreement between the parties concerned, "in an atmosphere of calm and collaboration", in which there could be no talk of either capitulation or terrorism or blackmail. It is obvious that the only real alternative to this would be either war, in defiance of the Covenant, or dictation exercised by strong Powers against weak ones.

A further factor is too often overlooked. How do the advocates of revision envisage the actual process of transfer of territory? The states concerned fall into two categories—those where all political opposition has been suppressed, and where a dictatorial and strongly nationalist regime prevails, and those where constitutional forms still survive. Can it be seriously maintained that national dictators are more predisposed to territorial concessions than the more liberal regimes which they have superseded, and which they now denounce as traitors? And again, can it seriously be expected that governments which are still responsible to parliamentary and representative bodies could ever obtain their sanction for drastic territorial changes, or even for rectification except on a basis of free mutual concession, leading to some new form of political and economic co-operation?

The fundamental difficulty was, however, that on which we have already insisted—that on no frontier, save possibly the Italian, could a clear-cut ethnic line of division be attained, and that, no matter how the frontiers may be drawn or re-drawn, very considerable minorities must in all cases remain on the wrong side of every one of them. It was a clear perception of this which led the much-abused experts of Paris to fall back upon the expedient of Minority Treaties guaranteeing the language, religion and culture of those racial fragments which it seemed unavoidable to leave under foreign rule. Unhappily a grave error of judgment was committed by the Conference when, instead of placing all the Powers concerned—great and small alike—on a footing of absolute equality in respect of minority rights, it imposed obligations on some Powers and left others as free as air. And there was this ominous feature about the distinction, that it was the major Powers who were dispensed, and the minor Powers to whom acceptance of a Minority Treaty was made a condition of recognising their new status in Europe. There was, it is true, an admirable precedent for this in those clauses of the Treaty of Berlin which compelled Roumania and Serbia, on attaining independence, to grant religious equality to their Jewish subjects. But in 1878 the questions at issue were, of course, far more circumscribed than in 1919, and there were other clauses imposing upon Turkey on her side definite pledges of religious, linguistic and administrative concessions to her remaining Christian subjects in Europe. That public opinion remembered nothing of this precedent was doubtless due to the fact that Turkey's pledges remained from the very outset a dead letter, and that the Powers never insisted on their fulfilment.

(1) The omission of the Great Powers from any such pledges in 1919 applied in particular to Britain, France, Italy and Germany. Of the first two it would suffice to say that they would greatly strengthen their moral standing in the whole question if they freely assumed minority obligations on their own behalf. In the first case this would apply to Wales and the Gaelic-speaking districts of Scotland, and perhaps to such groups of immigrants as the Irish and Lithuanians in Scotland and the Jews of East London; in the latter case to the Bretons, Provençals and Basques. In neither case would such action involve any danger to the state, still less any departure from liberal principles.

(2) The position of Italy is much more delicate. By the Peace Treaties she acquired, for purely strategic reasons, two pieces of territory in South Tirol and "Venezia Giulia" whose

racial composition was wellnigh 100 per cent German or Jugoslav. During the first occupation of this territory (November 1918), the Italian Commander-in-Chief issued a proclamation disclaiming all idea of suppressing other races and languages, and making many promises of special liberties. In his speech from the throne (1 January 1919), the King of Italy, in the name of "our liberal traditions", promised to respect "local autonomous institutions and customs". Finally, in concluding peace with Austria in September 1919, the Italian Government of the day voluntarily declared its intention of "adopting a far-reaching liberal policy towards its new citizens of German origin, with regard to their language, culture and economic institutions". In view of this general Italian attitude, it seemed to many unnecessary to press Italy at the Peace Conference for any specific undertaking. It is true that no such promises were ever made to the Jugoslavs of Italy as were made to South Tirol, but by the Treaty of Rapallo Jugoslavia was obliged to make far-reaching concessions to the microscopic Italian minority in Dalmatia, and in view of the *détente* produced by the Treaty it seemed reasonable to hope that there would be at least some approach towards reciprocity. But since the coming of Fascism there has been a gradual but progressive turning of the screw against the minorities; one liberty after the other has been annulled, until not one trace is now left of the three pledges quoted above. There are only Italian schools; the mother tongue is not even allowed for religious instruction, and is banished from the courts, the administration and all public notices. The minorities have no press, no right of assembly, no deputies, no societies or clubs, and in the case of the Jugoslavs they are forced to Italianise their surnames or eschew the Christian names of Slav saints (exactly as their kinsmen in Jugoslavia force the Macedonians to give their names a Serbian form). And the dictator who is, above all, responsible for this change is also the man who has till recently, for his own political ends, been encouraging certain Danubian minorities in demands far less modest than those which he has consistently refused to his own citizens. In this connection it is necessary to say quite bluntly that while it is almost impossible to find a point on any of the numerous disputed frontiers of Europe where a "clean cut" on racial lines could be effected, there is now one exception to this general rule, namely on the Italian border in South Tirol and on the Isonzo.

(3) In the case of Germany the minority question assumed yet another form. After the revision of her frontiers in favour of France, Belgium, Denmark, Poland and Czechoslovakia, there remained inside the curtailed Reich 896,141 Slavs (over 500,000 of them being classified as bi-lingual) and a negligible number of Lithuanians and Danes; while many millions of Germans by race remained, or became, citizens of Poland, Czechoslovakia, Hungary, Jugoslavia, Roumania and the Baltic States. (The case of Austria naturally falls under a special category, as it now forms *a second independent national German state*, in which the combined non-German population forms under 2 per cent of the total.) The pill was therefore not still further embittered by imposing unilateral obligations upon Germany, and her sole international commitment in the minority question is the mutual pledge regarding Upper Silesia, which accompanied the settlement of 15 May 1922.

We have already seen that there are close upon 7 million Germans scattered about the countries of East and South East Europe: and if to these be added the 2,600,000 Germans of Switzerland and the 6,270,000 Germans of Austria, we reach a rough total of 16 million Germans living in Europe *outside* the borders of the German Reich, while in the United States and South America there are many millions more, in all stages of assimilation or of resistance to the process. When Herr Hess, in December 1937, spoke of 100 million Germans, he was of course guilty of one of the gross exaggerations in which politicians on holiday so often indulge. But the fact remains that about a quarter of the entire German race lies outside the political borders of Germany. That their fate should not be a matter of indifference to the citizens of the Reich is only right and proper: and that the withholding of full equality from any section of them, still more any attempt to assimilate them, should arouse keen feeling, is equally natural, and is bound to provoke lively reactions, especially under the new Hitlerite dispensation, with its watchword of "*Volksgemeinschaft*" or blood brotherhood. So long as this doctrine remains a recognition of kinship and closest intercourse across artificially created political frontiers, it may be said to correspond to a national right whose denial will in the end spell disaster to those who deny it. In the moment when it became a claim to unite all the members of the race in a single political community, it would threaten Europe with chaos and conflict, because it would cut at the very roots of at least three independent states—Switzerland, Austria and Czechoslovakia—and would provoke internal conflicts in four or five others. It must at once be added that the post-war tendency of most of the new states to claim for themselves the character of *national states* is no less exaggerated in the other direction, and, indeed, constitutes an open challenge, in conflict with the patent facts of the present situation. For while in most cases the "Will to the State", to use a German expression, lies with some single majority race, that in no way confers upon it any right to restrict the inalienable rights of minorities of other races, whatever their proportion to the total population may be; and it is only when these minorities are out of all danger of assimilation or of reduction to an inferior rank, that the foundations of inter-racial and, therefore, inter-state, peace in Europe can be fully assured.

The Minority Treaties, then, were devised as an expedient—some would say a *pis-aller*—rendered necessary by the utter impossibility of producing exact ethnographic frontiers. The elaborate series of guarantees thus established falls into two main categories. On the one hand, the four defeated states were obliged to undertake specific obligations towards such minorities as still remained on their territory—Austria by Articles 62–9 of the Treaty of St Germain (10 September 1919), Bulgaria by Articles 49–57 of the Treaty of Neuilly (27 November 1919), Hungary by Articles 54–60 of the Treaty of Trianon (4 June 1920), and Turkey by Articles 37–45 of the Treaty of Lausanne (24 July 1923, the provisions of the original

Treaty of Sèvres having never been ratified, and having been finally overthrown by the Turco-Greek War). On the other hand, the new states were asked to undertake corresponding pledges of minority rights, as their contribution to the new order in Europe. The difficulties were specially great in the case of Poland and Roumania.

(1) Czechoslovakia—the most consistently democratic of the new states—forestalled criticism by intimating its intention of establishing Swiss constitutional principles: and it raised no difficulty whatsoever to signing a special Minority Treaty simultaneously with that of St Germain on 10 September 1919, embodying also what amounts to a special charter of autonomy for "Carpathian Ruthenia" (not yet fully implemented). These various provisions were supplemented by special regulations for minority protection, as an integral part of the Czechoslovak Constitution of 29 February 1920.

(2) Jugoslavia (then known as the Kingdom of the Serbs, Croats and Slovenes) vigorously resisted the Conference's demand that her minority obligations should apply to her whole territory and not merely to that acquired in the Great War. The point at issue was, of course, the vexed question of Macedonia. In the end the Powers imposed their view, and the Jugoslavs escaped from the dilemma by stubbornly insisting that the "Macedonians", being Serbs, are not a minority at all, and are therefore not affected by the Minority Treaty.

NATIONALITY AND CITIZENSHIP

The existence of all these elaborate treaties and conventions, under the guarantee of the League of Nations, is a new and hopeful factor in international relations which, in the end, should make for appeasement, by providing machinery for peaceful compromise. But it is unhappily true that (1) the exaggerated insistence by almost all states upon the principle of absolute state sovereignty; (2) the tendency of multi-national states to pose as purely national; and (3) the resentment due to the inequality of obligation between the greater and lesser states, have blocked the efficacy of the League in this vital question. Procedure has been too slow, publicity has been lacking, and two proposals of the first importance—for a permanent Minorities Committee on the lines of the Mandates Commission, and for the appointment of resident agents of the League in the disputed areas—have hitherto been defeated. There is a vicious circle, for a satisfactory reform of minority procedure seems difficult of attainment in the present unsettled condition of Europe, yet these very unsolved minority problems are one of the main causes of the unrest. Worst of all, for reasons which cannot be dealt with in this general sketch, some of the most important provisions of certain of these Minority Treaties have remained on paper: the irresponsible flood of ill-founded grievances with which Geneva was assailed in the first years discredited the method of petition: and certain interested Powers succeeded only too well in blocking all schemes for improved procedure and publicity in minority questions.

It follows from all this, not by any means that an *impasse* has been reached in the vexed "question of Nationalities", but rather that frontier revision, as generally advocated, does not provide the means of escape, and, indeed, that "the difference between ethnographic and political frontiers is inherent in the geographical distribution of the various races of Europe, and cannot be rectified". The real remedy must be sought in other directions. The motive force of "revisionism" comes from two main sources—on the one hand, political agitation and hopes of *revanche* (and this only time can cure, as the older generation dies off), and on the other hand, the absolutely legitimate fear for the fate of co-nationals on the wrong side of a frontier. This will continue until it can be proved to be groundless—in other words, until a policy of "assimilation" has by common consent been abandoned or rendered impossible. In the sixteenth century the attempt of temporal rulers to enforce upon their subjects the principle of *cujus regio, ejus religio*, led to constant wars of religion and drenched Europe in blood, till at last religion has almost everywhere become a private affair of the individual and not of the state. In somewhat the same way the attempt to assimilate *racial* minorities, by the denial of schools, culture and linguistic facilities—an attempt which is often, (though not always) veiled behind liberal professions and pursued far more widely than is generally realised—must inevitably keep large sections of Europe in a state of unrest—not merely the minorities concerned, who have been variously estimated at between 25 and 35 millions, but also of course large sections of their kinsmen in neighbouring states, who make up the greater part of Europe. What is needed is something more than the effective enforcement of existing Minority Treaties (though this would be an essential first step forwards), namely their extension to the maximum, not to the minimum, possible in each particular case, and the public recognition that a man's "nationality" is not identical with his "citizenship", but is something compounded of race, language, tradition and innermost feeling—something physiological and sacred, which should be as inviolate as his religion. If this view could once win general acceptance and be translated into practice, the frontiers would speedily lose much of their political significance, revision would fall into the background, cultural intercourse across the frontiers could be extended, and the path would be laid for that removal, or at least reduction, of economic barriers which must be the final goal.[1] In December 1934 M. Titulescu, then Roumanian Foreign Minister, gave eloquent expression to this idea in a speech before the League, when he advocated "the spiritualisation of frontiers". If the phrase was received sarcastically in some quarters, in view of the widespread contrasts between theory and practice, it none the less remains the goal towards which men of good will must press on. Without guarantees for the safety of Small States on the one hand, and for the survival of Minorities on the other, there can be no real appeasement in Europe.

---

[1] I developed this line of argument in "The Crisis of Democracy and the Slavonic World" (*Slavonic Review*, No. 27, March 1931); in "The Problem of Revision and the Slav World" (*ibid.* No. 34, July 1933); in "The Question of Minorities" (*ibid.* No. 40, July 1935); and more fully in a brochure entitled *Hungarian Frontiers and Treaty Revision* (1934).

X

THE ABYSSINIAN CRISIS

EVER since the War Europe has been like a nerve-ridden patient, passing through a succession of acute crises: no sooner has emergency treatment been applied to one limb, than the poison seems to break out in some other part of the body. If, then, the change of regime in Germany seems to mark a turning-point both in the disease and in the methods applied for its cure, it is also true that two questions—which in other times might have been isolated with comparative ease or even ignored by all save a few geographically interested countries—have for the last two years dominated the diplomatic situation in Europe, at times almost to the exclusion of all other issues. These two questions, the Abyssinian and the Spanish, in their latest forms are indeed a classical example of the manner in which all problems, however seemingly remote from each other, are today interlocked, thanks to the shrinkage of the world effected by science, and above all the improvements in transport and in news transmission. The Napier expedition to Magdala was merely one out of a long series of colonial incidents, while the Italian reverse at Adua in 1896 was mainly interesting as a check to the expansive ambitions of the youngest of the Great Powers, and in so far as it affected Italian internal politics. Even Spain, though early last century it had been the "ulcer" which sapped Napoleon's vitals and even a decade later had been the victim of "Legitimist" intervention from France, had at last been successfully insulated, with the result that her chronic civil wars had no serious repercussions outside the Peninsula except on one famous occasion when a candidature to the vacant Spanish throne was the spark that lit the Franco-German War. There may be some who will argue that the change was due to the impossible and meddlesome ideals of the League of Nations, leading fifty-two states to interfere in matters with which most of them had no direct concern. But the obvious rejoinder is that the League's endeavour to establish a new international order had been rendered imperative by that "European anarchy" of which the Great War was the logical outcome, that only the co-operation of all can avert a relapse into still worse anarchy. In any case, it is obviously impossible to evade either problem in any consideration of contemporary British policy.

Abyssinia, the oldest and last of the independent African states, had been admitted to the League of Nations in 1923, mainly at the instance of the French and Italian Governments, and against the better judgment of the British Government. It was a bundle of loosely knitted provinces and kingdoms, under powerful and reactionary feudal chiefs. Ras Tafari, who became Emperor in 1928 and assumed the title of "Haile Selassie I", stood for the centralising and reforming tendencies of the Shoan dynasty and probably wielded greater authority than the famous Menelik, who had driven out the Italian invaders in 1896: but he only had a small band of enlightened and competent helpers round him, corruption and superstition were hard to eradicate, slavery and slave-raiding still lingered, and the constitution promulgated by the Emperor in 1931 was a pious aspiration rather than an actual fact. None the less, his short reign had already proved an ample justification for Italy's action in concluding the Treaty of August 1928 with Abyssinia[1] (under Article V of which the parties were bound to arbitrate disputes, "without having recourse to force of arms"): and though it is quite true that the Abyssinians did not carry out their pledges of road and railway construction, the existence of this treaty greatly adds to the perfidy of Italy's action.[2]

---

[1] On 3 June 1928, in the Senate, the Duce spoke of Italy's specially friendly relations with Abyssinia ("clouds have vanished"). In the same speech he treated "the traditional friendship with England" as a reality, such as rendered special protocols unnecessary, *Scritti,* VI, 180, 184.

[2] Cf. Toynbee, *Survey of International Affairs for* 1935, II, p. 149.

ITALY'S PRETEXTS AND AIMS

The essential arguments put forward by Signor Mussolini himself to justify aggression were (1) "the vital needs of the Italian people", (2) "their security in East Africa", and (3) Italy's right to share in Europe's "civilising mission", and her claim that this would be fulfilled by the conquest of Ethiopia.[1] If the first of these phrases be analysed, it means that pressure of population at home—increased since the United States and South America have virtually closed their doors to emigrants from Italy and since the Fascist Government has (illogically enough) strained every effort to augment the birthrate still further—renders colonial expansion essential, and that as Libya and Eritrea are quite inadequate, fresh territory must be acquired elsewhere. It also means that Italy's admitted deficiency in coal and iron ore must be made good by the seizure of territory whose mineral wealth, when exploited, will either supply the deficiency or provide a rich basis of barter with other Powers. Yet, it is exceedingly doubtful whether Abyssinia can ever absorb Italy's surplus population, firstly because Abyssinia already has a very large native population (10 millions in 1925) which would have to be exterminated or displaced, or else would be a menace to isolated settlers, besides competing with them in the most fatal of all ways by a lower standard of living, and secondly because colonisation on any effective scale would cost untold sums, far beyond the resources of Italy. It has been calculated that the settlement of 250,000 Italians in Abyssinia— i.e. the surplus of a single year—would cost £350,000,000, exclusive of the cost of transport.

Behind these aims there are motives of revenge, sentiment, prestige and political strategy. It is perfectly natural that the humiliating defeat of Adua should have rankled in many Italian minds and that the chance of wiping out the disgrace should have been welcomed by those who have learned nothing from the Great War. In the mind of the Duce himself this

[1] *Popolo d'Italia*, 31 July 1935.

feeling is blended with the design of a Fascist Empire, of an "Impero Romano" in Africa: and a foreign adventure, well-staged and directed against less formidable enemies than are to be found in Europe, seemed the best means of rehabilitating the regime, diverting attention from the grinding economic distress of the masses, and temporarily solving the problem of unemployment by calling many to the colours and by increased armament production. From the standpoint of human life and by comparison with the Great War, the laurels of the Abyssinian campaign have been won at an incredibly low cost: but from the financial standpoint its cost has been enormous—far higher than any colonial war in history—and the drain caused by a huge army of occupation and by necessary public works in a primitive country, is likely to continue for years. Moreover, it may well be doubted whether the experiences of the army in Africa have really increased in a naturally mild and peaceful nation those "militaristic" traits which are so dear to the Duce's heart. Certainly the horrid massacre of Addis Ababa and the panic on the Spanish front are far from reassuring.

There is one direction only in which Italy may find some pretext for her action. By the secret Treaty of London of 26 April 1915, which brought her into the War on the side of the Allies, the latter recognised her right, in the event of Germany losing her African colonies, to "certain compensations" on the borders of Eritrea, Somaliland and Libya. This, the most shamelessly imperialistic treaty of the War, with its recognition of Italian rights of conquest against the Slav, and of a general grab against Turkey, hung like a millstone about the necks of the Allies, and complicated their relations with America at the Peace Conference, but did not prevent them from pocketing the entire colonial possessions of Germany in Africa and merely throwing to Italy a few scraps of arid desert: while the events connected with the disastrous Treaty of Sèvres prevented Italy—this time fortunately for her—from establishing a foothold in Asia Minor. From the standpoint of her relations with former allies, then, Italy had a just grievance, from the standpoint of a new World Order, none whatever: but this is an argument which sounds strangely when used by those who have supped well to those still waiting to be served. To the practical mind of the Duce the essential fact was that Britain had conquered the Sudan and the Boer Republics as recently as 1898 and 1902, while France had only completed her conquest of Morocco in 1934, and that Tanganyika alone was worth Jubaland fifty times over. "We find it monstrous", he declared in September 1935," that a nation which dominates the world should refuse to us a wretched plot of ground in the African sun." Towards Wilsonian principles, whether expressed in the Fourteen Points or in the Covenant, he has long since made it abundantly clear that he feels in very much the same way as Castlereagh towards the fine phrases of the Holy Alliance, which he regarded as "a piece of sublime mysticism and nonsense". But Castlereagh for that very reason prevented his master from entering the Holy Alliance, and at the same time scrupulously observed the international contracts which the victorious Powers intended as the basis of a new World Order. Italy, as a victor in the Great War, and of her own free will—and at first amid the acclamations of the Italian masses—accepted the League system, the Covenant and those other instruments which were at length to make a reality of world peace and co-operation. To the Duce, however, any attempt to distinguish between pre-war and post-war standards seems a mere hypocritical homily on the phrase "*beati possidentes*", though he on his side draws a most emphatic distinction between the ethics of an European and a Colonial war. He seems altogether impervious to the arguments of those who see in 1914–19 the "Great Divide" and would make of international law and peace the foundation of our World Order. Rejecting the conception of "a war to end war", he has resolutely proclaimed his belief in the steel-bath of war, his resolve to make of Italy "a military, nay a militaristic, nation" and his hope that they will breed as much cannon fodder as possible for the time when war will be even more wasteful of human flesh than it is today.

BROKEN PLEDGES

The full enormity of Mussolini's aggression is, however, best measured, not by his own perfervid rhetoric, but by a simple catalogue of the solemn pledges which he has violated. The list is a long one.

(1) As signatory of the Covenant of the League (Articles XII and XIII)—Italy undertook, in the case of "any dispute likely to lead to a rupture", to "submit the whole subject matter to arbitration".

(2) As signatory of the Kellogg Pact, Italy "renounced war as an instrument of national policy", and agreed that "the settlement of all disputes or conflicts...shall never be sought except by pacific means" (Article I).

(3) By the Tripartite Treaty of 13 December 1906 between France, Italy and Britain, the three signatories undertook to co-operate in maintaining "the political and territorial *status quo* in Ethiopia" (Article I).

(4) The fact that Italy (with France) was prominent in securing the admission of Abyssinia to the League in September 1923, gave at least an added moral emphasis to her obligations under Article XIII of the Covenant.

(5) The Anglo-Italian agreement of December 1925, promising mutual support as regards railway and hydraulic interests, aroused considerable disquiet both at Geneva and at Paris, and led to public disclaimers on the part of both Governments of any designs against Abyssinian sovereignty.

(6) By the Italo-Abyssinian Treaty of 2 August 1928 (Pact of non-aggression) both countries were pledged, not merely to "durable peace and perpetual friendship", but to the arbitration of any disputes, "without having recourse to the force of arms".

(7) Italy was a joint signatory of resolutions by the special Manchurian Committee of the League (16 February 1932), reaffirming the pledge of Article XII of the Covenant (to respect the territorial integrity of all other members) and of the League Assembly (11 March 1933), not to recognise "any

situation brought about by means contrary to the Covenant"
or the Kellogg Pact.

(8) By the joint Italo-Abyssinian Communique of 29 September 1934, both Governments disclaimed "any intentions of
aggression" and reaffirmed loyalty to the Treaty of 1928.

(9) On 15 April 1935 the Council of the League, at the instance of M. Laval, accepted as satisfactory (and therefore as an
excuse for postponing discussion) the assurances given to it
by Abyssinia and Italy, of "their intention of resorting to
procedure for peaceful settlement", in accordance with
Article V of the Treaty of 1928.[1]

Signor Mussolini, in addition to his deliberate violation of all
these treaties and undertakings, gave a whole series of public
assurances in the press which misled, and were presumably
intended to mislead, many friends of Italy and admirers of
Fascism in the West. But we now know from Marshal de
Bono's Memoirs—defiantly issued to the world with a preface
by the arch-criminal himself—that the plans of invasion and
conquest had begun to be laid between these two men as early
as the year 1933—"the year in which we began to consider what
practical measures must be taken in the event of war with
Ethiopia".[2] "Only he and I knew what was going to happen":
the secret "Plan of Action" was only in five copies. But first of
all "the equipment of Eritrea...had to be multiplied a hundred-
fold, and not by an indefinite date, but within a very brief space
of time specified and established almost as a dogma—October
1935".[3] He was naturally far too much of a realist to tell the
world beforehand what exact use he would make of victory:
but even before the actual outbreak of war and the League's
denunciation of Italy as aggressor it was as clear as daylight to
all save the wilfully blind that Mussolini was bent upon conquest to the uttermost limits of possibility, and would only be
deterred by defeat or armed intervention. *The Times*, in review-
ing de Bono's book, speaks the bare truth when it says that its

[1] See Toynbee, *Survey for 1935*, II, 149.
[2] de Bono, *Anno XIII*, pp. 12, 13, 14.
[3] These are the Duce's own prefatory words, *ibid*. p. xii.

frank admissions of Italian aggression and Abyssinian eagerness to avoid war "make British apologists for Italy's action look peculiarly foolish". Perfidy on the one side, *naïveté* on the other, could hardly go further.

ITALY'S VICTORY

A little later in this chapter we shall have to examine the factors which led Mussolini to take the final plunge. But we may at once note that already on 22 March 1935 Italy justified the despatch of troops to Eritrea on the absurdly false ground that "military measures had been taken on a very much larger scale by Ethiopia":[1] that on 14 May the Duce announced Italy's resolve to be "thoroughly safe in Africa" and to send as many troops as she pleased: that his war speech of 25 May was followed on 8 June by another affirming Italy's right to be the exclusive judge of her own interests and the resolve to take no account of world opinion: that on 6 July he proclaimed his "irrevocable decision" to avenge Adua: and that on 17 August he spoke quite openly of a war of conquest.

Quite a number of causes contributed to the rapid victory of Italy, which upset the calculations of many leading military experts in Europe. (1) First must be placed the utter inadequacy of the Abyssinian means of defence in face of Italy's overwhelming superiority of arms, technique and equipment, their almost complete lack of aeroplanes and the additional handicap due to foreign restrictions upon the supply of arms (a loathsome yet transparent hypocrisy on the part of Europe, since it scarcely affected Italy, but in the Abyssinian case amounted to virtual prohibition). These drawbacks were increased by the strategic blunders of the Rases, their disregard of the Emperor's orders and above all their failure to follow those guerilla tactics for which their country was so well suited. Such an attitude may of course be traced back to an insubordinate feudal outlook, to an arrogance compounded of ignorance and of Adua,

[1] Toynbee, *op. cit.* p. 145.

to widespread internal discontent, due almost equally to the old methods of government and to the Emperor's efforts at reform. (2) The second place may be assigned to the generalship of Marshal Badoglio—regarded by some as today the finest military brain in Europe—to the brilliant technical achievements of the Italian engineering and medical corps, and to the practice of throwing the brunt of any fighting upon the black conscripts of Eritrea. Foreign military experts (including those who advised both the British and German Governments) were entirely wrong in their calculations, having assumed that a serious advance could only be made over macadamised roads, that this would take an infinity of time and might be rendered most precarious by skilful guerilla tactics on the part of the Abyssinians. But Badoglio speedily transformed this situation by risking an advance over roads of an altogether inferior quality. (3) That this could be done with impunity was due not merely to the foolhardy massed onslaughts of the Abyssinians, but unhappily to "methods of barbarism" which have been fully authenticated and cannot therefore be omitted from any general estimate. There were a series of deliberate attacks by airmen upon Red Cross units—the American Adventists, the Swedish, the British and the Egyptian—obviously designed to frighten off foreign assistance. Worse still, poison gas was used on a large scale, not merely to force the Abyssinian troops out of their forest shelters and make it difficult to guard the passes, but also "to scatter horror and death"[1] over an unprotected and helpless civil population. The official returns of the Suez Canal show that 259 tons of mustard gas were declared in transit before

---

[1] Italian propagandists tried to draw a red herring across the trail by accusing the Abyssinians of the wholesale use of dum-dum ammunition, traceable to British manufacture; but inquiry showed that this was a complete invention, save for the fact that there were in the country certain small pre-war stocks of big game ammunition to which this description could be applied, and that in the dearth of army weapons many Abyssinians used hunting rifles and whatever they could lay their hands on (a fact which brings out still further the Italian superiority in arms). That here and there cases of mutilation of Italian wounded occurred would excuse summary punishment, but not promiscuous reprisals from the air.

the end of February 1936.[1] These flagrant violations of the
International Red Cross Convention and in particular of the
Protocols of 17 June 1925, forbidding the use of gas or microbes,
and of 27 June 1929 regarding the treatment of sick and
wounded[2], were followed logically after victory by a policy of
frightfulness[3] which is in marked contrast to that of Marshal
Lyautey in Morocco, and is likely to cost Italy dear in the
future. It is true that Vehib Pasha, a very able Turkish officer
fighting on the Abyssinian side, minimises the effect of gas and
attaches far greater importance to bribery, propaganda and
espionage among traitor chiefs and a divided people: and
Marshal De Bono in his Memoirs claims that "disintegrating
political action" set on foot by his Intelligence officers "deprived our enemy of at least 200,000 men".

RAS DESTA AND THE DUC D'ENGHIEN

The shameless usurpation of the Negus's throne by Victor
Emanuel III, the gratuitous insults levelled against its rightful
occupant in the Italian press and by its scribes at Geneva, even
the massacres following upon the attempt on Marshal Graziani's
life at Addis Ababa—all this seems to me to pale before the
supreme outrage of Ras Desta's execution. This man was a
son-in-law of the Emperor, commander of one of the chief
armies in the field: he was still at war, in legitimate defence of
his country, no treaty of peace having been concluded. Yet the
invaders of the country, taking him with arms in his hands,

---

[1] *Survey for* 1935, II, p. 346.

[2] *Ibid.* p. 69, annexe to Arms Traffic Convention.

[3] Lords Lytton and Cecil in a letter to *The Times* (18 April 1936) reminded
its readers that Italy's use of poison gases ("which blind and often practically
flay alive the barefooted peasants,... as well as blinding and killing and
torturing the women and children of the open towns"), and her "systematic
bombing of Red Cross units", was a direct violation of her most solemn
pledges, and that Abyssinia, "relying on membership of the League and on
the proposed Disarmament Convention, remained almost unarmed with
modern weapons until about two years ago".

shoot him like a dog, in defiance of all the laws of war and decency. The murder of the Duc d'Enghien by Napoleon was not a greater crime, and it places the Duce at least as much outside the pale of civilisation as was the "Corsican ogre" in the latter days of George III.[1]

> Und willst du nicht mein Bruder sein,
> So schlag' ich dir den Schädel ein.

This incident is the most infamous, but it is not unique, for the Italians also used a firing-squad to rid themselves of three other generals—Baltcha, Taye and Beiene Merid—as well as the two sons of Dr Martin, Ethiopian Minister in London, and the son of Blatten Gueta Herouy, the Minister of War. Another General, Ras Imru, has been sent to the Fascist penal settlement of Ponza.

In this connection it is pertinent to refer to the protest lodged by the Archbishop of Canterbury[2] against the Addis Ababa massacre. In it he committed himself to the statement that "bands of Blackshirts, armed with bombs and flame-throwers, rifles and pistols, ran amok among the natives, and many thousands of innocent men, women and children were killed". Those who know how efficiently the Primate is served by a special Committee of foreign affairs, to say nothing of his own known restraint and balanced judgment, will attach due importance to his intervention and will resent the Duce's insulting references to Anglican parsons.

Savage repression of this kind would hardly have won the approval of the Duce's special hero Machiavelli: it savours too

---

[1] Some time after I had written the above sentence, I found an interesting reflection on this very theme in Emil Ludwig's *Gespräche mit Mussolini* (p. 138). Mussolini defends Napoleon in the Enghien affair, comparing it with Cæsar's action in having Vercingetorix flogged to death. Without this, Cæsar's record, he argued, would undoubtedly be clearer, but it would be absurd to condemn so gigantic a figure on account of such a detail.

[2] In the House of Lords, 16 March 1937. See also appeal addressed by numerous signatories to League of Nations, 22 April 1937.

much of what he calls "measures by which empire may be gained, but not glory."[1]

BRITISH POLICY AND THE LEAGUE

It remains to consider British policy during the Abyssinian crisis: and while there can be no question of a detailed historical narrative, a certain chronological outline is essential. The first incidents at Wal-Wal occurred in December 1934: Abyssinia addressed two formal appeals to the League in March 1935, under Article XV of the Covenant, and pledged herself in advance "to accept any arbitral award". The first Italian reinforcements were sent on 23 February, and on 22 March Italy issued her note accusing Abyssinia of much larger military preparations—a statement which could only deceive the ignorant, considering that Abyssinia was almost entirely unarmed, and which is now overwhelmingly refuted by the admissions of Marshal de Bono and the Duce himself. Meanwhile on 7 January M. Laval had concluded a Franco-Italian agreement which, as the Duce rightly inferred, he was not anxious to sacrifice for the sake of Abyssinia: on 12 April there were triangular discussions between France, Britain and Italy at Stresa, and the silence of the two former on the Abyssinian question not unnaturally encouraged him still further. When the League Council was induced to postpone discussion till May, he doubtless assumed that Geneva would not be allowed to make serious trouble for him. On 25 May the League Council, in deference to French views, consented to further postponement, pending informal negotiations with the two parties. Early in June Mr Eden laid public emphasis on the Tripartite Treaty of 1906 (which pledged Italy, France and Britain to maintain Abyssinia's "political and territorial integrity"): and there followed on 24 June the British proposal that Abyssinia should cede part of Ogaden to Italy, in return for

[1] "I quali modi possono fare acquistare imperio, ma non gloria", *Il Principe*, chap. VIII.

Britain's cession of the "port" of Zeila, with a connecting strip of desert. This strange idea was stillborn, for the double reason that France, whose interests in Djibuti it vitally affected, had not been consulted and was therefore hostile, and that the Duce himself regarded it as grotesquely inadequate. On 6 July he declared himself "irrevocably decided", and when the new British Foreign Secretary Sir Samuel Hoare referred sympathetically to "Italy's desire for overseas expansion", but asked whether this was "sufficient cause for plunging into war", the only response from Rome was the mobilisation of further divisions. At a special session of the Council on 31 July M. Laval again tried to postpone, while Italy denied the League's jurisdiction in the Abyssinian dispute. When as the result of a compromise a Three-Power Conference met in Paris on 15 August, Baron Aloisi could not be persuaded to formulate Italian demands, and a complete deadlock resulted. But meanwhile the Duce was quite explicit, declaring that the dispute admitted "but one solution—with Geneva, without Geneva, against Geneva", and harangued the departing troops about a "war of conquest, in which every obstacle must be crushed".[1]

When on 4 September the Council again met at Geneva, Baron Aloisi roundly denied to Abyssinia any "equality of rights or duties with civilised states", while the defence of "backward races" was left in the hands of M. Litvinov. On 10 September Sir Samuel Hoare made the famous speech which rallied the League in defence of "collective security" and for a few months assured to Britain the moral leadership of Europe. But the Duce knew certain facts then still unknown to the outside world, and flatly rejected the suggestions which came to him from Geneva as "not only unacceptable, but derisory". On 2 October he ordered general mobilisation, giving as his reason "the continual and sanguinary aggression to which Italy has been subjected in the last ten years".[2]

[1] Article in *Popolo d' Italia* of 31 July, and speech of 17 August at Naples.
[2] Documents on International Affairs, 1935, vol. II. Professor Toynbee (*Survey for* 1935, II, p. 291) points out an historical parallel so ominous as to deserve emphasis in any discussion of the Abyssinian affair. To the *Petit*

The League had no serious alternative save to declare Italy the aggressor, as having resorted to war in disregard of Article XII, and machinery was set up for the enforcement of economic sanctions. Complications soon arose, above all on the thorny problem of "inequality of sacrifice"; indeed it soon resolved itself into a discussion of liabilities between France and Britain, the two Powers on whom, in this instance, geography and strategy had imposed the brunt of any decision. Already before the outbreak of the African war Britain had inquired whether she could count upon active French support in the event of her defence of League principles involving her in war with Italy: and this, as we saw in another connection, became (not as some say, through the skilful manœuvring of the Quai d'Orsay, but quite logically and inevitably) the starting-point of fresh mutual commitments between London and Paris. But though self-preservation forced the two Powers to co-operate in the Mediterranean, it did not remove the dead weight of M. Laval's passive resistance. As Professor Toynbee has well said, there were at the close of 1935 two conflicting policies striving at Geneva—the British, bent above all on frustrating Italian aggression through the application of Article XVI, the French, concentrating all efforts on a settlement of the dispute with Italy, such as would save the face of the League. Both of course failed, partly owing to steady political sabotage on the part of M. Laval, partly owing to the British Government's absorption in a general election, for which, from every standpoint save the Abyssinian, the psychological moment had undoubtedly been found. After Mr Baldwin's resounding victory at the polls yet another postponement of the issue at Geneva was decided upon (from 29 November to 12 December), and meanwhile the Petersen-St Quentin[1] compromise proposals were being

Journal of 27 September the Duce declared, "I have reflected well, I have calculated all, I have weighed everything". Francis Joseph, in his proclamation of 28 July 1914 (making war on Serbia), declared, "I have examined and weighed everything, and with a serene conscience I set out on the path to which my duty points".

[1] The two official experts deputed by the Quai d'Orsay and the Foreign Office.

worked out in Paris. Thus it came on 8 December to the famous Hoare-Laval conversations and Agreement, their deliberate betrayal to the French press, contrary to Sir Samuel's intention, and the storm of public indignation which forced Mr Baldwin to treat the Paris plan as "absolutely dead" and to drop his Foreign Secretary. Meanwhile the Duce, utterly un-abashed, spoke of "a war of civilisation and liberation", "a war of the poor, the disinherited, the proletariat", and announced his intention of "going straight ahead to victory". Badoglio replaced de Bono as Commander-in-chief, and taking full advantage of Abyssinian blunders, speedily put new life into a campaign that was dragging on very dangerously.

Europe, as represented at Geneva, grew increasingly negative, refusing to call off sanctions, yet shutting its eyes to the constant leakage, frightened to impose an oil embargo in the face of the Duce's threats, but banking on the opinion of most military experts that Italy could not conquer Abyssinia till 1937 at the earliest, and that even the "leaky" sanctions already in operation would have a fatal effect by the autumn of 1936. Once more France and Britain laid the main stress of policy in different directions—the former seeking at all costs to retain her alliance with Italy, the latter bent upon avoiding war with Italy. The motive in each case was the instinctive desire to avoid commit-ments in a secondary field, and to retain a free hand against Germany, now the most uncertain factor in world policy. It is impossible to dismiss this instinct as groundless, and indeed the German occupation of the Rhineland on 7 March 1936 con-firmed both Powers in their negative attitude towards the Italo-Abyssinian dispute, though also unfortunately accentuat-ing still further the different values which they attached to Hitler's repudiation of Versailles and Mussolini's defiance of the Covenant. In March the Duce's threat of withdrawal from the League if an oil embargo were imposed, brought M. Laval's successor, M. Flandin, to his knees, and Mr Eden consented to yet another postponement, while announcing *platonic* approval of oil sanctions. Even his protest against poison gas produced no effect, and the futility of the League, but still more of its leading members, was now patent to all the world. On 2 May Abyssinian resistance suddenly collapsed, and a week later the "Impero Romano" was proclaimed at Rome. Then, after a month of stupefied inaction and stock-taking, a series of official pronouncements followed one upon another. Mr Neville Chamberlain declared the policy of sanctions to have been tried out and to have failed. Sir John Simon, in a deliberately challenging phrase, declared that he was not prepared to see a single ship sunk in the cause of Abyssinian independence, and Mr Baldwin warned the country that the only alternatives were acceptance of the new situation or war. On 18 June, then, the Government, to which Sir Samuel Hoare now returned as First Lord and at least partial controller of Mediterranean policy, announced its decision to recommend at Geneva the abandonment of sanctions; and to complete the irony of events, France's endorsement of this step came neither from Laval nor from Flandin, but from the new Government of the Popular Front, formed on 4 June by M. Leon Blum after his all too tardy electoral victory. On 30 June, then, the League Assembly, after swallowing the insults of the Italian gutter pressmen and the Italian Note on the "sacred mission of civilisation", listened in pained silence to Haile Selassie's moving speech, and then called off sanctions and left Abyssinia to her fate.

BRITAIN, FRANCE AND THE DUCE

Such, in brief outline, are the main events of the long Abyssinian crisis: it is now possible to analyse the workings of British policy in relation to it.

In the first place it is obvious that what decided the Duce in favour of action was his reading of relations between London and Paris--each growing cold as the other grew hot, and unable to agree upon active co-operation. Even if M. Laval did not in so many words give him *carte blanche* in Abyssinia, this tacitly underlay their agreement of 7 January 1935; and after the German conscription *coup* in March France's anxiety not to offend Italy became more marked than ever. The attitude of the British Government was also such as to confirm the Duce in the belief that he could act with impunity: for although it was afterwards able to show that it had during the previous winter sent repeated warnings to Rome as to the grave consequences of an attack upon Abyssinia, it wiped out their whole effect by not even discussing the problem at Stresa, much less putting it on the agenda of the meeting.[1] In June the Duce was again encouraged by the divergent attitude of London and Paris, this time due above all to London's failure to notify to Paris in advance either the Naval Agreement with Germany or the Zeila offer to Italy. The third and worst blunder, in which the blame must be shared almost equally between the two, was the secret agreement reached between M. Laval and Sir Samuel Hoare at Geneva on 10 September, by which the two statesmen, expressly recognising that efforts at conciliation had failed, none the less decided to rule out military sanctions, a naval blockade and the closure of the Canal, or in their own phrase, "in a word, everything that might lead to war". This was really decisive, for it was at once known to the Duce, and showed him that the risks were worth taking and that Hoare's great speech of the following day before the Assembly was sheer bluff. To the Duce's realistic, not to say cynical, mind it savoured of something worse than bluff—something reminiscent of the old phrase "Perfidious Albion": in particular, the disingenuous affirmation that "the rule of law in international affairs" was "our sole interest", and that no selfish interests affected our attitude, invited a mocking dissent. Indeed, many of Sir Samuel's own countrymen felt that such a line of argument was most unfortunate in view of Britain's vital interests in the Mediterranean and in Africa, and would have preferred a frank recognition that such interests did affect our attitude, but that these coincided with the higher interests of League obligation,

[1] This we have on the authority of Sir John Simon on 1 August. Major Attlee obviously went too far in calling this "one of the most criminal blunders in the whole course of British diplomacy", but he had his finger on a weak point in the official case.

of general peace and of collective action. Moreover, the Duce was well aware that behind the façade of fine phrases at Geneva for the benefit of public opinion, Britain's military and naval situation was highly unsatisfactory, that the air defences of Malta, as also of Toulon and Biserta, were, to say the least, entirely out of date, and that the British Government found it necessary to transfer the Mediterranean fleet to Alexandria and to seek concrete assurances of help, not only from a reluctant France, but even from Jugoslavia, Greece and Turkey. In an interview given to the *Matin* he had already been explicit enough: a reference to Italy's long friendship with Britain, then the view that it was "monstrous that a nation which dominates the world should refuse us a wretched plot of ground in the African sun", and finally the assertion that "never from us will come an act of hostility against a *European* nation, but if one is committed against us, *it means war*".

During October and November, then, the National Government continued to bluff, hoping that Abyssinia could hold out till the rains, and that sanctions and bad finance would sap the Italian offensive: but at home it dealt more freely than ever in Genevan phrases and on the strength of them won the greatest electoral victory in our history. By the first week of December it found itself faced by realities. M. Laval, who had waited till 28 November before intimating to Italy that France would help Britain if attacked, was now informed from Rome that the Duce would answer the imposition of oil sanctions by an attack on the British fleet, and he in his turn informed Sir Samuel that a fortnight must elapse before French help could be effective, and that meanwhile the French naval dockyards could not hold British capital ships (which meant that a damaged battleship could find no place of refuge in the whole Mediterranean). It was this which stampeded Sir Samuel, then a sick man on his way to a Swiss holiday, into the fatal Agreement of 8 December with M. Laval. There are some who regret that the bargain was not implemented, and argue that in that case Haile Selassie would be today on his throne and the prestige of the League still undamaged.[1] But they surely forget two things: (1) that the Duce, as is today abundantly clear from his acknowledged dealings with de Bono and Badoglio, was bent upon complete conquest and could only have been deterred by military disaster; and (2) that for good or ill, Sir Samuel had by his Geneva speech of 11 September laid down principles entirely incompatible with any such bargain, and secured the adhesion of over fifty nations by convincing them that Britain this time meant business. To this should be added the tactical point raised by Professor Toynbee,[2] that at the very least the British Foreign Secretary, in giving way, should have laid upon his French colleague, in session at Geneva, the onus of either refusing his support to the British proposals for an oil embargo, or alternately refusing his support to the British fleet if attacked by Italy. His failure to do so was perhaps partly due to illness, but also to the knowledge that the pledges which he had made to Laval on 10 September really debarred him from taking too high a line on 8 December.

There is another possible explanation of the attitude adopted by the British Government—namely, that it knew that to impose an oil embargo meant war with Italy, and that the British fleet was not yet in a position to risk this single-handed. This is a charge as yet unproved, and not lightly to be made, especially by those who in the preceding period had steadily pressed for the reduction of British armaments: for it would convict the National Government of culpable neglect of our defences, and all post-war Governments of the utterly uneconomic use of very large sums expended by them on the three forces. A much more rational theory is that the Government did indeed wish to avoid war with an old ally, but this not

[1] Their argument is reminiscent of a phrase used 100 years ago by J. C. Hobhouse in a Commons debate on Non-Intervention in Spain! He compared the Government to a man with two friends who knew that one was going to rob the other, and therefore went to the latter and said, "I advise you to give away a little bit of your property: put a little money under your door, and I think I can guarantee you from having your throat cut in the middle of the night!" Hansard, VIII, p. 1347: 28 April 1833.

[2] *Survey for 1935*, pp. 294–5.

merely because it knew the Mediterranean situation to be unsatisfactory, but above all because it was resolved at all costs not to become involved in war in a (vitally important but nevertheless) secondary field, unless it either had no choice or had the reasonable certainty that the war would not spread to the North Sea and to the Pacific.

We now know that if the oil embargo had been imposed in November 1935 it "would have effectively frustrated Italy's attempt to conquer Abyssinia".[1] Even as it was, the technical experts held that the very imperfect sanctions actually applied would bring Italy to her knees by the autumn, while the military experts held that the conquest of Abyssinia could not be completed till the following year at the earliest. Events proved them to have miscalculated, and Mussolini's gigantic gamble succeeded. The policy of waiting upon events practised by London was not a heroic one, but a highly plausible case could be made out for it, given a European situation of such extreme danger. The two main indictments would seem to lie in other directions: (1) Far worse than the caution of December 1935 or May 1936 was the august pronouncement of the previous September, which misled almost equally British home opinion and the nations of Europe, when all the time there was a secret pledge to Laval not to bring matters to the issue. (2) Worse even than the surrender to Laval in December was the fatal choice of the very moment when the State Department at Washington was about to warn American citizens that they shipped to belligerent countries "at trader's risk"—a step which would have at once reduced the leakage in sanctions, increased the prospects of an oil embargo and revolutionised the American attitude towards "freedom of the seas".

There remains the old explanation of "Perfidious Albion": and indeed certain French journals of the Right were insistent that the clamour of British opinion in favour of action against the Italian aggressor was merely a skilful device for the furtherance of imperialistic aims under cover of the League. How

[1] For the Report of the Committee of Experts at Geneva (12 February 1936) see A. J. Toynbee, *op. cit.* pp. 330-4.

grotesque such a theory was in this particular case becomes apparent when it is borne in mind that the sole support for the Hoare-Laval policy came from the Rothermere, Beaverbrook and Houston press (the main advocates of isolation and extreme imperialism) and that almost all the leading Francophils in England[1] took the other view and were gravely disturbed at the Laval policy. But what eventually silenced the Anglophobes was not so much these self-evident facts, as the vital need for a common Franco-British front in face of German rearmament. And indeed it is hardly an exaggeration to say that what sealed the fate of Abyssinia was the German occupation of the Rhineland and the resultant crisis among the Locarno Powers. By this time the long series of postponements, accepted in deference to French reluctance, had had their effect: sanctions, though far from negligible, were no longer likely to be decisive: Italy the aggressor could only be brought to book by force of arms, and neither of the western democracies was prepared to fight for Abyssinia. On a pure basis of principle their position was ignominious. Their only excuse can be found in their resolve to reserve all their efforts for the German danger, and in the knowledge that in a war with Italy there was as yet no margin for the possibility of her finding allies in Germany and Japan. If this be the fundamental strategic calculation, the British rearmament programme follows with inexorable logic from the Abyssinian muddle. "Isolationists" and "peace-at-any-price men" are almost equally to blame for Britain's neglect, or inability, to warn the aggressor when it was still not too late for him to draw back without fatal loss of prestige.

Meanwhile, it is essential to challenge those who glibly assume the failure of sanctions. In the words of Mr Winston Churchill in the *Evening Standard*, "The sanctions which we have been pressing with so great a parade were not real sanctions to paralyse the invader, but merely such half-hearted sanctions as the invader would tolerate, because in fact they stimulated

[1] E.g. Sir Austen Chamberlain, Mr Churchill, General Spears, Mr Wickham Steed. This fact is effectively brought out by Professor P. Vaucher in his *L'Opinion britannique*, pp. 57, 69.

the Italian war spirit. It is true that included in the sanctions were many measures, especially financial, which in the long run would have destroyed the Italian financial power to purchase necessities in foreign countries, and that these would have eventually affected their war-making capacity. But the chief of these financial sanctions did not require Geneva to impose them. The credit of Italy had already fallen so low that the ordinary market factors would have been as valid as the League decision....*It is not true to say that economic sanctions have failed. It was the will power to enforce them in a real and biting manner which failed.*...There is no reason to despair of collective action against the aggressor. If a sufficient number of powerfully armed nations were ready to enforce economic sanctions, the aggressor would in many cases have to submit or attack the combination."

ITALY'S BURDEN

On the eve of the Italian War of 1859, when the British Government, with a general election on its hands, was labouring to achieve a compromise between Paris and Vienna, and when Russia put forward proposals for a peaceful settlement through a European Conference, Napoleon III stated very bluntly to a friend of King Leopold the alternative which lay before him— "une guerre ou une éclatante satisfaction pour moi". In the winter of 1935 another dictator was faced by a similar alternative, and the disunion of France and Britain, and their unreadiness for action, enabled him to emerge from the crisis with a striking personal satisfaction.

None the less, the fair hopes with which the Duce beguiled the Italian nation into the Abyssinian adventure, and which flamed higher than ever after the collapse of sanctions, have not been fulfilled. It was to have brought revenge for Adua, renewed glory and "Power" for Italy, and to have solved the double crisis of overpopulation and shortage of raw materials. Instead of this it has strained the whole finances of Italy to breaking-point, eaten deep into capital, savings and reserves, raised the cost of living and seriously affected standards among

the poorer classes. Millions have been poured out in unre-
munerative expenditure, upon maintaining a garrison of
250,000 men in Abyssinia, and 80,000 more in Libya. Trade is
altogether at a standstill in Abyssinia, the currency has broken
down and imports have to be restricted: some fine roads have
been built, but many millions more must be spent before there
can be any serious question of exploiting the minerals of the
country. A few hundred selected South Italian peasant families
have been sent out: but of colonisation on any serious scale
nothing more is heard, not only because of unsettled conditions—a hostile *bon mot* circulates, to the effect that "Abyssinia
belongs to the Italians by day and to the Ethiopians by night"—
but also because the cost of transport and settlement would be
prohibitive, because the high altitude renders heavy agricultural
labour difficult for European immigrants, and because the
newcomers could not hope to compete with the native
population except by fatally lowering their own standards.

No one can tell what will be the final repercussions of
Abyssinia upon Italy herself: but one thing is already clear.
The argument, so often ascribed to mere British hypocrisy, that
the days have long passed when a large-scale colonial war could
be made remunerative, has already been demonstrated far
beyond the expectations of those who first put it forward. Yet
the Japanese are at present engaged in pouring out blood and
treasure upon the inexhaustible soil of China! Perhaps other
nations who are arming for adventure, but have not yet done
anything irrevocable, will take warning at the eleventh hour
and refrain from plunging the whole world into ruin and
beggary.

XI

THE SPANISH WAR:
INTERVENTION AND NON-INTERVENTION

'WE are living today in a new and interdependent
world, with rapidly developing problems involving
peace or war." So wrote in 1936 Mr Henry
Stimson, the former United States Secretary of State, with his
mind especially directed to the bearings of Japanese aggression
in the Far East upon the efficacy of the League as an instrument
of World Peace. The economic crisis in Britain, following
closely upon the slump in America, encouraged Japan to
repudiate her many treaty obligations and grab Manchuria.
The League's failure in the Manchurian question (and this was
merely the outward seeming, the reality being the pitiable
weakness of the British and other Governments) served as a
direct encouragement to other lawbreakers. If Japan could
"get away with it" in the Far East, Italy could do the same in
Africa, and Mussolini made his preparations accordingly from
at least 1932 onwards. He was quicker than other people to
realise the extent to which Hitler's advent to power and the
successive stages of German repudiation and rearmament
increased his own prospects of success. The close interconnection between this German situation and the League's failure to
enforce sanctions has already been pointed out, and is too
glaringly obvious to require further elucidation.

Immensely elated by his Abyssinian success, and more than
ever bent upon dominating the Mediterranean, the Duce had
no sooner proclaimed an "Italian Empire" in the capital of the
last independent African state, than he found ready to his hand
a situation in Spain by fomenting which he might still further
alter the distribution of Mediterranean forces to the disadvantage of Britain and France. It is not as well known as it
ought to be that Italian armed assistance was on its way to the

Spanish malcontents before the civil war had broken out; and indeed it must almost certainly have been arranged before the collapse of sanctions could be reckoned with, and as a definite move in the conflict with the Western Powers. Italy first, and then Germany, sought to justify their action in Spain by the argument of two rival ideologies, one of which, the Communist or Bolshevik, was being artificially transplanted from Russia to the West of Europe, as a new stage in the expansion of the World Revolution. It is safe to assume that the Führer (though not the German General Staff) genuinely believed in this danger: and it is a fact that Trotsky has more than once expressed the belief that next to Russia, Spain offered the most fertile soil for a revolutionary outburst. But in the cooler brain of the Duce—of the statesman who first established diplomatic and trade relations with Soviet Russia and openly boasted of thus performing a useful service to all Europe[1]—denunciation of the Soviets or at a later date "Anti-Comintern Pacts" were a mere smoke-screen: the real motive was strategic. A Spain controlled by the Fascist Powers would not merely threaten France's communications with her North African possessions and weaken the already diminishing security of Gibraltar, but might even force France to fortify the Pyrenees and give her a third frontier to defend, in addition to the Rhine and Maritime Alps. The series of retreats sounded by Britain and France had indeed led him to believe that their hands could be forced yet again, or at least to think that the game was well worth trying, and that in any event there was a good prospect of strengthening Italy's Mediterranean position.

SPAIN IN THE NINETEENTH CENTURY

Needless to say certain organisms are more liable than others to infection, and for over a century past Spain has been a prey to fierce civil discord, intensified by foreign intrigue. The steady decline of Spain and her colonial Empire during the century and a half following the death of Philip II had been temporarily arrested by Charles III (1759–88). But his son and

[1] "Our tactics were Russian", he told Ludwig (*Gespräche*, p. 96).

grandson, Charles IV and Ferdinand VII, combined degeneracy, incompetence and bad faith to an alarming degree and subordinated the interests of their country to a dynastic policy narrowly conceived and veering with every wind of reaction. Napoleon's war of conquest rested above all upon strategic considerations (he hoped to control the Spanish fleet and colonies and to cut off Britain from the Mediterranean), supplemented no doubt by the search for vassal thrones for his family: and the Peninsular War was Britain's answer to an acute strategic danger. It was while Wellington and the Spanish patriots were fighting side by side against the French, and while the Spanish royal family was held captive by Napoleon, that the first real Parliament of modern Spain met and adopted the Constitution of 1812, which, despite its many obvious defects, was to have so great an influence upon constitutional development in Latin Europe in the post-Napoleonic epoch. But it is characteristic of British policy under Castlereagh and Wellington that it held aloof equally from the spasmodic efforts of the Spanish liberals to establish a new order and of the perfidious Ferdinand, on his restoration, to undermine it as speedily as possible. Even in the 'twenties, when Ferdinand's tyranny provoked a revolution, and a revival of the illegally abolished Constitution of 1812, and when the French invaded Spain on the pretext of preserving its throne for the Bourbon dynasty, Britain observed a disgruntled neutrality, while making it quite clear that she would not tolerate any attack upon her ancient ally Portugal or any attempt on the part of France to acquire Spanish colonies—in other words, treating strategical considerations as the paramount issue in her attitude towards Spain. Canning's phrase in Parliament—that Louis XVIII by his action in Spain had proclaimed "a principle which strikes at the root of the British Constitution"—was counterbalanced by the warning of Wellington that "there is no country in Europe, in the affairs of which foreigners can interfere with so little advantage as in those of Spain".[1] The

[1] Wellington to Castlereagh, 16 April 1820 (*Wellington Despatches*, I, p. 1173).

Duke of Angoulême, who led the invading French army in 1823, was soon only too eager to withdraw from a country where "we might stay ten years, but at the end the parties would begin to massacre each other again": and indeed France gained nothing by intervention. When the next acute crisis arose in Spain, owing to a disputed succession to the throne of Ferdinand VII, Britain and France found it expedient to frame a joint policy based upon non-interference in the affairs of the Iberian Peninsula—in practice, a support of the two young queens Isabella and Maria, and some semblance of constitutional government, against the savage absolutist ambitions of the two "wicked uncles" Carlos and Miguel.

Some other phrases of Canning from one of his most famous parliamentary speeches (30 April 1923) may be quoted with advantage, as forming a background to the situation a century later in Spain and in Europe. He quoted Vattel as saying: "The duty of a mediator is to favour well-founded claims,... but he ought not scrupulously to insist on rigid justice. He is a conciliator, not a judge: his business is to procure peace: and he ought to induce him who has right on his side, to relax something of his pretences, if necessary, with a view to so great a blessing." "With this conviction", Canning proceeded, "I confess I thought any sacrifice, short of national honour or national independence, cheap to prevent the first breach in that pacific settlement by which the miseries and agitations of the world have been so recently composed." "No man can witness with more delight than I do, the widening diffusion of political liberty....I would not prohibit other nations from kindling their flame at the torch of British freedom"; but "the general acquisition of free institutions is not necessarily a security for general peace." But here again he at once trims by adding, perhaps somewhat over confidently: "The principle which for centuries has given ascendancy to Great Britain, is that she was the single free state in Europe." And then he again seems to redress the balance by insisting on Britain's "essentially neutral" attitude—"neutral not only between contending nations, *but between conflicting principles*". It is easy to gather from this and other pronouncements that Canning, and Palmerston after him, were already confronted with the problem of the "Two Ideologies".

From the troubled history of Spain since 1833 certain broad facts emerge. The first is that civil war was chronic for the next generation, and that the contending factions showed an unusual intensity of feeling, often bordering on savagery, both towards each other and towards the many foreign volunteers whom the struggle attracted. In this connection it is pertinent to allude to the mission of Lord Eliot, who was sent out to Spain during the short-lived Premiership of the Duke of Wellington, for the purpose of securing, if possible, the abandonment of the practice of shooting prisoners *on both sides*. Opinion in Parliament was divided then, as now, and while John Bowring affirmed that there was no country in the world better suited than Spain for "popular institutions" and "in which more of the elements of freedom existed", Lord Mahon the historian, in a weighty speech, criticised the Spanish Government for the abolition of Basque privileges and the massacre of helpless prisoners, and spoke of the unanimous feeling of hatred with which all sections of the Spanish population regarded foreign intervention. The essential fact, however, is that Palmerston as Foreign Secretary openly declared the success of Queen Isabella's cause to be a British interest, and that Wellington during the interlude of Tory rule upheld the policy of the Quadruple Alliance which the Whigs had inaugurated and which rested upon support for a "constitutional Spain".[1]

The second fact is the prominent political rôle played by the Army, not only under Isabella and the First Republic, but even in the comparatively peaceful period that followed: the bare catalogue of military pronunciamentos, putsches, or petty risings, would probably fill some pages: and the dictatorships of Generals Primo de Rivera and Berenguer were merely new variations on a very old theme. Third on the list must come the

---

[1] I write this paragraph while attempts are being made from London to induce the warring factions in Spain to refrain from mutual bombing of defenceless cities and to exchange, rather than shoot, their respective prisoners.

great disparity of wealth, prosperity, tradition and outlook between the various provinces of Spain, due, doubtless, above all to the favouritism of Nature, but also to differences of historical evolution. From this it followed that in some districts the existence of vast *latifundia* poisoned the relations of the classes, whereas in others the land question had ceased to be acute. Moreover, this question reacted very vitally upon the position of the Church, which in certain provinces relied too much on its wealth and traditions, whereas in others it was so much the leader in good works and social service as to incur the rival charge of having become a business enterprise. It is certainly not too much to say that the Church, which in 1836 had suffered widespread persecution (notably confiscation of the property of the religious orders), but had in the following two generations regained much of its privileged position, still commanded the intense devotion of certain sections of the population (Castile, Asturias, the Basque provinces), yet had aroused no less intense antagonism in others (Oviedo, Malaga, Madrid), or again an attitude of no less rank indifference (Barcelona and parts of Aragon).

This acute difference of outlook towards a Church which many enlightened Catholics regard as the most backward section of European Catholicism is partly cause and partly effect of the undoubted cleavage which exists in Spanish opinion as to the ideal form of the state. The rival ideas of centralism and federalism give a keener edge to the deep political and social cleavage: and many keen observers see no hope for a free Spain save on the basis of a federation in which Castile and Andalusia, Biscaya, Catalonia and Valencia would each pursue its particular aims, while accepting unity of direction in face of foreign Powers. It is not a mere accident that the First Republic adopted a federal basis, and that under the Second, Catalan and Basque aspirations at once asserted themselves as irresistible.

Lastly, as a red thread affecting the entire pattern, there are the confused and fissiparous tendencies of political party life in Spain—always a striking feature, but since the downfall of the Monarchy more marked than ever before—and, worse still, the lack of any serious alternative. Neither of the two main contending groups possessed any real unity of purpose; Left and Right alike formed an *ad hoc* combination of highly incongruous forces, which victory would speedily dissolve: while the saner elements of the Centre were flung aside, and the Monarchy, having used up its reserves of respect and prestige during the long reign of Alfonso XIII, no longer offered a rallying-ground for supra-party patriotism.

THE SECOND REPUBLIC

The fair prospects under which the Second Republic began in April 1931—when republicanism was recognised as inevitable by large sections of the Right no less than by the Left, and by very considerable military opinion—were speedily clouded over when an epidemic of church-burning broke out in Madrid and Malaga and remained virtually unpunished. The new constitution proclaimed "a democratic Republic of workers of all classes, organised in a regime of liberty and justice": but those in power were not content with restrictions upon the influence of the religious Orders, for which a case could be made out, but from the first aimed at the secularisation of education and the eviction of the Church from all control over the youth of Spain—Señor Azaña declaring on 13 October 1931 that Spain was no longer a Catholic nation, which of course was equivalent to declaring that it was no longer Christian.[1]

It would be mere folly on my part to attempt to "assign responsibilities" for the tragedy that has assailed Spain: I have the high authority of Professor Allison Peers for condemning any such attempt in the light of present material. This much, however, may safely be affirmed, that civil war was merely the culmination of chaotic conditions due to the failure of successive Governments to enforce that "law and order" which had been proclaimed as the ideal. In a word a failure to govern on the

[1] It is not sufficiently realised that Protestantism is almost non-existent in Spain and therefore that the "tolerance" of the Valencia Government towards the Protestant 0·9 per cent. is not tolerance, but tactics, in view of the embargo on the Catholic 99·1 per cent.!

part of those in power produced the same reactions as in other countries, and the prompt interference of rival foreign Powers, for their own selfish ends, at once revealed the deep gulf dividing the Spanish nation—and the extent to which Spaniards were torn between the conflicting loyalties of national feeling and political aspirations. This is nothing new: it has been a prominent feature in Spanish history for a century past—alike in the Peninsular War, the revolution of 1821, the Carlist wars, the numerous pronunciamentos, the First Republic, the troubles fomented by Ferrer, the post-war political dissensions.

The two years of Left Government, from December 1931 to November 1933, during which the Catalan Statute was voted, the Jesuits were dissolved, and agrarian reform was introduced, ended somewhat unexpectedly in a landslide in favour of the Right. The refusal of those in power to draw the democratic conclusion and entrust the reins of government to the majority in the Cortes led logically to a series of short-lived Cabinets, Centre to Left Centre in composition, lacking adequate support on either wing and increasingly incapable of exercising a firm control. Sometimes indeed there was difficulty in finding a Premier. The extreme Left elements—Socialists, Syndicalists, Communists and Anarchists—grew steadily in strength, but were by no means agreed among themselves. The Socialist revolution which devastated Oviedo in October 1934—wrecking in particular the Cathedral and the University—revealed the Left as ready to secure by violence what it had hitherto failed to obtain by votes: it set an example of violence which its opponents were not loath to follow, and has disqualified the Left from posing as an austere champion of legality against rebellion. The only difference between the two rebellions is that that of the Right has been much more formidable and widespread.

The elections of February 1936 brought a fresh swing to the Left, though still more at the expense of the Centre than of the Right: the gulf between the two extremes thus widened still further. But the tendency abroad to treat the quarrel as one between Communism and Fascism is far too *simpliste*: it

ignores the patchwork character of the rival factions. In the
Popular Front the three Republican Parties, though combining
with the united Anarcho-Syndicalists (by no means as united as
is sometimes supposed) and the official Communists, and though
accepting an advanced programme of public works, a minimum
wage, land reform and a certain control of banks and industry,
stopped short of nationalisation, and failed to agree with the
larger and more militant unofficial Communist Party, which
professes pure Marxian and Trotskyite doctrine. In the Right
there were similar divergences between the Catholic "Ceda",
the Monarchists (divided into followers of Don Alfonso and of
Carlism), and the smaller Fascist and Falangist groups. It is of
course only too true that on both sides extreme views rapidly
gained ground. The Socialists tried to force the Azaña Government into a number of Marxist measures. There was renewed
burning of convents and churches—170 in four months—and of
newspaper offices, an "epidemic of murder" and disorder,
wholesale strikes and arson, and land seizure: while the alarm
caused by the deposition of President Zamora was not allayed
by the selection of Señor Azaña as his successor. The Opposition
charge that Spain was being reduced to a state of anarchy was
not met by the Government's retort that the "frenzy" of the
masses was due to the repression of the Oviedo revolt. As a
result, the Right withdrew from the Chamber, and violence on
both sides became chronic: while the unrest already spreading
in the Army, in accordance with Spanish precedent, was increased by the Government removing a number of military
leaders from their commands.

The actual revolt of 17 July, which began in Spanish Morocco,
but instantly spread through Castile, Leon, Navarre and parts of
Aragon, was precipitated, but certainly not caused, by the brutal
murder of the ablest politician of the Right, Señor Sotelo: there
are some grounds for thinking that it forced the "rebels" to act
before their plans had matured. At the outset we may discount
the indignation worked up abroad about revolt against a
legitimately constituted Government: for apart from the endless risings of the last century to which allusion has been made,

it is easy for either side to find precedents in the Republican revolt at Jaca in 1930, in General Sanjurjo's unsuccessful putsch in 1932, and in the more serious Socialist rising at Oviedo in 1934. The air has since been full of mutual recriminations, many of which fail to impress the outside observer. The Government has been blamed for arming the masses, though it is only too obvious that, faced by the defection of the officers' corps and most of the regular garrisons, they had to choose between this desperate step and complete surrender. What cannot be denied, however, is that for a good many weeks, until the first elements of discipline could be established among the new levies, the Government was totally unable to prevent wholesale murder, pillage and arson in Madrid and to a lesser degree in other cities. On the other side, General Franco has been fiercely condemned for employing Moorish troops on Spanish soil; but it is obvious that they formed an integral part of the Spanish army (no less than the Foreign Legion, which is mainly composed of Spaniards), that there is no hard and fast racial cleavage between the population of Southern Spain and that of Northern Morocco, and that these Moors, who of course are not "black" at all, have more than once been used on Spanish soil for similar purposes. The protest against their use against "Christians" does not come well from a Government whose policy is openly anti-Christian: the racial argument is meaningless save to those who uphold the racial dogmas of Hitler and Rosenberg.

Perhaps the most fundamental fact in the whole situation is that Spain is not merely deeply divided from the "ideological" point of view, but divided into two very nearly equal halves.[1]

This emerges from the results of the fatal elections of February 1936, which are best shown in tabular form:

	Votes	Deputies
Popular Front	4,356,000	270
Centre	340,000	60
Parties of the Right	4,570,000	140

[1] Cf. the article of that notable Spanish intellectual, Señor José Castillejo, in *The Times* of 18 May 1937.

Thus so far from there having been an overwhelming popular vote in favour of an extreme Left programme, it would seem that even without the moderates of the Centre the balance leant slightly in the opposite direction: in any case the issue was falsified by a system of unequal electoral distribution. It may indeed quite fairly be argued that an attempt to impose an advanced political and social programme by means of a faked majority provided its opponents with a desperate grievance. To my mind, as a believer in democracy, it makes nonsense of the extreme emphasis so often laid by ardent exponents of the Left upon the enormity of rebellion against a democratic and constitutional Government. It would be a contradiction in terms to speak of democracy in the present case, even if it were not a notorious fact that a majority of the Government parties place the dictatorship of the proletariat in the forefront of their programme. Moreover, these denunciations of rebellion are ill-placed in the mouths of those who glory in the two English Revolutions (so mild in doctrine and in action by the side of Spanish atrocities) and often enough justify the French Terror also. Let us be quite clear that "the right to rebel"—a doctrine held by all foreign supporters of the Spanish Left—has always been implicitly accepted and openly acted upon by all the rival factions in Spain for the last three or four generations. Spanish "Rebellion", whether of the Right or of the Left, is not to be judged by British or even French standards.

Infinitely graver is the question of foreign help: but even here it has to be said that both sides are tarred with the same brush, taking help where they could find it, as Lenin did in 1917, but unquestionably with the same unspoken resolve to escape as soon as possible from such temporary thraldom as its acceptance might involve. That any party in Spain seriously contemplates permanent subjection to the foreigner is in the last degree improbable—more improbable in the case of so proud, sensitive and xenophobe a people as the Spanish, than in most other cases. That the attempt to peg out further claims in return for assistance is likely to end in disaster for the claimants, is to say the least a reasonable inference from the whole course of

Spanish history. Of the bearings of foreign interference upon the international situation we shall have to speak in another context. But meanwhile the charge of lack of patriotism against either side must be used with great caution—not because of the numerous precedents in English and Scottish history[1] but because Spanish values, equally of the Left or Right, are not lightly to be translated into terms of Europe. For both sides sought help abroad, and the trite old question of who began it leads us nowhere, except to the interesting discovery that on the "Red" side the moving force was the Trotskyite group, acting in direct defiance of an angry Moscow, who only began to help in earnest when it saw its prestige endangered, and whose tardy action did, it is true, avert the fall of Madrid, but was within an ace of coming too late.

RIVAL ATROCITIES

The close balance of forces in the Peninsula goes far to explain two other factors—the fierceness of the passions aroused and the virtual stalemate that has been reached. Civil war is always more savage than foreign war: there is every reason to believe that it would be so even in our own country: how much more so, then, is it bound to be in a country where it has a tradition of over a century and where both sides pursue such radically opposite aims! Far be it from me to attempt an estimate of rival atrocities in the face of reckless statement, foreign gullibility and deliberate manufacture of horrors. It must suffice to affirm, in the words of *The Times*—demonstrated by a succession of detailed articles, and repeated not once, but many times— that there have been "frightful excesses" on both sides.[2] In

[1] Henry IV, Henry VII, the Elizabethan Catholics, Henrietta Maria, the restored Stuarts, William of Orange, the Jacobite Risings, etc.

[2] See *The Times* leader of 4 September 1936. Its leader of 17 August refers to "appalling murders of civilians and prisoners on both sides". On 19 August it admits "hundreds of executions in Madrid". On 8 September it refers to "irresponsible butchery", and to "the ruthless cruelty" of the rebels, which "has equalled, if not surpassed, the worst excesses of the other side". Its articles of 24 and 30 September and 1, 3 and 6 October give

Madrid there were midnight executions, continuing for many weeks, the Government being apparently helpless to prevent them: and at one time things were little better in Barcelona. In Malaga many of the Right were executed, and the refugees of the Left were mercilessly machine-gunned as they fled along the coast. On more than one Spanish Government warship the men massacred their officers and openly boasted of it to foreign residents. In San Sebastian both sides at different times shot their opponents in batches on the sands at low tide, so that the sea was full of floating corpses. The alleged massacre of 2000 prisoners by the insurgents after their capture of Badajoz has been hotly challenged from the Right: and it seems proved that an entirely bogus story was widely attributed to a reputable American journalist who afterwards denied having been at Badajoz or having written about it. On the other hand there have been a whole series of shootings in many towns and villages of "insurgent" Spain, and the testimony of Señor Villaplana as to executions in and around Burgos is especially striking. Finally, on 18 May 1937 a *Times* leader estimated that the number of executions without trial in Madrid and Barcelona amounted to 50,000.

However much this catalogue of horrors may be restricted, space must be found for the bombardment of Guernica in April 1937 by the insurgent forces—one of the most odious incidents in the whole war. Guernica is a small country town of 7000 inhabitants, specially dear to the Basques as their earliest capital, and in no way a military objective (incidentally, a munitions factory *outside* the town was left untouched). Yet it was attacked by a fleet of aeroplanes and "systematically

details of the executions in Madrid and Barcelona (where it puts the murders at 600–700). On 20 October it refers to the shooting of hostages on the Government side, and adds that while the insurgents are not known to have done this, they have been "pitiless in other respects": and it again speaks of "scenes of cruelty and horror on both sides".

On 14 October the *Manchester Guardian* writes of "both sides" as "utterly ruthless", and on 2 November refers to the shooting of workmen, *chosen at random*, as having taken place on both sides. It estimates the wholesale shootings by the rebels at Seville at 8000.

pounded to pieces" for about three hours. It was market day, and the civilian population and their livestock were chased and machine-gunned, and the whole town was left burning. To add insult to injury, the insurgent propaganda asked Europe to believe that Basque "Reds" had destroyed the town in order to poison foreign opinion against General Franco. Fortunately there were foreign eyewitnesses, and notably the correspondent of *The Times*,[1] to disprove this impudent fabrication: and yet there are still people sufficiently gullible to accept the story.

Mention of the Basques brings us back to the extraordinary confusion of Spanish parties, of which something remains to be said. To suggest that the issue is one between Fascism and Communism, between Black and Red, is to over-simplify to a dangerous degree. Speaking of the Popular Front, Professor Allison Peers has written that it is "rent by such schisms that

---

[1] *The Times*, 28 April 1937. See also Mr George Steer in *London Mercury*, August 1937, and the evidence of four Basque nurses in the Paris press, quoted by the *Manchester Guardian* for 28 May. Amusing confirmation is to be found in a remarkable article, "Realities of the War in Spain", published in the *Sunday Times* of 17 October 1937. Its author describes his visit to Guernica under the care of a Salamanca press officer, and how he met several natives who had survived the bombing, and two staff officers of General Davila who boasted of having done the bombing.

The Dean of Canterbury testified (*The Times*, 24 May) to having been at Durango while another air raid destroyed a church and convent, and was able to refute the very similar story that "Reds" had blown up the churches there and killed priests and nuns.

Dr Goebbels' official News Agency on 3 May accused *The Times* of deliberate invention, and suggested that "the failure of the British armaments loan" compelled the paper to stimulate subscription by such tales!

As this book goes to press, Mr Steer has published a detailed account of his experiences under the title of *The Tree of Guernica*. "He [the Basque] is proud of the year in which he governed himself; of how he kept order and the true Church's peace, gave freedom to all consciences, fed the poor, cured the wounded, ran all the services of a government without a single quarrel. Alone in all Spain he showed that he was fit to rule: where others murdered and butchered, terrorised the working class and sold their country to foreigners, the Basque bound together his little nation in strong bands of human solidarity, as strong as the sides of his great steel trawlers. His was a real People's Front, without any dark motive of policy to form it."

nothing but knowledge of what its disruption must mean is holding it together":[1] and this applies almost equally to the other side.

DISUNION ON BOTH SIDES

General Franco himself is not a Fascist in the ordinary sense, though he has come to lay increasing stress upon discipline as the only exit from chaos. His dominant position is very largely due to the accidents which removed Sotelo, Sanjurjo, Primo and Mola. He and several other Generals are Republicans rather than Monarchists: rightly or wrongly, many Catholics regard him as a Freemason. The question of the throne is the first source of discord among the leaders: for the Carlists uphold the pure legitimist doctrine, the Renovación Español favours Alfonso XIII or his third son, while the Falangists may or may not support the Monarchy when the time comes. Falangism is much the most turbulent element, and aims at the establishment of a Catholic totalitarian syndicalist state, resting on fierce intolerance, but full of mutually destructive aims. It seeks to abolish the parliamentary and party system root and branch, but accepts not only redistribution of the land, but the nationalisation of the banks and public works, and claims to be equally opposed to capitalism and Marxism. The sole bond between these various tendencies is a common fear of anarchy and communism, but Dr Borkenau, in his discerning book on "The Spanish Cockpit",[2] is probably right in concluding that any attempt to set up a totalitarian state will hopelessly split up the Coalition of the Right—quite irrespective of the rival groupings of the Left—and will also antagonise the Church.

On the other side there is the greatest possible discrepancy between the moderate Liberal Republicans—by now, it is true, for the most part crushed between the upper and the nether millstones—the Socialists, who began by being evolutionary, but as occasion offered, soon prefixed the letter "r" to

[1] *Catalonia Infelix*, p. 287.
[2] Cf. an article of Valentine Williams in the *Daily Telegraph*, 6 November 1936 ("Fiery Rivalries").

that adjective, the Communists, split into militant Trotskyites and more opportunist supporters of the Moscow Government, and, much more important, the Anarchists and Syndicalists, of whom the former stood for a peculiarly Spanish brand of theoretical individualism and held the State and all its organs to be anathema, while the latter also tempered the pure Sorelian doctrine with Spanish idiosyncrasies. To this already incongruous salad must be added the Catalans and Basques, who have all along been playing for their own hand, and who aim at a Federal Spain, offering at long last free scope for their national aspirations.[1] Even inside this wheel within a wheel there is no real unity, for while Barcelona, the Catalan capital, has always been a stronghold of anarchism, the extremist tendencies of the Republic since the victory of the Popular Front could not fail to alarm the Basques, of whom the great majority are devout Catholics and happily immune from the abuses which mark the Church in some other districts of Spain. Even before Biscaya was overrun by the insurgents, it was becoming increasingly obvious that Valencia was half-hearted in its support of Bilbao, while since then Catalonia seems to be husbanding her resources for the final struggle, in the hope that at least she may be able to preserve her much-prized autonomous Statute, even if it should prove necessary to compromise on many vital points. There are many who hope that, whatever the outcome of the civil war, a federal, rather than a strongly centralised, system may be evolved, since it offers the possibility of greater flexibility and tolerance in national affairs. But whatever conclusions we may draw, the picture of Spain today is kaleidoscopic and changing, and no man dare attempt an estimate of the future balance of forces.

One special feature of "Government Spain" cannot be omitted. Throughout the territory controlled from Valencia and Barcelona the churches have either been burnt, plundered, turned to secular uses, or else are kept closed. Hundreds of priests have been murdered or expelled, all monasteries and

[1] It is characteristic of the Italian attitude to Spain that the Duce's official mouthpiece, Virginio Gayda, treats the Catalan movement as "Muscovite".

convents closed and confiscated and their inmates either killed or driven into private life.[1] Church-burning, accompanied by every imaginable obscenity, became in the words of Professor Peers, "a familiar pastime". What deepens the horror produced by such events is the abundant testimony, from many different impartial sources, as to the utter indifference shown in all classes of society in Catalonia and Valencia to these outrages against the Church. In contrast to Biscay, where it is a living and venerated force, it seems in "Government Spain" simply to have faded out of the national life, thereby, of course, increasing still further the gulf which now separates the Eastern provinces from that "other Spain" where the churches are crowded and the old traditions upheld.

THE POLICY OF NON-INTERVENTION

I have laid special stress upon the complexities and uncertainties of Spanish affairs because to my mind it provides a complete justification for the policy of non-Intervention adopted, and adhered to despite much criticism and provocation, by the British and French Governments. The history of the Committee in which this policy centred is not edifying: it has been full of patent insincerities: decisions have often been postponed when the facts were perfectly obvious: and there have been periodic attempts to turn it into a platform for rival propaganda. But despite occasional hesitations and errors of judgment, the two Governments have strongly upheld the view that for them to side actively with one of the contending Spanish factions would almost inevitably plunge Europe into war. M. Blum warned his Communist critics that in order to assure the victory of the Republicans it would be necessary to send not merely munitions but large bodies of troops, and that this would be emulated by supporters of the rival "ideology". In the words of M. Delbos (3 August 1936) "there must be no crusade of ideals in

[1] The "Group of Anglican and Free Churches who visited Spain" have placed on record the fact that "unless the parish priest was actively unpopular, he was not killed by his own people" (*sic!*).

Europe", because this must inevitably end in war—an attitude wholly identical with Mr Eden's flat refusal to accept the division of Europe into two rival camps. It is quite true that Germany and Italy have periodically tried to force the issue of the two ideologies, but their very insistence produced the opposite effect, and led London and Paris into ever closer co-operation. The need for this was brought home to all save the wilfully blind by the immense resources in material and men placed at the disposal of the insurgents by Germany and Italy and their very obvious calculation that payment might be obtained by strategic concessions in Spanish Morocco and the Balearic Islands. The first sign that there were limits to what Britain and France would tolerate came in January 1937, as a result of persistent rumours of interference in Ceuta: the plain speech of the French Government and Ministry of Marine regarding Morocco, coupled with warnings both to General Franco and to the High Commissioner of Spanish Morocco, were not without effect, and Herr Hitler on 11 January assured the French Ambassador in Berlin that Germany had no designs upon Spain's territorial integrity.

During the spring and summer of 1937 the two dictatorial Powers on several further occasions tried to test the extent of the complaisance of the Western democracies. Germany's indignation at the air attack upon the "Deutschland" (29 May) was shared by many in England, though her idea that honour could be vindicated by the bombardment of the defenceless town of Almeria was no less resented. But when three weeks later she sought to use the doubtful and unexplored "Leipzig" incident (18 June) as the point of departure for a joint demonstration of the four Great Powers against the Valencia Government, she found that she had overreached herself. Not merely did France and Britain refuse, but when confronted by German and Italian withdrawal from the naval patrol scheme on the Spanish coasts, insisted upon drawing up a compromise plan, reinforced by Mr Eden's pointed warning (15 July) that if non-Intervention broke down, Europe "would enter upon a new and more perilous phase", when the general peace would be at the mercy of any incident. This view was reinforced by the Prime Minister, who condemned the Opposition's "reckless irresponsibility" in proposing frank intervention on the side of Valencia: this "would have plunged Europe into a crisis of the very gravest kind". For some weeks there was an awkward deadlock, in which, however, it became clear to the organisers of Mediterranean "piracy" that at any moment they might overstep the limit of what the Western Powers would tolerate, and also that the latter might at any moment make use of the damning proofs which they held in their hands. The "lamentable weakness" of the two Governments was a public theme of disgruntled critics, but when at last they decided to convoke a Conference of Mediterranean Powers at Nyon (12-14 September), the speed with which an agreement was reached on counter-measures against submarine piracy came as a shock to the obstructing Powers. Mr Eden's comparison between "the masked highwayman who does not stop short even of murder" and the new "gangster terrorism of the seas" was only one instance of the welcome plain speech which distinguished this Conference from many of its predecessors.

In actual fact, piracy died down from the moment when it was realised that Britain and France stood firm and had the support of all the minor Mediterranean Powers. In his survey of policy on 1 November 1937 Mr Eden was able to endorse the claim of M. Blum at the French Socialist Congress, that non-Intervention, despite numerous leakages and defects, had preserved Europe from a general war, and that to the prevention of such a war every other interest must be subordinated. Herein lies the essence of the Spanish problem in its international aspect. The only alternative to non-Intervention is the active espousal of one of the two contending factions in Spain, for neither is strong enough to win outright without some external assistance. But this is impossible for quite a number of reasons: because our own country is far too deeply divided on the Spanish question ever to tolerate such drastic action on the part of the Government; because it would run counter to our firm resolve not to become entangled in any aggressive Fascist or

Communist Bloc, resting upon warring "ideologies" which we reject as almost equally false and objectionable: and because in the Spanish case these "ideologies" are mere screens behind which the exponents of Power Politics pursue their strategic ambitions. Mr Chamberlain has well said that "the troubles that have arisen out of the civil war are only a by-product of deeper causes of unrest in Europe". They are also intimately connected with Italy's designs for the hegemony of the Mediterranean—designs which it suits Germany to support up to—but not beyond—a certain point. It is to this strategy that we must turn in conclusion.

FOREIGN HELP IN SPAIN

First let us consider very briefly what has actually been done in the way of intervention in Spain. On the Right it is often alleged that the rebellion was necessary in order to forestall an elaborate plot from Moscow for the Bolshevisation of Spain,[1] and there is no doubt that the Comintern had its agents in Spain for some years past, and that prominent Spaniards of the Left visited, and sympathised with, Soviet Russia. It must, however, be added that the more militant Communist wing was in touch with Trotsky and was therefore frowned upon by the Kremlin, to whose policy active revolution in Spain was a very genuine embarrassment. Hence, apart from Red volunteers (and these found their way to Madrid from every country in Europe), there was not much Russian assistance for the Spanish Government until Madrid was in danger of falling and Fascist intervention had made its defence a matter of Russian prestige. Indeed, it is hardly too much to say that the Spanish tactics of Hitler and Mussolini forced uniformity of policy in Spain upon Stalinites and Trotskyites at the very height of their internecine feud!

[1] No evidence on this point has ever been published—as in the case of the Reichstag Fire, "abuse the plantiff's attorney". If it were true that Russia had been arming Spain for five years, as some of Franco's supporters allege, how are we to explain the fact that when the insurgents attacked Madrid in November 1936, "the Government's troops only had 1400 rifles, 8 machine-guns and one cannon with which to defend the city"?

On the other hand, it is known that Spain had for at least two years previously been covered with a network of German Nazi spies and agents,[1] who poured out money in the press and in propaganda and in a more legitimate fashion, promoted trade. There is ample evidence that both German and Italian help had been promised long beforehand to the would-be rebels: and in actual fact the first German planes arrived in Spanish Morocco as early as 21 July 1936. On 30 July two Italian military planes, carrying a consignment of machine-guns for the rebels, made a forced landing in French Morocco, being part of a squadron of twenty-six which had left Milan *via* Sardinia for Spain, before the rebellion broke out: and on 8 August a German Junker plane came down by mistake near Madrid and had to admit that thirty others had already been sent to Seville. On 28 August twenty-four Italian planes landed at Vigo, while two days later twenty-eight German planes arrived at Cadiz. These are merely a few concrete instances: the fact is that war material was sent on a large scale from Germany and Italy, and supplemented by picked technicians, especially airmen: and this became so notorious that on 24 October the Soviet Ambassador announced to the Non-Intervention Committee that his Government proposed that the embargo on the supply of arms to the Spanish Government should be cancelled, and refused to be bound any longer while the other side was supplying the insurgents. The mutual recriminations to which this gave rise roused Moscow to greater activity, and there seems to be no doubt that Madrid was saved by the timely, if tardy, arrival of Russian war material, just as it is certain that the recognition accorded by Berlin and Rome to General Franco on 18 November was timed to coincide with the fall of Madrid and could no longer be recalled when the *coup* failed. For this recognition it is impossible to find any legal precedents,

---

[1] Full details, together with documents in facsimile, will be found in *The Nazi Conspiracy in Spain* (1937). Unfortunately this book is not merely tendencious in outlook, but very ill-digested, and the reader can hardly see the wood for the trees. It is based mainly on material seized at the Nazi headquarters in Barcelona after the rising.

either in the history of Western Europe last century, or in the support accorded to Kolchak and Denikin (who were the legitimate heirs not so much of the Tsarist as of the Provisional Government): the sole motive was "doctrinal enthusiasm", to use the sarcastic understatement of *The Times.*[1]

In the first period, up to Christmas 1936, most of the foreigners fighting in Spain were genuine volunteers, recruited from many countries and inspired by political zeal for Left or Right: but much the most notable of these groups was the International Brigade of anti-Fascist Italians, led by that gallant idealist Carlo Rosselli, editor of the Parisian weekly *Giustizia e Libertà*. It was his plan to fight for Italian liberty on Spanish soil, and the exploits of his band echoed along the whispering gallery of Fascist Italy. For this reason he was murdered by secret agents in June 1937, while recovering from his wounds at a Norman watering place, under circumstances of great mystery which are slowly coming to light and promise a profound sensation.

From the turn of the year onwards the situation changed, and large military contingents were sent both from Germany and Italy to the help of General Franco. In view of the numbers involved it soon became an odious farce to speak of "volunteers". Yet the farce had to be kept up at the Non-Intervention Committee, as the sole alternative to the break-down of the whole scheme and an open conflict. In reality the civil war had become merged in a regular Italo-Spanish war: for while the Germans sent a good many thousand trained experts, capable of invaluable help in key positions in the insurgent army, Signor Mussolini sent a regular "Expeditionary Force" with all the necessary equipment. In March 1937 careful foreign observers estimated them at 80,000 men, and if this be an exaggeration, it remains true that the Italian Government, after fiercely denouncing all such stories as an impudent calumny, and not allowing any reference in its own controlled press, suddenly in the summer made up its mind to admit the figure of

[1] Leader of 23 November 1936.

40,000![1] As an instance of Italian good faith, it will suffice to note that on the very day before the conclusion of the Anglo-Italian "Gentleman's Agreement" (save the mark!), 6000 Italians were landed at Cadiz, following upon another 4000 in the previous week. Though it was not known at the time, the Duce himself showed the keenest personal interest in the Italian units in Spain, and sent special messages to the various commanders, to be read aloud to their men. But pride goes before a fall, and the severe reverse which befell the insurgent armies at the battle of Guadalajara towards the end of March 1937 was due to the over-confidence of the Italian generals, followed by panic and rout on the part of their men.[2] Two vital contributory factors were effective bombing, and machine-gunning by Russian airmen, and above all the revolutionary *élan* of the anti-Fascist Italian brigade fighting for the Valencia Government. It was at Guadalajara that a large number of documents were captured, establishing beyond all possibility of doubt the vast scale of Italian intervention in Spain.[3] It is not too much to affirm that Mussolini's objective was political and strategic, intimately connected with his design of Mediterranean hegemony, and that if his troops had conquered Madrid and contributed to the downfall of Valencia, and if the Western Allies

[1] The author of a very well-informed article on "Intervention in Spain" in *The Times* of 9 March 1937 estimated the foreigners serving under Franco at 60,000 and those under the Government at 20–35,000, the latter being of course *real volunteers*. This figure is almost certainly immensely exaggerated. Mr Henry Blythe, in his very able *Spain over Britain* (p. 22), estimates the Italian forces in Spain at "nearer 100,000 than 50,000". This figure is almost certainly exaggerated.

[2] The first official admission of defeat was in *Popolo d'Italia* of 18 June.

[3] *Documents on the Italian Intervention in Spain*, containing summaries of 100 documents, and 66 pages of facsimiles. Of special interest are v and vi (details of organisation of units for Spain, by the Italian Ministry of War and the General Staff), xci (Mussolini's message, transmitted by General Mancini), xcvi (Message of Fascist Grand Council, "supreme interpreter of the spirit of the nation", to the troops in Spain), xcviii (General Mancini's admission of self-inflicted wounds, shamming and desertions among his troops), xcv (General Coppi's address to volunteer officers: "Do not over-value the enemy: they are a rabble of adventurers without faith").

had not taken a firm stand against his cryptic "piracy", he might have established himself in the Balearic Isles and completely dominated "Franco Spain".

There seems little doubt that during the summer of 1937 Germany slowly restricted the number of her troops in Spain, while still leaving carefully picked specialists in certain key positions. All along there have been fanatical Nazi leaders seeking to convince the Führer that it was a test case for the success of Bolshevism in Europe, whereas the General Staff, and still more the naval authorities, steadily warned against a policy which, if pushed beyond a certain point, would involve a conflict with Britain under the most unfavourable strategic conditions and on behalf of objects of very secondary importance to Germany. These latter views were reinforced by grave doubts as to the fighting value of the Italians, which Guadalajara seemed to bear out, and by the fear lest Germany should find herself in the position of pulling the Mediterranean chestnuts out of the fire for an Italy who was incapable of straight dealing in Central Europe. The result was a compromise: and the generals were in the end not so reluctant to use unhappy Spain as a "Versuchskaninchen" (an experimental rabbit) on which their new aeroplanes and tanks and anti-aircraft defences, and above all the value of *Ersatz* material, could be tried out. Whether the results of these experiments were encouraging or not, is a question which must be left to military experts.

MR EDEN ON ITALY AND SPAIN

The British Government was presumably under no illusions as to the motives of the Duce in assisting the Spanish insurgents, or again as to the value of his professions or promises, in view of the successful dissimulation with which he prepared the Abyssinian campaign, in violation of a whole series of voluntarily concluded treaties and agreements. None the less, during the late winter of 1936 it carried on negotiations with Italy which culminated on 2 January 1937 in what is most unsuitably known as a "Gentleman's Agreement" between Italy and Britain. Starting from the recognition "that freedom of entry into, exit from, and transit through the Mediterranean is a vital interest both to the different parts of the British Empire and to Italy, and that these interests are in no way inconsistent with each other", it goes on to disclaim "any desire to modify or see modified" the existing *status quo* in the Mediterranean, and to respect each other's rights and interests there. Appended to it was the exchange of notes between Sir Eric Drummond (now Lord Perth) and Count Ciano, in which the former made it clear that "any change in the *status quo* in the Western Mediterranean would be a matter of the closest concern to Britain", while the latter gave in Italy's name an explicit guarantee of Spanish integrity, especially as regards the Balearic Islands.

This was in pursuance of Mr Eden's clear statement of policy[1] to the effect that "for us the Mediterranean is not a short cut, but a main arterial road. Freedom of communications in these waters is of vital interest, in the full sense of the word, to the British Commonwealth of Nations." Unfortunately relations with Italy did not, and could not, improve while Italy was engaged in active war on a large scale against the Spanish Government, strengthening her hold on Majorca and conniving at submarine piracy. During the Commons debate of 19 July Mr Eden found it advisable to use plainer speech than hitherto on the subject of Spain. He insisted that our resolve not to interfere in her internal affairs did not prevent us from taking a very real interest in the integrity of Spanish territory, and that disinterestedness "must not be taken to mean disinterestedness where British interests are concerned on the land or sea fronts of Spain or the trade routes that pass her by. This country has every intention of defending its national interests in the Mediterranean as elsewhere in the world", but also no intention of challenging the interests of others. "If the Mediterranean is for us a main arterial road—and it is—yet there is plenty of room for all on such a road. If we intend to

[1] In the House of Commons, November 1936, repeated 19 January 1937.

maintain our place on it—and we do—we have no intention of seeking to turn anyone else off it"—least of all "those who geographically dwell upon it. There is ample room for all. Free traffic through and out of the Mediterranean is the common interest of Britain and of all the Mediterranean Powers." After strongly denying the insinuation that British policy was one of aggression or revenge, he took occasion to add that his remarks about the Mediterranean applied equally to the Red Sea: "it has always been, and is today, a major British interest that no Great Power should establish itself on the eastern shore" of that sea. The background to this statement was furnished by the long and poisonous campaign in Arabic conducted by the Italian radio station at Bari, for the purpose of rousing the Arab world against Britain.

In a later speech, on 1 November 1937, Mr Eden referred to the fears expressed in some quarters lest the insurgents, if victorious, should pursue a foreign policy directed against Britain. This he did not accept, since "there were strong forces of trade, of geography, working in another direction. Spaniards knew very well that England had no thought, direct or indirect, of interfering with the territorial integrity and political independence of Spain, and that no British war material had killed any Spaniard."[1] He might have added that the Spaniards are an unusually proud and sensitive people, whose reaction to foreign interference in the past has always been an acute outburst of xenophobia, that unless the national character has radically changed, history may well repeat itself, and that in actual fact the Italians in Spain (in contrast to the far less numerous, but carefully selected and therefore far better behaved, Germans) are already extremely unpopular among the population. Moreover, it would seem only reasonable to suppose that Spain will in the end look towards those countries

[1] Another passage in the same speech deserves quotation. "There is an inclination to threaten, to issue orders from housetops, to proclaim what is virtually an ultimatum, and to call it peace. Such orders will never have any response here. We are not prepared to stand and deliver at any one's call.... We offer co-operation to all, but will accept dictation from none."

which desire her complete independence and possess the material resources from which her many wounds can be healed, rather than to those who are in search of strategic bases and such an extension of the ideological front in Europe as may well place Spain in the very centre of the whirlpool. It is quite true that the emergence of a militarised Fascist state in Spain would be a grave danger to Britain and France: but it is not yet necessary to abandon all hope of Spain making a compromise on lines that are neither Fascist nor Communist, but take account of the wide divergences of tradition and evolution in her various provinces. Again, it is highly probable that Germany would not be averse to seeing the establishment of a Spanish regime so out of sympathy with France as to render necessary the fortification of the Pyrenees frontier and a consequent tying up of part of the forces which would otherwise be available on her eastern frontiers. But though this may be the counsel of perfection, the more immediate and practical German aim has been to secure some of the much-needed raw materials of Spain in return for the delivery of certain munitions of war, and by a process of bartering much more favourable to Germany than that which prevails in the case of other countries. The appointment of General Faupel, a recognised authority on metallurgy, as German Envoy to Salamanca, was the outward and visible sign of Germany's paramount interest in iron ore and other minerals.

MEDITERRANEAN STRATEGY

The Mediterranean question has rapidly become the most burning *strategic* problem of our time. Already in the Great War it had come to be admitted that even a fleet whose power was decisive on the high seas was at an increasing disadvantage in the narrow seas, and therefore peculiarly so in the Mediterranean, where the submarine menace was very acute and accounted for much the highest percentage of ships lost. Today, thanks to the combination of submarine and aircraft, that menace has been enormously increased. In the drastic phrase of

Captain Liddell Hart, war in that inland sea would be not unlike "shutting up a bunch of mad cats in a cage".[1]

Britain has now possessed vital interests, and maintained her naval power, in the Mediterranean for the best part of three centuries, and in that time the strategic problem has often varied. Sometimes France, sometimes Spain, has been her chief rival, sometimes the two have combined against her, and sometimes Turkey has had a far from negligible share of sea-power. But never until the last few years has she been confronted with a situation in which the Italian Peninsula, united in a single state, has made a determined bid for sea-power on a grand scale, in conjunction with an expansive colonial policy. The comfortable tradition that Italy and Britain were eternally friends, linked by common sympathies and interests, has been rudely shattered, and we now see Italy under the absolute control of a despot who despises and repudiates British traditions of liberty and of government; who moves a direct negative to the collective system and after undermining it by his defiances of treaty obligations, is deliberately planning its destruction and a return to "the European anarchy"; who, so far from believing in international peace, is training the rising generation of Italians for war. In a word, Italian aims today are diametrically opposed to those of Britain, and we must, without false sentiment, draw the grim conclusions. It is quite true that the strategic communications of the two countries are so inextricably interlocked that sanity and logic should impose a truce, and even an accord, based on the assumption that there is ample room in the Mediterranean for these two, and many others also, to go peacefully about their respective callings. But such an accord presupposes mutual respect for treaty obligations, and contentment with the existing international order: whereas the Duce has shown his word to be valueless and his ultimate aim to be domination in the Mediterranean.

It is obvious enough that Italy, so dependent on certain foreign imports that can only reach her by sea, is at a serious disadvantage so long as the three exits from the inland sea can

[1] *Europe in Arms*, p. 115.

be bottled, and this is a fact which geography has imposed, and which can never be undone. It is true that Italian reinforcements to North Africa have to pass the British naval base of Malta, and those destined for Eritrea and the new Ethiopian "Empire" through the Suez Canal and the Red Sea, where Britain holds most of the key positions. On the other hand, Britain's former superiority has greatly diminished. Gibraltar is no longer impregnable in these days of long range artillery, and there are many who consider that it might well be made untenable for the British Fleet—at any rate if the neighbouring coast of Spain were in hostile hands. The naval dockyards of Malta are only 70 miles distant from Sicily and 200 miles from Tripoli, and therefore dangerously exposed to Italian air-raids from both quarters. Egypt, in whose fate Britain is vitally concerned by reason of the Canal and the Sudan, is exposed on her western frontier to an Italian attack from Libya. Above all, British communications with the whole Eastern half of the Mediterranean, and therefore the main route to India, are now extremely vulnerable, having to pass along a narrow funnel between the African coast and the Italo-Sicilian coasts, narrowed still further by recent Italian fortification of the small island of Pantellaria. Without presuming to decide between the rival schools of naval strategy, we may at least treat it as quite open to argument that in the event of war with Italy the British fleet could not protect commercial shipping in the Mediterranean and would find it expedient to divert the Indian trade round the Cape, and itself to withdraw outside the Straits of Gibraltar. It is sufficiently serious that this would almost double the length of the route from London to Bombay (though not greatly lengthening that from London to Melbourne or Sydney), and that the transfer of troops to and from India and other dependencies would be rendered much less easy. Still more serious, however, is the fact that we have so many more commitments in the Levant than formerly, and that our power to defend Cyprus, Palestine, and above all the Canal against hostile attacks would be correspondingly diminished. This explains the intensive anti-British propaganda conducted by Italy throughout the Arab world: for there can be no manner of doubt that in the event of war she would attempt to foment a rising in Palestine, would incite the King of Arabia to attack Aden, and would perhaps attempt to take Egypt and the Sudan between two fires from Libya and Abyssinia. It is too soon to speak of Italy raising a Black Army in Abyssinia for the conquest of neighbouring territory: but if the present tendency continues in Italy, this too may be expected. It is, however, worth noting in passing that while only 20 per cent of British imports pass through the Mediterranean, 80 per cent of Italian imports pass through the Straits of Gibraltar.

The dangers inherent in the situation led, at the height of the Abyssinian crisis, to drastic changes in British naval dispositions, the centre of gravity being transferred from Malta to Alexandria: and Cyprus, after being completely useless to the protecting Power for fifty years, is now acquiring an entirely new value as an air base capable of checkmating the Italian naval station in the Dodecanese and stiffening the resistance of the smaller East Mediterranean Powers—Turkey, Greece, Jugoslavia, Egypt—who are all afraid of an Italian hegemony. The decisive factor, however, is at the other end of the Mediterranean: for if Italy could obtain control of the Balearic Islands (as the reward for her help to the Spanish rebellion) she might cut the communications of France with Algiers and Tunis and gravely affect French military dispositions in a future war, thereby virtually placing France and Britain combined on the defensive. But if she could establish a Fascist Spain in close alliance with herself, she might overcome all the main weaknesses of her enclosed strategic position—using Spanish ports to bring her imports from the Atlantic, not merely rendering Gibraltar untenable, but bottling the Straits between it and Spanish Morocco, and perhaps controlling the Azores and Canaries and so threatening even the Atlantic route of Britain to West Africa and the Cape.

There are good grounds for believing that Signor Mussolini had convinced himself of the aggressive intentions of Britain towards Italy, and was using this argument to convince his hard-driven subjects of the need of piling up armaments far in excess of what they can reasonably afford. He doubtless imputes to us motives similar to those on which he would act were the rôles reversed, and it may be doubted whether anything that we can do will avail to convince him of the contrary. The proof of the pudding is in the eating of it: and it only requires a modicum of intelligence to realise that the massing of 60–80,000 Italian troops in Libya is not due to the Duce's fear of Communism in Egypt, but is directed against Britain and France in the Mediterranean.

Under these circumstances we must maintain an attitude of ceaseless vigilance, act in closest co-operation with the French, keep the smaller Mediterranean states on our side not merely by behaving in a conciliatory manner, but by convincing them that a sort of Mediterranean "Peace Front", on purely defensive lines, is the only alternative to war and chaos, and offers an even stronger guarantee to the small than to the big Powers. At the same time we must scrupulously avoid all provocation, and lose no opportunity of demonstrating to the Italian people our absolutely pacific aims and our lack of territorial designs, while on the other hand taking a firm stand against such Italian propagandist activities as the Bari Radio and the still more insidious encouragement of sedition inside Palestine.

That we must for the present reckon with the settled hostility of the Duce is shown by the events of the last six months, and especially by his attitude to the "Anti-Comintern Pact", to Japan and to the League. His adherence to that Pact rests on quite other motives than those which led Germany and Japan to establish it in the first instance: for Japan had at least ample grounds for nervousness as to the rôle of Communism in China, and Germany's leaders are the victims of a positive obsession as regards the Bolshevik danger, and are no longer capable of forming a sane estimate of forces in Russia, whereas Mussolini, as we have seen, has often enough taken credit for his good relations with Soviet Russia, not to mention copying her methods in more than one direction, and is therefore quite obviously prompted by tactical motives rather than motives of principle. Still more flagrant is his attitude in recognising the

Japanese claim to Manchuria at the moment when Japan, without troubling to declare war, is engaged in a vast act of brigandage against China. A case can be made out for the German repudiation of Versailles—a bad case, as we have argued in earlier chapters, but none the less a case which reveals undoubted grievances. A case can be made out for Japan's claim to very special interests in Manchuria, and therefore for recognition of her special position in that province (on some such lines as are admitted by Mr Stimson in the very moderate opening chapters of his book).[1] But no case whatsoever can be made out for Japan's present war of aggression against China. It is no longer a question of the League, which Japan left long ago: but she is now acting in crass defiance of the Kellogg Pact and still more of the Nine-Power Pact, relating specifically to Far Eastern affairs, and therefore shows that she no longer respects any international order, but pursues the cult of naked force. Nor does that dangerous half-truth of "Haves" and "Have-nots" apply either to Italy, who is now engaged in the process of digesting a conquered territory larger in area than France and Germany combined, or to Japan, who after annexing Formosa, Korea, Manchuria and Jehol, now appears to aim at seizing three or four other Chinese provinces, to be followed perhaps by Hongkong, the Philippines, Java and Sumatra. Thus that the Duce should have chosen to recognise Japanese sovereignty in Manchuria at the height of Japanese brigandage in China, simply puts him out of court with the rest of the world: for it shows that he is completely indifferent to international law and order, and swayed by tactical considerations of Power Politics. His repeated abuse of the League of Nations—notably the reference in his Berlin speech of last September to "the false gods of Geneva"—had already made this clear to all save the wilfully blind: but the formal withdrawal of Italy from the League makes the situation even clearer than before, and Mr Churchill performed yet another service to the truth by his plain speaking in the House of Commons on 21 December 1937. The idea that the League

[1] *The Far Eastern Crisis* (New York, 1936).

should be "weakened by the departure of a country which had broken every engagement into which it had entered and whose spokesmen had rejoiced in mocking and insulting every principle on which the League was founded", is simply childish. "The one small service that Signor Mussolini was left to render the League was to leave it": and the League is well rid of him.

In some quarters it is rashly assumed that the absence of several Great Powers from the League means the definite failure of the experiment associated with Geneva. This is to misstate the problem before us. Obviously, if we accept defeat and abandon our efforts, what is left of the League will collapse, and the European anarchy will be complete. The cowardly or short-sighted advocates of such a course would probably be the first to wince when the result was expressed in the doubling of our already inflated armaments and the enforced renunciation of many ideals of social service for at least a generation. My inference is that the Mediterranean situation demands realism, courage, and constant vigilance, and that it can never be eased by a surrender of principle to one whose aims are as manifest as those of Mussolini, still less by lending him money to finance his fell designs: but that we must not despair of renewing friendship with the Italy we love, restored some day to freedom and sanity.

After the conquest of Abyssinia Mussolini declared that Italy belonged to the "satiated" Powers: but this was merely a *ruse*, for he not merely continued to arm on a vaster scale than ever, but sent whole armies to Spain for what is a regular war in all save name, while his press denounced Geneva and the democratic states as the real threat to peace in Europe. Meanwhile his methods, even in countries that are not yet at war, are becoming plain even to the man in the street. Commander Fletcher's pertinent questions in the House of Commons (23 December 1937) as to Italy's systematic campaign of anti-British propaganda from the Bari radio station exposed some of the facts to which our authorities, for some inexplicable reason, deny publicity. During his visit to Libya Mussolini had made an open bid for the status of "Friend and Protector of Islam" (in a theatrical speech at Tripoli that recalls the really much more harmless pronouncement of William II at Damascus in 1898). Since then there has been no concealment of the Italian tendency to encourage unrest throughout the Arab world, to poison opinion in Palestine against the mandatory Power, to exploit the Jewish problem, to fan the suspicions of Mecca and Bagdad, of the Yemen and Transjordania, to fish everywhere in troubled waters. It has long been notorious that the series of terrorist outrages in Jugoslavia in 1932–4 were the work of a group of exiles whose resources in money and weapons were of Italian origin: and even since the recent insincere *rapprochement* between Italy and Jugoslavia, the chief terrorist still has a refuge, or a gilded cage, in Italy. It is now beginning to be known that similar methods have been employed on the soil of France, that many of the weapons in the secret Cagoulard stores were of Italian origin, that there was an intimate connection between Fascism and the Csar terrorists, and that the murder of the Rosselli brothers at Bagnolles in June 1937 was not merely revenge for Guadalajara, but part of a projected Fascist offensive inside France.[1]

The plain brutal fact is that Mussolini would fain reduce anti-Fascist France by civil discord to the same prostration as has been produced in Spain. Then indeed he might achieve the mastery of the Mediterranean. Our only possible answer is an ever closer democratic accord between France and Britain; for on it alone depends the maintenance of the general peace and the survival of free institutions in Europe.

[1] In this connection it should be added that though the murder is not of course discussed in the controlled Italian press, it has none the less reverberated through Italy: and the name of Carlo Rosselli is linked with those of Battisti, Matteotti, and Amendola. History may perhaps record that the practical example which he set of armed and disciplined resistance to tyranny, through the International Brigade in Spain, marked the first turn of the tide in Europe.

XII

BRITISH POLICY OF TODAY

THIS book has been written in the belief that the dangers of the future cannot be adequately met without close study of the past—not in order to follow blindly in the old paths, but in order to know what methods it is now necessary to discard or adapt, and to find a key to those national psychologies which it is vital for us to comprehend. "A jealous, ever waking vigilance, to guard the treasure of our liberty, not only from invasion, but from decay and corruption, is our best wisdom and our first duty", so wrote Edmund Burke in face of dangers not smaller, and certainly more direct than those of our own day. One reason why the statesmen of Europe were so long unsuccessful against the French Revolution was, according to Albert Sorel, that "they judged upon false analogies and regulated their conduct towards it by groundless conjectures". It is this error above all which we must avoid today, and this is only possible if we examine the facts of the European situation in a spirit of utter realism, setting in the one scale hopes, ideals and aspirations, and in the other the facts of geography, strategy, raw materials and population, and framing our policy not only by what we wish but by what seems attainable. In this light we must attempt to answer the difficult questions what is, or should be, British policy today, and what are the best means of assuring the safety of the British Commonwealth of Nations.

At the outset it may be postulated that while "British interests" must be the constant and unwearying concern of every British statesman, he will be but a poor and unconstructive statesman who is content with this aim. Lofty though it is, it is not enough: he must aim not merely at "Pax Britannica", but at World Peace (they are not far apart!): he must above all else seek to keep or bring British interests into line with the new international World Order, and the real test of his statesmanship will come when the two are in conflict, and he fails to find a means of reconciling them. These alternative methods may, I boldly suggest, be summed up as the two standards of the old and the new dispensation—"Am I my brother's keeper?" and "No man liveth unto himself". This is not a sentimental intrusion, it is downright common sense, as fundamental as that contained in the old proverb, "Honesty is the best policy". Nothing shows more clearly how superficially the problem of foreign policy has been regarded, than the all too common assumption that complete selfishness—a-moral rather than moral or immoral—is the safest rule in international relations. This does not mean that the opposite extreme of *sancta simplicitas*—unarmed and unprepared—should be adopted, but only that though bandits sometimes get away with the swag, the statesman who combines ideals and honesty with practical precautions is positively at an advantage. Lest, however, my reader should dismiss my contention with scorn, I wish to assure him that my argument will pay a strict attention to considerations of Power Politics, as pursued by more than one Bandit State of the present day. He will already have observed that the League of Nations has played a somewhat subdued rôle throughout my narrative. This is not because I do not believe in its ultimate triumph (sheer necessity may in the end bring this to pass), but because the best way of demonstrating the dire need of such an institution is to survey events in the light of the existing European anarchy.

"BRITISH INTERESTS"

Any attempt to define British interests today must begin with certain abstract propositions and then pass gradually to concrete points of detail. Today, no less than in Pitt's time, "Peace and Security" are our foremost aims. Today even more, because there is scarcely a problem in any part of the world that could be referred to the arbitrament of war without directly affecting one or more British interests: so world-wide has our Empire become, and so close to the nerve-centres of every continent. These two famous words, reiterated by every British statesman down to the present day, are of course truisms which do not take us beyond the first signpost on our road: but it is none the less important to note, what is never so obvious as not to require emphasis, that Britain's face is set towards peace, and that she has today nothing to gain, and almost everything to lose, by warlike action of any kind.

In the period immediately following the War the principle of the Balance of Power temporarily disappeared, and many had sincerely hoped that the new international order, resting upon the League of Nations, would prove a permanent substitute. At times there was a nervous feeling that France was trying to establish her predominance under the camouflage of the League: and it is true that she was for about fifteen years much the strongest Power in Europe, though it is also true that her policy was rather one of insurance and insulation than one of direct aggression. In proportion, however, as the inefficacy of the League system has been demonstrated from 1933 onwards, the old principle of Balance has revived: and Britain, while not abandoning hope that the Genevan substitute will reassert itself, clearly has more interest than any other Power in maintaining some sort of balance in the meantime.

Let us then, before going any further, consider the European situation in those terms of Power Politics to which Italy and Germany are forcing us to revert. From such an angle the many smaller Powers may be ruled out, save as very convenient pawns in "the great game", or, occasionally, as victims of "ideological" interference—as, for instance, Spain at present. The great game has to be played by five Great Powers, and these five are deeply divided among themselves. Four permutations are possible: (1) A real and lasting triangular understanding between France, Britain and Germany—not, of course, at the expense of anyone else—would mean peace for a generation, and the other Powers would soon adjust themselves and recover confidence. (2) Similarly, a really cordial understanding between France, Britain and Russia—once more, not at anyone else's expense, in which case it would have the support of all the smaller Powers—would have overwhelming force on its side (especially as it would have the benevolent backing of America) and could preserve an armed peace. (3) Russia could be excluded from the comity of nations, and there would remain two precariously balanced groups—France and Britain versus Germany and Italy: tension and uncertainty would thus become chronic. (4) Russia and Germany could come to terms—either on some such basis as the eight Generals favoured, or at the expense of Poland, and leave the Western Powers to settle among themselves as best they could, pending a German bid for the Adriatic, the Middle East and a colonial empire.

In 1856, towards the close of the Crimean War, when Napoleon III was trying to re-establish friendship with Russia, he said to Count Orlov, the Tsar's delegate, "Could we not agrée *à trois*? we should dominate Europe": and in this there was no disloyalty to Britain, who would have been the third. In 1880 Bismarck put forward the maxim "Try to be *à trois* in a world governed by five Powers": and viewed simply as a diplomatic formula, this contained great wisdom. On 31 August 1936 the German semi-official *Deutsche Allgemeine Zeitung* laid down the axiom, "Moscow must be pushed out of European affairs". Thus the problem resolves itself into a question of strategy and mathematics: and it is time for us to say quite firmly and categorically that it is contrary alike to British and French interests that Russia should be ejected from Europe, because she is essential to the Balance of Power, because she desires peace for most obvious domestic reasons, and because she has no territorial or other interests which in any way run counter to those of the British Empire. In 1938 we may repeat the words of A. J. Balfour in his famous Memorandum of October 1916: "*The more Russia is made a European rather than an Asiatic Power, the better for everybody.*"[1] Her internal system is an obstacle to close friendship, but it does not prevent co-operation in the international field: for we have repeatedly rejected the idea that ideology determines policy, and indeed it

[1] D. Lloyd George, *War Memoirs*, II, p. 881.

is only on this assumption that we are able to deal with Hitler and Mussolini also. What is sauce for the goose is sauce for the gander.

Consequently, Britain stands committed to the collective system as the ideal goal: and in that case all the Powers meet as equals at Geneva. If there is to be exclusion of the lesser Powers from discussion or bargaining, it must be in favour of Five, not of Four, Powers. We already saw that the Duce's plan for a Directorate of Four was merely a somewhat crude design for placing France in a minority, at a moment when he reckoned with Britain as a more than usually uncertain quantity.

Our statesmen for the moment failed to see the trap, but it can never be prepared again in the old form.

STRATEGY IN EUROPE

The elements of the strategic position in Europe may be summed up as follows. Britain and France are bound together, more than ever in the past, not merely by the knowledge that the defeat of either means the downfall of free institutions in Europe, and perhaps in the whole world, but by the most elementary mathematical calculation that either of them alone is in a position of dangerous inferiority, and that even united they would, in the event of war, be in a far less favourable strategic position than in the Great War. It is true that on the one hand Germany is today much weaker at sea, and no longer has Austria-Hungary (once the fourth of the six Great Powers) as her ally: but on the other hand she has the support of Italy, who though much inferior to the old Habsburg Monarchy as a fighting force, and handicapped by African commitments, can none the less turn the whole Mediterranean situation greatly to the disadvantage of the Western Powers, and is second to none in the art of political blackmail. It is easy to see what would be the relative positions of Germany and Italy after a victorious war waged in common; the latter would be little more than the vassal of the former, and there would be competition among all the minor states for the favour of Berlin, not of Rome. In that event Germany would soon have more to say than Italy, even in the Adriatic and the Aegean. It follows that if France could be deprived of her alliances in Eastern Europe, and of course proportionately still more if Britain could be detached from France, Germany might feel irresistibly tempted to overthrow the *status quo* in Central Europe, and Italy might be shortsighted enough to swallow the bait of Mediterranean domination dangled before her eyes. It also follows that the best hope of peace for the Western Powers is to maintain a kind of "Peace Front" of those Powers who are interested in preventing any forcible disturbance of the *status quo* and in vindicating the damaged principles of international co-operation and collective security. Foremost among these Powers today stands Russia, who despite, or perhaps because of, the terrible internal crisis through which she is passing, and also because of the precarious situation along her Far Eastern frontiers, is vitally concerned in the maintenance of peace in Europe. This is also true of the Little and Balkan Ententes, of Poland, of Holland and Belgium, and of the seven states that surround the Baltic: but of course there are very great divergences between the respective attitudes of these four groups. As regards the first of them, Germany and Italy are actively engaged (as yet on parallel lines, but by no means always with the same objects) in trying to detach one state after the other, and above all to isolate Czechoslovakia, as the last stronghold of democratic government east of the Swiss frontier, and this is rendered easier by the fact that the other four members of this double Bloc have adopted varying forms of authoritarian government; and also by an unscrupulous exploitation of the thorny Jewish and minority questions, especially in Roumania. At the same time the Axis Powers have been successful in paralysing the recent tendencies towards political and economic *rapprochement* between Austria, Hungary and Czechoslovakia. As regards Poland, her main object is "to postpone the evil day" and at all costs to avert either a situation in which a war of rival ideologies might be fought out upon her soil, or alternately a situation in which a fresh partition might be the price of peace between

Moscow and Berlin. Deepseated internal discontent and social misery increase her inclination to hedge between the two extremes, and hence it comes about that a Foreign Minister who is the devoted ally of Nazi Germany is maintained in office by the heir to Pilsudski's semi-dictatorial power, Marshal Smigly-Rydz, who favours and maintains the French alliance. The modified and increasingly cautious attitude of such small Powers as Holland and Belgium, occupying notoriously exposed positions in the event of general war, and again of the three democratic Scandinavian Powers, reflects the state of uncertainty in which Europe finds itself, not merely owing to the aggressive policy of the two Fascist Powers, and to the hideous contrast between Russian domestic and foreign policy, but also to the vacillations of the two great Western Powers during the Abyssinian and Spanish crises. None the less, while realism forces us to take note of the obvious weaknesses of the Bloc formed out of so many different elements, we are entitled to assume that a great majority of European states favours a revival of the Genevan system and instantly reacts to any signs of leadership or energy on the part of Britain and France.

Strategically, then, we have only one of two alternatives— to maintain and extend this Peace Front on a strictly un-aggressive basis, while of course leaving the door, not ajar, but wide open, for all who may be disposed, at the next turn of the European kaleidoscope, to modify their views and join us on honourable terms; or, by submitting to the extreme Nazi claim for the exclusion of Russia from Europe, to achieve the immediate isolation of France and Britain (which is what the Nazi extremists really want) and to accept a situation in which we should very soon be impotent to avert far-reaching changes of the Balance of Power in our joint disfavour. It is quite clear that many of the states whose natural place is in the Peace Bloc, and indeed that we ourselves, have good reasons for suspicion of the Bolshevist regime: but with the lines of foreign policy repeatedly laid down by M. Litvinov at Geneva we can almost unreservedly agree, and it is in our vital interest, despite the immense difficulty of the task, to maintain a maximum of contact with Moscow, and, while jealously watching the activities of the Comintern, not to shut our eyes to Moscow's obvious interest, in the Europe of today, that France and Britain should be as strong as possible, and therefore not weakened by foreign support of subversive elements within their borders. At this stage it is well to bear in mind that recent outrage and conspiracy in France are known to have been fanned, not from Russia, but from quite another quarter.

This brief strategic survey leads to the conclusion that there are only two Powers in Europe, Germany and Italy, from whom an aggressive policy may be feared: all the rest are so eager for peace that they have been ready to accept humiliation rather than even the risk of war. We may note in passing that while Hitler arms to the teeth, he is full of verbal condemnations of war, and that though he has tried out new weapons of war in Spain, he has not yet made a war: whereas Mussolini has not merely waged two wars in defiance of many treaties and commitments, but loses no opportunity of preaching naked militarism as an ideal. Whether this represents a real difference between the two Dictator states, we shall have to consider later.

Obviously Italy alone has very great nuisance value, but is not a supreme danger to Britain and France combined, even though, as we saw, there are abundant grounds for distrusting her leader and suspecting his designs of conquest. It is only when allied in actual war with the infinitely more formidable Germany, that Italy becomes a danger. *Hence for the two Western Powers the crux of the whole European situation is the German problem.* An agreement with Italy is no substitute for an agreement with Germany: it is hardly even a palliative of the existing situation. Its attainment would certainly force Germany to alter her tactics, but it would not bring her to her knees, or even induce her to renounce her designs: it would at most lead her to postpone them, but incite her to further effort, in the consciousness of a real, and no longer an imaginary, encirclement. On the other hand, an agreement with Germany means the stabilisation of European peace, and the probability of restored international trade, for at least a generation to come: and it seems reasonable to suppose that neither Italy nor any other Power could challenge or upset it. It is admittedly the most difficult problem that faces the statesmen of today: but for that very reason it must be boldly faced, and every effort made to attain it, for the alternative is political bankruptcy and material ruin for Europe as a whole.

BRITISH AIMS AND COMMITMENTS

In the light of this thesis, let us examine realistically first British aims and commitments, then the alternatives that confront Germany, and, finally, the obstacles, material and moral, that must be boldly faced before a *détente* can be achieved.

The main lines of British policy are comparatively simple. The abstract principles of Peace and Security find a new definition in the fact that there is no part of the world in which war can break out without injuriously affecting British interests and British commerce, and that the first duty incumbent upon Britain is the defence of her world-wide Commonwealth of Nations and Dependencies. It follows logically and inevitably from this that Sea Power is her foremost instrument of defence, and that the size and character of her navy is determined almost equally by the strategic needs of these islands and by the necessity of maintaining the sea routes to America, Asia, Africa and Australasia. As Britain would already seem to have reached her utmost expansion, peace is more than ever desirable, in order to be able to develop the Empire's resources without the strain and risk of warlike expenditure or warlike adventure: and she therefore has a natural bond of interest with those other countries which seek no further expansion. Any instrument of peace must be of paramount importance to her, and it is therefore no exaggeration to affirm that Britain has a greater interest than any other Power in the maintenance and strengthening of the League of Nations and of that international order of which it is the expression. The alternative is a reversion to "the European anarchy", and we are already learning by bitter experience how infinitely more expensive, both materially and spiritually, are its unlimited liabilities than the pooled risks of collective action. Those who thought that the new order, or indeed any order whatsoever, is attainable without risk, had never attempted to think clearly or "deeply" on international problems.

Viewed from another angle, our special interest in universal peace is that of a nation which, it is true, in earlier times fought many wars for commercial aims, but which, at any rate for the last century, has expanded and flourished by peaceful trading, and which knows that full prosperity cannot return to the world (and hence the spectres of unemployment and social unrest cannot be banned) until the delicate mechanism of international trade and finance can in some measure be re-established. For this, and for the return of general confidence which would follow from it, international co-operation on some such lines as those of Geneva is indispensable: failing that, European anarchy will dominate the economic no less than the political field.

Next to the supreme interest of a guaranteed World Peace must always stand the maintenance of friendship, and the avoidance of conflict, with the United States. Here the bond of a common language is far superior to that community of blood about which there is so much sentimental exaggeration: it is, moreover, an immense asset and source of strength to both nations, if they know how to use it. Despite the considerable, and not always ungrounded, fear on the one side of designs of exploitation by the other, events are slowly bringing home to both nations the need for co-operation (I of course deliberately choose a word that is far short of "alliance") in the defence of free and representative institutions, which find themselves for the moment on the defensive. Such co-operation is needed to rally the lesser democracies throughout the world: its breakdown might easily mean their extinction. Co-operation will be easy in proportion as we eschew the methods and policy of those countries which, in President Roosevelt's words, "have impatiently reverted to the old belief in the law of the sword".

From these fundamentals we pass to Continental policy. As ever in the past, and perhaps more than ever before, any bid for the hegemony of Europe must at once arouse our opposition, since it must inevitably threaten those two strategic zones which are our vital concern—the Low Countries and the North Sea because of access to our shores and to London, the heart of our Empire: the Mediterranean because through it still passes our arterial route to the East. If the first of these concerns us no less today than in 1795 or in 1830, or in 1914, the second concerns us more than ever, since to our interest in the Suez Canal and the Red Sea is now added our interest in Palestine and in the evolution of the whole Arab world. Thanks to the modern problem of oil fuel the Eastern Mediterranean has come to interest us in much the same way as did the Baltic in the days when supplies of hemp and tar and timber were no less vital to the British Navy. A Power that challenges our security in the Mediterranean by excessive development of its sea and air power is to us no less a menace than a Power that seeks to control the North Sea or the Irish Channel: that our policy has for over a century been one of "live and let live", involving no danger to riparian states, is abundantly shown by the attitude of all the lesser Mediterranean Powers, and indeed by Italy herself in the forty years preceding the Great War.

Today these considerations apply with almost equal force to France, to whom the fate of Belgium and Holland is as vital as it is to Britain, and who is more interested than ever in the past in maintaining her connections with North Africa and in preventing control of any part of Spain by any foreign Power. These common interests between Britain and France are supplemented by overwhelming considerations of strategy and aerial defence, of population, of a common devotion to free institutions, and of an almost universal desire for peace among the population. Even the cynic who ascribes this pacific trait to repletion cannot deny its existence. France and Britain, in the circumstances of the modern world, are linked by such intimate and peremptory ties, as not even mutual antipathy, if it existed, could resist. "British isolation", which is of course merely a hypocritical phrase for the abandonment and betrayal of France, is really not far from being a physical impossibility: in any case, if made a reality, it would place Britain at the mercy of a hostile combination, which France would probably have no choice but to join. We should very quickly discover the truth of Guizot's words, that "the isolation of a Great Power is always the result of a fault committed by it". Alone, Britain is the most vulnerable of all Powers: and yet there are still individuals sufficiently devoid of sanity to advocate isolation on lines that would brand us to all time with the name of Perfidious Albion. If we cannot secure the reconstruction of the League on a sound and comprehensive basis, we must continue to make our reckonings on the old basis of strategy and Power Politics, and in that event we need all the alliances and understandings which we can find.

The great French historian Albert Sorel, surveying European policy in the eighteenth century, called Britain "the only redoubtable adversary of the French Revolution, because she was the only one who opposed it with analogous forces—with national principles and popular passions". Today we have entered a new phase in Europe, in which their national principles are harmonised and their popular passions abated, and in which they are therefore able to combine in defence of our common Western civilisation against those intolerant and retrograde theories upon which the dictators of the Right and Left are trying to rebuild a militarised and enslaved Europe. Moreover, there probably never was a moment in our history when isolation was less attainable or more dangerous if attained, or again a moment when our weight, thrown judiciously into the scales, was more likely to be decisive.

Are such general aims as these incompatible with Anglo-German friendship? Let us consider realistically Germany's aims and grievances in the world of today, and how far we can meet them. But let us at the outset be quite clear on one point. Once before in our history—from 1791 to 1814—Britain was "up against" the Revolution in its starkest and most aggressive form. Today Britain and a calmer France find themselves together in defence against the new revolutionary currents surging through Europe and assuming different forms according to the different nations upon which they work. The savagery which marked the Russian Revolution and the vastness of the social upheaval which it caused were facts which not even the veriest tyro in political affairs could overlook. But there are still many people who do not realise, despite the constant assurances of the Duce and the Führer themselves, that Italy and Germany are in the throes of a no less revolutionary process; and that throughout Europe there is a vast transformation of standards, moral, spiritual and material, the pace of which is being daily hastened on the one hand by the intoxication of absolute power and on the other by the pressing exigencies of finance: above all, that the difference between the three great tyrannies is one of degree rather than of essence. The oldest of the three has reached a new and more nationalistic stage of evolution, in which hundreds of the original theorists of Bolshevism are put against the wall, and lip-service is again paid to "democracy" amid "elections" which are a grotesque parody of the word. The leader of the second has for fifteen years, in an ascending scale of shrillness, poured contempt on liberal institutions, individualism, and freedom of thought, and sought to inculcate militarist ideas in a nation whose whole cultural tradition has for centuries run in other directions. The third and most dangerous, because the most central, virile and concentrated, is moving with breathless speed towards a position in which the State is an all-embracing Moloch, yet is deliberately identified with the person of a single man. There has not been for many centuries such a concentration of power in the hands of one man as that which Adolf Hitler has achieved: all constitutional checks, including budget control, have vanished, no elected body exists, all rival parties have been suppressed, the press, the universities, education, are "gleichgeschaltet" (thank God, there is no such word in the English language!), the army, the diplomatic and civil services, are his nominees. The Churches are muzzled, and the propagandists of the regime pursue methods of deification in all but name. Let us then be under no illusions.

If we can establish contact and conclude a firm bargain with a Dictator of this calibre, the nation will follow him blindly, until that inevitable day when God strikes him dead, or till that day when (*mutatis mutandis*) the populace of Paris learns that Robespierre is fallen, and once again rejoices in the sun. But if meanwhile the Dictator has other aims and does not will an accord with us, there will be no result: for the floating feelings of goodwill towards us in a spoon-fed and helot population will be of no avail. In Britain the keen desire of the great mass of our people to live in close amity with individual Germans is a directive, an incentive, to Government policy: in Germany there is no such equivalent. Only the Man and his innermost ring have the slightest say, and this is of course equally true of cowed Italy and distant Russia.

CONDITIONS OF AN ANGLO-GERMAN ACCORD

There are certain premises which must be laid down very clearly as the point of departure for any Anglo-German understanding. In the first place, such an understanding cannot be effected piecemeal; concessions in one field must be contingent upon agreement in every other field, and the structure stands or falls as a whole. To take only one example out of many, a colonial agreement (of which we shall have to speak in a moment) assumes an entirely different meaning according to what is agreed upon for other parts of the world.

In the second place, the two sides must acknowledge as their aim not merely a bilateral bargain, but a return to some kind of international order (possibly based upon a reform of the League: that is a matter for discussion). Negotiations would be quite unprofitable unless we were from the outset certain that Herr Hitler's offers of 21 May 1935 and 7 March 1936 (to re-enter the League, on terms) still hold good: for a pact with Berlin, much as we desire it, would be too dearly bought at the price of sacrificing the ideals of international arbitration and collective security. Germany may perhaps insist upon certain reservations, and there are points even of great importance upon which it may prove possible to agree to differ: but there must be no ambiguity as to our ultimate aim, and nothing must be conceded such as might serve to obstruct the path towards it.

In the third place, it must be made clear beyond all possibility of doubt that there can be no question of transferring our allegiance or friendship from France to Germany; and that an Anglo-German understanding is inconceivable, and indeed not of much value, save on a triangular basis. Perhaps the most fatal blunder of the German Government in the decade preceding the Great War was the obstinacy with which it clung to the idea that Britain's repeated overtures and negotiations were to lead to "a new orientation of English policy",[1] whereas in reality Grey was pursuing the fundamentally different aim of bridging the gulf between the two main camps in Europe. Under the changed circumstances of today, one thing remains unchanged—our anxiety to prevent the gulf between rival political tendencies from becoming unbridgeable. But we must recognise that the prospect of success is smaller, because the major part of Europe is now in the grip of men who do not wish it bridged, but merely to force us to take sides, whether we will or not. It will greatly simplify the situation if it is made clear to them that, whatever happens, we are neither so perfidious nor so mad as to abandon France or to leave her interests out of the reckoning.

With these three axioms established, let us consider how German grievances or claims can be met. First come certain matters of sentiment and prestige to which German opinion has all along attached great (some would say exaggerated—but that is for the Germans to decide) importance: and it may reasonably be argued that an entirely voluntary and frank recantation of certain errors connected with the Peace would create a more favourable atmosphere in which to discuss the major issues. The Covenant of the League should be detached from the Peace Treaties. Their economic clauses should be

---

[1] On 19 February 1913 the German Chancellor, Bethmann Hollweg, writing to the Austro-Hungarian Foreign Minister Berchtold, used this phrase to define his aim. William II's whole Moroccan policy rested on a similar aim.

declared to be inoperative. The so-called "War-Guilt Clause" (Article 231) should be specifically defined as aimed solely at establishing a legal basis for claims of damage: and a further statement should be added, distinguishing between the immediate and the ultimate causes of the War, and declaring this to be a fitting matter for investigation by an international committee of historical experts.[1] The assertion that Germany is unfit to possess or administer colonies should be unreservedly withdrawn.

THE COLONIAL PROBLEM

It follows quite logically from this that we cannot refuse on principle to discuss the possibility of Germany recovering old, or acquiring new, colonies. But perhaps more than any other this question is dependent upon Germany's attitude to the wider problems of world policy. As a final step towards removing that sense of inferiority and injustice of which there is so much loose talk, it deserves to be very seriously considered: but ultimately it depends upon her readiness to re-enter the collective system, to renounce war as an instrument of policy, to abandon the armament race, and accept some general system of limitation and control. In other words, colonial concessions are only possible on a basis of World Order and international, as opposed to bilateral, discussion: but for the attainment of this it would be worth paying a very high price. On the *present basis* of Power Politics (for my whole argument rests on the assumption that the League system is in abeyance) such concessions would be merely in the nature of Danegeld, and indeed Danegeld such as would obviously whet instead of satisfying hostile appetites. So long as this basis holds, we must be careful not to provide a possible enemy with new submarine stations and airports which could threaten our overseas com-

[1] A first step in this direction was taken by a small group of German and French historians, who met in November 1935 and embodied their discussions in 39 points, as "a first step" for further discussion. See the text as published in *American Historical Review* for January 1938, edited by Professor Bernadotte Schmitt, of Chicago. In France they were published in three leading educational journals, but *Vergangenheit und Gegenwart* refused publication, though *Nationalsozialistische Erziehung* did print them.

munications, and very chary of supplying them with certain raw materials whose shortage is at present the main deterrent upon warlike adventure.

It is impossible to admit that Germany has any *legal* claim to the lost colonies: they were conquered from her, and she ceded them unreservedly to the major Allied Powers, who of their own accord undertook to administer them under mandates supervised by the League. But a *moral* claim must be admitted, in view of the terms of the Fifth Point of President Wilson (see above, p. 68): and it is also possible to criticise the Allied Powers for their failure to observe the Congo Act of 26 February 1886, whereby the territories of the Four Powers[1] in Central Africa were "to remain neutralised in the event of war, and not to be used as a base of warlike operations".

There are, however, three further important grounds upon which the Germans base their claim for restoration. Firstly, they contend that a great nation such as Germany is entitled to what Herr Hitler calls "colonial equality" (a phrase greatly in need of definition, for there is no trace of real "equality" as between the present possessors of colonies), and that it is highly derogatory to withhold from them the advantages which small countries like Holland or Portugal possess. This is clearly an appeal to prestige, which naturally weighs with a dictatorial regime, but must be treated with respect as one which British democracy has not been slow to use in other connections. It is, however, legitimate to retort that by once accepting the arguments that every Continental Great Power has the right to be a great Colonial Power, or "that abstract justice demands that great industrial nations should have colonies", we are landed, as Mr Amery argues, "in a completely hopeless situation", since such arguments are "based on the idea that colonies are merely properties to be exploited, and not administrative responsibilities".[2] That was undoubtedly the old eighteenth-century view, on which we, no less than other colonial Powers,

[1] I.e. France, Britain, Belgium, Germany.

[2] "The Problem of Cession of Mandated Territories", *International Affairs* (January 1937), p. 12.

acted: but during the last generation the principle of trusteeship of backward races has made such strides and won such full acceptance, that we cannot now go back on it, even at the risk of being dubbed hypocrites by those who have entered the lists late in the day and with old-fashioned ideas. It is one of those "imponderables" which cannot be weighed, but which we neglect at our peril.

Secondly, they contend that the restoration of their colonies (and General von Epp, as head of the Colonial Department of the National Socialist Party, is careful to insist that Germany "has in mind *only her own* colonies") is a necessary step towards removing the shortage of raw materials from which she is suffering. No serious evidence has yet been adduced for this claim. In the last year before the War the German colonies only accounted for 0·6 per cent of Germany's export trade and for 0·5 per cent of her imports, and were responsible for a heavy deficit of revenue. On the other hand, Lord Lugard has pointed out that in the post-war period "there has been no restriction whatsoever upon exports from British territories in Africa, that any rebate of customs offered by Britain or the Dominions is at the expense of their own revenue, that a similar rebate can be offered by any foreign country, and that owing to the fall of the price of primary products they are more than ever eager to sell to any buyer".[1] "Nor is it the case that currency difficulties are an obstacle to the sale of imported goods in any British dependency", except in the sense that Germany and Italy, thanks to overspending and rearmament on a vast scale, have seen fit "to place an embargo on the export of money in order to save their currency from depreciation". But as Lord Lugard further points out, German trade with Tanganyika amounted to close upon £1,000,000 in 1934 and 1935, while Italy was able to purchase in British colonies large quantities of food for her army in Abyssinia. "The ability to purchase depends on the quality and the price of goods in free competition with those of other nations": and to take once more the

[1] See his two very weighty articles, "The Claims to Colonies", in *The Times*, 13 and 14 January 1936.

instance of Tanganyika, Germany between 1933 and 1936 greatly increased her imports there and created for herself a favourable balance of £873,000. In this connection it is well to stress a further point made by Mr Amery in his public reply to Herr von Ribbentropp's demand for Colonies at the Leipzig Fair (March 1937). In 1935–6 Germany imported as much raw materials as in 1929, on the eve of the Great Depression, but a large part of these imports, which should have supplied peaceful German industry, was diverted to intensive rearmament. The German Government cannot have its cake and eat it: while it continues to arm on the present fantastic scale, it cannot expect us to facilitate the supply of materials which might at any moment be directed against ourselves.

It is, however, only fair to add that, while in the A and B class of Mandates (to which Tanganyika, Cameroon and Togoland belong) "equality of commercial opportunity" is stipulated and observed, a much more serious problem has been created by the extension of the Ottawa Agreements to the British Crown Colonies. Here it must suffice for my present purpose to allude to the statesmanlike suggestion of one of the most ardent champions of Ottawa, Mr Amery, that our most practical contribution would be a free surrender of our claims under the Most-Favoured-Nation Clause.

Thirdly, the Germans contend that the recovery of their lost colonies is rendered essential by the pressure of population at home. To this the obvious reply is that during the decade 1904–13 the German colonies only accounted for 0·13 per cent of the total German emigration, and that when the War broke out, there were only 20,000 Germans in all their colonies combined! Those best qualified to judge inform me that in Tanganyika (which alone of their former colonies offers serious openings to white settlers) the number of new white settlers whom it might be possible to place there during the next ten years (if sufficient capital were forthcoming) could not possibly exceed 40,000. It will thus be seen that restoration to Germany would scarcely touch the edge of the problem of her surplus population. Similarly, the Italians, in the hill country of Eritrea (where there are 2000 square miles suitable for white settlers), have in fifty years settled 400 unofficial adult Italians (of whom only 84 were engaged in agriculture): and the prospects of settlement in Abyssinia on a scale likely to affect Italy's population problem are extremely slight. To quote Lord Lugard once more, "It is to the temperate zones in North and South America, in Siberia or in the Pacific, that the surplus population of Europe must look for colonisation."[1]

Even if all other obstacles were surmounted, it seems clear that the British Government, if it had the sole power to restore the German colonies (and this is of course not the case, since France, South Africa, Australia, New Zealand and Japan are also directly concerned), would only really be contributing to a solution of the first of the three claims—prestige—but in no way to the third—population—and only very inadequately to the second—raw materials. A section of German opinion is so little acquainted with the relevant facts as not to realise that Australia, New Zealand and South Africa are independent nations which cannot be coerced from the centre of the Empire.

To the second claim, however, Britain has already made a tentative contribution, through the mouth of Sir Samuel Hoare as Foreign Secretary, when at Geneva he offered an investigation into the means whereby a better distribution of raw materials could be effected. There can be no doubt that British opinion would welcome the establishment of an international commission, on which Germany and Italy were represented, with the double aim of establishing the actual facts and of making practical recommendations. There are, however, two conditions: it must be organised by the League of Nations, in close co-operation with the Mandates Commission, and the Governments represented must pledge themselves in advance to the integral publication of its findings in their respective countries, thus ensuring that dissentient or minority views of all kinds reached the interested public. So far Germany appears to be unwilling to share in any such discussion, if it is held under

[1] "The Bases of the Claim for Colonies", *International Affairs*, January 1936.

the auspices of Geneva: but the deadlock thus caused could probably be overcome.

It is not too much to affirm that the third claim, of an overseas outlet for the German population, cannot be solved in Africa, and therefore is not merely a matter between Germany and Britain. This is only another way of saying that, apart from a reversion to the old method of conquest, it can only be solved by international discussion between all the colonial Powers, either at Geneva or at a specially convoked Conference. This course would probably be acceptable to British opinion, if it formed part of Germany's return to the basis of international discussion and arbitration as a substitute for war, but certainly not otherwise. Subject, however, to this all-important proviso, there are many in this country who would not rule out of the discussion the possibility of cessions not only of mandated territory, but even of territory which we hold in absolute sovereignty. But let it be made clear from the very outset that a German Colonial Empire in West Africa, to which by far the major contribution would have to come from Britain, would have to be on a really generous scale—not something which the donor could then describe to his home public as of trifling importance.[1] It is obvious that no such solution is possible without consulting, and obtaining the consent and presumably the co-operation of France, Belgium, Portugal, South Africa and perhaps Spain—a co-operation which it will not be easy to obtain.

Another idea, much canvassed and not unfavourably regarded by some sections of opinion, is that certain of the existing mandates should be transferred to Germany, and that, to prove that nothing derogatory was intended, Britain should voluntarily place some of her African Crown Colonies under the mandatory system, pending the moment when all colonies not self-governing or near the stage of self-government, should be placed under a general mandatory system, under which

---

[1] Incredible as it might seem, the suggestion is constantly being made in discussion and in the press, that South-West Africa might be restored, and in the same breath that it is worthless desert!

questions of immigration and trade would be considered from a broad international angle. It is necessary to add that such a solution, desirable as it may be, bristles with difficulties, and that the first of them is the complete disinclination of Germany, in her present mood, to accept any international settlement.

That disinclination is partly due to ultra-nationalistic susceptibilities, which optimists hope will slowly calm down. But it is also due to the knowledge that there are two *sine qua non* conditions of a colonial settlement with Germany, upon which British public opinion would be absolutely certain to insist. The first is that Germany, in taking over such colonies, should give the most explicit guarantees to maintain the existing legislation in favour of the native population and to ensure that their status should not deteriorate. Even then it is likely to arouse determined opposition, and indeed above all in that very section of public opinion which is most enlightened and best informed. On the other hand, it is possible to argue that the natives, not having been consulted when we took them over, need not be consulted when we surrender them, always providing that their rights are duly guaranteed. There are some who argue that Germany's record of treatment of natives ought to debar us for ever from ceding colonial territory to her: but without for a moment minimising the brutalities of Karl Peters or the methods adopted towards the Herreros, it is impossible for us to pretend that Germany alone of African Powers was guilty of atrocities, or to deny that she had already produced more than one most enlightened administrator, men such as Dernburg or Solf. Certainly neither Kenya nor the Union of South Africa has the right to assume a high moral tone in this question.

Much more serious in the eyes of many is the argument that a nation which is engaged in reducing to helotry and utter ruin a section of its own home population and deliberately branding them as second-class citizens before the law for purely racial reasons, irrespective of conduct or of cultural standing, is not fit to be entrusted with the government of subject races in any Continent. This argument is not easy to meet, save on the assumption that anti-Semitism is a passing aberration, deeply humiliating to many Germans, and that the separation which exists between black and white in Africa is in itself a guarantee that the Bantu races will not be treated as the Jews.

The second condition which is likely to be upheld at all costs is that such colonies as Germany might acquire by agreement should under no circumstances be converted into naval stations or military airports, and that the black population should not be armed, save on the diminutive scale of our East African possessions, where the black regiments are really mere police forces. If Germany should object that the latter undertaking places her in a position inferior to both France and Italy, who have black armies, the answer is that this is an inferiority which we share, and that it is with us above all that, for good or for bad, the bargain will have to be made. All that Dr Schnee, in his able statement of the German case,[1] says of the conscription of Black Africa is likely to be endorsed by almost everyone in Britain who likes to inform himself on African questions: and we can be relied upon to miss no opportunity of urging this point of view upon France (with the Italy of Mussolini it would be waste of time, and the existence of that Italy prejudges the French answer!). But in the meantime we are bound to stress the strategic aspects of the whole colonial question, until such time as Germany sees fit to damp down the frenzy of her militarism. Above all, she must of her own accord preclude herself from ever in future putting forward the argument that the possession of colonies forces her to provide armaments for their safety.

The above survey of the colonial problem makes no pretence at being exhaustive: but it should suffice to bring home its extraordinary complexity to those who glibly demand an immediate colonial settlement.

THE OBSTACLES

Let us in conclusion return to the crux of the whole issue between ourselves and Germany, namely the question whether Herr Hitler's assurances of 21 May 1935 and 7 March 1936 still

[1] *German Colonization, Past and Future* (1926).

hold good, and whether he is ready to re-enter the international fellowship and renounce force as an instrument of policy. This question, after remaining in doubt for nearly two years, has been answered with even more than his habitual vehemence in the Reichstag speech of 20 February 1938. In it he repudiated the idea of ever returning to the League, declared his deep distrust of "so-called Conferences" and summarily dismissed such "international plans" as the Van Zeeland Report. In face of these very explicit statements we are bound to conclude that the Führer is not at present disposed to negotiate upon the only basis which we can accept—namely one of equality and peaceful intercourse inside the European Commonwealth of Nations. In demanding that we should scrap all the machinery of peaceful international accord and accept as a permanence the "European anarchy" to which his policy of unilateral repudiation has brought us all—for this, in almost so many words, is what he demands—he is asking too high a price for a settlement. We are therefore forced back upon the alternative of organising a "Peace Front" of the peace-loving nations, sufficiently strong to deter any would-be aggressor from warlike adventure, and of holding out grimly until the disordered finances of the dictatorial states bring them to a more reasonable frame of mind. Such a policy is less negative than would at first sight appear—and indeed involves much arduous constructive work: and though of course it has its dangers, it is less dangerous than any possible alternative in the present parlous state of world affairs.

It may be that the obstacles put in the way of an international understanding by Germany are in some degree tactical, in other words, upheld until certain demands can be extracted from us and certain guarantees given. If this be so, the obstacles can be overcome, given good will on both sides. But there must be no manner of doubt that our aim is a reconstruction, or revivification, of the League, not the triumph of Power Politics on the corpses of the smaller nations.

This difference of outlook is intimately connected with the Two Ideologies. As Mr Baldwin and Mr Eden have both repeatedly pointed out, we reject the choice, and prefer a middle way. But with the extreme intolerance and arrogance which characterises these modern dictatorships, they are bent upon forcing this choice upon us and the rest of the world. Nay, more, they are directing a frontal attack upon the very foundations of our whole political system. A century ago Tsar Nicholas and Metternich often refused to distinguish between the various shades of progressive opinion, lumping not merely the extremists of the Left, but liberals, radicals and advocates of constitutional government together as in effect revolutionaries; but neither they nor Napoleon III at his worst period conducted subversive propaganda in liberal countries. The most that they attempted was to provide active help for kindred thrones and regimes when threatened by open revolution, and their main complaint against the Western powers was that they supported liberal movements, notably in Spain and Portugal. The chief offender in this respect, Palmerston, was able to make the effective rejoinder that his aim was not to achieve revolution, but to forestall or avert it by timely concession and reform. *Nous avons changé tout cela.* Today the dictatorial states are engaged in driving the free states on to the defensive: their leaders denounce not only revolution, but "democracy" (a word which is today more than ever in need of definition), and not only democracy but liberalism, constitutional and representative institutions as poisonous and out-of-date, and even as identical with Marxism or leading logically to it!—an identification far more arrogant than any attempted by Tsar Nicholas. They go much further than this, pouring forth money like water on political and press propaganda in many countries, and conducting intensive wireless campaigns across this or that frontier, and as they themselves possess unrestricted control of all that is written or publicly spoken within their own bounds, they are able to prevent any possibility of rejoinders reaching their own people. As if this were not enough, Herr Hitler, in his recent Reichstag speech (20 February 1938), not only denounced the foreign press for its criticisms of his own regime,[1]

[1] Here he was careful to confuse the issue by quoting the absurdities of the "popular press"—incidentally the very press which gives him support.

but protested against "intolerable press agitation conducted under the guise of free expression of opinion",[1] and darkly threatened reprisals on the part of Germany. Needless to say, the original arch-offender was Russia, who for years conducted a determined Communist propaganda in the West, taking especial advantage of the complete press freedom prevailing in England. But since Russia entered the League and adopted a more moderate foreign policy, this aggressive propaganda has been greatly modified, if not entirely abandoned, the main reason being that it no longer suits Russian interests that the internal strength and unity of her political allies in the West should be undermined. For some years past, then, it is Germany, and to a lesser degree Italy, who have been copying Russian Bolshevik methods of propaganda abroad.

Time and again, in many changing situations, our statesmen have made it clear that with all our attachment to the free institutions which we have slowly built up in these islands, we do not presume to make identity of political views or systems the condition of our friendship, and that geographical or other interests may sometimes outweigh other considerations. Our cordial relations with the three autocrats of the Grand Alliance against Napoleon I, or forty years later with Napoleon III, or again the relations of the French Republic with Alexander III or with Stalin, serve to illustrate this point. But in the words of Signor Mussolini (already quoted on page 181), while "analogous systems of politics and ideas" do serve as a bond of union between two countries, it is also true that "such sympathies and elective affinities must not guide in a dominant, still less in an exclusive, fashion the foreign policy and international relations of great peoples". None the less, friendship becomes increasingly difficult if totalitarian statesmen are to denounce and calumniate the fundamental institutions of the West and subsidise dictatorial putsches in those few countries where a democratic, or even semi-democratic, regime still

[1] It is possible to sympathise with his hit at "the insolent habit of writing letters to the head of a foreign state", practised by some members of Parliament. But that is because all power rests in his hands.

survives. When Herr Hitler in March 1936 declared that "it is not wise to believe that in so small a house as Europe it is possible to have differing conceptions of right", he was in effect arguing that in Europe there is no longer any room for Liberty or the representative institutions which he and the Duce are never tired of attacking. Herein lies the real gravity of the European situation.[1]

What makes a truce between a totalitarian and a free regime so difficult is that the former, presuming upon the advantages which modern communications and modern weapons (especially the three most reactionary of all, the telephone, the machine-gun and the aeroplane) confer upon any central government, extend the claims of obedience which they exact from their subjects to every sphere of public and private life, and to a degree undreamt of under the older absolutisms. The conception of "Masse-Mensch" (Mankind in the Mass) which, as portrayed by the Socialist playwright Ernst Toller, is now taboo in Germany, is the very conception which the National Socialists themselves are engaged in enforcing. The rights of the individual as against the all-powerful State are abruptly denied. Liberty of thought has been replaced by the dragooning of the universities and the schools and a careful censorship of all the instruments of instruction. Liberty of speech and writing has been replaced by holocausts of books such as recall the days of the Spanish Inquisition, by an absolute control of press, publishing and wireless, and by the conversion of the broad thoroughfares of scholarship and literature into political one-way streets. The old norms of justice, with their roots deep in the past, have been undermined by the ruthless identification of State and Party: and the degradation of one section of the community, the Jews, to an inferior status before the law, is a defiance of the elements of law and justice as hitherto accepted in civilised countries. Above all, liberty of religion is openly challenged by a pagan and intolerant creed, which is

[1] The reader is urged to read a brilliant and courageous little book entitled *We or They*, in which Mr Hamilton Fish Armstrong, editor of the American quarterly *Foreign Affairs*, takes Mussolini at his word.

bent upon creating a gulf between the rising generation and its parents: and the ideal of leadership—one of the greatest of which the human mind is capable—is being perverted by a demand for complete and unreasoning surrender of intellect and will to the "*Sic Volo, Sic Jubeo*" of a single man. If the Protestant in me protests against this repudiation of Luther's cardinal principle of the right of private judgment, I can at the same time share the indignation of the Catholic at the attempt to subordinate the Church and all its traditions of learning and faith to the orders of a fallible but autocratic state.

That all this militates against close and cordial contacts between the nations situated on either side of the great "divide", and that "*incompatibilité de mœurs*" between them goes very deep, it would be the merest folly to deny. But this does not mean that it renders an accommodation impossible. All depends upon whether the aims pursued by the dictatorial states are compatible with peace and international order—in other words, whether or not Germany has designs upon the territorial *status quo*. (The only other states of Europe which could be suspected of such designs are Hungary and Italy, and of these the former has repeatedly disclaimed violence as a means towards revision and lacks the military force to achieve it against the Little Entente, while the latter's plans of further aggrandisement, if they exist, relate to extra-European lands.) A number of alternative policies lie open to an aggressive Germany, and it seems probable that the adoption of one rather than another would depend upon the accident of a given situation. In the first place, there have always been rival eastern and western schools of thought in the matter of German foreign policy. The leaders of the former—the Emperor William I, Bismarck, Schweinitz and others—held that close friendship with Russia was essential if Germany was to be secure on the West and to avoid being caught in the pincers of a Franco-Russian alliance. This of course had a dynastic basis, but for eighteen years after the War and the fall of the dynasties the German General Staff continued to work on similar lines, until Hitlerian policy pro-

duced the Franco-Soviet Pact. The other school held that Russia
was the arch-enemy of the German race, that the best hope of
German expansion lay on her Eastern frontier, and especially
in those Baltic lands where German colonisation had once played
so vital a part. It therefore advocated close friendship with
Britain on Russophobe lines, and avoidance of naval and colonial
rivalry, in the calculation that in face of a friendly Britain and
an allied Austria-Hungary France would be helpless when the
final struggle with Russia came. Unfortunately the folly of
William II mixed up the two policies: first his renunciation of
Bismarck's Reinsurance Treaty with Russia opened the path
for the latter's alliance with France, and then at a later date his
naval policy forced Britain into ever closer relations with the
"Franco-Russe" and made Germany increasingly dependent
on the Austrian alliance. In the end Germany fell between
two stools. To judge from various passages in *Mein Kampf*,
Herr Hitler would seem to have realised the errors of his less
autocratic predecessor on the German throne, and to favour
friendship with Britain and Italy and a renunciation of overseas
ambitions, in order to concentrate upon the conquest of Eastern
territory from Russia. By this means the Germans, by reverting
to their great colonising days in the twelfth and thirteenth
centuries, would expand during the next hundred years into
a nation of 250 millions and thus presumably dominate Europe,
and perhaps the world. There is nothing to show that Hitler
has in any way renounced this dream: and his steadfast denunciation of the Bolshevik danger—which really was a danger
when his book first appeared, but has since lost much of its
offensive power outside Russia and is certainly well under control
in Nazi Germany—must be regarded as a smokescreen behind
which his designs upon the rich soil of the Ukraine are con-
cealed.

Fortunately for us all, Germany and Russia are not contiguous,
and it is not entirely obvious how Germany could carry into
effect such designs of conquest. An attack upon the Baltic
states could only be undertaken by sea; and therefore could
hardly take the world by surprise: the three states would have

no choice save to throw themselves into the arms of Russia, or if their hesitation in choosing between the devil and the deep sea were too marked, might easily be overrun by Russia before ever the Germans could arrive. An attack through Poland would undoubtedly meet with fierce resistance, for that country is obsessed with the fear of another war fought upon her soil, leading perhaps to yet another Partition. Nor would an offer of alliance against Russia and of territorial spoils in the event of success be likely to tempt Poland, since it would almost inevitably end in one or other of the two contingencies: war on her soil or partition. It is to be added that every Pole has at the back of his mind an incentive to vigilance and suspicion in the thought that, as in the past, Germany and Russia might exploit Polish dissensions and come to terms over Poland's dead body. Nor can this be dismissed as merely fantastic, for there are many who think that if Germany should ever attempt to translate the theories of "Blood and Soil" into practice, the natural scene for such an experiment of wholesale eviction and exploitation would be in the lands between the Oder and Vistula rather than in the rich, but all too remote, Ukraine.

There is a third possible line of advance to the South-East, but only after the resistance of Czechoslovakia and Roumania had been overcome by force; and it is difficult to see how this could be attained without a general European war, since Russia and France are pledged to help the former and Poland to help the latter. There remains yet another alternative—to abandon, or postpone, the idea of colonisation, but to permeate the Danubian states one by one, using the considerable German minorities in each of them as an instrument of political agitation, and thwarting all attempts at Danubian union, until "Mittel-Europa" becomes first an economic and then a political reality. Here, of course, it is all a matter of degree: for no one can seriously deny that Germany has an absolute right to be interested in the fate of her kinsmen abroad, and that these countries offer her a legitimate sphere of commerce, a source of raw materials and an outlet for her cultural influence. Her commercial interests are very great in all that region, and we have no right to look grudgingly on their development.

It is only if she came to threaten their independence or integrity that the other Powers could reasonably take exception: but it is significant that this fear is uppermost in the minds of all of them—Austria, Czechoslovakia, Hungary, Jugoslavia, Roumania, Bulgaria and Greece. It is widely believed that this necessarily slow and indefinite process of permeation which we have described as alone legitimate is not a policy which those who are at present in control of Germany will be content to apply, but on the contrary that it is of the very essence of their domineering totalitarian creed to hasten the pace and to impose their wishes, and that even if tactical reasons could avail to check their ardour, the urgency of their own economic situation spurs them on to action. Indeed, many close observers go still further and contend that their only real hope of escape from internal difficulties lies in foreign adventure, launched with such *élan* as to be irresistible and thus avoid a lengthy war in which their economic reserves would fail. If there is one thing calculated to encourage such designs in dictatorial minds, it is the attitude of our defeatist press in suggesting that the fate of Central Europe is no concern of ours—forgetting that the abandonment of Austria and Czechoslovakia to a German conqueror would mean the immediate submission of all the states lying between them and the Aegean, a Continental hegemony more absolute than that of Napoleon and the certain loss of our position in the Mediterranean. In that event the "perfidious" advocates of buying our colonial immunity with other people's property would speedily be faced by colonial demands couched in unmistakable terms of menace, and might see the Empire, isolated and distrusted, crumble before a concentrated attack.

Moreover, those who suppose that in the event of war arising out of a German bid for the mastery of Central Europe it would be possible to divide the Continent into two watertight compartments of "East" and "West", either cannot have fairly faced up to the problems to which this book is devoted, or are altogether incapable of clear political thinking. War, if it does come, will come so swiftly that alliances may have to be clinched by telephone, and bombs may be dropping on a capital city before even a Parliament actually in session has had time to meet and discuss the issues. In such circumstances the stark "indivisibility of peace" will emerge with overwhelming force, and within a few days the question whether the conflict began because of an Eastern or a Western commitment will be indistinguishable amid the din of aerial warfare.

The plain, brutal fact is, that for reasons of self-preservation Britain dare not abandon France, even if she were mean enough to desire it, that France in her turn cannot abandon her Eastern allies without being reduced to a precarious defensive in Europe, and that those who describe *"désintéressement"* as "realism" are simply inventing a synonym for "funk". Every man of sense in this country is deeply concerned at the thought of another war and realises that whatever its issue may be, it would inevitably shake the whole structure of the modern state to its foundations. But he must also realise that to assure the world that nothing will make him fight, and that he cares nothing for his neighbour's fate, is the surest way to encourage those who have no such aversion for the "steel-bath" of war, to lose him his loyal friends and to bring upon him the very catastrophe which he seeks to avoid.

There are only two ways of avoiding such a war—the honourable one of banding together all pacific elements in a final effort of conciliation, based on adherence to a World Order, or the craven one of divesting ourselves of the possessions which our fathers have brought together, and of the responsibilities and duties which have accrued from them, and crouching together in this crowded little island, while others scramble for the fragments. There are still many in the world today who, when they contemplate London and the Empire, re-echo the words of Blücher, "Oh, what a city to sack!"

Here is the true problem which faces the rising generation, and to which they alone can give a decisive answer. Is the British Commonwealth of Nations a worthy ideal, capable of further development, capable of setting an example of peace, liberty and ordered government for men of every race and creed, or was it from the first a mere foolish illusion, and has it in any case passed its prime? Is it possible to argue that, having been built up on principles of "grab and piracy", it is not worth defending against the glories of totalitarian doctrine? Was nothing saved for the world by those who gave their lives in the last war, even though the ideal of ending war is still unrealised? Have we forgotten the emancipation of whole nations? And are we to confess that the League and the Covenant also were acts of folly, hypocrisy or illusion, which it is time to repudiate, now that their inefficacy has been proved? It might as well be argued—with all reverence I say it—that Christianity is a lost creed because the Crucifixion was not followed by the Second Advent. Was not the saving of a free Commonwealth a great achievement, and may not its survival, if we show the necessary courage and endurance, yet avail to redress the balance in favour of Europe's lost liberties?

If the answer of British Youth be negative, it will mean a denial not merely of the democratic position, but of the Christian and ethical creed upon which our political institutions ultimately rest—a relapse into true anarchy of thought. Then indeed the leadership must pass to races which are ready to sacrifice themselves to a narrower, but more virile, creed. But negation will not save us from attack: it will only mean that, after first flinging away our honour, we shall be left to perish ingloriously and unaided.

XIII

AUSTRIAN EPILOGUE

Let us not in the foolish spirit of romance suppose that we alone could re-
generate Europe.   CANNING (1821)

Nothing is to be gained by any government by anything which looks like
doubt, hesitation or fear, while on the other hand a bold firm course founded
on right, and supported by strength, is the safest way of arriving at a satisfactory and peaceable result.   PALMERSTON (28 June 1853)

THIS book was finished on 17 February, but scarcely was
the ink dry than a fresh series of big events plunged
Europe into panic. The resignation of Mr Eden, the
renewal of Italo-British conversations, the Reichstag Speech
of 21 February, the Purge of the German High Command and
Diplomatic Service, the summons of Schuschnigg to receive
the Führer's orders at Berchtesgaden, his last-hour resort to a
plebiscite, and finally the sudden invasion and "Gleichschaltung" of Austria by the forces of the Reich—all this, coinciding
with renewed Italo-German activities in Spain and with a
recrudescence of the Russian terrorist purges, has created an
entirely new situation, of which statesmen in every camp are
now anxiously taking stock. There can be no question here of
detailed treatment: what is essential is that we should face these
events in a spirit of calm realism.

(1) In the first place, we may regret that Herr Hitler's
Reichstag Speech of 20 February 1938 should have coincided
with the Cabinet crisis in London, with the result that public
attention was mainly concentrated on the latter and failed to
realise that this utterance of the Führer—lasting almost three
hours—was much the most uncompromising and aggressive
which he had hitherto made, and presumably a foretaste of
things to come. In it he repudiated quite categorically all idea
of Germany ever re-entering the League—thus withdrawing
the explicit offers of earlier speeches—and he denied altogether
that the League was an instrument of justice. He made the

usual attacks upon democratic institutions and statesmen and roundly denounced the foreign press for the dropping of incendiary poison. The new feature was the emphasis laid upon German colonial claims, and the refusal to consider them as in any way part of a general settlement, but simply as a demand to be unconditionally fulfilled. Thus we must face the fact that the speech is a direct negation of all such proposals and conditions as are enumerated in my concluding chapter, and that a deadlock would seem to have been reached, unless we are prepared for unconditional surrender, without guarantees. At the same time he bluntly rejected all such proposals for international economic co-operation and appeasement as are laid down in the Van Zeeland report. That the speech was not merely a tactical one, intended to divert attention from Danubian designs, seems quite certain in view of the Führer's attitude to Lord Halifax during his Berlin visit last November, and to the British Ambassador in Berlin in February 1938. There are good grounds for believing that the solution outlined to Lord Halifax by Herr Hitler centred upon West Africa, and was skillfully contrived to create the maximum of friction between Britain and the four other countries interested in that region. Thus while Britain herself would only give up her share of Cameroon, French and Belgian Congo, Spanish Guinea and Portuguese Angola would also pass under German control. This would be a long stage towards the scheme propounded in 1918 by the well-known German colonial experts Albrecht Wirth and Emil Zimmermann, by which the new German African Empire would stretch unbroken from Liberia to the Orange river and link up across the continent with Tanganyika and Mozambique.[1] To Sir Nevile Henderson the Führer seems to have been far more categorical, and to have indicated that he would discuss nothing with Britain, save on a basis of full colonial restoration.

(2) The seizure of Austria, in its ruthless suddenness and overwhelming use of force, has few parallels in history since

[1] *Was muss Deutschland an Kolonien haben? Deutschland und der Orient* (Wirth): *Mittelafrika als Deutsche Kolonie* (Zimmermann)—Frankfurt, 1918.

the day when Frederick the Great wrested Silesia from Maria
Theresa, in defiance of solemn treaty pledges. Within a very
few days it became abundantly clear that the *coup* had long
been in preparation and had been worked out to the minutest
details. The plot of Dr Tavs, of the so-called "Pacification
Committee", which by terrorist action was to provide an
excuse for intervention from the Reich, but which was un-
masked by the Schuschnigg Government on the eve of the
final tragedy, shows that methods similar to those leading to
the murder of Dollfuss were about to be revived: and within
a few days of the *coup* the Nazi authorities no longer attempted
to conceal this attitude, for one of the first acts of Herr Himmler,
the dreaded chief of the Gestapo (Secret Police), was to lay a
wreath on the grave of the chief murderer of Dollfuss and to
appoint as Police Chief of Vienna one of those most implicated
in the plot of 1934. It appears that the name of Planetta is to be
added to those of Schlageter and Horst Wessel as heroes of the
rising generation! Every day brought fresh proof of the
thoroughness with which the *coup* had been planned: thousands
of troops and police occupied key positions, several hundred
aeroplanes circled over Vienna, and Nazi organisers, with arm-
bands and marching orders, appeared by magic to take over
thousands of posts throughout the country. The naïve Schuschnigg had gone to Berchtesgaden with the Tavs dossier under
his arm, thinking that he only had to lay the facts before the
Führer, in order to win his co-operation: but to his horror
he found that Hitler did not attempt to conceal his approval of
the plot.

Most essential of all to remember is the fact that this action
was launched by the Führer while his Foreign Minister, Herr
von Ribbentrop, was lunching with King George VI, and con-
ferring with the unsuspecting Mr Chamberlain and Lord
Halifax, and while the Duce, resigned to the view that Italy
could not take the risk of opposing the destruction of Austria,
had already pocketed the pledge of the Brenner in perpetuity
and of a free hand from Germany in the Mediterranean, but
graciously continued to negotiate with the British Cabinet.

It would therefore be absurd to deny that the Führer's action towards Austria has rendered immensely more difficult the negotiation of any agreement between our two countries, for the double reason that Germany's word today means the word of a single man, no less ruthless, and even more un-controlled, than Louis Quatorze, Napoleon or the Tsars of last century, and that he has time after time refused to be bound by his own most explicit and voluntary pledges. In seizing Austria he did not merely break the Treaties of Versailles and St Germain and brush aside the undertakings of France, Britain and Italy[1] in respect of Austrian independence, and again the Rome Protocols and other pledges of his Italian ally (17 March and 6 October 1934),[2] but also his own declaration of 21 May 1935—in the most solemn and important of all his speeches on foreign policy—that "Germany neither intends nor wishes to interfere in the internal affairs of Austria, to annex Austria or to conclude an Anschluss". Above all he broke the convention which he himself concluded with Austria on 11 July 1936, and the additional convention which he dictated to Herr von Schuschnigg as recently as 12 February 1938. The allegation that it was Austria, not Germany, which broke these two conventions will not stand examination for one moment: it is the old story of the wolf and the lamb. Herr von Schusch-nigg, it is true, was never entitled to call himself a democrat, and it may well be doubted whether he was wise in trying to rush through a plebiscite—a highly questionable instrument of policy in these days of mass suggestion and propagandist terror. But it is sheer hypocrisy on the part of the Führer and his followers to criticise Schuschnigg for doing the very thing which they had been demanding for Austria for several years past: and the violence of their response is in itself the best proof that they knew him to be certain of a large majority. The disgusting farce of a totalitarian plebiscite—already employed several

[1] 17 February 1934.
[2] On the latter date the Duce declared: "We have defended and will defend the independence of Austria, consecrated by the blood of a Chancellor who may have been small in stature, but whose spirit and soul were great."

times by Hitler in the Reich—will now be applied to unhappy Austria with all the overwhelming apparatus of intimidation at the disposal of Dr Goebbels and Herr Himmler. It is time to recognise that plebiscites are not merely ineffective but directly mischievous and misleading, when carried out under authoritarian control.

Regarding the *coup* realistically, we have to recognise that Hitler had certain very definite factors in his favour. The Nazi element in Austria probably did not exceed twenty-five per cent. of the total population, but it made up for its small numbers by its fanatical devotion and had a strong hold on the youth of the intellectual class. Moreover, there had always been a large element of waverers, torn between dislike of Nazism and Prussianism and a real belief in the "Great German" idea, and ready, when once the volcanic energy of Hitler had overborne all barriers, to accept Unity as the supreme good, throwing into the shade every question of political creed. Indeed, to almost every Austrian of whatever political views, the idea of armed resistance was hateful, not merely because of the disproportion of resources, but because it would have meant a veritable civil war as between Germans. And finally, it was clear that foreign aid could only have come from some *non-German* quarter, and that would automatically have provoked defections from the anti-Nazi camp. From all this it followed that from the moment when the Führer was prepared to snap his fingers at Europe and ruthless enough to bear down all internal resistance, there was nothing that could stop him from wreaking his will upon Austria. All this is no less essential to the picture as a whole than our knowledge of the terror meted out to Austrian Catholicism, to Austrian Socialism and to the Jews of Vienna. Not the least monstrous and incredible feature of the new regime is the announcement that Dr von Schuschnigg is to be put on trial before a Court to which, as lawful Chancellor of an independent state, he owes no possible jurisdiction.

It would be utter folly to minimise the bigness of the achievement. It is true that the Great War was needed to destroy the

balance of forces between Austria and Prussia, between Habsburg and Hohenzollern: but now this "Bohemian Corporal",
as Junker Hindenburg contemptuously called him, has shown
his superb mastery of political strategy and technique[1] and
completed a process which neither Metternich nor Bismarck
had come near achieving, and which we may consider as
irrevocable, except perhaps as regards some return to a federal
system within the "Great German Reich". In passing, we may
note how utterly worthless his assurances are: only fourteen
months have passed since he assured Europe that "the period
of surprises is now over", and now he has stunned the world
with another lightning stroke. Let us, accepting Mr Chamberlain's admission that the Rape of Austria "has created a new
situation in Europe", try to strike a balance of the changes.

(1) In the first place Germany acquires a further population
of $6\frac{1}{2}$ millions, and thus becomes a solid block astride the centre
of the Continent—"the 70 million Reich" of Great German
tradition.

(2) For National Socialism the gain is no less tremendous
than for Germany: for it swallows up the last centre of a South
German and Catholic culture, and destroys the possibility of
independent development on non-totalitarian lines. This corresponds to the lifelong aspirations of Adolf Hitler, who always
detested Austrian culture and the Habsburg State, desired the
Anschluss of German Austria to the Reich, and wrote of
Vienna, "the giant city, as the personification of incest".[2]

Obviously the many German racial fragments scattered
about Central and South-east Europe will be more than ever
impressed by the Nazi mentality and are likely to become an
increasing source of unrest to all the states in which they live:
we cannot count even upon Switzerland remaining immune
to this process.

(3) All the projects of Danubian confederation, co-operation
and economic union, however loosely planned—and there was

[1] Nowhere has this aspect been more admirably summarised than in
"The Shadow of the Sword" in the *Economist* of 19 March 1938.

[2] *Mein Kampf*, p. 135.

never any question of a reversion to the pre-war conditions of the defunct Habsburg Dual Monarchy—are now definitely destroyed, and with them such temporary expedients as the Rome Protocols, over which no tears need be shed. Only time can show what advantages the Reich will draw from its closer contacts with Danubian and Balkan markets: but even from Austria itself Germany can draw immense resources in timber and in iron ore; the valuable deposits in Styria are near the surface and capable of rapid exploitation on a far greater scale.

(4) Above all, the strategic position of Germany has been immensely strengthened. On the south she is now protected by the great mountain barrier of the Alps and on the south-east controls the gates into the great Hungarian plain. Perched upon the Brenner, she looks down the path followed for centuries by German invaders, and Italian public opinion asks itself nervously how long the ruthless Italianisation of "South Tirol" will be allowed to continue despite the Führer's pledge to the Duce, and whether the way to Trieste also is not now wide open. Germany's right to an economic outlet on the Adriatic cannot be denied, so long as it is not made the excuse for political hegemony. But this hegemony, from the new German frontier to the Adriatic, Aegean and Black Sea, is exactly what is feared by all the lesser countries which occupy that area. Incidentally, if once effective, it would enable Germany to snap her fingers at a naval blockade, in view of the vast resources in minerals, oil, wheat and timber which would then be at her disposal.

For the moment the strategic key lies in Czechoslovakia; it is only necessary to look at a physical map of Europe to see that the Bohemian lozenge, girt on three sides by high watersheds, stands out from the very centre of the Continent, and that Bismarck was not far wrong when he called it "a fortress created by God Himself". Bohemia's existing frontier is one of the oldest and best in Europe, and that is why it has stood for at least 800 years: within it there has been an age-long struggle for political power between Czech and German, of which the end is not yet, and the two races are still so inter-

mingled that no purely ethnographical frontier could be drawn
between them. In Hussite days the Czechs unaided held at
bay the crusading armies of all Europe (one of them led by a
royal English Cardinal, Henry of Beaufort): today they are
far more united, but the forces arrayed against them are more
formidable. The essence of this problem is that there is no serious
alternative between the present frontiers and the incorporation
within the Reich of the whole western half of the Republic,
Czech and German districts alike: any intermediate line between
these two extremes would not merely place the watersheds in
German control and destroy all possibility of military defence:
it would dislocate the Republic's industry and create an impossible economic situation, and yet it would inevitably leave
the two races still entangled in many districts.

What gives the Czech problem such importance is that
Czechoslovakia is the last democratic state to survive in Europe
east of the Rhine: and it is this situation to which the leaders
of the Reich are so anxious to put an end. They are well aware
that the German minority in Czechoslovakia—though it has
certain legitimate grievances and suffered more acutely than
the more agricultural Czechs during the height of the world
depression—is in no national danger whatsoever and indeed
has always enjoyed far more national rights, especially in
education, than any other German minority in Europe. But
so long as the country is governed in the spirit of Masaryk and
Beneš, on Western democratic lines, it is a rallying ground for
such remnants of democratic tradition as still survive under the
four reactionary Balkan dynasties. This explains the periodic
wireless and press campaigns conducted against Czechoslovakia
as a "Bolshevik" state, when all the time no country in Europe
is so immune from the Bolshevik danger. The best proof that
this is so is the strong position of the Catholic Church inside
Czechoslovakia—purified and strengthened by the religious
troubles of 1919–21—and the consistent support given by the
Holy See to a Republic whose leaders stand for progressive
thought, but who fully respect the tradition of a free Church
in a free State. Once let the Czech fortress fall, and the tide of

totalitarian state doctrine will flood across the Danubian and Balkan area: Britain's negative policy, and her failure to give due encouragement to those democratic elements which are quite logically at one and the same time democratic, Francophil and Anglophil, will reap its fatal fruits. It is not by any means impossible that the fall of Czechoslovakia would have immediate repercussions in the Eastern Mediterranean and that there might be a stampede of the lesser Powers to make their terms with the rising star of Hitlerism. The present eclipse of Russia, owing to the insane purges in the army and in industry, is of course an essential factor in German calculations, which have hitherto succeeded with clockwork regularity. The absolutely explicit pledges of help to Czechoslovakia, in the event of aggression, made by the French and Soviet Governments after the rape of Austria, have created a new situation for the British Government which, since the resignation of Mr Eden, had veiled itself in a stubborn silence. The assurances given by Berlin to Prague and to Prague's ally Belgrade, that Germany has no intention of attacking Czechoslovakia, will be readily accepted by those who are merely seeking any kind of excuse for doing nothing, but with far greater reserve by those who take the trouble to count up the long array of broken pledges. Much more serious is the certainty that the Czechs and Slovaks, in the words of their Slovak Premier Dr Hodža, will "defend, defend, defend", and if need be, go down fighting.

Faced by this "new situation", and by the knowledge that British opinion was outraged by events, and increasingly restive at the Government's failure to give any clear lead, Mr Neville Chamberlain had urgently to consider some further definition of policy. From the one side he was urged to give to Czechoslovakia an undertaking of assistance no less binding than that of her two great allies, from the other to dissociate herself altogether from Central European commitments. He very wisely took a middle course, refusing a blank cheque, but insisting on "the profound disturbance of international confidence", reaffirming more explicitly than ever British obligations towards France and Belgium and, more guardedly, the

Covenant obligation, "which is of more general character but which may have more significance". While declining any "automatic" pledge under which His Majesty's Government would cease to be a free agent, he made it quite clear that "if war broke out, it would be unlikely to be confined to those who have assumed legal obligations. It would be quite impossible to say where it would end and what Governments might become involved. The inexorable pressure of facts might prove more powerful than formal pronouncements, and in that event it would be well within the bounds of possibility that other countries besides those who were parties to the original dispute would almost immediately become involved. This is especially true in the case of two countries like Great Britain and France, with long associations of friendship, with interests closely interwoven, devoted to the same ideals of democratic liberty, and determined to uphold them."

The Prime Minister by his speech broke quite definitely, and probably once for all, with the fantastic idea of British isolation, leading, as it inevitably would, to a universal coalition for the overthrow of the British Empire. He also tacitly admitted the impossibility of separating off East and West into watertight compartments and the certainty that we could not stand aside and allow France to perish, whatever the nature of the quarrel which first involved us in war. Above all, it follows logically from his speech that those who talk of "fighting for Czechoslovakia" do not understand the elements of the problem. If we should eventually become involved in a war in which Czechoslovakia was one out of many bones of contention, it would almost certainly be for the same fundamental reason that had involved us in the past—namely to repel a fresh attempt at European hegemony on the part of an aggressive and militaristic Power. During the debate that followed the Prime Minister's weighty speech, Mr Winston Churchill as usual hit many nails on the head, and in particular when he spoke of "the Nazi dictation of the Danube States" as "a danger of the first magnitude to the British Empire" and of "the vast degeneration of the forces of parliamentary democracy" which was proceeding throughout Europe. He and other speakers in no way exaggerated when they suggested that Germany might subject the small States one by one to an economic stranglehold, and create a situation in which the use of armed force would be unnecessary.

Mr Chamberlain's speech, as far as it went, showed a firm tone and a refusal to be panicstricken: but it surrounded the Spanish issues, and the highly questionable negotiations with the Duce, with an air of mystery that is not a little disquieting. Public opinion throughout the country—entirely unrepresented by a small clique of neutralist press magnates—is at last fully alive to the revolutionary and explosive character of those forces in Europe from which proceeds the challenge to our free institutions, and realises that the Western democracies may have to fight for their lives against the attempt to substitute Power Politics for the reign of law through the collective system. What it asks of the Government is not merely constructive statesmanship, but a clear lead upon the moral issues involved. The neutralist press denounces those who lay more emphasis on the breaking of pledges by the dictators than on their repeated pacific assurances, and almost in the same breath clamours for still vaster armaments. As such precautions obviously cannot be directed against the perfect gentlemen in whom we are invited to put unreserved trust, and who are helping us to reinterpret such words as "piracy" and "non-intervention", we must presume that they will be required to reduce our quondam friends, the Small Nations, to a due state of vassalage towards the totalitarian Powers. The writers to whom we allude are either insincere or foolish. The British people demand to be told the truth. They demand that "British interests" should be duly safeguarded, but still more that determined effort should continue to be made to bring them into line with the higher interests of a peaceful international order. They genuinely and rightly regard the League as the loftiest experiment of human policy yet devised: they believe that with general goodwill, it would be capable of infinite development and reform: they keenly resent the insults levelled against it by the dictators, and they feel instinctively that our leaders have been too half-hearted in its defence. They desire to "rally the peaceloving Powers in a system of mutual assistance against aggression", and are perfectly ready to discuss with the totalitarian Powers on an equal footing the problems of "economic nationalism" and colonial grievances.[1] With Germany in particular they most earnestly desire a permanent reconciliation, but not at the price of abandoning the cause of the League, and sinking into a pagan materialism which accepts war as a biological necessity and rejects the redemption of mankind. Then indeed "are we of all men most miserable".

It is not for the mere historian to continue the argument. But it may boldly be affirmed that if the statesmen of our age have not the courage of a Christian faith and fail to establish a direct connection between the errors of foreign policy and the neglect of moral values in the past, their failure may drag down our whole world in ruin.

[1] The phrases quoted are those used by Sir Archibald Sinclair in the House of Commons on 24 March 1938.

Machiavelli has for long ages prevailed over Dante. To save Italy and awaken the soul in Europe, you must return to that immortal spring of a people's noblest aspirations.

MAZZINI

Barbaren von altersher, durch Fleiss und Wissenschaft und selbst durch Religion barbarischer geworden.

HÖLDERLIN

> Nehmen sie den Leib,
> Gut, Ehr, Kind und Weib,
> Lass fahren dahin
> Sie haben's kein Gewinn:
> Das Reich muss uns doch bleiben.

LUTHER

> We are selfish men:
> O raise us up, return to us again,
> And give us manners, virtue, freedom, power.

WORDSWORTH

So then because thou art lukewarm, and neither hot nor cold, I will spue thee out of my mouth....

Thus with violence shall that great city Babylon be thrown down, and shall be found no more at all...

Seal not the sayings of the prophecy: for the time is at hand.

REVELATION

INDEX

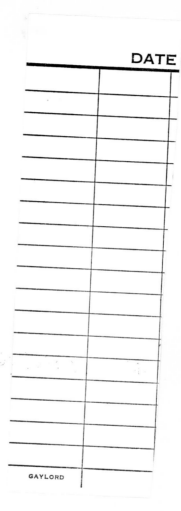

DATE

GAYLORD